ANTHROPOLOGICAL PAPERS OF
THE UNIVERSITY OF ARIZONA
NUMBER 41

THE ASTURIAN OF CANTABRIA
Early Holocene Hunter-Gatherers In Northern Spain

Geoffrey A. Clark

THE UNIVERSITY OF ARIZONA PRESS
TUCSON, ARIZONA
1983

About the author...

GEOFFREY A. CLARK, an Old World prehistorian, has done field work in France, Spain, and Turkey, and in the southwestern United States. His interests include preagricultural coastal adaptations (with which this monograph is concerned), paleoecology, archaeozoology, and archaeological site catchment analysis. Since 1968 he has been involved in research on Late Pleistocene hunter-gatherers in northern coastal Spain. Clark received his bachelor's degree (magna cum laude with Honors, 1966) and master's degree (1967) from the University of Arizona, and his doctoral degree from the University of Chicago (1971). He is a Professor in the Department of Anthropology at Arizona State University and has published papers on quantitative methods, the role of statistics in archaeological research designs, and human evolution.

THE UNIVERSITY OF ARIZONA PRESS

This book was set in 10/11 V-I-P Times Roman
Manufactured in the U.S.A.

Library of Congress Cataloging in Publication Data

Clark, Geoffrey A.
    The Asturian of Cantabria.

    (Anthropological papers of the University of Arizona; no. 41)
    Includes index.
    1. Mesolithic period—Spain—Cantabria. 2. Kitchen-middens
—Spain—Cantabria. 3. Cantabria (Spain)—Antiquities. 4. Spain
—Antiquities. I. Title. II. Series.
GN774.22.S7C53 1983   936.6   83-1052

ISBN 0-8165-0800-3

This Volume is Dedicated to
the Memory of

D. Ricardo Duque de Estrada y Martínez de Moratín,
Eighth Count of Vega Del Sella

[1870–1941]

CONTENTS

FIGURES

TABLES

PREFACE

Mesolithic studies have undergone several major fluctuations in credibility since the mesolithic was first identified as a separate area of research. In one of the earliest attempts to systematize the growing corpus of prehistoric archaeological data, Sir John Lubbock (1865) created the fundamental distinction between a "palaeolithic" and a "neolithic" era. These eras were defined on faunal grounds (paleolithic peoples were the contemporaries of extinct animals, the remains of neolithic peoples were associated with extant faunas), means of subsistence (paleolithic peoples were hunter-gatherers, neolithic groups had domestication economies), and technology (paleolithic man was a flint knapper, neolithic people made ground stone artifacts and pottery; J.G.D. Clark 1978, 1980). As is often the case with bipolar models, applications of Lubbock's scheme resulted in a false contrast, and much subsequent work in the 1870 to 1914 interval was devoted to refining and elaborating criteria by which this dichotomy might be maintained and made less ambiguous (for example, de Mortillet 1883). For all intents and purposes, industries intermediate in age between the paleolithic and the neolithic were rendered conceptually "invisible." The notion of a hiatus in the archaeological record (and by implication, a period of abandonment) developed and persisted in the literature of the time, despite mounting evidence in Europe itself of material clearly interstratified between industries assigned to Lubbock's phases (for example, Mas d'Azil cave, the Azilian type site; Piette 1889), and occasional arguments for continuous human occupation of Europe during the period of alleged abandonment (Brown 1893).

By the early 1920s, enough evidence had been accumulated that it was no longer possible to argue for the hiatus, or to ignore the existence of "intermediate" assemblages. Mesolithic studies gradually acquired the same legitimacy as other areas of archaeological research, becoming part of the regional culture histories that were the objective of "classificatory era" (1914–1960) archaeological research in both England and the United States (Willey and Sabloff 1974). Writing in 1932, Professor Grahame Clark was concerned to "fill the gap between the close of the Pleistocene and the arrival of the Neolithic arts in [Britain]" (page 5). With the publication of the first major English synthetic work, *The Mesolithic Age in Britain* (J.G.D. Clark 1932), the legitimacy of mesolithic research became firmly established—at least in some circles.

Resistance to the mesolithic as a stage concept resulted from the economic and technological connotations of Lubbock's original evolutionary scheme, which by implication carried over to the mesolithic. If the mesolithic were to be accommodated in Lubbock's by-now-universally-accepted classification, then what were its defining characteristics to be? A number of prominent scholars had trouble with that question, and they typically reacted by rejecting the validity of the concept. V. Gordon Childe (1927:13) considered it a conceptually meaningless extension of the Upper Paleolithic, and grudgingly accorded it only limited temporal significance "...because in time—and only in time—[do mesolithic cultures] occupy a place between the latest paleolithic and the oldest neolithic cultures." Similar views were expressed in all succeeding editions of *The Dawn of European Civilisation*. Hugo Obermaier (1924: 322, 323) also believed the mesolithic to be analytically useless, because it did not display "a natural evolutionary development—a progressive transformation from Palaeolithic to Neolithic." These authors tended to view mesolithic materials as inconsequential survivals of the paleolithic age, separated from the neolithic (where all the "action" was) by a significant developmental, if not temporal, distance. The mesolithic was a European phenomenon and the locus of significant Pleistocene-Holocene boundary culture change was thought to lie outside the boundaries of Europe.

Since World War II, mesolithic studies have been influenced by the same succession of paradigm shifts that has characterized Anglo-American archaeology in general. Because of the enormous impact of a single scholar, Grahame Clark, mesolithic research has tended to have a strong ecological component. Having developed from a state of 'conceptual invisibility', through a period of legitimacy during which mesolithic studies were accorded equal status with other areas of archaeological research, the mesolithic is now seen to be central to our understanding of the transition to domestication economies everywhere. Most regional studies, including this one, attempt to show how mesolithic adaptations acted to facilitate or constrain the development of economies dependent on food production (Clark and Yi 1982).

Current research approaches to the European mesolithic are discussed at greater length in Chapter 1. Problematical generalizations about a mesolithic stage concept and about relationships of mesolithic adaptations to Late Pleistocene hunting and gathering societies and to the initial western European evidence for domestication economies provided the stimulus for the research presented here. In essence, this study of the Asturian and of other preagricultural coastal adaptations was undertaken because I questioned the validity of these generalizations as they had been applied to the prehistory of northern Spain. During the course of the project I was able to analyze and use eight major sources of information.

1. The bibliographic sources in the research libraries at the University of Chicago and at the provincial museums of Oviedo and Santander in Spain provided both a primary source of specialized information and a fundamental orientation to the late and post-Pleistocene industrial and paleoclimatic sequences in northern Spain.

2. Asturian and Asturian-like materials from 27 sites in seven museums were examined and classified. Over the years the museum collections had been subjected to extensive selection through analysis and in storage. Selection was evident from the fact that no debitage was preserved in any of the collections. A single tool type, the Asturian pick, accounted for more than 26 percent of the total number of pieces examined.

Selection also occurred through excavation techniques. Most of the excavations took place more than 40 years ago, and large crews of unskilled laborers were used, apparently with minimal supervision. As a result much material appears to have been lost at the outset. I excavated a small (100 cm by 100 cm by 50 cm) test pit at the cave site of Balmori (Asturias) in 1969. Placed purposefully in an unquestionable spoilheap, it yielded over 150 prehistoric artifacts, including 25 obvious stone tools along with medieval and twentieth century ceramics. I believe that the supposed crudeness of the Asturian lithic industry is attributable, at least in part, to this apparent sampling error; only the more obvious pieces were saved by the early excavators.

Apart from selection, provenience information available at museums was minimal; few pieces were labeled and acquisition books were kept only at the Museo Arqueológico Nacional in Madrid. Many pieces apparently were lost because collections were divided and traded piecemeal to other museums, a situation that renders restudy difficult and often impossible. Unfortunately, no records were kept of these transactions that might have facilitated the reconstruction of assemblages. Finally, Santa-Olalla told me in 1969 that many pieces were lost during the Revolution of Asturias (1934) and during the Spanish Civil War (1936–1939). The museum collections yielded a total of 624 pieces.

Given the paucity of the sample and the probability that the collections were not representative of the assemblage as a whole, steps were taken to improve the quality of the data.

3. Samples from conchero (shell midden) deposits were removed from eight known or suspected Asturian sites. Three Upper Paleolithic and two post-Asturian concheros were tested for comparative purposes. The objective was to construct molluscan species frequency graphs to permit the temporal classification and statistical comparison of samples in order to facilitate the iden-

tification of different kinds of concheros for future investigation. The samples were also used to reconstruct the microenvironmental zones exploited by the prehistoric Asturians and to determine seasonality.

Test excavations were conducted in Spain at four Asturian cave sites (La Riera, Balmori, Coberizas, and Penicial, all in Asturias) and at the newly discovered open-air site at Liencres (Santander). In addition to the desired increase in the lithic industry sample, the combined results of these two operations provided five additional data classes.

4. At La Riera, Coberizas, and Balmori, secure evidence of stratigraphic position was obtained. Until 1969, the relative stratigraphic position of Asturian assemblages was ambiguous.

5. Fourteen radiocarbon samples were obtained from six Asturian, three Upper Paleolithic, and two post-Asturian levels. These determinations, the first of their kind for these time ranges in this area, are invaluable because the chronological position of Asturian assemblages has been the subject of heated discussion.

6, 7. Twenty pollen and 16 sediment samples were taken from four of the test excavations and from two of the concheros. Palynological studies had never been attempted for any Asturian site, nor were there published references to soil or sediment studies.

8. Finally, a considerable quantity of mammalian faunal remains resulted from the sampling program. Together, the pollen, sediment, and faunal remains proved useful in reconstructing the paleoclimatic regimen under which that portion of the extinct sociocultural system represented by the Asturian of Cantabria developed and flourished.

ACKNOWLEDGMENTS

Since its inception in 1968, as part of a doctoral research program, until its completion in 1979, many individuals have contributed generously to the effort that has produced this monograph. First, I thank my graduate committee, Dr. Leslie G. Freeman, Dr. Karl W. Butzer, Dr. Robert J. Braidwood, Dr. F. Clark Howell (University of California, Berkeley), and Mr. T. P. Muller, all members or former members of the Department of Anthropology, University of Chicago, for their patient support and constructive criticism of the dissertation phase of this research. Dr. Freeman deserves special tribute for providing invaluable advice and encouragement during the period of initial fieldwork in Spain in 1968 and 1969.

Gratitude is also expressed to numerous Spanish friends and colleagues without whose help the study could not have been completed. Chief among these were Dr. Jesús Altuna, Museo de San Telmo, San Sebastián, Guipúzcoa, who was responsible for the identification of the mammalian faunal remains; and Dr. Benito Madariaga de la Campa, Instituto Oceanográfico de Madrid (Santander branch), who identified the molluscan fauna. Dr. Lawrence G. Straus, Department of Anthropology, University of New Mexico, has contributed greatly to a refinement of my thinking about Asturian adaptations in general. As Co-directors of the La

Riera Paleoecological Project (1976-1980), we have managed to survive one another's company for nearly five years now. Dr. Joaquín González Echegaray, Vice-director, Museo Provincial de Prehistoria y Arqueología, Santander, has been a steadfast friend and was most helpful in providing access to museum collections and sites in that province. Doña Matilde Escortell Ponsoda, Director, Museo Arqueológico Provincial, Oviedo, provided similar assistance in Asturias. Permission to excavate in Asturian sites was granted by Professor Martín Almagro Basch, erstwhile head of the Comisaría Nacional de Excavaciones Arqueológicas, and Director of the Museo Arqueológico Nacional, Madrid. Provincial officials and many Spanish students also greatly facilitated my research. Some of the latter have gone on to become practicing professional archaeologists, among them Manuel González Morales, Victoria Cabrera Valdés, Federico Bernaldo de Quiros, Maria del Carmen Marquez Uría, and Maria Dolores Garralda. Garralda and Francisco Giles Pacheco provided helpful information about the site of Cuartamentero.

I wish to acknowledge the support of Dr. Raymond Thompson, Department of Anthropology, University of Arizona, who was instrumental in facilitating publication of this volume. Dr. Gwinn Vivian and Dr. Arthur Jelinek reviewed the manuscript and made many useful suggestions that I have tried to incorporate whenever possible. Mrs. Carol Gifford, editor of the *Anthropological Papers of the University of Arizona*, has kept an editorial eye on my tendencies toward digression and verbosity, and has "pruned" the manuscript to its considerable benefit. Mrs. Ida Edwards is given special thanks for typing the extensive references. The efforts of these individuals have resulted in a cleaner and more readable work, for which I am profoundly grateful.

Finally, I wish to thank my former wife Valerie for her assistance in all phases of the project. She is responsible for most of the illustrations in the text and for the mapping of many of the cave sites. Without her patient encouragement, I might have given up this frustrating task long prior to its completion. I owe her a tremendous debt of gratitude that I fear I can never even partly repay.

Throughout the initial research period (1968–1971) my investigations were supported by a series of National Science Foundation Graduate Fellowships. A National Science Foundation Dissertation Aid Grant (1970) supplemented the earlier awards. Ford Foundation travel grants, to Dr. Freeman and Dr. Braidwood, paid for all travel expenses incurred from 1968 through 1970. Subsequent research in Spain from 1972 until 1978, much of it concerned with various aspects of Asturian adaptations, was supported by the Wenner-Gren Foundation for Anthropological Research, the National Science Foundation, and the Graduate College of Arizona State University.

Marshall Townsend, Director of the University of Arizona Press, and his able staff are especially thanked for their fine production of this volume. The continuing support of scholarly publication offered by the Press through the *Anthropological Papers* is highly commendable and especially appreciated by the anthropological community.

G.A. Clark
17 August, 1982
Tempe, Arizona

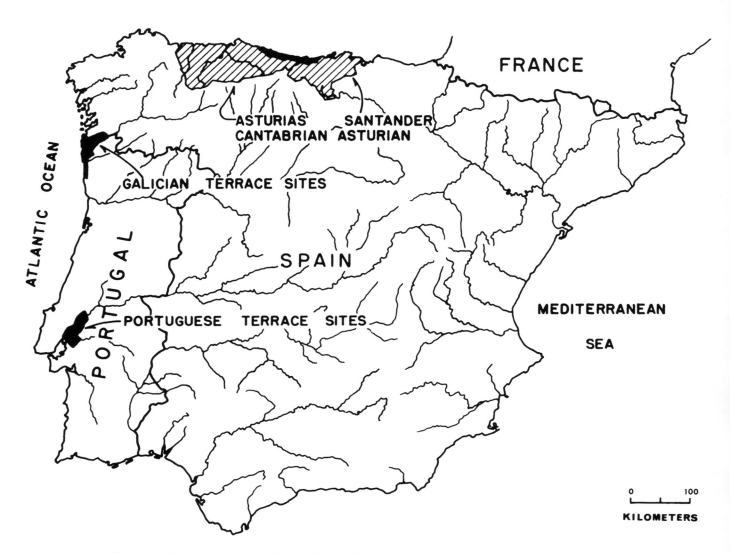

FRANCE

ATLANTIC OCEAN

ASTURIAS   SANTANDER
CANTABRIAN ASTURIAN

GALICIAN TERRACE SITES

P O R T U G A L

S P A I N

PORTUGUESE TERRACE SITES

MEDITERRANEAN

SEA

0   100

KILOMETERS

Figure 1.1. Iberian Peninsula, showing Spain, Portugal, and the provinces of Asturias and Santander.

1. RESEARCH APPROACHES TO THE EUROPEAN MESOLITHIC

The subject of this monograph is the Asturian of Cantabria. The sites that comprise this archaeological assemblage are found in caves situated along the coastal portions of the provinces of Asturias and Santander in northern Spain. The assemblage is characterized by a crude industry in quartzite. Artifacts are found in shell midden deposits called concheros, and are generally stated to be Mesolithic in age.

The term "Asturian" has often been misapplied in the literature. It has been used to refer to at least three chronologically, typologically, and spatially distinctive collections of artifacts: (1) the Asturian of Cantabria (described above), (2) the Portuguese terrace sites (Lower Tejo Valley, Portugal) and (3) the Galician terrace sites (Atlantic coast; Louro and Minho Valleys, Galicia). The locations of these site clusters are indicated in Figure 1.1.

Superficial resemblances between the Cantabrian Asturian and the Portuguese and Galician sites have led to a number of publications that have distorted or misrepresented primary source material, thus confusing attempts at serious investigation of the subject. The word "Asturian," as it is used here, refers only to Cantabrian sites and assemblages unless otherwise indicated.

The volume of literature concerned with the Asturian and with supposedly related industries is considerable. Unfortunately, however, most of these publications tend to be summary accounts based on dated secondary sources that incorporate neither fresh perspectives nor new material. As a consequence, interpretations of Asturian origins, development, and possible relationships with other Spanish and Portuguese assemblages are founded largely on speculation, rather than on the modern-quality archaeological, stratigraphic, and paleoenvironmental analyses required to substantiate conclusions.

Five major generalizations characterize the paradigm under which most recent mesolithic research has been conducted (Binford 1968: 313–342). First, it has been argued (Waterbolk 1968: 1096, but see J. G. D. Clark 1975) that there was a major shift in the distribution of the centers of population growth from Preboreal times (10,250–9450 B.P., Before Present base is A.D. 1950), when hunter-gatherers in western Europe tended to be distributed inland and were oriented toward the exploitation of forest, riverine, and lacustrine resources (for example, the Maglemøsian), to Atlantic times (8150–5250 B.P.), when they were primarily distributed along the coasts and emphasized shellfish gathering (for exam-

ple, Ertebølle). Second, the notion that there was a major change (microlithization) in the form of stone tools subsequent to 10,000 B.P. is often taken as a criterion for defining a mesolithic stage. This idea first became current with the early writings of Childe (1931: 325–348) and J. G. D. Clark (1936); it was stressed by the French, and originated as far back as 1848, with the establishment of the first Danish Kitchenmidden Committee (Sehested 1884, in Brinch Petersen 1973: 77). Third, it has been argued that there is "greater geographical variety" among cultural remains of Early Holocene date than among those dating to the Late Pleistocene, in turn implying that societies are adapting ever more efficiently to specific sets of resources—Braidwood's "settling" or "living-in" process (Braidwood and Reed 1957: 19–31). Fourth, the mesolithic is supposedly identified by a marked increase in the exploitation of aquatic resources (especially shellfish). Finally, there is a trend toward the hunting of small to medium sized game animals, and increased concentration on solitary or seasonally gregarious forms (especially deer).

This characterization of the mesolithic is at best only valid in part. Even for northwestern Europe (where assertions of demographic changes were first made and were thought to be best documented), Newell (1973: 409–412) has observed that in those areas where Early Holocene coastlines have been preserved, coastal adaptations extend well back into the Pleistocene and simultaneously occur with adaptations at inland sites oriented toward the exploitation of terrestrial resources (J.G.D. Clark 1975: 190–193). In Spanish Cantabria both coastal and inland adaptations are documented from Upper Paleolithic times. There are many archaeological assemblages of Early Holocene date, including the one described in this monograph, that contain few microlithic pieces, refuting the generalization about microlithization. Conversely, genuinely microlithic assemblages clearly predate the Pleistocene-Holocene boundary in many parts of the Old World (for example, the Nile Valley and Palestine, as well as in Cantabria itself).

The idea of greater geographical variety in the Early Holocene remains questionable. "Greater geographical variety" usually means that industrial (and perhaps faunal) remains are variable from area to area and may, perhaps, be more variable (in some impressionistic sense) than those of Late Pleistocene date. This assertion, bound up as it is with critical typological questions, has never been adequately demonstrated. Also, it is risky to imply that because lithic industries vary from place to place, responses to the environment necessarily varied in a simple, linear fashion.

The fourth criterion is better documented than the rest, but again there are problems of generality. Coastal adaptations involving intensive and sustained exploitation of marine shellfish go back more than 125,000 years at the Middle Stone Age sites at Klasies River Mouth (Volman 1978: 911–913; Wymer and Singer 1972: 207–217), Cape Province, South Africa. J. G. D. Clark (1948: 44–85) cited the Mousterian levels at Devil's Tower, Gibraltar (Garrod and others 1928: 33–114), as an early European example of shellfish exploitation. Edible molluscs also occurred in Mousterian contexts in Cantabrian Spain, and were intensively and systematically exploited from Solutrean times (Straus 1975a; Straus and Clark 1978a: 308, 309).

Finally, in those areas where Late Pleistocene steppe-tundra biotopes gave way to a succession of different and increasingly arboreal floral communities, it may be true that an exploitative shift from gregarious herbivores to smaller, solitary forms took place. This form of environmental determinism, however, seems to apply only to periglacial Europe, and it is by no means certainly appropriate there either (Rozoy 1978). For these reasons, the mesolithic as previously defined has no general validity as either an economic-developmental or chronological stage concept. If the term is retained at all, it should be used simply to identify those assemblages that postdate the end of the Pleistocene and that predate the local appearance of domesticates (except the dog) and ceramics in any given area, a usage similar to that of J. G. D. Clark (1975: 30).

Different kinds of adaptations are demonstrable for mesolithic societies, and they are not neatly correlated with specific geographical regions or vegetational configurations. Although there are considerable differences in tool and debitage (tool-making refuse) frequencies, Asturian lithics are not qualitatively distinct from the repertoire of Magdalenian industries on the Cantabrian coast, as was previously argued by Crusafont (1963) and Jordá (1963). Subsistence practices do vary through time in terms of shellfish species collected, probably as consequences of (1) macroclimatic change involving variations in sea water temperature (and perhaps salinity) and (2) pressures brought to bear on estuarine resources due to long-term population growth and resultant overexploitation (Straus and others 1981). A cyclical pattern only very loosely correlated with Late and post-Pleistocene climatic fluctuations seems to be emerging. It involves an apparent differential in the intensity of exploitation of open country and forested biotopes, and appears to vary independently of the culture-stratigraphic units on which much archaeological research in these time ranges is based (Freeman 1973; Clark 1971a: 428–460, 1971b, 1972; Clark and Clark 1975; Clark and Straus 1977a, 1977b; Straus and Clark 1978a, 1978b).

The earliest Asturian assemblages are dated to the mid-Boreal around 8700 B.P. and overlap slightly with the latest Azilian in the region (Straus, Clark, and González 1978; González and Marquez 1978). It persists as a recognizable archaeological assemblage well into the Atlantic phase (until about 7000 B.P.), and is almost contemporaneous with the earliest evidence for food producing economies on the Iberian Peninsula (Coveta de l'Or, Cueva de la Sarsa in Valencia, and at Carigüela del Pinar, Granada; Almagró 1963; Savory 1968: 75–77). These sites, dating to the middle and late fifth millennium B.C., contain the bones of domesticated cattle, sheep, goats, and pigs, as well as carbonized remains of emmer and einkorn wheat and barley.

Evidence for domesticates was expected in at least the latest Asturian sites, and certainly in deposits of post-Asturian date that were also sampled (Clark 1976a: 125–131), but none was recovered. Although a second shift in exploited marine species, analogous to that of early Holocene date, was detected after about 5900 B.P., evidence for domesticates in Asturias and Santander does not appear archaeologically until Bronze Age times (about 3450–2700 B.P.), and even at this late date it takes the form of petroglyphs depicting wheeled vehicles drawn by what may be oxen. Bronze Age I and II are known almost exclusively from sepulchral caves and isolated finds of Argaric daggers, polished stone axes, and pottery (Escortell 1973; Jordá 1977: 172–199). In the western part of Cantabria no sites pertaining to the period 5900 to 3500 B.P. have been excavated, although a few are known from the Basque provinces. Consequently, little is known of the transition to a food producing way of life, except that it did not happen especially early. Inferences about domesticated (or any economic) plants are hampered by a scarcity of preserved pollen. As of 1974, over 30 samples from a dozen Asturian sites had been submitted to several laboratories for analysis. Except for a sample analyzed in 1978 from the Asturian conchero at the key site of La Riera (Straus and others 1981), the total pollen count has yet to reach 50 grains, and these document the arboreal vegetation expected in any early Holocene mixed deciduous-coniferous forest. Although quantities of fauna from Asturian sites were examined by competent paleontologists, no primary (morphological) evidence for domesticates was forthcoming. The only faunal evidence for early domestication economies in northern Spain comes from the recently published Basque Country cave sites of Arenaza and Marizulo, located far to the east of the study area and in distinct topographical settings (Altuna 1980). The "neolithic" levels in these caves are dated to the early fifth millennium B.P. (3015±195 B.C., 3335±65 B.C.) and contain the remains of domesticated cattle (*Bos taurus*), ovicaprines (mostly sheep, *Ovis aries*) and pig (*Sus domesticus*), together with a wild fauna indistinguishable from that of the regional mesolithic.

It seems that the transition to a food producing economy was late and certainly partial, even at the time of initial Roman contact (2100–2050 B.P.). It is difficult to escape the impression of a long term, stable, and extremely productive hunting and gathering economy, flexible enough to adjust to the kinds of short-term and relatively mild environmental stresses that are documented by changes in the resource base, and to long-term population growth inferred from increases through time in the number of sites assigned to the various Upper and post-Paleolithic culture-stratigraphic units (Straus 1977; Clark and Straus 1982). As Tringham (1973: 563, 564) has noted, rejection of an ovicaprid-grain economy cannot be satisfactorily explained by inherent hunter-gatherer conservatism (Piggott 1965) nor (in this case) by environmental unsuitability. Apparently human extractive technology had become sophisticated enough in Cantabrian Spain by Late Pleistocene times to permit a degree of productivity and reliability not usually associated with a hunting and gathering way of life. If so, the adoption of food production would have conferred no special advantage on the Cantabrians, and it might have entailed considerable dislocation from the strategies that they had been practicing since Solutrean times. It is suggested that food producing economies would only have been adopted under circumstances that would have favored more labor intensive, higher yield strategems (Binford 1968). One such circumstance for which there is some archaeological evidence (Straus 1977; Straus and others 1981) is an increase in regional population density to the point where the flexibility built into the mixed hunting-gathering strategy noted above is no longer adequate to provide for regional subsistence requirements (Boserup 1965; Spooner 1972).

Current research on the European mesolithic seems to be trending in two major, and somewhat opposite, directions. One is characterized by a strong and continuing concern with lithic typology, sometimes accompanied by considerable methodological sophistication and often regarded as an end in itself. Many of the papers in *The Mesolithic in Europe* (edited by Stefan Kozłowski, 1973) exemplify this approach. Tringham (1972) has expressed skepticism, shared by me, that such morphological variation as is likely to be recorded in stone tool typologies would reflect cultural affiliation in any meaningful way.

The other trend is concerned with what might loosely be called "culture process questions" (Flannery 1973). These studies are regionally based, share a concern with temporal and spatial variability, have strong ecological and demographic components and, while they stop short of environmental determinism, usually regard environmental change as an important variable influencing the structure of human groups. The genesis of this approach can be detected in J. G. D. Clark's (1936) characteriza-

tion of the Scandinavian mesolithic, and in his subsequent work at Star Carr and at Broxbourne (J. G. D. Clark 1953, 1972; J. G. D. Clark and others 1954). Recent examples include articles by Brinch Petersen (1971, 1973), Newell (1973), Price (1973), J. G. D. Clark's much-revised and up-dated *The Earlier Stone Age Settlement of Scandinavia* (1975) and *The Early Postglacial Settlement of Northern Europe* (edited by Paul Mellars, 1978). The work of the La Riera Paleoecological Project, a development out of the research reported here, has a similar orientation (Clark and Straus 1977a, 1977b, 1982; Straus and Clark 1978a, 1978b; Straus and others 1980, 1981).

In this study these two approaches are combined. A considerable portion of the text is devoted to a standardized description of Asturian lithics, because they are not "typical" of, or even closely similar to, those of any other Spanish mesolithic industries and they have never been described before (Chapters 3–5). Of more interest, however, has been the identification of subsistence practices as monitored by variation in faunal inventories and the relationship of changes in the faunal inventories to postulated macroclimatic change over time (Chapter 6). An Asturian pattern is defined and juxtaposed with patterns characteristic of Magdalenian and post-Asturian (Atlantic period) adaptations. Using geographic data derived from the reconstructed regional environment (Chapter 2), an archaeological site catchment analysis was made to evaluate settlement-subsistence models that approximate different and contrasting systemic poses operative during the Asturian period (8650–7000 B.P.). Empirically derived patterns of resource exploitation are compared with expectations under three alternative permutations of a general model (Chapter 7). It has been possible to delineate a distinctive Asturian lithic and faunal configuration differing in certain important respects from Upper and post-Paleolithic configurations that bracket it in time. Some possible causal factors include macroclimatic change and its influence on faunal (especially marine-estuarine) resources, and regional population density that increased markedly in these regions and time intervals. The notion that Asturian sites might represent the remains of a set of activities functionally complementary to those represented by penecontemporaneous Azilian sites is also addressed.

2. CANTABRIAN GEOGRAPHY

The area known as Cantabria consists of the north coastal provinces of Oviedo (the former kingdom of Asturias, and referred to as Asturias herein) and Santander, and the Basque provinces of Vizcaya and Guipúzcoa (see Fig. 1.1). Insofar as Asturian industrial remains are confined to the former provinces, this study is concerned only peripherally with the Basque country. Although in general terms the Cantabrian region can be considered a physiographic whole, and has been so treated by most Spanish prehistorians, marked regional differences in bedrock, rainfall, temperature, and altitude create a varied topography.

When the distribution of Asturian sites is examined in detail, it is apparent that they are associated with particular geographic, geological, and vegetational configurations that in turn have associated molluscan and mammalian faunas for which there is archaeological evidence of selective exploitation. A comprehensive overview of the regional geographical setting is given in Clark (1976a: 21–35), and the economic elements in Cantabrian faunas are discussed in Chapters 6 and 7. For an inventory of contemporary Asturian mammalian, avian, and molluscan faunas, see Clark (1976a: 275–348). The wild mammalian faunas of Asturias are discussed in Noval (1976), and the contemporary flora of Asturias and Santander has been described at length by Guinea Lopez (1953) and by Mayor and Diaz (1977).

GEOMORPHOLOGY

Geological Structures

The Cantabrian region is characterized by a series of complex geological structures. In general, they have not been the subject of extensive investigation except in Asturias (Martínez Alvarez 1965: 95–122). Bedrock in the province of Santander and in eastern Asturias is dominated by folded series of limestones and sandstones, with restricted exposures of conglomerates, quartzites, shales, slates, and gypsums (Martínez Alvarez 1965, Fig. 8). Most formations pertain to the Mesozoic Era (Cretaceous Period) in Santander. Asturias, however, is characterized by deposits of Paleozoic (Carboniferous) age; these are distributed east of the city of Oviedo. Farther west, the nature of the bedrock changes abruptly from sedimentary to metamorphic. Slates, schists, and quartzites of Paleozoic (Silurian) age predominate as far west as the Galician plateaus (Mapa Geológico de España 1966; Houston 1967: 180).

Most Asturian sites are concentrated along the coastal region from San Vicente de la Barquera (Santander) to Lastres (Asturias). A complex series of Paleozoic limestones dominates bedrock, although Silurian quartzites and shales underlie the Quaternary alluvia of the Cabras and Nueva river valleys in Asturias (Martínez Alvarez 1965, Map). The limestone formations date from two different geological periods, the Devonian and the Lower Carboniferous, according to Llopis-Lladó and Aranguren (Mapa Geológico de España 1966).

A series of subparallel, flat, east-west trending ridges (*rasas*) interrupt the narrow coastal plain from Ribadesella (Asturias) to San Vicente (Santander). Of probable Devonian age, the ridges do not extend more than 15 km inland, and seldom attain a height of more than 300 m. They grade into a series of higher anticlinal formations that constitute the coastal mountain ranges in the area (Martínez Alvarez 1965, Fig. 6). These latter, of Lower Carboniferous age, have an average elevation of between 800 m and 850 m above mean sea level, and extend in a broken and irregular chain for about 60 km, paralleling the coast.

Inland from the coastal ranges lies a deep, narrow, east-west trending valley, some 5 km to 8 km wide, through which the Cares and Casaño rivers flow. Behind the rivers lie the foothills and the massive, block faulted, horst and graben formations forming that portion of the Cantabrian Cordillera called the Picos de Europa. Extensively dissected by gorges, the mountains attain a maximum elevation of over 2500 m (Houston 1967: 181). They extend for more than 40 km from the Sierra de la Corta (Santander) to the Sierra de Beza, on the Asturias-Leon border (Mapa de la Provincia de Oviedo 1968).

The landscape, then, may be described along a north-south section as being composed of four principal components: (1) the coastal ridges, (2) the coastal mountain ranges, (3) the intermontane valley, and (4) the foothills and peaks of the Picos de Europa. These distinctions are remarkably clear-cut in eastern Asturias; they become blurred in Santander, however, because of softer bedrock (Houston 1967: 180, 181).

Karst Topography

Both Santander and Asturias are characterized by landscapes in which extensively developed karstic phenomena are superimposed on the gross structural features outlined above. Without a single exception, Asturian sites are associated with the sinkholes, rock shelters, and caves that dot the Cantabrian landscape in the study area, and some comprehension of karstic processes is crucial to an understanding of the so-called "karstic rejuvenation theory," promulgated by Francisco Jordá and Noël Llopis-Lladó, that has been used to assign a Middle Paleolithic (Late Pleistocene) date to Asturian archaeological assemblages.

Perhaps the most common features of karstic topography in Cantabria are sinkholes (*dolinas,* avens, closed depressions) produced by the channeling of surface waters into preexisting depressions and by the subsequent dissolution of the underlying bedrock (Gorchkov and Yakouchova 1967: 168–170). Although their form is variable, sinkholes tend to be shallow, saucer-shaped depressions, mantled with a thick layer of soil, roughly circular in plan, and with gently sloping sides. Deep vertical shafts occur, but are not common. An estimate of average diameter is 30 m, and here, as elsewhere, they seldom exceed 15 m in depth.

If tectonic activity has resulted in faulting, sinkholes and other depressions tend to form alignments along faults where, due to the weakening of the bedrock, the most intense processes of karstification are concentrated (Gorchkov and Yakouchova 1967: 172). Solution cavities also tend to concentrate along fault lines, and if they collapse depressions are formed that are indistinguishable on the surface from sinkholes. Further development leads to the formation of karstic valleys, dotted with caverns and rock shelters.

Well-developed karst lends a distinctive cast to the landscape, having a jagged, cratered appearance, often somewhat muted by the thick vegetal mat that covers bedrock in northern Spain. This pattern is particularly noticeable in the area surrounding Posada de Llanes (Asturias), where a number of important Asturian sites are concentrated.

The creation of large, underground galleries may result in the resurgence and exsurgence of rivers. Although often a seasonal phenomenon related to precipitation variability and resultant fluctuations in the level of the water table (Gorchkov and Yakouchova 1967: 174), the disappearance of the Calabres River at Posada is an example of a permanent resurgence.

Soil Types

Cantabria may be divided into eight major soil associations, according to the classification developed by Guerra Delgado and others (1968). The Delgado typology is oriented toward the definition of physiographic provinces, each characterized by a single dominant, and several related, associated soil subtypes. The terminology is generally in accord with that of the standard work by Kubiena (1953). There is a major change in bedrock and in associated soil types on the longitude of the capital city of Oviedo in Asturias that appears to coincide with a boundary in the distribution of Asturian sites (see Figs. 1.1, 3.1). With one dubious exception, all known Asturian sites are located on the coastal plain east of Oviedo in association with calcareous substrates and soils.

The predominant association in western Asturias, from Oviedo to the Lugo border, is called a humid ranker. These are AC soils, characterized by gray mull or mull-like moder humic horizons, produced primarily by mechanical weathering with little or no translocation of materials in solution (Kubiena 1953: 171, 172, 175). In Asturias, they occur almost exclusively over siliceous parent material (quartzite, sandstone, gneiss, granite).

Just west of Oviedo, however, the nature of the bedrock changes from siliceous to calcareous (limestones), with a corresponding change in the dominant soil type to a dark calcareous forest soil (*calc-braunerde* in the lexicon of Kubiena, 1953). The sequence of soil horizons is A(B)C; the soil group is distinguished from the dark humid soils by the presence of unleached carbonates in the A horizon, which has abundant mull humus. Dark calcareous forest soils predominate throughout eastern Asturias and extend into western Santander, corresponding in distribution to that of most Asturian sites. The soil is associated with rare (A)C lithosols, A(B)C *terras rossa,* ACaC humid mull rendzinas, and somewhat more common A(B)–BC *terras fusca* (limestone *braunlehms*), which are associated with hard, "pure" limestones. The humic horizon, generally poorly developed, is a mull-like moder under natural forested conditions; with deforestation mull humus is the norm. The (B) horizon is a dense, sticky yellow or yellow-red clay and is extremely impermeable (Kubiena 1953: 208, 209). Although located over calcareous parent material, *terras fusca* are almost always decalcified. The important Asturian open-air site at Liencres (Santander) is associated with a *terra fusca* soil, which is characteristic of post-Pleistocene pedogenesis in the area (Clark 1979b).

Climate

The Cantabrian coast is marked at present by a climatic regimen that is mild and oceanic, due in part to the influence of the Rennell Current, an arm of the Gulf Stream. The region is humid (80 percent annual average), with maximum precipitation concentrated in the winter and spring. Average annual rainfall in Asturias is about 1000 to 1200 mm, concentrated in the months of November, December, March, and April. There is no dry season (that is, no month in the year that is typically devoid of precipitation). June through September are the driest months, but the average annual number of rainy days exceeds 150 on the low-lying coastal plain (data from Gijón). Colder, higher inland regions receive still more precipitation, usually in the form of snow. In both Asturias and Santander, however, precipitation occurs on the average at least 120 days a year. Mean annual temperature varies markedly with altitude, from 8°C to 19°C in Asturias, with an annual average of 13.8°C at Gijón (which is perhaps typical of the coast) to an annual average of 7.6°C in the mountain valleys of the Asturian Cordillera. January is generally the coldest month, August the warmest. Because of the maritime climate, the annual number of days free of killing frosts never falls below 240 and often exceeds 300 for the coastal portions of the provinces (Quirós Linares and Murcia Navarro

1977; Houston 1967: 10–23). Although there is geomorphological, sedimentological, and palynological evidence for cold-climate phenomena (terracing, periglacial screes, little or no arboreal vegetation) at low elevations in Late Pleistocene Santander (Butzer 1971b; Leroi-Gourhan 1971) and Asturias (Clark and Straus 1982; Clark 1982), similar climatic monitors do not indicate significant variations from the present climatic regime for the prehistoric time ranges considered here.

Vegetation

Prior to extensive deforestation by man, the vegetational cover in Cantabria under climax conditions was a mosaic consisting of a mixed coniferous-deciduous forest and patches of open grassland. Man's interference has radically altered the landscape, however, so that at present the predominant cover is artificial grassland (*prado*). The pattern is especially marked in Santander. In Asturias, deforestation is not quite so widespread, owing to a more mountainous interior inaccessible enough in the past to make intensive lumbering impractical.

The vegetational picture is rendered more complex because a number of arboreal species have been introduced over the past century in efforts to halt erosion and to develop a timber industry formerly in danger of extinction for lack of an adequate conservation program. The eucalyptus (*Eucalyptus globulus* Labill.), characterized by wide climatic and soil tolerances, extremely hard wood, and rapid growth, has proven to be ideal for reforestation and has been extensively utilized for that purpose throughout Iberia.

The major arboreal species naturally present in Cantabria number at least twenty (Mapa Forestal de España 1966; Houston 1967: 94, 95, 98; Mayor and Diaz 1977). Altitude appears to be the most important single factor influencing their distribution, although moisture, drainage, exposure, bedrock, and soil conditions also play significant roles.

Among the conifers, four species of pine are present; two of them (*Pinus laricio* Poir., *Pinus radiata* D. Don) were introduced from other areas (*P. radiata* from California) during the past century. Formerly prevalent in mountainous regions to an elevation of about 1200 m, the Scots pine (*Pinus silvestris* L.) is now limited to a few scattered relict populations located in south central and southwestern Asturias, and central and southeastern Santander. Present day elevations range from 600 m to 1300 m. More common is the coastally distributed maritime pine (*Pinus pinaster* Sol.), which is still relatively abundant in northwestern Asturias. East of Oviedo, however, maritime pines are absent except for small stands near Santander. The species usually occurs over calcareous bedrock at elevations from sea level to about 500 m.

Because of the maritime climate, with its mild winters and minimal summer drought, a deciduous broadleaf flora rather than a coniferous one is the climax and paraclimax vegetational association in Cantabria (Houston

1967: 94). Of the 14 predominantly deciduous species represented, the oaks (six species) are the most important economically (Clark 1976a: 27–31; Mayor and Diaz 1977: 513–591).

Associated primarily with low elevations, the common or pedunculate oak (*Quercus robur* L., *Quercus pedunculata* Ehrh.) is distributed on alluvial or siliceous soils in areas where humid conditions preclude the occurrence of a pronounced summer dry season and the resultant seasonal lowering of the water table (Butzer 1964: 66; Houston 1967: 94). Large concentrations occur in the sierras of southwestern Asturias and central Santander. The high altitude distribution of *Quercus robur* is an artifact of selective cutting by man, who has all but destroyed large stands at low elevations.

The evergreen holm or live oak (*Quercus ilex* L.) also has a predominantly lowland distribution when it occurs in its natural state (Butzer 1964: 66). Due to deforestation, however, the present day distribution in Spain ranges from 200 m to more than 1200 m (Mapa Forestal de España 1966: 46). The live oak is nearly absent in western Asturias, but a large forest covers the Peñamellera Alta in the eastern end of the province. In Santander, stands of considerable size are located in the Liébana Valley, and on the Vizcaya border. In all three instances, the species is found in intermontane valley environments at elevations between 200 m and 400 m above sea level.

Although oak and pine form the characteristic arboreal vegetational configuration in Cantabria under natural climax circumstances, human interference with the land has been such as to permit other members of the association to proliferate, occupying niches made vacant by fire or lumbering operations. The beech (*Fagus silvatica* L.) has been particularly successful in exploiting cleared land. Although absent on the coast, the beech is the most prevalent of the Cantabrian species. Large forests are located on practically all of the sierras of the Cantabrian Cordillera. They are especially dense in southeastern Asturias and southwestern Santander where the species is restricted to elevations over 1000 m (Mapa Forestal de España 1966: 32).

Considered a valuable food source in the past, the sweet chestnut (*Castanea sativa* Mill.) has also benefited extensively from human agencies (Houston 1967: 95). Chestnuts form extensive forests in montane regions of central Asturias at elevations between 500 m and 1000 m, corresponding rather neatly in distribution to the slopes and narrow bottomlands of the intermontane river systems (Trubia, Huerna, Nembro, Aller, Nalón) that transect the area.

Although oak, pine, chestnut, and beech typify the arboreal vegetation of Cantabria, other elements associated with the middle latitude mixed forest climax are also present. Poplars (aspen, *Populus alba* L., *Populus tremula* L.) are relatively rare and are confined to a few small stands northeast of Reinosa (Santander) and to the area around Covadonga (Asturias). Alder (*Alnus glutinosa* Gaertn.), birch (*Betula vulgaris* L.), willow (*Salix fragilis*

L.), elm (*Ulmus glabra* Huds., cf. *Ulmus campestris* L.), hazel (*Corylus avellana* L.), lime (*Tilia cordata* Mill.), and ash (*Fraxinus excelsior* L.) are commonly found throughout northern Spain wherever the original climax or paraclimax vegetation has been preserved (Guinea Lopez 1953).

Finally, a vegetational configuration the Spanish call *monte bajo*, or *matorral*, is a widespread feature of the Cantabrian landscape. Classified according to their origins, *matorrales* are of two major kinds, both represented in Cantabria.

One is the natural climax vegetation of montane slopes and valleys at high elevations, where the action of cold, snow, and wind produce (A)C lithosols lacking the soil depth necessary to sustain even a coniferous forest. The landscape consists predominantly of an evergreen ericaceous heather (*Erica* spp.), but with ferns (*Pteridium* spp.), gorse (*Ulex* spp.), sedges (*Cyperus* spp.), broom (*Genista* spp.), and some grasses (*Agrostis* spp.) also much in evidence.

The other matorral configuration is similar, except that it occurs at all elevations from sea level to 1800 m and the diminutive arboreal forms are absent. Some lowland heathers are climax vegetational associations produced by the excessively saline conditions prevalent in the coastal *rías* (drowned valleys) that are such spectacular scenic hallmarks of the Cantabrian coast. Extremely localized conditions such as soil type, parent material, exposure to sun and wind, slope, and moisture regime all play important roles in determining matorral composition.

In the archaeological record there is macrofloral evidence from Asturian midden deposits for prehistoric exploitation of oak and chestnut. Pollen analysis documents the presence of birch, hazel, willow, alder, and elm in the vicinity of the Asturian sites of Liencres, Balmori, and La Riera; most of the components of lowland matorrals are represented by Liencres and La Riera (Clark and Menéndez-Amor 1975). Many of the coastally distributed Asturian sites occur in microenvironmental contexts that are today characterized by lowland matorrals.

FAUNAS
Mammals

In spite of centuries-old human interference, the present-day fauna of Cantabria includes at least 76 mammalian species, excluding domesticated forms. Terrestrial mammals (44 species) account for more than 59 percent of the total. Bats add another 16 species (20 percent); the remainder (16 species, 20 percent) are sea mammals. Although the fauna is impoverished compared with that of the Late and even post-Pleistocene (Obermaier 1925; Fraga-Torrejón 1958; Cabrera 1914; Vega del Sella 1916; Altuna 1972), the mountainous southern portions of Asturias, and to a lesser extent Santander, have acted as refuge areas for a number of species extinct for centuries in the more accessible parts of the Peninsula (Noval 1976; Jordá 1977: 23–32).

Of the 44 species of terrestrial mammals, 13 can be considered to be potentially important in terms of food and raw materials. There is archaeological evidence for the systematic exploitation of only six of them, however. Significant economic species during the Asturian were red deer (*Cervus elaphus*), roe deer (*Capreolus capreolus*), chamois (*Rupicapra rupicapra*), and ibex (*Capra ibex*), and to a much lesser extent, boar (*Sus scrofa*) and horse (*Equus caballus*). Of these species, two prefer deciduous forest and forest margin habitats (red and roe deer), two are alpine creatures primarily found on rocky, treeless terrain (ibex, chamois), and one (boar) is restricted to matorral vegetation (dense, thorny undergrowth) near flowing water. Both in numbers of individual animals represented and in quantity of meat yield, red deer are the most important species prehistorically in Cantabrian archaeological assemblages, an observation made not only for the Asturian culture-stratigraphic unit (Clark 1971b), but for the Magdalenian and Solutrean periods as well (Freeman 1973; Straus 1975a: 381–420; 1977).

At least 16 species of marine mammals occur sporadically along the Cantabrian coastline, and, with certain exceptions (seals), never in great numbers. Marine mammals were not systematically exploited prehistorically in Cantabria, although a few seal bones are present in Late Pleistocene contexts at Altamira (Altuna and Straus 1976), Tito Bustillo (Altuna 1976), and La Riera (Straus and others 1980). Bird, amphibian, and fresh and saltwater fish remains also occur, but in quantities so small that they suggest only sporadic, infrequent exploitation of these resources, probably on an opportunistic basis.

Molluscs

The other major component in the Asturian diet for which there is archaeological evidence was shellfood. Cantabrian coasts support no less than 14 orders of shell-bearing marine molluscs; some 141 species are represented (Clark 1971a: 595–613; 1976a: 330–348). Only about a dozen (8 percent) occur in archaeological contexts assigned to the Asturian period, however, and only three are commonly found in great numbers: the European topshell (*Trochocochlea crassa*) and two limpets (*Patella vulgata*, *Patella intermedia*) together account for at least 90 percent of the identified shell in any given Asturian site. All are estuarine and intertidal species, exposed twice daily by the tides. The limpets, in particular, are often found concentrated in great numbers (12 to 30 per square meter) and can be collected by anyone with comparative ease. While these species were of undoubted economic importance, just how important they were as a staple food is difficult to assess. Certainly their combined dietary contribution compared with red deer was minimal, and they must represent either (1) dietary supplements accumulated over the long term either seasonally or perennially, or (2) an "insurance resource" exploited intensively only when other (mammalian) staples were not available. A seasonal pattern of collection is suggested by preliminary analysis of oxygen isotope ratios from Asturian shell samples from the La Riera cave (Straus and others 1980; Clark and Straus 1982).

More detailed discussion of contemporary Cantabrian faunas, their distributions and habitats, is provided by Noval (1976) and Clark (1971a). The latter paper also lists significant marine and terrestrial species by order and family, gives taxonomic designations, a synonymy, and common English and Spanish names (see also Chapter 6). Avifaunal data pertinent to northern Spain is recorded by Voous (1960) and Vaurie (1959, 1965).

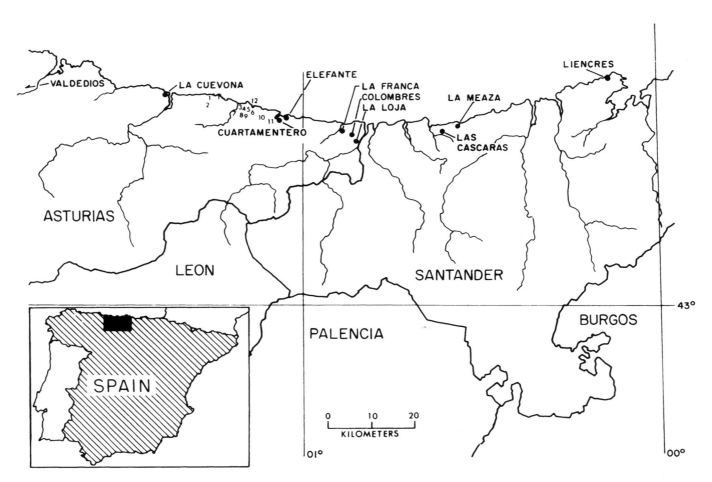

Figure 3.1. Location of Asturian sites in the Cantabrian provinces of Asturias and Santander:

1. Cuevas del Mar	5. La Riera	9. Lledías
2. Penicial	6. Tres Calabres	10. Balmori
3. Bricia	7. Coberizas	11. Allorú
4. Cueto de la Mina	8. Arnero	12. Fonfría

3. THE ASTURIAN OF CANTABRIA: SURVEY OF PRIOR RESEARCH

Asturian industrial remains are found principally in the mouths of caves and rock shelters cut into the limestone ridges and plateaus of the coastal plain. Sites never occur more than 10 km from the sea, and they are strung out for over 100 km along the Asturian coast and eastward into Santander (Fig. 3.1).

The industry is associated almost exclusively with concheros, artificial middens composed of variable quantities of bone fragments, fine sediments, and *éboulis,* and always containing, as the name implies, tens of thousands of marine shells. In Cantabria such deposits have formed since Aurignacian times (Vega del Sella 1916: 22), and some are cemented into breccialike deposits from percolation by carbonate-charged waters and subsequent dessication. Normally, little discernible stratigraphy is present in them and artifact density is low.

To judge from published descriptions of the industry, an Asturian assemblage should be composed of the following quartzite tool types: (1) unifacial picks (20–30 percent); (2) choppers, chopping tools, hammerstones, nucleiform endscrapers, bitruncated cobbles, and debitage (together about 65 percent); and (3) rare sidescrapers, denticulates, partial bifaces, notches, sharpened bone splinters, and perforated batons (together less than 5 percent). Globular flake cores are relatively common; prismatic blade and bladelet cores are apparently absent (but see Chapters 4 and 5). Little manufacturing debris is found in the museum collections, although its presence during excavation is noted in published accounts (Vega del Sella 1923: 14). In all cases, the pieces are unrolled and appear to have been taken from their original depositional contexts.

Unfortunately, rapid identification of the Asturian rests most securely at the moment on an archaeological "index fossil"—an unrolled, unifacial pick made on a flattened, ovoid quartzite cobble that does not appear in any Upper Paleolithic levels (see Fig. 5.1). A grossly similar form does occur, however, extensively rolled, in Portuguese Quaternary beach deposits of Lower and Middle Paleolithic age (Breuil and Zybszewski 1942, 1945). This situation has caused considerable confusion in the literature.

ASTURIAN CONCHEROS

The Asturian as a Mesolithic Industry

The original discoverer and principal systematizer of the Asturian was Ricardo Duque de Estrada, the eighth Conde de la Vega del Sella. The industry, with its characteristic picks, was first recorded at the cave of Penicial in 1914 (Vega del Sella 1914). The Count recognized the unusual nature of his discovery but attributed it, on morphological grounds, to the Lower Paleolithic. Over the next 20 years he excavated in or visited at least 19 other Asturian sites; published accounts exist for only seven of them (Vega del Sella 1914, 1916, 1923, 1925, 1930).

The Conde's collections were stored at his summer home in Nueva. When he died on September 28, 1941, they were shipped to the Museo Arqueológico Provincial in Oviedo and to the Museo Nacional de Ciencias Naturales in Madrid, where some still remain. During the 1940s, the lots of material were divided and traded with other museums. At some point, too, debitage and pieces unsuitable for display were combined for efficiency in storage into about 20 large bushel baskets now found in the basement of the Oviedo museum. Much of the provenience data was lost in the process as it was not customary at the time of the excavations to label individual pieces.

The relative chronological position of the Asturian was defined at the cave site of La Riera (Asturias), where Asturian concheros directly overlie Azilian levels (Straus and Clark 1979). Asturian assemblages were thought to correspond in time to the so-called "post-glacial climatic optimum," a conclusion drawn from the stratigraphy and from the characteristics of the shellfish inventory (Vega del Sella 1916: 83–87; 1923: 38–41). An estimation of 10,000 to 8000 B.P. would probably correspond to the period envisioned by the Count.

A summary monograph entitled *El Asturiense: Nueva Industria Pre-neolítica* was published in 1923 (Vega del Sella 1923). At that date the stratigraphic position of the assemblage appeared to have been established beyond question. A site report dealing with the La Riera and Balmori cave sites was published in 1930 (Vega del Sella 1930), the last major publication on the subject for more than 45 years.

One other early prehistorian directly concerned with the Asturian was Fr. Jesús Carballo (1926, 1960), who excavated a human burial containing Asturian picks as grave offerings at the rock shelter of Colombres (Asturias) in 1926, so far a unique find. He also is credited with the discovery of some picks on the surface at Ciriego outside the city of Santander in the early 1920s (Carballo 1924), the first indication that the industry might occur in other than cave contexts.

[9]

More recently, Dr. Francisco Jordá-Cerdá encountered
an Asturian conchero at the cave site of Bricia, overlying
a sequence of Magdalenian levels (Jordá 1954: 169–195).
This important sequence was a further indication of the
correct stratigraphic position of Asturian industries that
Jordá, in subsequent articles (1958, 1959, 1963, 1975),
has chosen to ignore.

The Asturian as a Lower Paleolithic Industry

In the middle 1950s, Jordá, in collaboration with the
Asturian geologist Noël Llopis-Lladó, began a much
needed, but unfortunately somewhat cursory, reexamina-
tion of the Asturian problem. The apparent crudeness of
Asturian assemblages had always been difficult to explain given a Mesolithic context. After a geological-ar-
chaeological survey of the Asturian coast (Hernández-
Pacheco and others 1957; Llopis-Lladó and Jordá 1957),
they developed a theory of "karstic rejuvenation"
whereby a Middle Paleolithic time range could be assigned to Asturian concheros.

According to this theory, Asturian deposits, often
found cemented to the walls or ceilings of caves separated by some meters from stratified deposits below,
were laid down in Lower or early Middle Paleolithic
times. Subsequently indurated through cementation by
carbonate-charged waters, the deposits were then eroded
by a rising water table (correlated with a renewed "cycle"
of karstic activity), except for the most indurated segments still seen on the cave walls today. These events
would have occurred prior to the deposition of Upper
Paleolithic levels. Thus, the Asturian deposits would now
appear to overlie and postdate the Upper Paleolithic sequence because of their relative elevation when, in fact,
they are claimed to be much older (Jordá 1957: 66, 67;
1958: 19–21, 23–29; 1959: 63–66). The date of the proposed rejuvenation was not specified in the published
accounts by Jordá and Llopis except that it was believed
to have taken place not later than Middle Paleolithic
times (that is, prior to the deposition of Mousterian
assemblages).

This improbable and untestable hypothesis has the superficial advantage of appearing to satisfy the question of
the crudeness of the lithic industry. Somewhat elabo-
rated, it has become widely accepted in Spain today
(Crusafont 1963; Pericot 1964: 48–50; J. M. González
1965; Hernández-Pacheco and others 1957: 24), although
present research indicates that the karstic rejuvenation
theory is invalid.

Historical Review of Asturian Sites

Most of the sites described below have traditionally
been cited to contain Asturian levels (Vega del Sella
1923: 49; Almagro 1960: 311–315, in Menéndez-Pidal,
editor, 1963: 411–414). It is instructive to examine the
contextual situations in which these deposits occur. Levels are considered Asturian if they contain: (1) concheros, with or without industrial remains, in which the
modern varieties of *Patella vulgata* and *Trochocochlea
crassa* predominate and in which the large and distinctive
Pleistocene forms of *Patella vulgata sautuola* and *Lit-*

torina littorea are absent, or (2) the characteristic Asturian pick in primary depositional context. Co-or-
dinates, elevations, and distance from the sea for all sites
are listed in Table 3.1.

Penicial

The Asturian type site is the cave of Penicial, located
in the pueblo of Nueva, *concejo* of Llanes, in eastern
Asturias (see Fig. 3.1, Table 3.1). One of a number of
caves formed by the Río Nueva, Penicial is situated approximately 75 m from the present-day river course.

The cave is cut into a small hill of Carboniferous limestone and has two major and several minor entrances.
The main or lower entrance (vestibule) opens to the
southwest and leads by a constricted passage into a larger
room, 15 m wide by 20 m deep, which is the point of
origin for a labyrinth of narrow, water-cut corridors.

The second or upper entrance is situated 4.5 m above
the floor of the vestibule to the east of the main entrance.
Opening to the southwest, it leads into a small chamber
some 2 m in height that is easily accessible from the cave
interior. This little chamber contains abundant remains
of an Asturian conchero, still unquestionably in situ,
sealed in by a thick stalagmitic cap (Fig. 3.2).

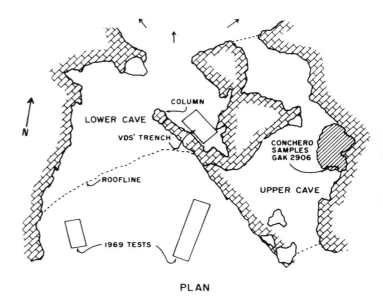
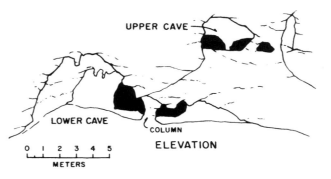

Figure 3.2. Penicial: plan and elevation of the cave.

TABLE 3.1
Conchero Sites Mentioned in the Text: Coordinates, Elevations, and Distances from the Sea[1]

Asturian Sites	Coordinates			Elevations	Distance from Sea
	Longitude	Latitude	Above sea level	Above nearest flowing water (source)	(kilometers)
PENICIAL (Cueva Benigna, Cueva Cabrón)	01°15′18″	43°26′44″	<10 m	3.9 m (Río Nueva)	1.5
CUETO DE LA MINA	01°10′02″	43°25′42″	60–70 m	11.6 m (Río Calabres)	1.6
ARNERO	01°10′48″	43°25′12″	60–70 m	1.6 m (Río Bedón, east branch)	2.4
FONFRÍA	01°08′38″	43°26′03″	~20 m	20.4 m (Río Calabres estuary)	0.4
COBERIZAS (Cueva Sabina)	01°11′30″	43°25′42″	50–60 m	30.6 m (Río Bedón)	1.6
TRES CALABRES	01°09′50″	43°25′41″	50–60 m	~10.0 m (Río Calabres)	1.8
BALMORI (Cueva de la Ería, Cueva del Pradón, La Cuevona)	01°08′47″	43°25′57″	~40 m	2.0 m (no name)	0.5
LA RIERA	01°09′58″	43°25′47″	30–40 m	4.5 m (Río Calabres)	1.5
MÉSÉ	01°13′18″	43°23′10″	~100 m	6.5 m (Río Cabras)	6.9
LLEDÍAS (Cueva del Cuetú, Cueva del Cueto, El Cuetú, Cueto de Lledías)	01°10′08″	43°24′46″	50–60 m	5–10 m (Río Calabres)	3.1
BRICIA (Cueva Rodríguez)	01°10′08″	43°25′36″	60–70 m	11–12 m (Río Calabres)	1.6
CUARTAMENTERO	01°04″14″	43°24′44″	40–50 m	<1 m (water table intersected in cave	1.0
COLOMBRES	00°52′49″	43°22′18″	80–90 m	4 m (Río Cabra)	2.3
LA FRANCA (Cueva de Mazaculos II)	00°53′18″	43°23′16″	~40 m	20 m (Río Cabra)	0.5
CIRIEGO	00°11′00″	43°28′34″	13 m	13 m (sea)	0.1
LIENCRES	00°12′20″	43°28′31″	13 m	13 m (sea)	0.02
LA LLOSETA (Cueva de la Moría)	01°22′55″	43°27′46″	12 m	10 m (Río San Miguel)	0.5
Other Sites					
EL CIERRO	01°25′15″	43°27′34″	~100 m	10–15 m (Río San Miguel)	1.6
LES PEDROSES	01°25′15″	43°27′34″	~100 m	10–15 m (Río San Miguel)	1.7
SAN ANTONIO	01°21′55″	43°27′20″	45 m	40–45 m (Río Sella, estuary)	1.1

1. All longitudinal designations are West longitude; all latitudinal designations are North latitude. Longitude is measured from the Meridian of Madrid, as is the Spanish custom (Spanish topographic maps were used throughout). The Greenwich Meridian was not used; there is a difference of about 4°. Elevations are standardized to the mean elevation of the Mediterranean Sea at Alicante, to which all Spanish benchmarks refer.

The Conde decided to place his trench along the west side of the main entrance, a location he judged to be protected from the prevailing winds and thus a likely spot in which to find an occupation level. The remains of this trench could not be located with certainty in 1969; it does not appear on the plan of the cave provided in the original publication (Vega del Sella 1914: 5). The cut measured about 4.2 m long by 1 m wide; bedrock was encountered at a depth of 2 m. For the stratigraphy described below, modified slightly from Vega del Sella

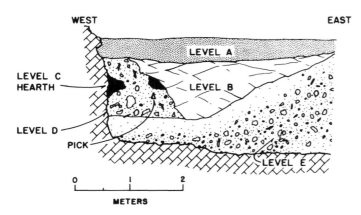

Figure 3.3. Penicial: cross section through the original excavation (after Vega del Sella 1914).

(1914: 4, 6), level measurements are approximations based on the published section; depths are in centimeters below the then-existing surface (Fig. 3.3).

Level E, 200 cm to 180–40 cm. The original cave fill; a sandy clay with small rounded quartzite cobble inclusions, grading to fine sandy clay near the top of the deposit; apparently archaeologically sterile.

Level D, 150 cm to 40 cm. A fill of broken and rolled cobbles; some bone, a few quartzite flakes; ash and charcoal inclusions.

Level C, 120 cm to 70 cm. The remains of a hearth (charcoal lense), containing bone fragments, quartzite flakes; *Patella vulgata* and *Littorina littorea*; in Level D.

Level B, 160 cm to 40 cm. A flowstone formation inclined toward the front of the cave; either intrusive through and thus postdates formation of Levels C, D, and E, or deposited in a depression contemporaneously with their formation; overlain by Level A, except in the end of the cut.

Level A, 40 cm to 50–0 cm. A deposit called *tierra vegetal* (a reddish clay resulting from decalcification, possibly with a soil developing on top of it in the exposed portions of the entrance); with small roof-fall inclusions; archaeologically sterile.

The industry at Penicial was originally believed to represent a single component, a transitional stage between the Acheulean and the Mousterian (Vega del Sella 1914: 12), but this interpretation was rejected by the Conde in all of his subsequent publications (Vega del Sella 1916, 1923, 1925, 1930). Most of the pieces are stated to have occurred in close proximity to one another in the basal central portion of Level D, in association with the hearth (see Fig. 3.3). The supposition of a single component (while not demonstrable) is probably justified, and is supported by the nature of the tools themselves.

Vega del Sella (1914: 4) was convinced that the sediments in all of the levels, if not waterlaid originally, were extensively reworked by the action of water at some time subsequent to their deposition. While it appears likely that the archaeologically sterile Level E was the product of water action, such a conclusion is not warranted by the descriptions of Levels C and D (Clark 1971a: 73, 74). The presence of sharply broken cobbles, the remains of an identifiable feature (the "hearth"), and the mint condition of the pieces themselves all militate against extensive disturbance.

Because of his conviction, the Conde discounted the scarce faunal remains as of no importance because their association with the industry could not be demonstrated (Vega del Sella 1914: 6, 7). He mentions only that the bones of horse (*Equus caballus*), red deer (*Cervus elaphus*), and an unspecified bovid (*Bos* sp.) were recovered from the west (interior) end of the trench. A similar fauna, but with some caprid (*Capra* sp.) remains, occurred in the east (exterior) end of the trench. The limpet (*Patella vulgata*) and the winkle (*Littorina littorea*) are also recorded.

Penicial has suffered extensive damage during the 65 years that have elapsed since its excavation (Clark 1976a: 46). Little remains of the site today except for the conchero deposits preserved in the upper entrance. A radiocarbon sample taken from these sediments in 1969 yielded 35.1 gm of charcoal. Submitted to the radiocarbon laboratory at Gakushuin University (Tokyo, Japan) for analysis, the resulting determination (GaK 2906), corrected for the new half-life (5730 ± 40), is 8909 ± 185 years before 1950.

Cueto de la Mina

The Cueto de la Mina rock shelter is located in the hamlet of Bricia, in the town of Posada de Llanes, eastern Asturias (see Fig. 3.1, Table 3.1). The site, among the most important Solutrean stations in northern Spain, occurs in one of five caves and shelters cut into the southern face of a small limestone plateau called the Llera. The area, characterized by karstic formations (Fig. 3.4), exhibits a variety of microenvironmental zones that appear to have provided a wide range of faunal resources potentially exploitable with comparatively little expenditure of energy, compared with other, less well favored sections of the coast. It is to this hypothetical plethora of densely concentrated food resources that the Conde attributed the dense occupation of the Calabres Valley (Vega del Sella 1916: 11).

Cueto de la Mina was selected for excavation because of the presence of a large artificial mound, apparently a shell midden, underneath the shelter overhang (Vega del Sella 1916: 1–5). The mound, which in 1914 was more than 5 m high, filled the greater part of the shelter, almost completely obscuring a small cave cut into the rear of the cliff (Fig. 3.5).

The excavations, conducted during the winter of 1914 and the summer of the following year, were in arbitrary levels 8 to 10 cm thick except where color differences made it apparent that more than one stratigraphic unit was involved. Altogether three trenches were cut. The first trench extended in an east-west direction across the mouth of the cave under the shelter overhang, cross-cutting a series of deposits related to slope wash external to

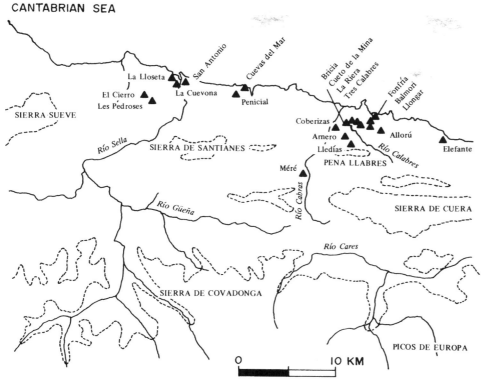

Figure 3.4. Topography of the Ribadesella-Posada de Llanes area, showing the locations of pre-Asturian, Asturian, and post-Asturian sites (modified from Straus 1975a).

the cave and to the sequence found in the cave itself. The second trench ran parallel to the long axis of the cave down its center; it appears to have completely emptied the cave of deposits, and the sequence there was strictly related to internal deposition. The third and largest trench was situated outside the cave parallel to the west wall of the shelter.

The stratigraphy was concordant (with stated exceptions) throughout the site (Vega del Sella 1916: 13, 14). Eight archaeological levels were described, supposedly extending as far back as the Upper Aurignacian (as then defined). Although arbitrary levels were used, these excavations were carefully done. Marquez (1974: 811–836), who recently uncovered some of the Conde's original excavation diaries at his summer home in Nueva, speaks of dry screening and even washing of sediments after excavation, resulting in the recovery of tiny bladelets and bone needle fragments. These pieces have apparently been lost or discarded through the years, as they are badly underrepresented in museum collections from the old excavations (Chapa 1975).

Although the following summary is based on the original monograph, in this and subsequent reviews, the archaic tool typology used by the Conde has been replaced where possible with that developed by de Sonneville-Bordes and Perrot (1954, 1955, 1956), widely used in Cantabria today. In making the conversions, I was able to exploit both the excellent illustrations and the written

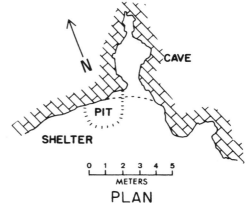

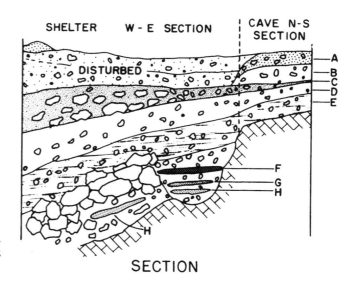

Figure 3.5. Cueto de la Mina: plan of the cave and cross section through the original excavations (after Vega del Sella 1916; no scale given).

descriptions of the pieces. Also, in June and July of 1974, I had the opportunity to inspect Upper Paleolithic collections from some of these sites. Except for the Asturian collections, however, all pieces were not personally examined and what follows should not be construed as representing the results of such a detailed study. Level thicknesses are approximations based on statements in the text and on the composite cross section provided in the original monograph (Vega del Sella 1916: 15).

Level H, 750 cm to 600 cm (shelter). Level H was the oldest archaeological deposit in the site, restricted in distribution to two small 10 cm lenses in front of the cave, underneath the overhang. They slope sharply to the south, which accounts for the apparent depth of the level (Fig. 3.5).

The deposit consists of a "ferruginized clay matrix," rusty brown in color, mixed with ashes, charcoal, bone fragments, shellfish, and quartzite (predominantly) and flint tools. The level is underlain by a sterile gray clay, a decomposition product of the limestone substratum.

Although industrial remains were abundant, few pieces were retouched and even fewer were readily classifiable. In quartzite there were some sidescrapers and denticulates made on flakes; flake endscrapers appear to have been somewhat more numerous. The so-called "discoidal axes" and "biconvex pieces" (Vega del Sella 1916: 22, plate 4) are discoidal flake cores. The flint inventory comprises the smaller, more delicate tools, for the most part made on blades: small, thick circular endscrapers, simple endscrapers made on blades, keeled endscrapers, straight and canted dihedral burins, burins made on breaks and retouched truncations (all sometimes multiple); along with occasional notches, denticulates, atypical perforators (becs), and continuously retouched pieces. Unworked blades occur and some are small enough to be considered microliths (see Chapter 4).

What is distinctive about the collection is the retouch technique. Although designated "Upper Aurignacian" by the Conde (Vega del Sella 1916: 21, 76) the invasive, scalar retouch characteristic of the early phases of that industry is completely absent. Carinate and nucleiform endscrapers are rare. None of the bone point types that are so distinctive an Aurignacian feature in France are present. Retouched pieces are almost universally worked by a marginal, at times nibbling, technique, one of the hallmarks of a Perigordian IV industry. Jordá (1957: 61) attributes both Levels H and G at Cueto de la Mina to Perigordian IV, an opinion seconded by González Echegaray. McCullough (1971: 324), however, in his reevaluation of the Cantabrian Perigordian, cannot find sufficient evidence for assignment to either the typical Aurignacian or the Upper Perigordian.

Mammalian fauna include abundant remains of horse (*Equus caballus*), red deer (*Cervus elaphus*), and bison (*Bison priscus*). Roe deer (*Capreolus capreolus = Cervus capreolus*), ibex (*Capra ibex pyrenaica = Capra pyrenaica*), and the cave hyaena (*Hyaena spelaea*) are less commonly found. The giant Pleistocene limpet (*Patella vulgata sautuola*) occurs in low frequency in the deposits, along with a few examples of the ornamental *Littorina*

obtussata. The land snail, *Helix nemoralis,* also has been recovered in apparently unquestionable association with the archaeological remains (Vega del Sella 1916: 77).

Level G, 590 cm to 580 cm (shelter). Level G is also attributed to the Upper Aurignacian by Vega del Sella (1916: 23, 24). It occurs as a lens in a small natural depression about 10 cm above Level H. It is found only outside the cave entrance. The lithics are similar to those of the previous level, although burin frequency is much diminished. The bone industry, more abundant than in Level H, is characterized by beveled base circular and oval sectioned spear points. As noted, Jordá (1957: 61) assigns the level to Perigordian IV, although the "Gravette blades" figured by the Conde (Vega del Sella 1916: 23, 24) are not convincing.

Mammalian faunal remains include the wild boar (*Sus scrofa*), *Equus caballus, Cervus elaphus, Capra ibex pyrenaica,* and the chamois (*Rupicapra rupicapra = Capella rupicapra*). Mollusca are identical with Level H (Vega del Sella 1916: 77).

Level F, 560 cm to 535 cm (shelter). Like H and G, Level F is found in the natural depression created by the rockfall "buttress" shown in Figure 3.5. The matrix is a rusty brown ferruginized clay about 25 cm thick.

Designated Lower Solutrean by Vega del Sella (1916: 25–28), Level F marks the beginning of a Solutrean sequence. The level includes numerous circular endscrapers and endscrapers made on blades, not markedly different from those in Level G (although retouch tends to be somewhat more invasive). There are also keeled and nucleiform endscrapers and some ill-defined sidescrapers, but the characteristic pieces are the bifacially worked protolaurel leaves. The retouch is flat and invasive, produced by pressure flaking, and congruent with Solutrean collections elsewhere. Pieces are often retouched entirely over one or both surfaces. Even if the ventral surface is not retouched, the bulb of percussion is usually removed. Subtriangular forms predominate, although some may be simply the tips of foliate pieces broken obliquely in use or manufacture. The bone industry is inconsequential.

Jordá (1953, 1955, 1957) developed a four-part sequence for the Cantabrian Solutrean. He classifies Level F in his Phase II (Middle Solutrean), characterized by bifacially worked shouldered points, foliates with convex bases, rhomboidal forms in high frequency, and centrally flattened bone spear points (Jordá 1957: 63). According to the site report, however, there are few if any shouldered points in the level, bifacial or otherwise, few rhomboids occur, and the single bone spear point recovered has a circular cross section. Jordá's sequence has been vigorously criticized by Straus (1975a, 1978a, 1979a), who has suggested that Jordá's phases have neither general currency nor temporal significance.

Fauna present are *Bison priscus, Equus caballus, Cervus elaphus, Rupicapra rupicapra, Vulpes vulpes* (red fox), *Arvicola amphibius* (water vole); *Patella vulgata sautola* (abundant), *Littorina littorea* (scarce), and *Littorina obtussata* (Vega del Sella 1916: 76).

Level E, 500 cm to 440 cm (shelter); 280 cm to 170 cm (cave, measurement gives thickness of deposit containing the industry). Level E is the main Solutrean occupation in the site, occurring both under the shelter and in the cave itself; differences in elevation result from the sloping effect in front of the cave, a characteristic of all the sediments under the overhang (Fig. 3.5).

The matrix both inside and outside the cave consists of a dark brown sediment separated from Level F by an archaeologically sterile layer filled with éboulis about 35 cm thick. Level E deposits consist of ash, charcoal, bone fragments, some éboulis, and lithic debris.

The Conde divided Level E into four sublevels (*subtramos*), each 12 to 15 cm thick. The two lower divisions formed a unit marked by quartzite endscrapers analogous to those found in Level F. In flint, nucleiform, keeled, and double endscrapers occur in some frequency, with simple endscrapers made on blades. Fine blades are common. Backed bladelets are present but scarce. Perforators, burins made on breaks, and flake denticulates occur in low frequencies. The most characteristic items are the numerous shouldered and laurel leaf points. Antler is distinguished by double pointed pieces with flattened or oval cross sections near the center. Beveled base, circular sectioned points also occur. There are a number of needles and incised, perforated objects that appear to be pendants.

Fauna listed by Vega del Sella (1916: 32, 76) in the lower sublevels comprised scarce remains of woolly mammoth (*Mammuthus primigenius* Blum. = *Elephas primigenius*), an indicator of cold climatic conditions. Horse (*Equus caballus*) and red deer (*Cervus elaphus*) were common, with bison (*Bison priscus*), ibex (*Capra ibex pyrenaica*), chamois (*Rupicapra rupicapra*), and red fox (*Vulpes vulpes*) present. Mollusca were represented by *Patella vulgata sautuola* (abundant), and by scarce remains of *Littorina littorea, Littorina obtussata, Nassa mutabilis,* and *Pecten maximus.*

The upper sublevels are marked by most of the features noted above, in particular by the numerous and varied endscraper inventory and by the scarcity of burins. Microlithic tools, especially backed bladelets, occur in greater frequency and there are some magnificent sidescrapers made on curved blades. The characteristic pieces are the abundant shouldered, laurel leaf, and willow leaf points.

The bone antler industry is numerically more abundant than in the lower sublevels, although the types represented are the same. From the wear patterns on their surfaces, some large cylindrical pieces, oval in cross section, might have served as compressors. The distribution of both bone and stone tools showed marked variation from area to area within levels, an observation made but unfortunately not acted on by the Conde (Vega del Sella 1916: 36).

The faunal spectrum in the upper sublevels is more varied than ever before; it includes *Mammuthus primigenius, Equus caballus, Cervus elaphus* (very abundant), *Capreolus capreolus, Capra ibex pyrenaica* (abundant), *Rupicapra rupicapra* (abundant), *Hyaena spelaea, Vulpes vulpes,* and *Arvicola amphibius.* Mollusca include numerous examples of *Patella vulgata sautuola* and *Turritela triplicata; Littorina littorea, Littorina obtussata,* and *Trivia europaea* are present in low frequency. The last two species were made into ornaments (Vega del Sella 1916: 76, 80).

The industrial sequence in Level E was considered to be Upper Solutrean by Vega del Sella (1916: 29–43) because of the occurrence of shouldered points. Jordá (1957: 63), however, assigns the lower sublevels to his Phase II (Middle Solutrean). He places the upper sublevels, in which the frequency of concave based points supposedly increases, into his Phases III and IV (Upper Solutrean), defined in relative terms on the basis of that characteristic. Straus (1975a) has observed that Jordá's attempts to produce a series of over-fine Solutrean phases are probably invalid, because they are not supported by recent, modern-quality excavated Solutrean data.

In historical terms, Cueto de la Mina is a "key" site for an understanding of the Cantabrian Solutrean, both because of the long stratified sequence of superimposed Solutrean levels and because of the complex literary debates that have surrounded them—marked most prominently by the numerous "evolutionary" schema proposed by Francisco Jordá (1953, 1955, 1957, 1960, 1963, 1967, 1977) and his student Corchón (1971a, 1971b). In his comprehensive and excellent reevaluation of the Vasco-Cantabrian Solutrean, Straus (1975a: 120–155) can find no basis for *any* meaningful "evolutionary" trends in the morphology (and indeed in the relative frequency) of the lithic and bone artifact types at Cueto de la Mina. Interlevel variation is attributed to postexcavation selective factors, and—perhaps more significant in behavioral terms—to intralevel activity differences to which allusions are made in the original monograph (Vega del Sella 1916). Although Jordá (1977: 91–109) and his students continue to support evolutionary schema to account for changes in type forms and frequencies during the Cantabrian Solutrean, "change through time for its own sake, by means of some innate, vitalistic 'evolutionary' process acting on inanimate objects" (Straus 1975a: 155) seems a poor kind of explanation for what are probably basic functional and activity differences that vary independently of time and that cross-cut most of the Upper and post-Paleolithic culture-stratigraphic units (Clark and Straus 1977a, b; Straus and Clark 1978a, b).

Level D, 300 cm to 200 cm (shelter); 170 cm to 120 cm (cave). Level D occurs in a dark, greasy organic sediment, similar to that of Level E. It is found in all three trenches. Considered a Lower Magdalenian level (Vega del Sella 1916: 45–49), the deposits are extensive, consisting of charcoal, ash, bone fragments, and stone tools; the relative frequency of worked pieces is low.

Burins are the most abundant tools. There are also denticulates made on blades (called sidescrapers in Vega del Sella's text); pieces that are probably convergent denticulates; keeled, circular, and nucleiform endscrapers; simple endscrapers on blades; some massive sidescrapers; at least one chopping tool (called a "discoidal handaxe"); a number of continuously retouched pieces; and a considerable quantity and variety of backed bladelets, some of which resemble microgravettes.

In the abundant bone industry, beveled-base, circular and oval sectioned spear points appear to be the most common form. Smaller pieces, awls and "punches," are frequent. Plain and deeply engraved cylindrical "wands" (*varillas*) also occur in this level, as do shell and teeth pendants. There are no harpoons (Chapa 1975: 755–780).

Level D mammalian fauna are *Bison priscus*, *Equus caballus*, *Cervus elaphus* (abundant), *Capra ibex pyrenaica*, *Rupicapra rupicapra*, *Canis lupus*, *Vulpes vulpes*, and *Arvicola amphibius*. Molluscan species include the giant Pleistocene forms of *Patella vulgata* and *Littorina littorea*, as well as *Cyprina islandica*, *Pecten maximus*, *Purpura lapillus*, *Turritela triplicata* (abundant), *Buccinum undatum*, and *Littorina obtussata* (Vega del Sella 1916: 48).

There is little justification for attributing this collection to the Lower Magdalenian, at least as Vega del Sella intended, to the Magdalenian I or II of the French sequence, which is characterized by *raclettes*, multiple "star shaped" borers, and beveled, oval sectioned points. In Cantabria the Solutrean persisted until a time coeval with Magdalenian III in France, and assemblages called "Lower Magdalenian" in the more recent Spanish literature refer to collections that resemble Magdalenian III in the French sequence (Jordá 1957: 63, 64, 1958: 79–84; Janssens and others 1958: 95–99; Almagro 1960: 205–206).

Jordá (1958: 81–84) attributes the lowest Magdalenian level in Cueto de la Mina (mistakenly designated Level E) to the "Lower Magdalenian," in the usage described above. In a recent restudy, Chapa (1975: 755–780) assigns this assemblage to her "Cantabrian Middle Magdalenian" stage, an assessment based primarily on an elevation of the characteristics of the worked bone (there are no harpoons or harpoon fragments in this level). A higher incidence of burins also separates Levels D and C from Level B (Upper Magdalenian). Utrilla (1976a: 60–64), on the other hand, considers Level D "Cantabrian Magdalenian III," and Level C "Cantabrian Magdalenian IV." Her conclusions came from an overfine typological subdivision of lithic and bone implements based ultimately on differences in Magdalenian assemblages without harpoons across modern Spanish political subdivision (Asturias, Santander, and País Vasco)—differences that were surely meaningless in the Late Pleistocene.

Level C, 200 cm to 100(±) cm (shelter); 120 cm to 100 cm (cave). Level C occurs within a massive deposit of red clay containing large and numerous limestone blocks, fallen from the roof and sides of the shelter apparently during the Level C occupation (Vega del Sella 1916: 14).

The sparse Magdalenian industry is characterized by a great variety of burins (Vega del Sella 1916: 15, 49). Straight and canted dihedral burins on blades appear to be most common; burins on retouched truncations, busked burins, and endscraper-burins are also represented. There may be nucleiform pieces as well.

The industry in bone is also sparse and, like Level D, contains no harpoons. Beveled base, circular sectioned bone points occur, along with a few perforated baton fragments made from cervid antler. Most of the pieces are deeply engraved with geometrical designs. The high frequency of burins and the stratigraphic position of the industry suggest an equation with Magdalenian IV in the French sequence. The level accords well with Jordá's (1957: 64; 1958: 84–87) "Middle Magdalenian," defined in part on an examination of the Cueto de la Mina collections.

Mammalian fauna include abundant remains of *Equus caballus* and *Cervus elaphus*. Less frequently found are *Bison priscus*, *Capra ibex pyrenaica*, *Rupicapra rupicapra*, and *Arvicola amphibius*. The mollusca show an apparent reduction in the size of *Patella vulgata*. *Littorina littorea* (large and abundant), *Littorina obtussata*, *Pecten islandicus*, *Dentalium* spp., *Trivia europaea*, and *Sipho* spp. make up the rest of the inventory. The last three species were used for adornment (Vega del Sella 1916: 76, 81).

Level B, 90–100 cm to 40 cm (cave). This level consists of a dark organic sediment rich in shellfish remains. It occurs in situ only in the interior of the cave; outside it is replaced by disturbed deposits containing Roman tiles and potsherds of various ages, in addition to lithic debris. The Conde believed that Level B was originally present under the shelter, but that it had been disturbed and largely removed by an erosional cycle of post-Pleistocene date (Vega del Sella 1916: 51). The in situ deposits consisted of a rich industry in bone and antler, including uniserial harpoons with perforated bases and basal protuberances, perforated antler batons, engraved wands (*varillas*), beveled base quadrangular sectioned points, and needles.

Endscrapers made up the largest component in the lithic industry. Keeled and nucleiform endscrapers, endscrapers on blades, and combination forms were all represented. Dihedral burins made on blades, flake denticulates, a few Mousterian-like "points," continuously retouched blades, backed and denticulated bladelets, and some microgravettes round out the inventory.

The assemblage corresponds generally to Magdalenian V collections in France except for the basally, perforated harpoons, a distinctively Cantabrian feature. Jordá classified Level B as "Upper Magdalenian" in his four-part typology developed exclusively for the Cantabrian area (Jordá 1957: 63–65; 1958: 87–89). This assignment agrees with that of Chapa (1975: 779, 780); it is based on the high incidence of endscrapers and the presence of harpoons.

The Level B faunal spectrum includes numerous bones of *Cervus elaphus* and *Capra ibex pyrenaica*; *Bison priscus*, *Equus caballus*, *Capreolus capreolus*, *Vulpes vulpes*, and *Arvicola amphibius* are less frequently represented. The molluscan inventory is much curtailed; *Patella vulgata* (size not specified), *Littorina littorea* (large and abundant), *Cyprina islandica*, and *Cardium tuberculata* are the only species represented.

Level A, exists as shells adhering to the shelter wall 5 m above the shelter floor (shelter), 40 cm to 0 cm (cave). Level A is found only in the interior of the cave, although the shell midden outside that first brought the site to the Conde's attention also pertains to the Level A period of deposition. The level consisted primarily of a mass of shell. In the exterior trenches, Level A was replaced by a red clay that penetrated the interior of the cave in the form of a wedge. It contained fragments of modern tile but was archaeologically sterile.

Organic sediments at the base of the deposit contained an industry stratigraphically inseparable from Level B. Industrial remains were scarce and consisted of small circular endscrapers, dihedral burins made of small blades, and some microliths. The pieces are decidedly Azilian-like, although the characteristic harpoons are absent. The Conde postulated the presence of an Azilian assemblage "in an empirical manner" by setting aside, during the course of excavation, those pieces that appeared to him to be characteristically Azilian (Vega del Sella 1916: 59, 60). As a result, the collection from the level has little value because of selection; probably there was an Azilian deposit near the top of the sediments containing Level B. The conchero contained an Asturian industry in quartzite consisting almost entirely of the characteristic picks; unmodified flakes were common, but no blades were present.

The Level A faunal inventory is post-Pleistocene. *Equus caballus, Sus scrofa, Cervus elaphus, Capreolus capreolus, Rupicapra rupicapra, Capra ibex pyrenaica,* and *Vulpes vulpes* occur, along with six forms appearing for the first time in the sequence: *Bos* sp. (auroch), *Putorius putorius* (= *Mustela putorius,* the polecat), *Lutra lutra* (= *Lutra vulgaris,* the otter), *Meles meles* (= *Meles taxus,* the badger), *Felis silvestris* (= *Felis catus,* the wildcat), and *Lepus europaeus* (= *Lepus timidus,* the brown or European hare).

The inventory of molluscan fauna is also distinctive from that of preceding levels. Limpets (*Patella vulgata*) are still the most common species but they now occur reduced in size to modern dimensions. The winkle (*Littorina littorea*) has been replaced by the topshell (*Trochocochlea crassa* = *Trochus lineatus, Monodonta* sp.) as the next most prevalent form. The mussel (*Mytilus edulis*) occurs in low frequency, along with scarce remains of *Nassa reticulata, Tuberculata atlantica,* and *Triton nodiferus.* Echinoderms are represented by the sea urchin (*Paracentrotus lividus* = *Echinus* sp.), whose spines occur by the thousands in most Asturian levels. There are also the remains of two crabs, *Cancer pagurus* and *Portunus puber.* The land snail *Helix nemoralis* recurs for the first time since the Aurignacian levels.

The combined occurrence of *Patella vulgata* (of modern dimensions) and *Patella intermedia* with *Trochocochlea crassa* and the absence of *Littorina littorea* defines a configuration used extensively by the Conde to distinguish Asturian concheros from those of Late Pleistocene age. The present research confirms the validity of this distinction.

The Cueto de la Mina monograph contains the Count's earliest formulation of the theoretical paleoclimatic conditions that obtained prior to, during, and after the period of Asturian occupation. Based on observations of caves and sediments exposed in road cuts in the Nueva Valley, the Conde first postulated a period of downcutting, during which the Río Nueva eroded its bed and produced, in conjunction with a generally lowered water table, a series of shelters, caverns, and subterranean channels stabilizing at an elevation approximately 1.5 m above the present day river level. Subsequent to this erosional cycle there followed a period of alluviation during which the cobble conglomerates found in the mouth of Penicial and at other sites in the area were deposited. The third stage corresponded to the period of Asturian occupation and the accumulation of the shell middens. It was followed by an episode characterized by a relatively drier climatic regimen, which facilitated cementation of the concheros where they had accumulated in the open air in contact with fissured bedrock. The final stage consisted of a second erosional cycle that destroyed unconsolidated portions of the middens and lowered river bed levels to their present elevation (Vega del Sella 1916: 78).

However poorly understood are the processes leading to the preservation or destruction of conchero deposits, it at least seems clear that cementation is not so much dependent on macroclimatic factors external to caves as it is on conditions within caves themselves. At Cueva Morín near Villanueva in Santander (Vega del Sella 1921; González Echegaray and Freeman 1971, 1973), a column of sediments about 3 m in height has been preserved, while levels deposited contemporaneously elsewhere in the site have vanished. This is almost certainly due to a large fissure in the ceiling above the deposits that admitted, over a long period of time, an almost constant trickle of runoff laden with carbonates absorbed during passage through the roof of the cave.

It seems unnecessary, then, to postulate either a period substantially drier than the present to account for the induration of the concheros, or a period of "great rains," to use the Conde's phraseology, to account for their destruction. If percolation through fissured bedrock of cave walls and ceilings is the agent primarily responsible for conchero cementation, then the key variable is the solubility of the limestone, a factor with extreme local variation. Rainfall is only important insofar as it controls the rate of cementation, when other factors are equal. It would not be an important variable except under desertic conditions where minimal rainfall would set limits precluding effective dissolution and transportation of carbonates. There is no evidence for such a period of dessication in the entire Pleistocene sequence of northern Spain. The assertion that induration could only have taken place under conditions drier than those of the present (Vega del Sella 1916: 78; Obermaier 1924: 355, 356) does contain an element of truth, however; a drier climatic regimen would be expected to accelerate evaporation and precipitation of carbonates held in solution at cave mouths. Both events occur, at least seasonally, under present climatic conditions.

Arnero

Arnero is located on the southeast side of Posada de Llanes, a town three-quarters of a kilometer to the southwest of Cueto de la Mina (see Fig. 3.4, Table 3.1). Cut

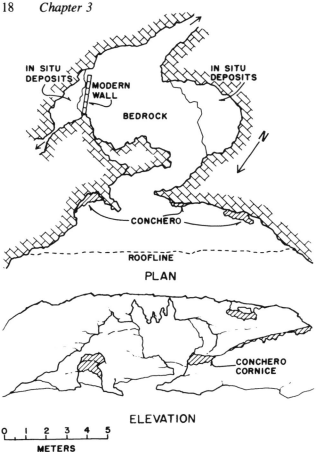

IN SITU DEPOSITS

MODERN WALL

IN SITU DEPOSITS

BEDROCK

N

CONCHERO

ROOFLINE

PLAN

CONCHERO CORNICE

ELEVATION

0 1 2 3 4 5
METERS

Figure 3.6. Arnero: plan and elevation of the rock shelter.

into a limestone hill of Devonian age (Martínez-Alvarez 1965, Map), the cave opens to the northwest and consists of a single modest chamber (Fig. 3.6). The site was discovered by Vega del Sella in 1913 and excavated sporadically through 1918 by the Count and Hugo Obermaier. The cut appears to have been placed at the back of the cave rather than in the entrance (Vega del Sella 1923: 44). The sediments in the cave contained at least two, and possibly three, cultural deposits. (Level designations are my own.)

Level C, no depth given. Containing the oldest archaeological deposit in the site, Level C represents an extensively disturbed supposedly Mousterian level. The sedimentary matrix was a "reddish clay." The pieces, few in number and only debatably Mousterian, have never been described nor can any trace of the collection be located today (Jordá 1956: 20). Vega del Sella notes that the industry occurs with Merck's rhino (*Dicerorhinus kirchbergensis = Rhinoceros merckii*), a woodland form and temperate climate indicator (Vega del Sella 1921: 155). No other faunal information is provided.

Level B, no depth given. Also occurring in the reddish clay, but said to be in situ, is an assemblage called Middle Aurignacian (Obermaier 1924: 171; Vega del Sella 1923: 44). Obermaier notes only that the bone industry is

characterized by points with a "cleft base." No account of the lithic material was provided. Jordá attributes the industry to the "typical Aurignacian" on the basis of split-based bone points; the same characteristic is used by de Sonneville-Bordes (1963: 351) to define Aurignacian I.

Faunal remains listed in Obermaier (1924: 171) include *Dicerorhinus kirchbergensis, Bos primigenius, Equus caballus, Cervus elaphus, Capreolus capreolus, Capra ibex pyrenaica,* and *Rupicapra rupicapra.* No molluscs are mentioned in the account.

Interposed between Levels A and B, according to the section provided by Vega del Sella (1923: 44), are at least one, and possibly two, unidentified strata. Conceivably there were archaeologically sterile deposits ignored in the sketchy description of the site. The levels are conspicuously absent in the later publication by Obermaier (1924: 357).

Level A, no depth given. Level A sediments, containing Asturian tools, were of two types. Most of the pieces occurred slightly buried in the surface clays that floored the site at the time of its discovery. Also, remains of a conchero occur about 3 m above the floor to the right of the entrance. A smaller but more heavily indurated segment is left of the entrance. Both conchero deposits contain a sparse industry in flint and quartzite.

No faunal remains are detailed for the Asturian levels, nor was worked bone recovered (Vega del Sella 1923: 21). Characteristic picks did occur and have escaped the fate of the collection from the other levels.

The original excavations apparently emptied the cave interior except for a small deposit along the right wall (see Fig. 3.6). The cave's small size and the fact that it was almost entirely filled with conchero during the Asturian occupation preclude its use as a habitation site (Clark 1971a, 1976a: 58–61).

Arnero was never adequately published; restudy is no longer possible because most of the collections and all the field notes appear to have been lost (Marquez 1974: 811–835). The basic sources are a few paragraphs in Vega del Sella (1916: 63; 1923: 42–44) and Obermaier (1924: 170, 171).

Fonfría

The cave of Fonfría is situated on the east bank of the Barro estuary, pueblo of Barro, *concejo* of Llanes (see Fig. 3.4, Table 3.1). The cave, which opens to the west, was excavated by Vega del Sella in 1915 (Obermaier 1924: 175; Vega del Sella 1916: 63, 1923: 42, 43). There has been some confusion in the literature about Fonfría because of a second cave with the same name located within a few hundred meters of the archaeological site and on the same side of the river. The Río Calabres emerges at this second cave in a great torrent, after having gone underground on the south side of the Llera karstic plateau below Cueto de la Mina, about 1.5 km distant. The exsurgence powers a mill at the cave mouth. The current has emptied the main chamber of any deposits it might have contained in antiquity. To the right and left of the entrance, however, conchero remnants of Asturian type are preserved in small niches in the cavern walls. No Asturian artifacts are known with certainty to have come from the mill cave, although the Conde was aware of the fact that some archaeological remains were preserved in the entrance.

The Asturian site lies about 200 m southeast of the mill, and about 20 m above it. The cave consists of a narrow (3 m to 5 m), sloping (about 40°) chimney 7 m long with a small chamber at the base. The entrance was nearly closed in antiquity by enormous blocks of roof fall that are still visible left of the present mouth. Cultural deposits occur among the interstices of these blocks, and are preserved on both sides of the chimney for nearly its length to a height of about 1.7 m. Although never described, the excavation apparently consisted of a single, massive trench running down the center of the chimney, leaving splendid profiles on both sides. Description of the stratigraphic sequence below pertains to the sediments preserved on the right wall.

Level D, 134 cm to 130 cm. The earliest deposits exposed consisted of a thin level of black organic sediments containing an industry designated Lower Magdalenian by the Count (Vega del Sella 1916: 64). The "industry" (in flint) consisted of only two retouched pieces. The tools are neither sufficiently numerous nor diagnostic enough to make any statements of cultural affinity. Fauna listed are *Cervus elaphus* and the large Pleistocene variant of *Patella vulgata sautuola.*

Level C, 130 cm to 60 cm. An archaeologically sterile layer of red cave clay.

Level B, 60 cm to 5 cm. Level B consisted of an Asturian conchero represented on both sides of the entrance. The matrix was a black organic sediment, contrasting sharply with the underlying clay, and containing bone fragments, ash, and shell. The industry consisted of quartzite picks and a variety of other tools. Of interest was a perforated shaft straightener (*baton*) in unquestionable association with the picks and analogous to finds from Magdalenian levels in Cantabria.

Data on Level B mammalian fauna were omitted from the report. Mollusca included abundant remains of *Patella vulgata* (of modern dimensions), *Trochocochlea crassa,* and *Cardium edulis. Mytilus edulis* occurs in very low frequency. Sea urchin (*Paracentrotus lividus*), crab claws, a conch (*Triton nodiferus*?), and mandibles of the flounderlike *lenguado* (*Solea* spp.) were present (Vega del Sella 1916: 63; 1923: 43). The land snail, *Helix nemoralis,* occurs in association with the marine fauna near the top of the level; its presence may represent an intrusion subsequent to the deposition of Level B.

Level A, 5 cm to 0 cm. This level was an archaeologically sterile travertine cap sealing in the underlying deposits.

The Count considered Fonfría important because of the antler tools, the first ever recovered from an Asturian level. At Fonfría there could be no question that the archaic-looking picks and the concheros were deposited contemporaneously; some of the pieces occurred embedded in the indurated shell matrix.

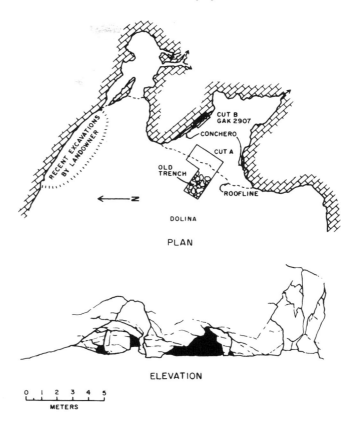

Figure 3.7. Coberizas: plan and elevation of the cave.

Coberizas (Cueva Sabina)

Coberizas is situated at the base of a sinkhole formed on the northeast slope of the Cuesta la Sabina, a promontory located 1.5 km west of Posada (see Fig. 3.4, Table 3.1). The east wall of the sinkhole is a sheer limestone escarpment in which two solution cavities have formed; Coberizas is the smaller of the two (Fig. 3.7). Both caves contain the remains of shell middens but in the more extensively developed cavern the shells appear to have been redeposited.

Coberizas measures about 7 m across the entrance, its widest point, and is only 7 m deep. On the left wall are the remnants of a stalagmitic cap; cemented into this deposit are the remains of a conchero. Prior to 1973, nothing had been published about the cultural deposits in Coberizas, although acquisition books in the Museo Arqueológico Nacional in Madrid record a visit to the site by Hugo Obermaier in 1919. Obermaier made collections from the concheros preserved along the left wall of the cave (see Chapter 5). A number of Asturian picks are attributed to the site; they were probably taken from the concheros by Obermaier or perhaps by Vega del Sella that same year.

Coberizas is a potentially important site because it is likely that significant deposits dating from Upper Paleolithic times remain in situ there. I tested the site in 1969; cultural levels dating back to the Solutrean were exposed by limited excavations in the mouth of the cave

(Cut A), and along the left wall (Cut B; Clark and Cartledge 1973a, b). A composite stratigraphy is presented below; level subdivisions are averages taken from the surface.

Level 5, 60(?) cm to 48 cm (Cut A); *Level 3,* 75(?) cm to 60 cm (Cut B). These levels are represented by a compact, dense, and homogeneous yellow clay, with limestone éboulis scarce in the uppermost 5 cm but more common with depth. Depth is unknown, apparently sterile in Cut A with some charcoal flecks and a few nondiagnostic artifacts in Cut B. Fauna include weasel (*Mustela nivalis*), two voles (*Arvicola terrestris, Microtus arvalis*), and a mole (*Talpa europaea*), as well as red and roe deer (*Cervus elaphus, Capreolus capreolus*), boar (*Sus scrofa*), fox (*Vulpes vulpes*), horse (*Equus caballus*), chamois (*Rupicapra rupicapra*), and ibex (*Capra ibex pyrenaica*). Of the economic forms present, only the red deer is common in these levels. Most of the species indicate woodland or woodland-margin biotopes or are indifferent in their habitat requirements.

Level 4, 48 cm to 40 cm (Cut A). The Level 4 designation is used to identify the upper portion of the yellow clay in Cut A, which is characterized by less éboulis than Level 5 and by a significant cultural component. Level 4 contains a poor Solutrean industry along with quantities of charcoal and ash flecks and animal bones. The stratum is considered Solutrean because of the presence of an unmistakable archaeological "index fossil"—a concave-based quartzite foliate point typical of the Cantabrian Upper Solutrean (Straus 1975a: 119). The terrestrial fauna is similar to that of Level 5. Fragmentary Pleistocene limpets (*P. vulgata sautuola*) are the only molluscan fauna represented.

Level 3, 40 cm to 25 cm (Cut A); *Level 2,* 60 cm to 40 cm (Cut B). Level 3 in Cut A probably corresponds with Level 2 in Cut B. The sedimentary matrix in both cuts is a poorly consolidated brownish-gray clay, with quantities of charcoal flecks, bone, shell, and debitage. The industry, sparse in both cuts, is typical Upper Paleolithic, with many unretouched bladelets and some backed and truncated pieces. It is tentatively assigned to Magdalenian III (Cantabrian Middle Magdalenian; Chapa 1975), based on a statistical comparison with the Magdalenian assemblages at Balmori (Clark 1974a; Clark and Clark 1975) and Altamira (González Echegaray 1971: 323–327; 1972–1973), which also lack harpoons.

Fauna were dominated by red deer remains in both cuts, with some exploitation of alpine ibex. Other species either represent creatures naturally occupying cave and rock shelter habitats (*Arvicola terrestris, Talpa europaea*) or whose presence in the site can be attributed to nonhuman predation (*Mustela nivalis*). The molluscan faunal spectrum is not clear-cut. The low frequency of *P. vulgata sautuola* and *Littorina littorea* argues for sediments of post-Pleistocene date. Quantities of giant forms characteristic of late Upper Pleistocene deposits in the area are conspicuously absent. The accumulation of terrestrial gastropods (*Helix nemoralis*) is interesting because this species appears to have been exploited for food in some

Azilian sites in Cantabria (Garcia Guinea 1975). The Level 2 specimens are small for the most part, although a few large examples occur. Snails occupy the cave mouth naturally, as they select for moist, secluded environments. The shells are whole, which would be unusual if exploited, and show no signs of burning or systematic damage unquestionably due to man (Clark and Cartledge 1973b: 402, 403).

Level 1, 40 cm to 0 cm (Cut B). Level 1 of Cut B consists of a typical Asturian conchero; Levels 1 and 2 of Cut A are disturbed and contain principally modern industrial and faunal remains (buttons, cartridge cases, scraps of metal). In Cut B the stratigraphic sequence is terminated by a travertine cap that marks the end of geological deposition within the cave.

Fauna from Level 1 of Cut B is typically Asturian, with quantities of modern limpets (*P. vulgata, P. intermedia*) and topshells (*T. crassa*) comprising respectively 71 percent and 23 percent of 3293 identified marine shells. The terrestrial fauna is again dominated by red deer, but with a nearly equal incidence of wild boar (*Sus scrofa*), a large, dangerous, matorral-adapted species that is exploited only comparatively late in the Cantabrian prehistoric record (Freeman 1973).

Faunal samples taken from the Level 1 conchero in Cut B at a point 10 cm below the travertine cap were shown statistically to be similar to those from other concheros containing Asturian picks elsewhere in the Posada region. While a good case can be made on faunal grounds for assigning Level B1 to the Asturian, excavation failed to produce any unifacial quartzite picks typical of the industry. Industrial remains were extremely sparse—a condition unfortunately characteristic of Asturian concheros. The single piece of worked bone recovered was a punch or awl fragment. These deposits produced a charcoal sample (29.9 gm) that yielded a determination (GaK 2907) of 7313 ± 175 years B.P., corrected for the new half-life. Coberizas is thus the youngest Asturian site so far dated. Clark and Cartledge (1973a, b) discuss further the 1969 excavations at Coberizas.

Tres Calabres

Tres Calabres is on the southern edge of the Llera plateau (see Fig. 3.4, Table 3.1), a few hundred meters due east of the important Asturian site of La Riera (Llopis-Lladó and Jordá 1957). Excavated by the Conde in 1921 and 1922 (Jordá 1953: 46), only the sketchiest references to the site were published by the original investigator (Vega del Sella 1923: 25, 49; 1930: 17). Although the Solutrean collections housed in the Museo Arqueológico Provincial in Oviedo were studied by Jordá (1953: 46–58) and Straus (1975: 165–168), details of the stratigraphic sequence are lacking. Obermaier (1925: 383–389) records only two cultural deposits.

Level C, no depth given. A sparse Upper Solutrean level, the earliest cultural deposit in the site totals about 50 artifacts (Jordá 1953: 53). Straus (1975: 166) was able to locate an additional 19 pieces. Endscrapers account for

11 of the 23 retouched pieces recorded in the 1953 publication; characteristic Solutrean tools include a single bifacial shouldered point of flint and a single unifacial laurel leaf of quartzite. Jordá (1957: 63) assigns the level to his Solutrean Phase II (initial Upper Solutrean).

Level B, no depth given. There was also an Asturian deposit containing the typical picks, other retouched pieces, and flakes, all made of quartzite. The bone industry included a perforated cervid-antler baton similar to that found earlier at Fonfría (Vega del Sella 1930: 16, 17). A small part of this collection is stored in the Museo Arqueológico Provincial (Oviedo). No faunal remains were reported in detail from either Level B or C.

Level A, no depth given. A sterile stalagmitic crust reportedly seals in the underlying deposits (Vega del Sella 1930: 17).

Jordá's (1953: 46–58) evaluation of the Solutrean level was part of a continuing effort to restudy collections from the Conde's excavations housed in the Museo Arqueológico Provincial in Oviedo. His reevaluations, which have promulgated a bewildering number of ever-changing but supposedly temporally sequent Solutrean "evolutionary" stages (Jordá 1955, 1957, 1960, 1977), were based mainly on the examination of pieces displayed in museum showcases. His classification of the Tres Calabres collections was founded on the absence of any concave based foliate points in a collection comprising only *two* Solutrean points—hardly a credible sample on which to develop a scheme of chronological relationships (Straus 1975: 166–168).

Balmori (Cueva de la Ería, Cueva del Pradón, La Cuevona)

Balmori, often confused with the nearby cave art site of Quintanal (Alcalde del Río and others 1911: 83, 84; González Morales and Marquez 1974), is a large and important Upper to post-Paleolithic occupation site located on the southern face of the Llera plateau about 600 m northeast of the town of Balmori (see Figs. 3.1, 3.4; Table 3.1). Discovered by Hermilio Alcalde del Río and the Abbé Breuil in April, 1908, the site was first tested by Father Evaristo Gomez, a local Jesuit high school teacher, in 1910 and subsequently was excavated by the Conde de la Vega del Sella and Hugo Obermaier from 1915 to 1917 (Vega del Sella 1930: 76).

Like Penicial, the cave has two entrances, both open to the southeast (Fig. 3.8); the lower and more spacious forms a regular triangle some 13 m across, the apex standing 7 m above the present floor of the cave. The entrance connects directly with a large, rectangular room (Room 1) about 26 m long. The left wall of Room 1 is a massive limestone block, displaced along a fault line. At 26 m from the entrance, Room 1 veers to the north, forming a wide but low passageway (Corridor 1) that divides at about 16 m into two large branches (Fig. 3.8).

The second entrance is situated 4 m northwest of the first and about 5.5 m above it. It also opens on a room of substantial proportions that, unlike Room 1, still contains abundant cultural deposits. Room 2 measures 17 m

long and is about 4 m in height. The two chambers are connected by a second corridor (Corridor 2) running parallel to the first but situated about 9 m west of it. The entire corridor was originally filled with an immense shell midden. At its northern end, Corridor 2 leads into an interior chamber of moderate dimensions, Room 3, which in turn connects with Corridor 1 and the upper entrance. The southern end of Corridor 2 was filled with sand and clay deposits believed to have been of fluvial origin (Vega del Sella 1930: 48).

Prior to excavation, cultural deposits filled Corridor 2 and large parts of Rooms 2 and 3. Indurated conchero remnants occurred along the north wall of Room 1 and on the walls and ceiling of Room 2, indicating archaeological levels destroyed prior to investigation of the site. Finally, a mass of red deer antlers of exceptional size was found along the right wall of Room 1 (Vega del Sella 1930: 48–50).

Excavations were conducted first from the lower entrance (Room 1) in order to improve access to Room 3. This trench is still visible (Fig. 3.8). Excavations were also conducted in Rooms 2 and 3 and in Corridor 2, apparently in the form of long, narrow trenches. The description provided of the operation is minimal and confusing; no plan of the site is given in the basic sources (Vega del Sella 1916: 66, 67; 1930: 47–89). Four cultural assemblages were recovered from the site. A composite stratigraphic sequence is given below; level designations are my own.

Level G, no depth given. The earliest level recorded was a thick deposit of sterile yellow sand thought to overlie bedrock (the floor of the cave was never exposed in any of the excavations). The depositional agency was believed to have been a flood or a series of floods of pre-Solutrean date (Vega del Sella 1930: 49, 50).

Level F, no depth given. Level F consisted of a yellow cave clay; it contained a sparse Solutrean industry in flint and quartzite and occurred both in the Room 2 trench and the trench connecting Rooms 2 and 3. The industry is described under Level E.

Level E, no depth given. A thin calcrete horizon, weakly cemented throughout the limited exposure, was recorded in Room 2 and in the trench connecting Rooms 2 and 3. Both Levels F and E contained an industry described as Upper Solutrean (Vega del Sella 1930: 50, 78–81). The inventory includes large quartzite endscrapers made on flakes and approaching circular forms. A few endscrapers on retouched flakes and blades occur, along with at least two endscraper-multiple burins. The burin series, the most numerous tool class, is interesting because the retouch techniques used on the blades show marked variation. Most of the pieces are retouched by the flat, invasive Solutrean technique, producing straight or slightly concave edges. Microliths include backed bladelets in low frequency. Characteristically Solutrean pieces consisted of a few apparent laurel leaves, one of which had a concave base, and a nondescript foliate point, roughly triangular in plan. There is a single, shouldered point in flint.

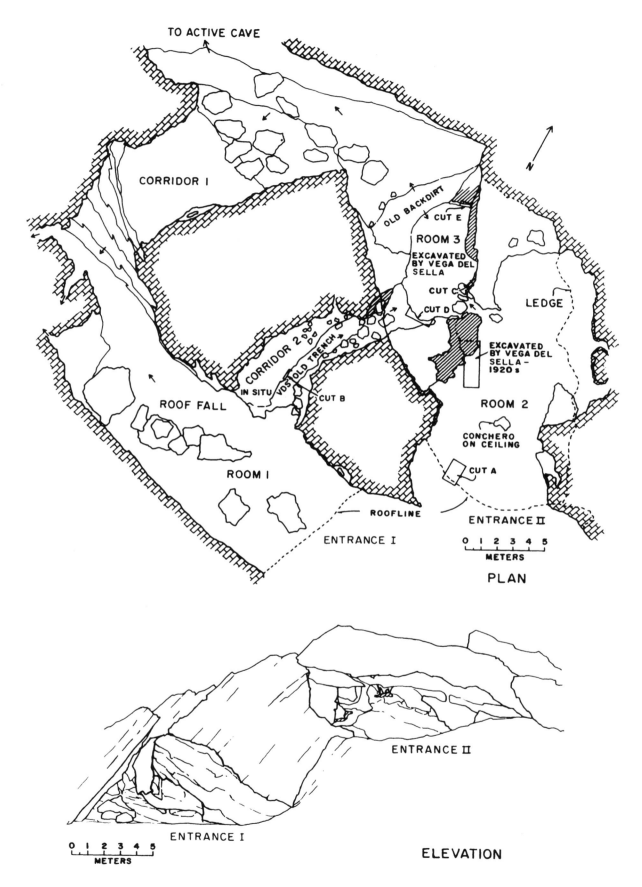

TO ACTIVE CAVE

CORRIDOR I

OLD BACKDIRT
CUT E

ROOM 3
EXCAVATED
BY VEGA DEL
SELLA

CUT C

CUT D

LEDGE

CORRIDOR 2
VDS OLD TRENCH

IN SITU

CUT B

EXCAVATED
BY VEGA DEL
SELLA –
1920s

ROOF FALL

ROOM 2

ROOM I

CONCHERO
ON CEILING

CUT A

ROOFLINE

ENTRANCE I

ENTRANCE II

N

0 1 2 3 4 5
METERS

PLAN

ENTRANCE II

ENTRANCE I

0 1 2 3 4 5
METERS

ELEVATION

Figure 3.8. Balmori: plan and elevation of the cave.

The industry in bone was sparse (see Clark 1974a for an extended discussion of the lithic and bone industries). No faunal data are given.

Jordá (1957: 63) classifies the Solutrean levels from Balmori in his Phase IV (Final Solutrean), as does Corchón (1971a: 101). Straus (1975a: 175, 176) considers these classifications overfine and inconsistently applied. He labels the collection simply "Upper Solutrean," because of the presence of shouldered points.

Level D, no depth given to 0 cm. This thin layer of yellow cave clay was described only as similar to that of Level F (Vega del Sella 1930: 50). Overlying Level D in parts of Rooms 2 and 3 and in Corridor 2 were the masses of Upper Paleolithic conchero mentioned above. The Conde was unable to discern any stratification within these black, organic sediments that in places measured more than 2 m thick. Consequently, he excavated them as a single unit. Using his knowledge of the Cantabrian Upper Paleolithic as a basis for classification (Vega del Sella 1930: 54, 55, 68), he separated the industrial components from one another during and after the excavation. These collections from the Paleolithic concheros, therefore, are suspect, produced to conform with assemblage definitions conceived prior to excavation.

Level C, no depth given. Level C describes the industry removed from the central portion of the mound to about 20 to 25 cm from its edges. The collection is attributed to the Final Magdalenian by Vega del Sella (1930: 61), a classification that is inexplicable given the total absence of harpoons of any kind in the deposits.

The Level C collection consisted of four kinds of endscrapers. Nucleiform and carinate pieces are common, as are endscrapers made on long flakes; simple blade endscrapers are rare. Both flint and quartzite were utilized as raw materials. Burins were common and almost always occurred on retouched flint blades. Also important is a series of numerous, markedly denticulated, blades. It is noteworthy that no microliths are mentioned in the description of the assemblage.

If the lithic industry is nondescript, the industry in antler is remarkably distinctive and consistent. Quadrangular sectioned points with a single bevel at the base were the most common forms recovered (Vega del Sella 1930: 65–67). Many of the pieces are engraved. Two perforated antler batons were also recovered, along with needles and awls.

Jordá (1957: 64; 1958: 84–87; 1977: 127) assigns this collection to his Middle Magdalenian phase; Utrilla (1976a: 60, 61) considers it Magdalenian III, as does Clark (1974a: 411–420).

Level B, no depth given. Level B designates the peripheral 20 to 25 cm of the Paleolithic shell midden, thought to contain an Azilian industry (Vega del Sella 1930: 56, 61). Pieces taken from other parts of the mound, however, if they appeared Azilian to the Conde were classified as such. The result is a collection of circular and keeled endscrapers, nucleiform endscrapers made on tiny bladelet cores, small flake perforators, numerous burins, and backed bladelets, which, as might be expected, resemble Azilian collections from other Cantabrian sites. It should be noted, however, that no "Azi-

lian points" nor any characteristic flattened harpoons were recovered from the site (Jordá 1957: 66; 1958: 89–91).

Because no distinction was made between levels in the Paleolithic midden, the faunal inventory pertains to the deposit as a whole. Species said to occur in high frequency include *Bos* sp., *Bison* sp., *Equus caballus* (two varieties), and *Cervus elaphus* (two varieties). The cave lion (*Felis leo spelaea*) and bear (*Ursus spelaeus*) occur in low frequency along with the familiar grouping of Holocene species. *Canis lupus, Vulpes vulpes, Capra ibex, Meles meles,* and *Capreolus capreolus* are listed.

Mollusca identified included numerous examples of *Patella vulgata sautuola* and *Littorina littorea. Cardium mucronatum, Cardium tuberculum, Cyprina islandica, Pecten maximus, Quenoptus pes pelicani, Littorina obtussata, Cyprea europaea,* and *Nassa reticulata* occur in low frequencies; the last four were used as objects of adornment (Vega del Sella 1930: 89).

Level A, no depth given to 0 cm. In contrast with Levels C and B, the final cultural deposit in the site was distinctive with respect to both industry and sediment and was excavated as a unit. Level A consisted of an Asturian assemblage localized on the surface and in the peripheral concheros of Room 3. The Room 3 floor consisted of red cave clay overlain by a veneer of limestone cobbles. "Numerous picks" were found on top of and buried within this surface deposit and in pure Asturian concheros preserved in crevices along the east wall of Room 3, overlying those of Paleolithic date. Elsewhere in the chamber, the deposits reportedly were mixed (Vega del Sella 1930: 51, 52).

Concheros of Asturian type were also found along the west wall of Room 2 and suspended from its ceiling. Overlain by flowstone deposits, they are now reduced to cornices about 3 m above the present floor of the cave; they mark the final period of deposition in Balmori.

No inventory of terrestrial fauna was provided for the Asturian level; the only molluscan species recorded are *Patella vulgata* (of modern size) and *Trochocochlea crassa.* The collection from the Asturian level at Balmori cannot be located today.

Excavations were conducted in Corridor 2 and in Rooms 2 and 3 of Balmori in 1969. The most important tests, Cuts D and E, were situated in undisturbed deposits on opposite sides of Vega del Sella's old trench in Room 3 (Fig. 3.8); they exposed a series of in situ Upper Paleolithic levels. The sequence from Cut E also includes an Asturian conchero (Level 1) overlying a sequence of Magdalenian III levels (Levels 2–5; see Clark 1974a: 383–426).

Analysis of five sediment samples from Cut D and three from Cut E indicates a climatic regime similar to that of today. This may be due (1) to the coastal situation of Balmori and to the relative stability of the maritime climate characteristic of the low-lying coastal plain; (2) to the stable internal regime of the cave itself (note that both cuts are situated at considerable distances from the cave mouth); and (3) to the high "cultural" component in the Upper Paleolithic levels that may well have obscured

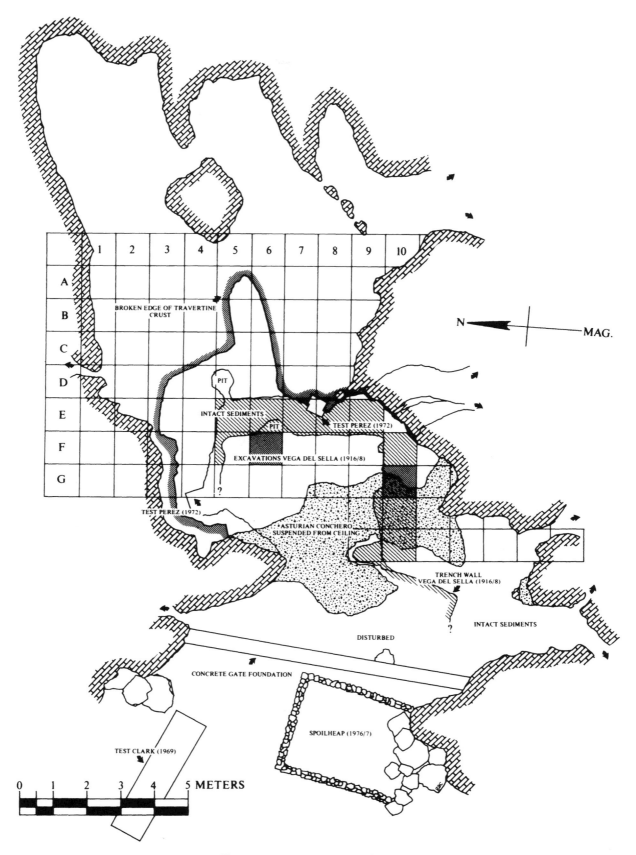

Figure 3.9. La Riera: plan of the cave.

prevalent physical processes. Phosphorous and potassium studies suggest marked differences in the intensity of human occupation between Cut E (where those elements are present at high levels of concentration) and Cut D (where they are much less in evidence).

La Riera

La Riera, the most important Asturian site investigated so far, is situated a scant 50 m east of Cueto de la Mina, at the eastern end of the Posada Valley (see Figs. 3.1, 3.4; Table 3.1). The site consists of a cave, facing west, formed at the foot of a rock shelter in the southern face of the Llera plateau. La Riera was discovered by Vega del Sella in 1916 and was excavated by the Conde in collaboration with Hugo Obermaier during the following two years (Obermaier 1924: 175, 346).

When discovered, the rock shelter was small and inconspicuous, measuring only 8 m across by 5 m deep (Fig. 3.9). There were no surface indications of the important cultural deposits within it. Moreover, the entrance to the cavern was completely blocked by a massive deposit of conchero. A layer of soil had formed on top of the shell mound, so that the cave was not readily apparent. The Conde, however, found a small opening at the shelter base that connected with the hidden cavern by means of a torturous crawlway (Vega del Sella 1930: 6, 7).

The cave itself consisted of a single, irregular chamber, about 12 m long, between 6 m and 10 m wide, with a ceiling less than 2 m high (Fig. 3.9). The interior was characterized by flowstone formations (now largely destroyed), which the Conde pierced to determine if archaeological levels were present. In doing so, he exposed the mass of shell that penetrated the interior of the cave in the form of a wedge. The cultural deposits at the foot of the shelter and in the cave entrance and interior were sealed in by this stalagmitic crust, precluding any possible mixture due to disturbance subsequent to its formation (Vega del Sella 1930: 9).

Excavations were conducted in two phases. First, a trench was dug parallel to the long axis of the shelters exposing deposits and creating a passageway for backdirt, deposited to the right of the entrance. This trench provided a stratigraphic guide to facilitate excavation and simultaneously permitted natural light to enter the cave. A second trench was then excavated parallel to the long axis of the cave to tap the deposits there, and to verify the stratigraphic sequence revealed by the first sounding. The second trench, perpendicular to the first, formed a "T" with it (Straus and Clark 1978a: 302). The stratigraphic sequence described below occurs at the conjunction of the two tests, indicated on Figure 3.9.

At least four, possibly as many as six, cultural deposits were recovered from the site. The oldest assemblage recorded in situ pertained to the Upper Solutrean. Bedrock was never reached. Level thicknesses are approximations from original surfaces. Those in the shelter are taken from ground level; those in the cave are calculated from the top of the stalagmitic crust.

Level K, ? to 157 cm (shelter); ? to 91 cm (cave). The oldest deposit was a yellow cave clay of undetermined thickness. It contained a few charcoal flakes near the top and some éboulis, but apparently no industrial remains.

Level J, 157 cm to 122–117 cm (shelter); 91 cm to 56–51 cm (cave). Level J was the oldest cultural level recorded. The sedimentary matrix, 35 to 40 cm thick, was a sandy clay similar in texture to Level K, but of a darker gray or gray-brown color. Industrial remains, attributed to the Upper Solutrean by the Conde (Vega del Sella 1923: 48; 1930: 35), were localized at the foot of the shelter. They did not extend far into the cave itself, where the cultural component was represented only by ash and charcoal flecks.

The industry in stone consists of a few nucleiform endscrapers; endscrapers made on thick flakes and simple blade endscrapers also occur. As is the case generally with Solutrean industries (de Sonneville-Bordes 1963: 252), endscrapers are more numerous than burins. Finely-made single and double perforators occur on both flakes and blades. Sidescrapers are probably the most common type group; notches and denticulates are also present in some frequency. A few microliths (backed bladelets) were noted during my 1974 inspection of the Oviedo museum collections. The characteristically Solutrean pieces include unifacially retouched shouldered points in flint and magnificent laurel leaves with concave bases. A broken willow leaf point is also represented.

The industry in bone and antler is both plentiful and varied. Most commonly represented is a Magdalenian-like beveled base, circular-sectioned antler point. The characteristic Solutrean curved antler point, with marked medial flattening, is also present.

Fauna listed include *Equus caballus, Cervus elaphus, Capra ibex pyrenaica, Vulpes vulpes,* and *Canis lupus.* Mollusca exploited consisted of *Patella vulgata sautuola, Littorina littorea,* and *Littorina obtussata.*

Jordá (1957: 63), citing the shouldered and concave-based points and the medially flattened bone pieces, places the Solutrean at La Riera in his Phase III (Cantabrian Upper Solutrean), a designation maintained in his latest writing on the subject (Jordá 1977: 96). Corchón (1971b: 10) identifies the industry as the "latest Solutrean level in Asturias," for reasons that are not made clear. Straus (1975a: 164) simply considers these old collections to be "typically Upper Solutrean, in the generally accepted definition of the stage." Level J bone and lithic industries are treated at greater length by Straus (1975a: 155–165) and by Clark and Richards (1978).

Level I, 122–117 cm to about 115 cm (shelter); 56–51 cm to about 50 cm (cave). Level I is a thin level of gray clay, lighter in color than Level J; archaeologically sterile.

Level H, about 115 cm to 108 cm (shelter); about 50 cm to 40 cm (cave). This level of black, organic clayey sediment is similar to, although darker than, that of Level J. The industrial component is identified as Late Magdalenian (Vega del Sella 1930: 31, 35). The level merges with

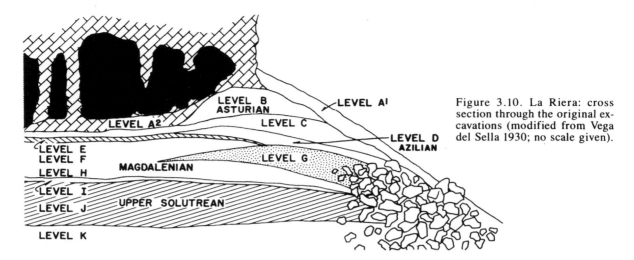

Figure 3.10. La Riera: cross section through the original excavations (modified from Vega del Sella 1930; no scale given).

Level F at the rear of the cave (Fig. 3.10). The lithic industry was not separated from that of Level F because no sedimentological distinction could be made.

Level G, 108 cm to 78 cm (shelter); 40 cm to 35 cm (cave). Level G was interposed between Levels H and F in the rock shelter and at the mouth of the cave. It consisted of a wedge of red clay contrasting sharply with the darker sediments of the levels occurring above and below it.

Level G contained an industry described as Acheulean by the Conde. Its occurrence in the middle of a deposit of Magdalenian age is explained by postulating a landslide. The Acheulean pieces were believed to have been deposited originally on the platform above the site. During the late Magdalenian, they allegedly fell from the slope above the shelter and thus became incorporated in the Level H–F depositional sequence (Vega del Sella 1930: 8–10, 45, 46; Obermaier 1924: 175).

The industry, exclusively in quartz and quartzite, consists of only six pieces. All are retouched and are shown in Vega del Sella's text. Five of the pieces are manufactured on cobbles. Only one piece appears to be bifacial, a quartzite handaxe, amygdaloid in plan and biconvex in section, that is flaked over both faces and retouched secondarily on the margins. These pieces are in the Museo Nacional de Ciencias Naturales in Madrid.

In spite of the distinctive nature of the industry and of the sedimentary context in which it occurs, I believe the small collection belongs with the Magdalenian levels with which it is associated. The evidence suggests a "heavy duty" tool kit reserved for a specific set of activities involving chopping or cutting. Large quartzite implements of "archaic" appearance are a common component of Magdalenian deposits in Cantabria. It is not necessary to postulate an Acheulean intrusion to account for the appearance of such tools in Upper Paleolithic assemblages.

Level F, 35 cm to 23 cm (cave). Level F consisted of a black, organic sediment, identical to Level H. It occurred as a separate entity only in the mouth of the cave where deposits from 7 cm to 12 cm thick are recorded. It is absent beneath the shelter overhang and grades imper-

ceptibly into Level H farther back in the cave (Fig. 3.10). Like Level H, the industry is classified as Late Magdalenian (Vega del Sella 1930: 30, 31).

Because the Conde considered Levels H and F representative of a single period of deposition, he made no effort to distinguish the artifacts recovered from below the red clay wedge (Level G) from those taken from the sediments above it. The distinction may have been important because the Conde himself later remarks that the deposits designated Level F contained harpoons, whereas the Level H sediments did not (Vega del Sella 1930: 31, 32).

The most numerous tool category appears to be nucleiform endscrapers. They occur both on small flint bladelet cores and on large and massive quartzite flake cores. Flake endscrapers are present in some frequency; endscrapers on blades are rare. Burins are also present in "their various forms" (Vega del Sella 1930: 26). No mention is made of the microlithic component to be expected in a Late Magdalenian assemblage.

The industry in bone includes two uniserial harpoons, both recovered from Level F; remaining pieces cannot be fixed as to level. The most common pieces are quadrangular sectioned points of cervid antler, usually engraved with parallel or hatched line motifs.

Faunal remains were *Equus caballus, Bison priscus, Cervus elaphus, Capra ibex pyrenaica, Meles meles, Rupicapra rupicapra, Vulpes vulpes, Canis lupus,* and an unidentified long-legged wading fowl. Mollusca recovered consisted of *Patella vulgata sautuola, Littorina littorea, Littorina obtussata, Trivia europaea, Pectunculus glycimeris,* and *Turritela triplicata* (Vega del Sella 1930: 35).

Jordá (1957: 64; 1977: 141, 142) classified the Magdalenian levels from La Riera in his "Initial Upper Magdalenian," which he believed corresponded to Magdalenian V in the French sequence. The agreement was good except for the fact apparent at that time that no microliths occurred in either Level H or Level F. Actually microliths *do* occur in these strata (Clark and Straus 1977a, b). Utrilla (1976a: 61) also considers this assemblage Upper Magdalenian, while inexplicably classifying the Level H assemblage as Magdalenian III.

Level E, 78 cm to 76 cm (shelter); 23 cm to 21 cm (cave). A thin clay layer on top of Level F separates it from Level D (Azilian); the sediment does not extend much beyond the base of the rock shelter (Fig. 3.10). Lighter in color than Level F, no mention is made of faunal or cultural debris.

Level D, 76 cm to 69 cm (shelter). Level D is classified as Azilian (Vega del Sella 1923: 47; 1930: 18–25). The sedimentary matrix was a red clay, contrasting with the darker sediments of Levels E and F (Vega del Sella 1930: 9).

The industry included an impressive array of small endscrapers made on flakes and blades. Flake endscrapers, retouched around three-quarters of their circumferences, are common. A few truly circular forms occur. Burins are also said to be numerous. Like the endscraper series, they are diminutive, occurring on small blades (frequent) and flakes (rare). Straight and canted dihedral burins are most common. Finally, in marked contrast with Level F, the microlithic component is abundantly represented. It consists mainly of simple backed bladelets, but truncated, backed and truncated bladelets, and microgravettes also occur. "Azilian points," however, are apparently absent.

The industry in bone includes the characteristic flat Azilian antler harpoon with basal perforation; also of note is a long, cylindrical piece engraved with a zigzag pattern, said to be characteristic of the Azilian of Cantabria (Vega del Sella 1930: 25). The rest of the pieces consisted of various kinds of points.

Faunal remains included *Equus caballus, Bos.* sp., *Cervus elaphus, Capreolus capreolus, Rupicapra rupicapra, Canis lupus, Vulpes vulpes, Meles meles.* Salmon vertebrae (*Salmo* spp.) and leopard bones (*Felis pardus*) are noteworthy, as they are not recorded from earlier levels in the site. Only two molluscs are listed: *Patella vulgata* (no size indicated) and *Littorina littorea.*

Level C, 69 cm to 39 cm (shelter); 21 cm to 15 cm (cave). A deposit of red clay, attaining a maximum thickness of 25 cm to 30 cm under the rock shelter, is much thinner inside the cave (Fig. 3.10). Archaeologically sterile.

Level B, 39 cm to 20 cm (shelter); 15 cm to 10 cm (cave). Level B consisted of an Asturian shell midden extending across the shelter mouth and penetrating the cave interior (Figs. 3.9, 3.10). This deposit completely obstructed the mouth of the cavern prior to excavation. The matrix consisted of a black, greasy organic sediment; the main constituents of the midden were millions of loose shells and bone fragments. Inside the cave the deposit was indurated near the top by flowstone formations that capped the stratigraphic sequence there.

The industry, exclusively in quartzite, was present in greater abundance and variety than at any other excavated Asturian station. Bone and antler tools were also recovered (see Chapter 5; Vega del Sella 1930: 11–18).

No terrestrial fauna are listed for Level B, but the molluscan constituents are presented in some detail. *Patella vulgata* (of modern dimension) and *Trochocochlea crassa* are present in great numbers; *Cardium edulis* is abundant. A few examples each of *Mytilus edulis, As-*

tralium rugosus, and *Triton nodiferus* were also recovered. Sea urchins (*Paracentrotus lividus* = *Taxoneptes lividus*) and crab claws (*Cancer pagurus*) are present (Vega del Sella 1930: 18).

Level A, 20 cm to 0 cm (shelter); 10 cm to 0 cm (cave). Level A consists of two kinds of sediments; both mark the end of the depositional sequence at the site. Level A1 refers to the modern soil cover formed atop the shell midden where it occurs beneath the rock shelter in the open air. It attains a maximum thickness of about 25 cm and is archaeologically sterile. Level A2 designates the stalagmitic crust formed on top of Levels B and C in the interior of the cave. It attains a maximum thickness of about 10 cm; it is also archaeologically sterile (Vega del Sella 1930: 9).

The stratification at La Riera was claimed to be absolutely unambiguous with respect to the Asturian level; the Conde reported that the conchero directly overlies the Azilian deposits, thus foreshadowing a refutation of the karstic rejuvenation theory of Jordá. The site has also contributed the largest and best Asturian industrial collection from the original series of excavations (Clark 1974b). Much of the site itself remains intact; possibly pre-Solutrean deposits have only been sampled recently (Straus and Clark 1978b).

La Riera was tested by me during the summer of 1969 (Clark 1974b; Clark and Richards 1978) and by Perez and Gomez Tabanera in 1972 (Gomez Tabanera 1976). In addition, the site has been the focus of a large, multidisciplinary project (1976–1980, sponsored by the National Science Foundation; Clark and Straus 1977a, b, c; Straus and Clark 1978a, b, c; Straus and others 1977).

My 1969 tests at La Riera were confined mainly to the slope in front of the cave, where a 4 m by 1 m by 1 m excavation revealed in situ Asturian deposits stratified in soil to the left of the cave entrance (Fig. 3.9). This test (Cut A) produced two distinct Asturian strata with associated industry and fauna; the contents are discussed in more detail in Chapters 5 and 6. The excavation altered the notion of primitiveness associated with the industry and provided, for the first time, a representative sample of Asturian debitage. The Asturian conchero suspended from the cave roof was also tested (Cut B) to provide unbiased samples of molluscan and mammalian faunas. Both excavations produced the characteristic picks that serve to identify the assemblage. Conchero samples from Cut B yielded more than 37.7 gm of wood charcoal. The resulting determination (GaK 2909), corrected for the new half-life, is 8909 ± 309 years B.P., a date in almost perfect accord with that obtained from the analogous conchero in the upper cave at Penicial.

Perez and Gomez Tabanera also tested La Riera in 1972 with a tiny but deep sounding (about 50 cm by 25 cm by 100 cm) in the slope in front of the cave (Gomez Tabanera 1976); unfortunately it almost certainly was placed in the spoilheap from the 1916–1918 excavations (Sector B). Perez' main contribution, however, was an equally diminutive but deep test in the cave interior (Sector C), which indicated that the stratigraphy was a good deal more complex than the Conde had originally reported it to be. Somehow 20 levels were defined in this narrow shaft, allegedly pertaining to Upper Solutrean (Levels 20–17), Middle Magdalenian (Level 16), Magdalenian III (Levels 15, 14), Magdalenian IV (Level 13), Magdalenian IV–V (Level 12), Magdalenian V (Level 11) and Final Magdalenian (VI, Levels 10–4) occupations (Gomez Tabanera 1976). These refined culture-stratigraphic assignments should not be taken seriously, although Upper Solutrean and Magdalenian deposits of some kind were in fact sampled. While Perez' test clearly shows the stratigraphy to be complex, these assignments are based on miniscule industrial and faunal samples taken from thin lenses in an area about 0.125 square meter in extent. Tabanera seldom visited the site during the course of the excavations, and his published report is rendered still less credible by bizarre assertions of the existence of hut floors, walls, and other structures allegedly uncovered in the tiny test; by unsubstantiated correlations of stratigraphic units with specific Late Pleistocene paleoclimatic episodes (correlations not grounded in analysis of any kind); and by discourses on demographic density and economic and spiritual activities, evidence for which was supposedly recovered from an excavated surface area about one-eighth of a meter in extent.

The La Riera Paleoecological Project excavations (1976–1980; Clark and Straus 1977a, b, c; Straus and Clark 1978a, b, c) were conducted in order to test a series of explicit hypotheses that bear on the changing nature of man-land relationships on the Cantabrian coastal plain during the 12,000 or so year span of occupation represented by the radiocarbon-dated culture sequence at the cave. Although the project has a regional orientation, some 36 natural strata have been defined at La Riera; they contain industries assigned to Upper Solutrean (Levels 2–17), Lower Magdalenian (Levels 18–23), Upper Magdalenian (Level 24), Azilian (Levels 26–28), and Asturian (Level 29, conchero) culture-stratigraphic units. Most of the sediments in the cave interior pertain to Upper Solutrean occupations, which span a period of some 4000 years (Straus and others 1978). This research has been most extensively reported in Clark and Straus (1982), Straus and Clark (1978a), and in Straus and others (1981).

With respect to the Asturian, excavation in 1978 was able to establish that the Asturian conchero suspended from the cave ceiling did directly overlie a distinctive Azilian midden, as the Conde had claimed, where a continuous stratigraphic column was preserved along the right wall of the cave. There seems little question, then, of the relative age of these deposits compared with those of the final Paleolithic. Pollen samples taken from the conchero contain pine (*Pinus*), birch (*Betula*), oak (*Quercus*), and especially hazel (*Corylus*), mainly thermophilous arboreal species typical of the regional Early Boreal that accord well with the date indicated by the 1969 radiocarbon assay. An enormous quantity of ferns clearly indicates very humid conditions. The molluscan fauna point to intensive exploitation of two species of

limpet (*P. vulgata, P. intermedia*), topshells (*T. crassa*), and finally, mussels (*Mytilus edulis*). According to Nicholas Shackleton, the limpets and topshells were probably collected during the winter months. *P. intermedia* and *T. crassa* are species adapted to rocky, moderately exposed littoral zones, which apparently were not exploited prior to Lower Magdalenian times (Level 20). Limpet size also remains stable in Upper Solutrean-Lower Magdalenian Levels 2 through 20, but size decreases during the remainder of the sequence as the large estuarine *P. vulgata* specimens are now mixed with smaller ones from the open littoral and with *P. intermedia*, a species that is always smaller. It is suggested that during the earlier occupations (Levels 1–20), while the needs of the human population were presumably adequately met, gathering took place only in sheltered zones like estuaries, where large specimens of *P. vulgata* and *Littorina littorea* were collected. Later (after Level 20), and possibly because of an increase in human population density requiring the exploitation of new food sources, gathering extended to the open, moderately wave-beaten shore beyond the estuarine zone. The diversity of molluscan species exploited reaches a maximum during the Asturian; diversity is minimal during the long Upper Solutrean and Lower Magdalenian periods (Straus and others 1980; Clark and Straus 1982).

Mésé

Mésé is a small cavern located in a limestone hill on the east bank of the Río Cabras north of the hamlet of Mere, *concejo* of Llanes, Asturias (see Fig. 3.4, Table 3.1). It is the most inland Asturian site reported to date.

The single, cursory reference to the cave (Jordá, in Hernández-Pacheco and others 1957: 24, 25), describes two small chambers, each with a separate entrance. The two openings lie at different elevations with respect to the present level of the river. The lowermost, at 5 m above river level, reportedly contains a Magdalenian industry; the higher entrance, 8 m above the river, contains an Asturian conchero. No excavations have been conducted at the site.

Jordá (Hernández-Pacheco and others 1957: 24, 25) contends that the distribution of the cultural deposits is significant:

> The two caves are elements of different ages [pertaining to] the same [karstic] resurgence. The oldest element is evidently the upper cavern. The Asturian conchero would have been deposited once this cavern [had dried out] and while the lower one was still functioning [that is, while it was still a conduit for a water course]. When the exsurgence ceased, and the lower cave dried out, it was probably occupied during the Magdalenian because tools of that age are found there. This implies for the Asturian an age earlier than the Magdalenian. (Translation by G. A. Clark.)

I suggest instead that both caverns were formed at an unspecified period much anterior to that of human occupation, and that the absence of an Asturian conchero in the lower entrance, here, as elsewhere in the region, is due to a post-Pleistocene erosional cycle that evacuated those loose, easily transported sediments, while leaving the conchero in the upper entrance intact. Evidence for post-Pleistocene erosion is extensive in Cantabria and Karl Butzer has indicated that evidence for erosion during the Würm is ephemeral.

Lledías (Cueva del Cuetú, Cueva del Cueto, Cueto de Lledías, El Cuetú)

Lledías is located 1.5 km southeast of the pueblo of Posada, in the *concejo* of Llanes (see Fig. 3.4, Table 3.1). The cave, which contains forged Upper Paleolithic artwork, is formed in the north slope of the limestone mountain called Cueto de Lledías. The primitive entrance is a rock shelter facing north. A crevice in the shelter floor connects directly with a chimney that descends at a steep inclination some 42 m into the Cueto massif.

Although known since the last century, most of the cave interior was not discovered until the summer of 1936. In June of that year, Cesareo Cardín, the landlord of the property, erected a stock enclosure under the shelter. In the process he made some shallow excavations and discovered the hidden cavern. Cultural deposits recovered from both the shelter and the cave were turned over to Dr. Juan Uría-Riú at the University of Oviedo. The stratigraphy at the site, as revealed in Cardín's cut, was first reported by Uría-Riú (1941). Jordá (1955: 49) also excavated there during the early 1950s, and he presents the most detailed account of the stratigraphy. Except for Level I, level designations are those used by Jordá.

Level I, sediments at 42 m from the cave mouth. Jordá (in Hernández-Pacheco and others 1957: 25) makes note of alternating strata of sands and clays, thought to be of marine origin. They occur near the bottom of the cavern and are archaeologically sterile, long predating the period of human occupation.

Level H, at less than 221 cm. A sterile sediment, not described (Jordá 1955: 49). H through A form a stratified column extending upward from the base of the connecting passage (at 221 cm) to the floor of the rock shelter (at 0 cm).

Level G, 221 cm to 195 cm. Traces of an Upper Solutrean level, not otherwise described (Jordá 1955: 49).

Level F, 195 cm to 175 cm. A sterile sediment, not described (Jordá 1955: 49).

Level E, 175 cm to 150 cm. Levels E through C were evidently mixed because Uría-Riú (1941) treats these deposits as if they were separable only on a priori typological grounds. The sediments, described as a heap of shell, bone, and lithic debris, were found in the cave interior where they had fallen through the crevice at the base of the rock shelter. He does not describe the sedimentary matrix. The industry consisted of about a dozen split-based bone points called Aurignacian in the original publication (Uría-Riú 1941). Jordá (1955: 49) first assigned the collection to his Lower Magdalenian (equivalent to Magdalenian III). Later (in Hernández-Pacheco

and others 1957: 25), he revised his opinion and classified the tools as Middle Magdalenian (equivalent to Magdalenian IV), finally expressing doubt (Jordá 1957: 65) about the authenticity of the tools from Levels D, E, and G.

Level D, 150 cm to 110 cm. Level E grades directly into Level D. The industry, again in cervid antler, consisted of eight beveled base points, some double ended points, and a variety of harpoons. Reminiscent of Azilian tools are three flat, clumsily-made harpoons. On typological grounds Uría-Riú (1941) defined an Azilian component, and assigned these pieces to it. Jordá (1955: 49; 1957: 65; 1958: 91; and in Hernández-Pacheco and others 1957: 25) refers the artifacts to a Final Upper Magdalenian stage, while expressing grave doubts about the authenticity of the collection (see Clark 1971a: 191–196 for an account of the checkered history of the site). The absence of stone tools in all the Upper Paleolithic levels is striking. Of the fauna, remains of *Cervus elaphus* were abundant; no other species were recorded. Molluscs were present in quantity but were ignored by the early investigators.

Level C, 110 cm to 70 cm. This level is a sterile sediment "plug," not otherwise described, which sealed off the interior of the cave from the base of the rock shelter.

Level B, 70 cm to 25 cm. Level B overlies the floor of the rock shelter. It contains an Asturian industry in quartzite that is unusual because it contains partial bifaces and diminutive picks.

Two loose conchero fragments on display at the cave are said to come from Level B. The specimens are heavily indurated and contain three indisputable Asturian picks. There is no question that the conchero fragments are genuine, but they might have been brought to Lledías from another site in the area in order to supplement the cave's tourist appeal. Uría-Riú (1941) states that breccias are lacking in the cave mouth as a result of dryness.

Level A, 25 cm to 0 cm. A surface level called Neolithic (Uría-Riú 1941; Jordá 1955: 49) contained potsherds (not described), and two large, polished stone axes.

Inspection of the cultural deposits still preserved below the shelter is discouraged today. The primitive entrance has been closed, although it is visible from the galleries below it. Further investigation of this enigmatic site is made difficult by its function as a tourist attraction.

Bricia (Cueva Rodríguez)

Bricia is a small cave formed in the southern face of the Llera plateau. It is located about 250 m due west of Cueto de la Mina, and at about the same elevation (see Fig. 3.4, Table 3.1). The cave has a single entrance opening to the south (Fig. 3.11). It connects directly with a chamber about 11 m long that terminates in a thick, stalactitic column. The stalactite obstructs a constriction in the solution cavity that leads to a second, smaller chamber. Cultural deposits appeared to be restricted to the larger of the two rooms.

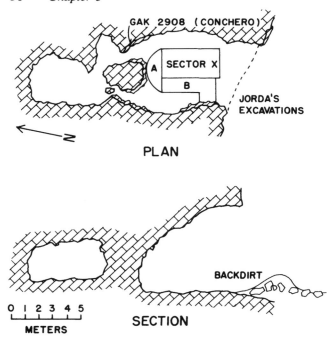

Figure 3.11. Bricia: plan and section of the cave (after Jordá 1954).

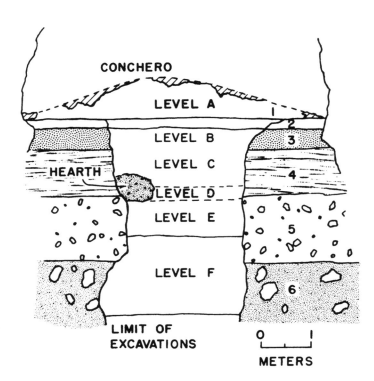

Figure 3.12. Bricia: section through the original excavations showing the double stratigraphic sequence of Llopis (after Jordá 1954).

Bricia was discovered during the earlier part of the century and was tested by the Conde de la Vega del Sella in November, 1915, although he never published on it (Marquez 1974: 828). Jordá visited the site during the early 1950s and excavated it in 1953 (Jordá 1954: 169–195). Sediments exposed by his excavations were analyzed by Noël Llopis-Lladó (1953; Llopis in Hernández-Pacheco and others 1957: 26) in what was to be the beginning of a long and somewhat unfortunate collaboration.

The succession of depositional events postulated for the site is curious and perhaps requires some preliminary comment (Fig. 3.12). Both geological (Levels 6–1) and archaeological (Levels F–A) sequences are presented and, according to the authors, they are related. First, it would appear that Levels 6 through 3 were deposited prior to the occupation of the site, as they are sterile of cultural remains. Second, an erosional process supposedly related to a cycle of karstic rejuvenation created a deep, straight-sided depression in these sediments near the center of the site. Third, the depression was filled with a sequence of cultural deposits. Fourth, both the sterile, preoccupational levels and the cultural deposits were overlain by travertine that sealed in what lay below. Fifth, an Asturian conchero may or may not have accumulated on top of the flowstone. Finally, a cycle of limestone dissolution indurated much of the shell midden at its peripheries, forming breccia cornices at points of wall contact.

The geological sequence is given below (see Fig. 3.12). One strictly cultural level (1) is included in the evaluations by Llopis-Lladó (in Jordá 1954: 174–176); in Hernández-Pacheco and others 1957: 26). Level 1 corres-

ponds to Level A in the archaeological series; level designations are from Jordá (1954: 175, 176).

Level 6, 490+ cm to 370 cm. Large limestone cobbles, minimally 20 cm in diameter; otherwise not described. Neither the base of Level 6 nor bedrock were exposed in the excavations.

Level 5, 370 cm to 230 cm. A dark yellow clay with limestone cobbles from 5 to 20 cm in diameter; much cemented by a diffuse travertine.

Level 4, 230 cm to 130 cm. A yellow clay like Level 5; limestone inclusions smaller and less frequent.

Level 3, 130 cm to 80 cm. A calcareous breccia with limestone cobbles averaging 10 cm; not otherwise described. Flint associated with this level on the east side of the cave.

Level 2, 80 cm to 50 cm. A band of porous, white travertine, horizontal in section; thickness varies from 20 cm to 40 cm. Level 2 corresponds to Level B in the archaeological series.

Level 1, 50 cm to 0 cm. An Asturian conchero (see below).

The archaeological deposits are described in greater detail. The site contains three cultural horizons and is best known for its Magdalenian industries.

Level F, 480+ cm to 320 cm. Level F contrasts sharply with Level 6. It consists of a light red clay, sterile, with small éboulis inclusions; not otherwise described.

Level E, 320 cm to 245 cm. The Level E matrix consists of a gray brown clayey sediment with small limestone inclusions. It contains an industry described as "Initial Upper Magdalenian" (Jordá 1957: 64, 65) or Upper Magdalenian (Jordá 1958: 88; equivalent to Magdalenian V). In flint, simple flake endscrapers predominated. More common quartzite pieces included flake sidescrapers and endscrapers, a few burins, and perforators. Debitage and mixed nuclei were prevalent; artifacts were few.

The industry in bone was also sparse but diagnostic. In addition to spear point fragments, there were two uniserial harpoon fragments and a piece thought to be part of a perforated baton.

Faunal remains listed included *Equus caballus, Cervus elaphus, Capra pyrenaica,* some other caprid remains, and *Bos* or *Bison* sp. Of the shellfish, only *Patella vulgata* (*sautuola?*) and *Cardium edulis* were noted.

Level D, 245 cm to 205 cm. A nearly sterile level of gray clayey sediments containing ash, charcoal, and the same fauna as Level E. The remains of a hearth contained numerous limpet shells (*Patella vulgata*) reportedly of small size. Jordá (1954: 85) suggests that the feature is intrusive into Level D and dates from the Upper Magdalenian Level C.

Level C, 205 cm to 80 cm. The main Magdalenian occupation in the site was assigned to the Upper Magdalenian by Jordá (1957: 64, 65; 1958: 88). The sedimentary matrix differs little from Levels D and E, and the lithic industry resembles that of Level E. Flake endscrapers and burins predominate in flint; sidescrapers, notches, and perforators are the most prevalent quartzite pieces.

The bone industry contained a diagnostic uniserial antler harpoon fragment, along with sharpened bone splinters and pieces of spear points. The faunal array is similar to that from Level E.

Level B, 80 cm to 50 cm. Travertine deposit, archaeologically sterile (see Level 2).

Level A, 50 cm to 0 cm. A black, greasy organic sediment, between 20 cm and 80 cm in thickness, contained a conchero of Asturian type, "consisting of limpets (85%), limestone cobbles (14%), and lithic material (1%)" (Jordá in Hernández-Pacheco and others 1957: 26). The sparse industry in quartzite contained one of the characteristic picks. Ash, bone fragments, and charcoal were also reported, although the mammalian fauna were not analyzed. Shellfish species included *Patella vulgata* (of small size), *Trochocochlea crassa, Cardium edulis,* and *Oricium* sp. The deposits are inclined toward the interior of the cave at an angle of 15° to 20°.

The Bricia site report is important because the earliest doubts were cast here on the then-established chronological interpretation of the Asturian. In 1953, Llopis published an article proposing that the concheros, as they occur today, are secondary deposits washed into cave mouths from the nearby river banks where they had originally accumulated. Subsequently, they were indurated with calcareous deposits, then eroded, resulting in the durable breccia cornices observable today.

Jordá (1954: 178, 179) saw in this suggestion the answer to a question that puzzled him since he first became interested in the Asturian: how to account for the disap-

pearance of the concheros, because he believed they were lapidified through percolation with lime-charged waters. The answer in terms of Llopis' theory seemed an obvious one. The breccias were dissolved and much of the loose shell washed away by rivers again operating at higher levels than those of the present day. Apparently Jordá thought that the concheros were indurated *throughout* their entire mass, not only at their peripheries as was almost certainly the case. This misconception lies at the root of his mistrust of the original, largely accurate, evaluation of the assemblage.

This solution, however, thrust Jordá on the horns of another dilemma. If events transpired as Llopis suggested, then why were the more soluble sediments of the Upper Paleolithic sequence preserved intact when the rocklike breccias were dissolved and carried away? The peculiar stratigraphic situation at Bricia seemed to provide an answer. The cultural deposits, except for the Asturian level, occurred in a chimneylike depression (see Fig. 3.12) cut through a series of sterile geologically deposited strata. Excluding as unlikely an intentional large scale excavation at some point prior to the deposition of the Magdalenian sequence, Jordá (1954: 178) contended that such a situation could only have resulted from an exsurgence of subterranean waters that evacuated most of the sediments present in the cave, leaving a gaping hole in the floor later to be filled with sediments containing a Magdalenian industry. Given this dubious reconstruction, which admits no evidence for a post-Magdalenian erosional cycle, the concheros must have been destroyed by the exsurgence just postulated, implying that they were accumulated (by whatever process) prior to the Magdalenian.

In this ingenious chain of thought, based on a misconception and riddled with improbabilities, lies the essence of the theory of karstic rejuvenation, much amplified during the subsequent decade by Jordá and others. In direct opposition to the karstic rejuvenation theory and in support of a post-Pleistocene date is a radiocarbon determination taken from Level A. The date, based on a sample of 29.9 gr, corrected for the new half-life (5730 ± 40), is 7004 ± 165 years B.P. (GaK 2908).

Cuartamentero

Cuartamentero is located in the hamlet of La Portilla near Llanes in eastern Asturias (see Fig. 3.1, Table 3.1) and is situated on a low, east-west trending limestone plateau. The cave is large, with three main chambers, and two entrances separated from one another by a bedrock spur 9 m thick (Fig. 3.13). The western entrance (1) faces southeast, opening on a chamber (Room 1) that has never been tested for cultural deposits. At 7.5 m from the mouth ground water is encountered, precluding exploration beyond that point. The eastern entrance (2) faces southwest and opens on a sloping corridor that connects directly with two large rooms lying, respectively, west (Room 2) and east (Room 3) of the corridor. Both are comparatively dry. Cultural deposits are found in the corridor and in Room 3 (Fig. 3.13). Only Asturian remains have been recovered from the site.

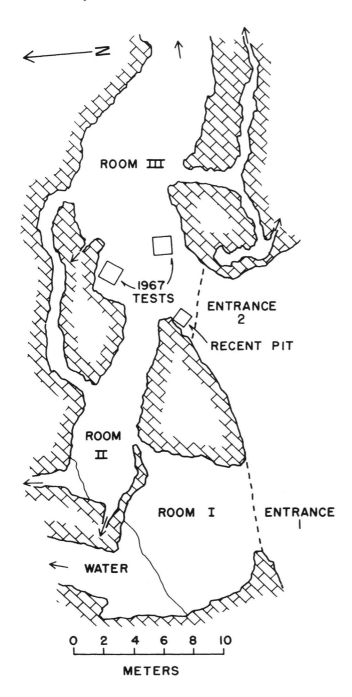

Figure 3.13. Cuartamentero: plan of the cave.

Excavations were conducted by the Grupo Espeleológico Querneto in 1967. Two small tests were placed along the eastern wall of Entrance 2 and along the western wall of Room 3. A visit to the site in June, 1969, revealed a third cut, located along the west wall of Entrance 2. No cut exceeded 50 cm in depth (Fig. 3.13). Francisco Giles Pacheco has provided a preliminary description of the stratigraphy, but he cautions that it is "idealized" and subject to revision.

Level D, ? to 27 cm. Undescribed sediments.

Level C, 27 cm to 25 cm. A sterile white flowstone deposit about 2 cm thick.

Level B, 25 cm to 15 cm. A fine yellow sand containing carbonized plant material; thickness varies between 10 and 15 cm. The deposit also contains small limestone fragments and shells. *Patella vulgata sautuola* were observed in June, 1969. There may be Upper Paleolithic industrial remains associated with this level but none have been recovered from the preliminary tests.

Level A, 15 cm to 0 cm. A coarse, yellow sand, containing large limestone and quartzite cobbles, shells (*Patella vulgata*), and unanalyzed mammalian faunal remains. Associated with these sediments is an abundant Asturian industry that includes eight of the characteristic quartzite picks. An isolated calvarium, unusual for its marked supraorbital tori, was also recovered from this level. It is undergoing metrical analysis at the Museo Arqueológico Nacional in Madrid. The surface of the site is covered with large limestone and quartzite cobbles.

During visits to the site (June, September, 1969; June 1972), conchero deposits were observed beneath an overhang adhering to the west wall of Entrance 2. These sediments were contiguous with sediments similar to those of Levels A and B exposed in the post-1967 cut. The shell content of the conchero consisted almost exclusively of limpets. Both the modern (*Patella vulgata*) and the Pleistocene (*Patella vulgata sautuola*) variants were present, with the latter occurring in low frequency.

Cuartamentero so far has been spared the devastating effects of pre-1940 excavation techniques. Local enthusiasts have already become interested in the site, however. To realize its tremendous potential, a full-scale program of excavations should be implemented as soon as possible.

Colombres

Colombres is a rock shelter site located in the pueblo of La Franca, *concejo* of Rivadedeva, a scant 5 km from the Santander border in eastern Asturias (see Fig. 3.1, Table 3.1). It was discovered on January 2, 1926, by the landlord of the property who, while constructing a path beneath the shelter overhang, discovered some bones he recognized as human. Because there had been a murder in the area recently, he immediately informed the local doctor. After judging the remains to be of archaeological interest, the doctor telegraphed Fr. Jesús Carballo at the Santander archaeological museum. Carballo arrived the next day.

Excavations began immediately. They lasted for less than a week, during which time the site was almost completely exhausted. The results were published privately by Fr. Carballo in 1926 and appeared again during Carballo's tenure as Director of the Museo Provincial de Prehistoria in Santander (Carballo 1960).

The site is a small rock shelter, oriented east-west and facing south. It lies about 75 m north of the Río Cabra in a limestone escarpment. Archaeological remains were restricted to a band of sediments about 4 m long by 2 m wide, following the long axis of the shelter. All levels sloped from north to south at about a 30° angle. Four levels were distinguished on sedimentological grounds; they contained only a single cultural component (Carballo 1960: 131, 132).

Level D, 150 cm to 60 cm. Level D overlay bedrock at 150 cm below the original surface. It consisted of a black, greasy organic sediment, containing an abundant quantity of shell, fragments of charcoal, "petrified" animal bones, and an Asturian industry in quartz, quartzite, and sandstone (Carballo 1960: 132). Level D also contained an undisturbed human burial (discussed below).

Mammalian faunal remains associated with Level D included *Sus scrofa, Capra ibex,* and *Cervus elaphus,* all present in frequency. Three heavily worn bear molars (*Ursus arctos*) and a lower jaw and canine attributed to *Felis silvestris* rounded out the inventory.

Molluscan remains consisted of *Patella vulgata* and (probably) *Trochocochlea crassa.* The uncertainty arises because the word *bígaro* refers to both *Trochocochlea crassa* and *Littorina littorea.* However, it would be most unusual to find *Littorina littorea* in an Asturian site. Oysters (*Ostrea edulis*) occurred in lower frequency, along with a few mussels (*Mytilus edulis*), cardial shells (*Cardium edulis*), and earshells (*Halyotis* spp.).

The skeleton was found near the back of the shelter, at the base of the angle formed by the overhang, 55 cm from the wall. Oriented east-west and parallel with the long axis of the shelter, it lay supine with arms and legs extended, resting 10 cm above bedrock. The head was at the east end. The postcranial skeleton lay within a clearly demarcated rectangle composed of 28 unmodified tabular limestone blocks. The skull rested on its right side, facing north, on a platform of five blocks. Seven more blocks defined a circle above (east of) the head and this enclosure contained three Asturian picks. A cervid tibia was placed in the grave beside the face, possibly intended as a source of food in the afterworld. These features and the disposition of the skeleton itself, are shown in Figure 3.14. After the corpse was placed in the grave, a mound of rocks and earth was heaped over the torso, and especially over the head.

Although a primary interment, acidic soil conditions inimical to good preservation had destroyed much of the rib cage, the thoracic and cervical vertebrae, and the pelvis. The long bones, discovered intact, were extremely fragile and crumbled when touched. The feet were never found. The postcranial skeleton as a whole was not recovered (Carballo 1960: 136).

The skull, on the other hand, was comparatively well preserved. It bore traces of pathological conditions summarized by Carballo (1926: 18, 26; 1960: 153, 154) and by Clark (1971a: 172, 175). A massive but regular oval hole, apparently a trepanation rather than a casual injury, occurred at the junction of the coronal and squamous sutures, destroying the posterior portion of the left wing of the sphenoid. No resorption of the osseous tissue was observed, suggesting that the trepanation was done after death, if it was not itself the cause of death (Carballo 1960: 140, 141).

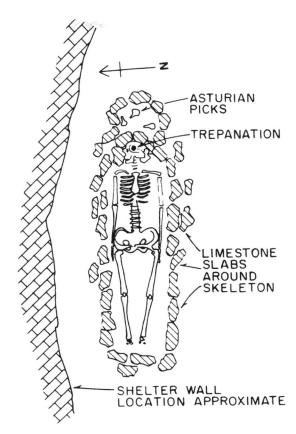

Figure 3.14. Colombres: burial and associated features (after Carballo 1960; no scale given).

Because of the fragmentary condition of the bones, a complete metrical analysis was impossible. The remains are stated tentatively to be those of a woman about fifty years old at death (Carballo 1960: 135). Age estimation was based on the amount of tooth wear and may be in error; no other aging criteria were used. Sex is equally debatable because the pelvis was not preserved. The fineness of certain cranial features suggested classification as female (Carballo 1960: 137). Unfortunately, the skull cannot be located today.

Level C, 60 cm to 50 cm. Overlying Level D was a thin band of gray clay reportedly containing the same faunal spectrum and industrial remains as Level D. Of variable thickness, it was not otherwise described.

Level B, 50 cm to 30 cm. Level B, like D, consisted of black, greasy organic sediments. Cultural inclusions consisted of a great quantity of shell, charcoal fragments identifiable as oak, a number (not specified) of Asturian picks, other industrial remains, some burned sandstone fragments, ochre lumps showing striations due to use, and "petrified" animal bones. Level B was variable in thickness, exceeding 20 cm in many parts of the site. No flint or ceramic debris was recovered from any of the levels. The faunal inventory is indistinguishable from that of Level D.

Level A, 30 cm to 24–18 cm. Level A consisted of two components. The first, designated A1, was an archaeologically sterile stalagmitic cap, about 6 cm thick. It occurred only near the shelter wall and was overlain by sediment or soil of undetermined thickness. The second component, designated A2, consisted of the soil mantle outside the shelter. This level, also archaeologically sterile, averaged some 12 cm in thickness. It is not otherwise described.

The remaining 18 cm are not accounted for in the text. Presumably they are absorbed by level thickness variation. Figures given for level thicknesses are averages only. The section provided by Carballo (1960: 131) is only schematic.

The industry at Colombres, clearly Asturian, is called "Cuerquense" (Cuerquian) by Carballo (1924, 1926, 1960). The term refers to the theoretical replacement of the Final Pleistocene coniferous forest by one in which oak (*Quercus* spp.) predominated, a process that was thought to have been completed by Asturian times (more than 10,000 B.P., according to Carballo).

Colombres has been nearly destroyed by events subsequent to excavation. The roof of the shelter was largely removed in 1944 or 1945 to produce bedding for a new highway that was built in place of the 1926 road. The original fill of the rock shelter was removed at that time and an artificial roadbed put in its place.

La Franca
(Cueva de Mazaculos)
La Franca (Vega del Sella 1916: 65) is situated on a hill of Cretaceous limestone (Martinez-Alvarez 1965, Map) in the town of La Franca, *concejo* of Rivadedeva, in the northeastern part of Asturias (see Fig. 3.1, Table 3.1). Originally discovered by Hermilio Alcalde del Rio in April, 1908, the cave bore some painted signs and dots that brought it to the attention of the Abbé Breuil (Alcalde del Rio and others 1911: 81–83). The hill, called Mazaculos, forms a natural amphitheater opening to the north. The cave developed in the east wall of the amphitheater and faces northwest. It was excavated by the Conde in December of 1915, although no details of that project are available today. The excavations also produced a human mandible but its stratigraphic position could not be determined with certainty (Obermaier 1924: 351).

Level C, ? cm to 45–55 cm. The earliest deposit reported was a colluvial red clay, thought to be a product of slopewash from above the cave mouth. The clays penetrated the cavern interior to a considerable extent. No mention is made of cultural deposits and no faunal lists are given.

Level B, 45–55 cm to 5–10 cm. The principal archaeological deposit in the site was an Asturian conchero, said to have been in an extremely fine state of preservation (Vega del Sella 1916: 65, 66). The conchero con-

tained "numerous Asturian picks" and choppers; the rest of the industry was described as "eolithic."

Mammalian fauna listed include *Cervus elaphus, Cappreolus capreolus, Rupicapra rupicapra,* and *Bos.* sp. Molluscan species were *Patella vulgata* (of normal dimensions) and *Trochocochlea crassa.* Examination of a conchero fragment from the site preserved in the Museo Municipal in Madrid yielded 75 percent (60 examples) of *Patella vulgata* and 25 percent (20 examples) of *Trochocochlea crassa.* Ash, bone, and charcoal were also observed. The Conde notes the appearance of oysters (*Ostrea edulis*), along with scarce remains of *Mytilus edulis* and *Triton nodiferus.* Sea urchins (*Paracentrotus lividus*) are also recorded in low frequency, along with some examples of *Helix nemoralis.*

Level A, 5–10 cm to 0 cm. At the top was a sterile(?) layer consisting of a thin organic soil or sediment (*tierra vegetal*) and some stalagmitic deposits. The relationship between the flowstones and the unconsolidated sediments is not made clear.

The site of La Franca and the cave that contained it were believed destroyed during the 1950s as a result of commercial limestone quarrying. In 1974, however, Professor Manuel R. González Morales, of the Department of Prehistory at the University of Oviedo, and I relocated La Franca. Preliminary tests directed by Morales in 1976 indicated that a large, intact Asturian midden was preserved at the cave—a circumstance that makes La Franca virtually unique among known Asturian sites. These deposits were excavated more fully in 1977 and 1978; excavations are continuing.

Morales renamed the cave Mazaculos II (to distinguish it from another cavern on the hill), and it has produced a series of both disturbed and intact Asturian deposits, some interrupted by sterile lenses. Level designations are from González Morales (1978).

Level 4, no depth given. A reddish basal clay, sterile of archaeological remains. These sediments almost certainly correspond to Level C described from the 1915 excavations; bedrock not reached in any test.

Level 3.3, no depth given. An Asturian occupation surface contains the remains of a hearth atop the Level 4 clay, in association with manuports (limestone blocks), an Asturian pick, debitage, and quantities of bone and shell. Remains of terrestrial fauna are abundant in this level, in contrast with overlying strata. The most common species represented is red deer (*Cervus elaphus*), many of which are young individuals; goat (*Capra ibex*) and horse (*Equus caballus*) are also present in low frequencies.

The inventory of marine molluscs is dominated by limpets (*P. vulgata, P. intermedia*) and the warm-water topshell (*T. crassa*), with other species found in small quantities. In a striking departure from previously recorded Asturian middens, fish bones are common and include the genus *Labrus* (a bottom-dwelling flatfish) and other similar flounderlike forms.

Level 3.2, no depth given. A thin lense of fine gray-brown silts, with little cultural material.

Level 3.1, no depth given. In this thick deposit of loose shell, ash, and charcoal, bone and charcoal are unusually common. Species represented are similar to those reported from Level 3.3.

Level 2.2, no depth given. These carbonaceous lenses are included within Level 2.1; no discernible hearths.

Level 2.1, no depth given. Brown, fine to medium-fine silts and sandy silts contain a major shell component; species are similar to Level 3.3; little artifactual material.

Level 1.3, no depth given. Another conchero stratum is composed almost entirely of limpets (*P. vulgata, P. intermedia*) and topshells (*T. crassa*); little sedimentary matrix. An Asturian pick was recovered at the Level 2.1 and 1.3 contact.

Level 1.2, no depth given. A wedge-shaped lense of fine sediments (silts) is archaeologically sterile.

Level 1.1, no depth given. A deposit of loose shell has very little sedimentary matrix, contains little bone, and is almost devoid of artifacts.

Stratified above Level 1.1 are a series of four disturbed deposits (Levels 0.4–0.1) that are rich in Asturian fauna and industries, but unfortunately they cannot be considered in situ; they contain broken pieces of flowstones probably resulting from the 1915 excavations. Levels 0.2 and 0.4 are compacted clays appearing to be 1915 walking surfaces. The main section, reproduced in Figure 3.15, is believed to intersect part of the Conde's 1915 trench. The partly exposed Level 3.3 living floor is reproduced in figure 3.16.

The industrial component is dominated by quartzite tools and debitage (81 percent), with chert lithics accounting for an additional 11 percent. Scarce quartz, sandstone, and limestone pieces make up the balance of the industry. Only 68 pieces of debitage (out of 271) were

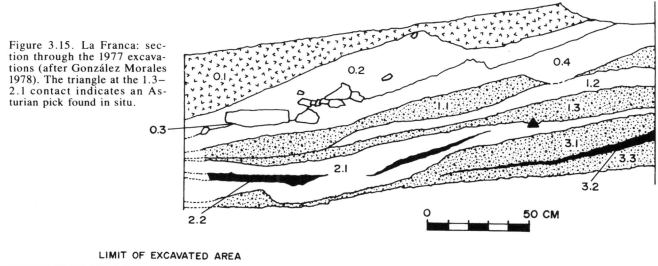

Figure 3.15. La Franca: section through the 1977 excavations (after González Morales 1978). The triangle at the 1.3–2.1 contact indicates an Asturian pick found in situ.

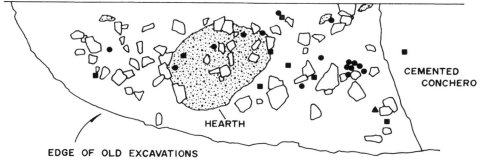

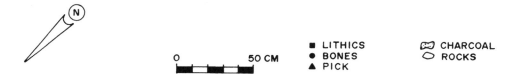

Figure 3.16. La Franca: Asturian occupation surface (Level 3.3) exposed in 1977 (after González Morales 1978).

recovered in situ; 48 are unretouched flakes. The remainder are cores and core fragments, and unworked quartzite cobbles that were probably brought into the site as raw material for heavy duty tools. Of 23 Asturian picks recovered, 20 were from disturbed contexts. The remaining core tools are nearly all unifacial choppers. A few notches and denticulates round out the retouched tool inventory (González Morales 1978: 382, 383).

The base of the Level 3.3 occupation surface has been radiocarbon dated from charcoal samples taken from a thin travertine layer in contact with the underlying clay deposit. The date, based on the Libby half-life, is 9290 ± 440 B.P. (GaK 6684). Although some 650 years older than the heretofore oldest Asturian determinations (from nearby Penicial, La Riera), the Mazaculos date pertains to the beginning of Asturian occupation of the cave (González Morales and Marquez 1978).

Playa de Ciriego

Ciriego refers to a series of surface sites on top of the sea cliffs one kilometer west of the municipal cemetery (Ciriego) for the city of Santander. Carballo (1924, 1926: 36) records the fact that Asturian picks occur in some of these deposits. I surveyed the region in January, 1969, and found five such surface scatters, all apparently unmixed and completely aceramic. Because of exposed pieces, four scatters were considered to be Upper Paleolithic; they were not collected. The fifth scatter contained Asturian picks, along with a variety of other artifacts in flint and quartzite. This site was named Liencres, and I mapped, collected, and excavated it during February and March of 1969 and August, 1972 (Chapters 4, 5; Clark 1975a).

Vega del Sella (1930: 95) considered Ciriego a mixed site, containing artifacts of Lower and Middle Paleolithic age along with those of more recent manufacture. The tidal inlets below the cliffs contain Mousterian-like artifacts, rolled and mixed among the limestone cobbles exposed at low tide. During a half-hour period on January 5, 1969, at least a dozen quartzite flakes, choppers, cleavers, and disks were recovered from these gravels. Ciriego cultural material as defined here is not mixed and the two deposits should not be confused.

Liencres

Liencres is a coastal open-air site located in the Rostrio de Ciriego, about one kilometer west of the municipal cemetery for the provincial capital of Santander (see Fig. 3.1, Table 3.1). The coastline near the site is characterized by sea cliffs cut into an old marine platform, the top of which rises 13 m above the level of the sea. The limestone platform has been heavily subjected to erosion; dolinas and other karstic phenomena are common. Wind and water erosion have stripped off much of the vegetation surrounding the edges of the dolinas and deflation has occurred, creating patches of bare ground in many places. The subsurface sediment commonly exposed in these blowouts is a dark brownish or grayish loam (Level 1); it extends to a depth of about 35 cm, where it grades into a brown, then a yellowish-brown loam (Level 2; Butzer and Bowman 1975; Clark 1979b). Level 2 directly

overlies bedrock, encountered at from 47 to 65 cm below surface. Cultural deposits are confined primarily to Level 1.

In January, 1969, the site consisted of a scatter of lithic debris about 20 m long by 9 m wide. Lithics were dispersed around the eastern edge of a large sinkhole situated on a rocky spine above an inlet. Surface materials included flint and quartzite waste flakes, some flint tools, and a number of flint blades. The prevalence of flint at the site is ascribed to the presence of rare source material nearby. Most noteworthy, however, were four quartzite picks similar to those depicted so frequently in the works of Vega del Sella (1914, 1916, 1923, 1930) and others (Carballo 1926, 1960). A massive quartzite grinding slab, overturned and surrounded by chipping debris, occurred near the center of the site. Adjacent to it lay a large quartzite boulder.

After permission was secured, surface collections were made on six occasions during January and February, 1969, and the site was tested in February and March. The procedures used for surface sampling, excavation, stratigraphic analysis, and typology are discussed in Chapter 4 (see Clark 1975a: 1–17; 1976a: 190–194). The 1969 excavations and surface pickup at the site yielded a total of 1604 lithic artifacts, including over 140 retouched pieces. No faunal material was preserved, nor were substances suitable for radiocarbon dating recovered. Additional collections were made in 1972.

Four sediment samples were removed from Level 1 and a single sample was taken from Level 2; they pertain to the sandy A-horizons of the *terra fusca* soil characteristic of post-Pleistocene pedogenesis in the area. Evidence of human presence is suggested by tiny bone and shell fragments as well as by phosphate concentrations. Two pollen samples were taken from Level 1 and one from Level 2; they reflect early to mid-Holocene vegetation in the area site vicinity and are discussed in Appendix A.

La Lloseta
(Cueva de La Moría)

La Lloseta is a cave site located in the limestone hills on the west bank of the Río Sella, northwest of the village of Ardines, in eastern Asturias (see Fig. 3.4, Table 3.1). Known since antiquity, it opens to the southwest and consists of a single chamber 35 m long by 16 m wide. The ceiling is about 8 m high. Narrow passageways in the north and east walls connect with more ample galleries deep inside the massif that eventually lead to the complex series of painted caverns called "El Ramu" or "Tito Bustillo" and to the Mousterian site of La Cuevona (Freeman 1964).

La Lloseta was extensively tested by Jordá and Alvarez from the summer of 1956 intermittently through 1958. Jordá (1958) prepared a detailed preliminary report on the 1956 excavation. The cultural sequence at the site is also summarized in Hernández-Pacheco and others (1957: 27, 28). Although the site is primarily Magdalenian, conchero deposits said to be analogous to those from Asturian sites are also noted (Jordá 1958: 24).

Jordá confined his activities to two areas in the main chamber of the cave and to one test outside the entrance

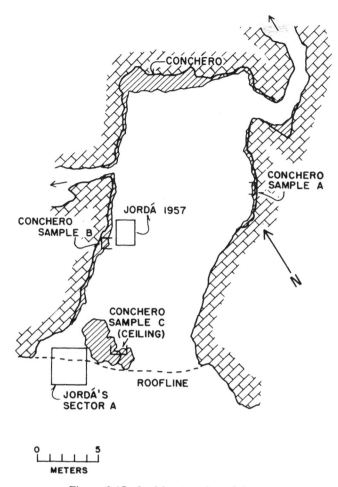

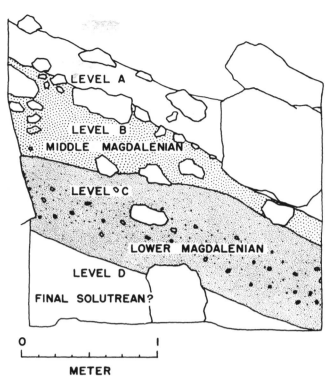

Figure 3.18. La Lloseta: north-south section through Jordá's Sector A (after Jordá 1957).

Figure 3.17. La Lloseta: plan of the cave.

in the talus slope. The major cut, designated "Sector A," was placed in the west part of the entrance beneath the overhang (Figs. 3.17, 3.18). The stratigraphic sequence given below is from Sector A. Alvarez told me that in 1957 or 1958 a second trench was excavated adjacent to the west wall of the cave; no report of the sequence from this test has been published.

Level D, 223 cm to 185 cm (average thickness). Level D is the oldest stratum revealed in Sector A. The sedimentary matrix consists of a reddish clay containing numerous small fragments of limestone roof fall (Jordá 1958: 53, 54). Excavation was hindered by large limestone blocks and by flowstone deposits. In this and in subsequently deposited levels, strata slope markedly from south to north. Level thickness is variable (Fig. 3.18).

Industrial remains consisted largely of nuclei and flakes. No mention is made of *any* retouched stone tools. The industry in bone contained three large "points" made from long bone fragments said to show considerable polishing due to use (Jordá 1958: 53). The abundant faunal remains have not been analyzed.

The level is tentatively considered to be Final Solutrean, but there is no evidence to document this assertion

(Jordá 1958: 57). There is no clear sedimentary distinction between Levels D and C, suggesting continuity of occupation (Clark 1976a: 114–117).

Level C, 185 cm to 75 cm (average thickness). Level C is the most important level in the site and one of the few good Lower Magdalenian levels in northern Spain. The matrix is a gray-black sediment that grades imperceptibly into the redder sediments of Level D. The major occupation levels are represented by darker, blackened lenses in the middle of the deposit, suggesting a stratigraphy more complex than that reported. Most of the lithic debris and practically all of the copious faunal material were concentrated in these black lenses.

The industry in quartzite outnumbered that in flint by a ratio of two to one. Quartzite lithics included numerous blades and bladelets; many tended to be short and wide, approaching blade-flakes. Unretouched flakes amounted to almost 80 percent of the total quartzite inventory (Jordá 1958: 440, 41). Pyramidal and prismatic nuclei were abundant; many showed step retouch, qualifying them as nucleiform endscrapers. Retouched pieces included a series of flake sidescrapers in which straight and convex forms predominated; concave forms were rare. Endscrapers and burins were common and varied. Tool classes occurring in low frequency were unifacial and bifacial points, "naturally pointed" flakes, and perforators.

The industry in flint is more diminutive and carefully made than that in quartzite due to an effort to conserve scarce raw material. Debitage includes numerous small blades and bladelet fragments. Jordá (1958: 42) defines a bladelet as a blade less than 4 cm in length. Flakes account for 85 percent of the total flint inventory. Nuclei are relatively scarce; prismatic forms predominate (Jordá 1958: 47).

Retouched pieces include more than a hundred bladelets with semiabrupt and abrupt marginal retouch. They are divided into several subcategories and include what de Sonneville-Bordes and Perrot (1954, 1955, 1956) refer to as partially backed bladelets, denticulated bladelets, "Azilian" points, and atypical microgravettes. Backed bladelets, usually common, are not particularly numerous. Rare microlithic "thumbnail" and simple endscrapers also occur. The plethora of microliths was thought to be unusual for a Magdalenian III level in Cantabria (Jordá 1958: 42, 43), although it is characteristic of analogous French sites. Macrolithic endscrapers and burins like those in quartzite are relatively common, and include straight and canted dihedral burins on retouched truncations (rare). Of special interest are a few flake *raclettes*.

The industry in bone is represented by commonly found bone and antler spear point fragments. Unibeveled bases predominate, with oval and rectangular cross sections. Basal engraving is common. More prevalent are crudely sharpened longbone fragments that probably served as punches or awls. Some needle fragments were also recovered, and at least one piece of a perforated baton.

Faunal remains have not been analyzed in detail. A summary list given by Jordá (1958: 52) notes *Cervus elaphus* (predominant), *Bison priscus, Equus caballus, Capra ibex,* and *Rupicapra rupicapra.* Shellfish include *Patella vulgata* (*sautuola?*, common), *Littorina littorea,* and *Pecten maximus.*

Utrilla considers the Level C assemblage to be Magdalenian II, based on a comparison with similar harpoonless Magdalenian levels at the Santander sites of El Juyo, Altamira, and Pasiega. Magdalenian II is regarded as an activity or facies variant in the Utrilla scheme; it is not thought to be chronologically distinct and is interstratified with Magdalenian I and Magdalenian III assemblages (Utrilla 1976a: 60, 61).

Level B, 75 cm to 40 cm (average thickness). Level B consists of two sediments. Near the top the depositional matrix is a reddish sediment that grades into a yellowish clay near the Level B and C contact. Limestone cobbles of various sizes are frequent inclusions. Level thickness varies from 20 to 50 cm.

Industrial remains were scarce and diagnostically inconclusive. The level is tentatively assigned to the Middle Magdalenian IV (Jordá 1958: 30–36). Most of the lithics were quartzite; flint pieces were not distinguished in the inventory. Unretouched flakes and blades were common; bladelets, on the other hand, were scarce. Nuclei were common; prismatic cores predominated. Retouched pieces included simple, straight-edged sidescrapers, and a few endscrapers and burins.

The industry in bone is inconsequential. It includes only a few crudely pointed long bone fragments.

There is little evidence except for that of superposition to justify a classification of Level B as Magdalenian IV. The plethora of burins and microliths that characterize French assemblages is absent. Bone points and uniserial "proto-harpoons" are also lacking.

Faunal remains noted in the preliminary classification included *Cervus elaphus, Capra pyrenaica,* and some unidentified rodents. Bone tentatively identified as *Bison* spp. and *Equus caballus* was also recovered. Molluscan species included *Patella vulgata* (*sautuola?*) and *Littorina littorea.*

This assemblage has been classified as Magdalenian III by Utrilla (1976a, b), based on an exhaustive evaluation of the inadequately published Jordá collection stored in the Oviedo museum. Because of the high incidence of debitage in both Levels C and B, she argues that all the Magdalenian strata at Lloseta are the remains of *talleres* (workshops) where fabrication of finished stone tools was a principal activity.

Level A, 40 cm to 0 cm (average thickness). The final level stratified in Sector A consisted of the modern soil cover, devoid of cultural material.

In addition to this sequence, there are a series of conchero deposits in the cave. They occur along both walls and on the ceiling in the positions indicated in Figure 3.17. Dated by radiocarbon, they provided faunal samples important in understanding the Late Pleistocene–post-Pleistocene climatic transition.

Although Jordá (1958: 24) notes that no Asturian picks have been recovered from the site, a collection of tools from La Lloseta, including one such "guide fossil," was located in the Museo Arqueológico Provincial (Oviedo) in November, 1969. The collection, labeled "Cueva de La Lloseta, Ribadesella" and dated 23 June, 1958, was probably made subsequent to the date at which the book went to press. Jordá (1958: 23–25) notes the presence of "concheros analogous to those of Asturian sites," but the exact provenience of the collection within the site is not known. Conchero samples taken in 1969 failed to identify deposits of Asturian age.

Minor Asturian Sites

The literature contains references to 13 additional caves and one open site that are alleged to contain Asturian deposits. These sites are of secondary importance because little or no Asturian artifactual material can presently be located that pertains to them. In some cases the sites themselves can no longer be located, in spite of repeated efforts to do so. They exist only as names on lists of Asturian sites compiled by the Conde (Vega del Sella 1923: 49). In several instances, previously unreported concheros of Asturian type were discovered by the survey team. Because no full-scale excavations were conducted at these sites, no industrial samples are forthcoming. Any cultural assignment, therefore, is tentative, based on the characteristics of the faunal inventory. Minor Asturian sites are listed in Table 3.2, together with pertinent references (see also Clark 1971a, 1976a). While industrial and faunal data are minimal in nearly every

TABLE 3.2
Minor Asturian Sites With References

Sites	References
WITH ASTURIAN INDUSTRIES AND FAUNA	
Allorú	Vega del Sella 1916: 63; Clark 1971a: 104, 105; 1976a: 61; Marquez 1974: 829; Jordá 1976: 34, 115; 1977: 158, 165
Colomba	Vega del Sella 1916: 63; Clark 1971a: 108; 1976a: 62; Marquez 1974: 827; Jordá 1976: 114; 1977: 158, 165
Cuevas del Mar	Vega del Sella 1914: 1–7; 1916: 78; Clark 1971a: 123, 124; 1976a: 70
Cueva del Río	Obermaier 1924: 176; Jordá 1957: 63, 64; 1958: 81–84; 1977: 159; Clark 1971a: 121–123; 1976a: 69
Infierno	Vega del Sella 1923: 49; Clark 1971a: 115, 116; 1976a: 66; Almagro 1960: 312; Jordá 1976: 115; 1977: 158
Leona	Vega del Sella 1916: 63; Clark 1971a: 105–108; 1976a: 62; Marquez 1974: 829; Jordá 1976: 34, 15; 1977: 158
Vidiago	Vega del Sella 1923: 49; Clark 1971a: 126, 127; 1976a: 71, 72; Marquez 1974: 830; Jordá 1976: 34, 115
WITH ASTURIAN-TYPE FAUNAS ONLY	
Elefante	Clark 1971a: 211, 212; 1976a: 109
Las Cáscaras	Vega del Sella 1923: 49; Carballo 1960: 130; Clark 1971a: 179, 180; 1976a: 95; García Guinea 1975: 192–197
Meaza	Alcalde del Río and others 1911: 50–52; Calderón 1945; Anderez 1953: 208–214; Clark 1971a: 180–189; 1976a: 95–99
WITH DISPUTED CLAIMS TO ASTURIAN INDUSTRIES AND FAUNA	
Cuevona	Vega del Sella 1916: 85; Obermaier 1924: 175; Jordá 1957: 64; 1958: 82; Clark 1971a: 210, 211; 1976a: 108, 109
La Loja	Alcalde del Río and others 1911: 53–59; Obermaier 1924: 170; Jordá 1957: 64; Clark 1971a: 145–150; 1976a: 79–81; Marquez 1974: 831
Luarca (open site)	González 1965: 35–39; Clark 1971a: 221, 222; 1976a: 113
Valdedíos	Uría-Riú 1958: 12–38; Clark 1971a: 208–210; 1976a: 108; García-Caveda 1886; Barras 1898; Hoyos-Sainz 1947: 165, 166

case, it was usually possible to relocate these caves and to establish the existence of Asturian-period deposits in them. Thus their placements within the regional landscape provided information useful in the constructing and testing of models pertinent to the subsistence and settlement patterns outlined in Chapters 6 and 7.

In summary, it is apparent that the quality of Asturian lithic data preserved in museum collections is variable and that criteria for even so simple a task as site classification by culture-stratigraphic unit leave much to be desired. A more reliable indicator of an Asturian assemblage is the faunal spectrum, which *is* reasonably consistent from site to site, and which probably bespeaks a fundamental unity of adaptation among those sites recorded so far—an adaptation not necessarily unique to the Asturian. But faunal remains are only preserved in conchero sites, certainly representative of only a part of the activity spectrum recorded archaeologically among Asturian sites as a whole, and a part badly overrepresented in the sample. Variation among site types is only just beginning to be understood, as is perhaps evident from a comparison of the industry from the open station at Liencres—Asturian on sedimentological and palynological grounds and by virtue of the appearance of the characteristic picks—with that of the fauna-bearing cave and rock shelter sites outlined in Chapters 4 and 5. A synthetic description and evaluation of Asturian lithic industries is presented in Chapter 5 in an effort to distinguish possible activity facies among these enigmatic and poorly understood assemblages.

OTHER CONCHEROS

Concheros that predate and postdate the Asturian were also sampled. They can be identified by their molluscan components as well as by the industrial remains they contain.

Upper Paleolithic Conchero Sites

The Upper Paleolithic configuration was originally described by Vega del Sella (1916: 82–92; 1921: 32–46; 1925; 1933) more than fifty years ago. Although much is made of the supposed paleoclimatic significance of a few rare molluscan species (*Cyprina islandica, Pecten islandicus*), the shellfish most frequently found in the Cantabrian middens from the Aurignacian on are the large Pleistocene variants of the limpet (*Patella vulgata sautuola*) and the winkle (*Littorina littorea*). This conclusion is supported by investigations at the Solutrean-Magdalenian sites of El Cierro (Jordá 1958: 19), La Lloseta A (Jordá 1958), and Balmori (Clark 1974a; Clark and Clark 1975).

El Cierro

El Cierro is situated in the limestone hills overlooking the hamlet of El Carmen; the site is about 500 m northeast of the village (see Fig. 3.4, Table 3.1). It gives the appearance of a partially collapsed solution cavity, and has two entrances opening to the north and east. According to José Antonio Alvarez of the Museo Arqueológico Provincial (Oviedo), he and Francisco Jordá-Cerdá tested the site in 1958 and 1959; the results have not been published.

I visited the site with Señor Alvarez on February 10, 1969. At that time, there were four distinct levels exposed in the side of the old excavation. Lowermost was a yellow clay filled with tiny fragments of limestone roof fall. Of undetermined thickness, it was attributed to the Aurignacian primarily because it was stratified below a more or less defensible Solutrean deposit (Jordá 1977: 79, 82). Above this level lay a black organic horizon filled with bone, shell, and charcoal. About 20 cm thick, this deposit was originally considered a transitional "Solutrean-Magdalenian deposit," and was used to argue for

TABLE 3.3
El Cierro: Conchero Sample, Faunal Inventory

	Absolute Frequency		Relative Frequency	
Species	Whole	Fragments	Whole	All
Patella vulgata sautuola	124	145	0.544	0.328
Patella spp.	1		0.004	0.001
Littorina littorea	36	9	0.158	0.055
Mytilus edulis		10		0.012
Trivia europaea	1		0.004	0.001
Paracentrotus lividus	1	370	0.004	0.452
Helix nemoralis	62	56	0.272	0.144
Helix arbustorum	3	2	0.013	0.006
Total	228	592	0.999	0.999

Other Faunal Remains	Number
Indeterminate bones, small fish	280
Indeterminate bones and teeth, rodent	32
Cervus elaphus	1
Capreolus capreolus	1
Indeterminate bones, large bovid (*Bos* sp.)	1
Indeterminate antler fragments	4
Indeterminate bones, teeth fragments	141
Total	460

industrial continuity between the Upper Solutrean and Lower Magdalenian culture-stratigraphic units (Jordá 1960: 15, 16). Jordá has since reevaluated this assemblage, along with the stratigraphy at the site (Straus 1975a: 107–110). After a careful examination of the unpublished Jordá collections at the Oviedo museum (which resulted in the discovery of 3 Solutrean points), and after studying Jordá's level designations, Straus (1975a: 112–115) concludes that a rather atypical, Magdalenian III–like Upper Solutrean assemblage was sampled. In his latest opinion on the El Cierro Solutrean, Jordá seems to concur (1977: 92). Atop the black sediments lay a second yellow stratum about 35 cm thick and of uncertain cultural affinity (either Upper Magdalenian or Azilian or both, according to Alvarez). Jordá (1977: 114–117) presently regards this deposit as Lower Magdalenian or Magdalenian III (at any rate, a Magdalenian assemblage without harpoons), citing apparent similarities with the Santander "Magdalenian III" sites of El Juyo, Rascaño, and Altamira. Capping the sequence is a conchero 75 cm thick, sealed in by a stalagmitic cap where in contact with the cave wall. This last deposit is believed, because of a radiocarbon date, to be Azilian by Jordá (1977: 159), and Upper Magdalenian by Clark (1971a: 238) and Straus (1975a: 110).

Faunal, charcoal, and sediment samples were taken from the conchero to determine whether the midden conformed to Vega del Sella's (1916: 82–92) description of an Upper Paleolithic conchero, and if possible to date it by radiocarbon. Shellfish species and their absolute and relative frequencies are given in Table 3.3, and agreement with the Conde's description is good. *Patella vulgata sautuola* and *Littorina littorea* predominate, along with the terrestrial gastropod *Helix nemoralis*. The high incidence of sea urchins (*Paracentrotus lividus*) is an artifact of their fragility. The industrial remains recovered

from this small conchero sample numbered 45 pieces. Unfortunately, no "diagnostic" fossil indicators were among them (see Clark 1971a: 239).

The conchero sample from El Cierro yielded a total of 18.2 gm of charcoal fragments. The determination (GaK 2548) was 10,400 ± 500 years B.P. Multiplied by the correction factor, the conchero dates to 10,712 ± 515 years B.P. This would place it toward the end of the cool, humid Younger Dryas phase; the corresponding industrial association should be Final Magdalenian V-VI (González Echegaray 1966; 1975: 59).

Balmori
The sequence defined in the 1969 Cuts D and E at the cave site of Balmori also supports the conclusions reached above. Cut E, located on the northwest side of the Conde's old trench, exposed six levels (see Fig. 3.8). Excluding a flowstone cap, the uppermost is a rich Asturian deposit. Level distinctions are based on subtle, sedimentological differences related to the internal dynamics of the cave rather than to macroclimatic events outside it (Butzer and Bowman 1979). I believe that the Cut E sequence, except for Level 1 (Asturian), is primarily Magdalenian III, although industrial remains are not sufficiently numerous to state this conclusively (Clark 1974a: 411–420; Clark and Clark 1975: 68–74). Of interest here are the faunal remains that, in keeping with the Conde's interpretation, vary through time from Upper Paleolithic exploitation of *Patella vulgata sautuola* and *Littorina littorea,* to the Asturian pattern emphasizing the smaller post-Pleistocene species (*Patella* spp., *T. crassa*). The increase in frequency of *Patella* spp. and *Trochocochlea crassa,* at the expense of *P. vulgata sautuola* and *Littorina littorea,* is clearly marked. Similar trends are apparent in Cut D. Level D1 is assigned to the Asturian; underlying levels D2 through D5 are considered Upper Paleolithic (Fig. 3.19).

SPECIES	E5	E4	E3	E2/3	E1	D5	D4	D3	D2	D1	KEY
Patella vulgata, P.intermedia	.011	.235	.509	.797	.645	.015	.051	------	------	.883	————
Patella vulgata sautuola (var. mayor)	.887	.647	.360	.093	.006	.936	.820	.900	.941	.017	- - - - -
Littorina littorea	.102	.094	.096	.027	.004	.049	.128	.100	.059	.083	□——□
Trochocochlea crassa	------	.023	.035	.082	.344	------	------	------	------	.017	············

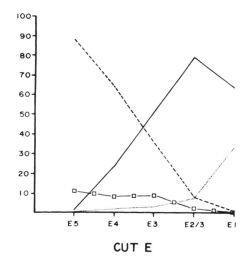

CUT E

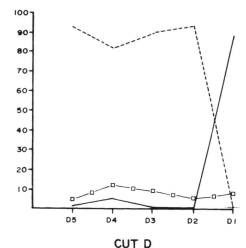

CUT D

Figure 3.19. Balmori: major shellfish species exploited from about 17,000 to 8200 B.P. (Cuts D and E after Clark 1974a).

La Lloseta

The cave of La Lloseta also contains several different kinds of concheros. The sequence defined in the cave mouth was described above (*Historical Review of Asturian Sites*). In addition, samples were taken from three of the shell-bearing deposits adhering to the walls and ceiling of the main chamber, designated A, B, and C. Samples B and C pertain to post-Asturian concheros (see below, *Post-Asturian Conchero Sites*).

Sample A was removed from an intact pocket of black greasy organic sediments, rich in shell and bone, located 23 m back from the cave mouth along the east wall. The intent was to obtain a sample of what appeared to be an Upper Paleolithic conchero that could be dated and that contained sufficient faunal material to permit comparison with other similar samples. The results were somewhat unexpected (Table 3.4).

The high frequency of *Patella* spp. and the relatively less common occurrence of *Patella vulgata sautuola* is striking. *Littorina littorea* is quite numerous, as would be expected in a Magdalenian conchero; *Trochocochlea crassa* is reassuringly absent. The apparent lower frequency of the so-called "sautuola" variant may be due to a high proportion of breakage; fragments assigned to that subspecies are relatively numerous compared with *Patella* spp. This configuration might be explained by local microenvironmental differences. Intertidal shellfish populations could vary somewhat in composition from area to area, even given identical substrates.

TABLE 3.4
La Lloseta: Conchero Sample A, Faunal Inventory

Species	Absolute Frequency		Relative Frequency	
	Whole	Fragments	Whole	All
Patella vulgata sautuola	5	81	0.036	0.274
Patella spp.	59	48	0.427	0.341
Littorina littorea	74	46	0.536	0.382
Mytilus edulis		1		0.003
Total	138	176	0.999	1.000
Other Faunal Remains				Number
Indeterminate bones, rodent				4
Cervus elaphus				51
Capreolus capreolus				1
Capra ibex				1
Indeterminate bone, teeth fragments				536
Total				593

The industrial remains in the sample contained no diagnostic pieces. The industry is probably, although not demonstrably, Lower Magdalenian (Clark 1971a: 243, 245, 246; 1976a: 123–125). A charcoal sample from La Lloseta A (15.9 gm) yielded a corrected determination of 15,656 ± 412 B.P. (GaK 2549). This date places the faunal spectrum in the Cantabrian Lower Magdalenian III, an assignation at least tentatively supported by the sparse industrial remains (González Echegaray 1966; Jordá 1958: 84–87; 1977: 130).

The evidence from El Cierro, Balmori, and La Lloseta A, and the most recent excavations at La Riera (Straus and others 1981), support the Conde's correlation of particular conchero configurations with particular Upper (Solutrean, Magdalenian) and post-Paleolithic (Asturian) culture-stratigraphic units. The decline in frequency of *P. vulgata sautuola* and *Littorina littorea,* and the corresponding increase through time of *Patella* spp. and *T. crassa* are clearly marked at Balmori and at other conchero sites in eastern Asturias. There is, however, considerable evidence for regional variability (La Lloseta A).

Post-Asturian Conchero Sites

Concheros pertaining to periods subsequent to the Asturian also have a characteristic array of molluscan species. Post-Asturian concheros are those in which the edible mussel (*Mytilus edulis*) is predominant or well represented. Such deposits also contain quantities of small Holocene limpets (*P. vulgata, P. intermedia*), topshells (*T. crassa*), and even the diminutive modern variant of the winkle (*L. littorea*) that is scarce or absent in Asturian deposits (Vega del Sella 1916: 89). Three concheros in which this configuration appeared to be present were inspected. These deposits were in the caves of Les Pedroses, La Lloseta B and C, and San Antonio; only the first two were sampled.

Les Pedroses

Les Pedroses is an element in the complex karstic system developed in the Sella valley. Like El Cierro, the cave is situated on a ridge north of the village of El Carmen; it opens to the east (see Fig. 3.4, Table 3.1). It is best known for Upper Paleolithic engravings, supposedly of Magdalenian age (Jordá 1977: 115, 126, 137). The site also has produced some Bronze Age pottery, although the detailed provenience of the vessels is not known. Les Pedroses was tested in the mid-1950s by Jordá and Alvarez, but the results have not been published.

With Señor Alvarez, I sampled the site on February 10, 1969. The remnants of a conchero, now largely removed, is visible on both sides of the entrance to the cave. All sediments are heavily indurated with calcium carbonate. A sample was obtained from the top 25 cm of the cornice preserved along the south wall, at a point 3 m back from the mouth of the cave. The sediment sample derived from this location (No. 1727) is described in Butzer and Bowman (1979). The breccia was broken apart with a pick mattock because it was extremely hard. The sediment contained little industry (Clark 1971a: 250) but was rich in charcoal and faunal remains (Table 3.5).

Noteworthy is the complete absence of *P. vulgata sautuola* and *L. littorea,* and the relatively higher frequency of *Mytilus edulis.* The sediments were extremely rich in carbon; 31.2 gm remained after the cleaning process. The sample yielded a (corrected) determination of 5932 ± 185 years B.P. (GaK 2547). No pottery was recovered from the sample.

San Antonio

San Antonio is a small cave located on the west bank of the Río Sella about 1.2 km from that river (see Fig. 3.4, Table 3.1). It consists of a single main chamber about 17 m across, and a series of lesser galleries leading back into the hill. The entrance faces north. San Antonio has

TABLE 3.5
Les Pedroses: Conchero Sample, Faunal Inventory

	Absolute Frequency		Relative Frequency	
Species	**Whole**	**Fragments**	**Whole**	**All**
Patella spp.				
(*P. aspera* most common)	345	237	0.698	0.479
Trochocochlea crassa	98	108	0.198	0.169
Mytilus edulis	43	73	0.087	0.095
Tapes decussatus	1		0.002	0.001
Gibbula umbilicalis	1		0.002	0.001
Cardium edulis	1	3	0.002	0.003
Paracentrotus lividus		289		0.236
Helix nemoralis	3	3	0.006	0.005
Helix arbustorum	2	11	0.004	0.011
Total	494	724	0.999	1.000

Other Faunal Remains	Number
Indeterminate crustaceans	2
Indeterminate bones, small fish	4
Indeterminate bones, rodent	2
Indeterminate bones	11
Indeterminate antler	1
Total	20

never been systematically excavated (Jordá 1958: 19). Nothing has been published on the cultural deposits although various tourist guides make note of Upper Paleolithic paintings.

The cave contains the remnants of a conchero, the former extent of which can be traced by a stalagmitic cornice on the west wall (Clark 1976a: 127, 128). Little conchero remains in the cave today, however. Inspection of these remnants shows that the conchero was composed mainly of large (more than 10 cm long) valves of *M. edulis; T. crassa, P. vulgata, P. intermedia,* and *P. aspera* were also observed in some frequency. There are rarer specimens of oyster (*Ostrea edulis*) and cardial shell (*Cardium edulis*), and the deposit also contained some bone and charcoal. No samples were taken; the sediments remaining in the cave were extremely hard. These facts and the complete absence of large specimens of *L. littorea* and *P. vulgata sautuola* suggest that the conchero at San Antonio is a post-Asturian one, although it cannot be demonstrated without radiocarbon determinations.

La Lloseta

La Lloseta contains two conchero deposits, designated B and C, that appear to be post-Asturian. Sample B was taken from the top of a conchero deposit cemented to the west wall of the cave 15 m from its mouth, at an elevation of 175 cm above the floor. It was removed from the uppermost 20 cm of a band of conchero sealed in by the last depositional episode in the cave—a thick flowstone cap. The faunal inventory is given in Table 3.6.

As at Les Pedroses and San Antonio, the high frequency of *Mytilus edulis* is striking. No *L. littorea* nor any of the Pleistocene variants of *P. vulgata* were noted in this small sample. Splinters of mussel shell (*M. edulis*) were not counted. The "whole mussel" count includes complete valves and the basal portions (apices) of valves. Most of the bone occurs as tiny, triturated fragments.

Sample C was removed from the ceiling of the cave 2 m back from the mouth, underneath the overhang. The sediments were detached (with considerable effort) from a massive deposit of conchero suspended about 2.8 m above the present floor. It is evident that prior to removal this shell midden obstructed the entrance to the cavern.

The Sample C inventory appears similar to that from Sample B (Table 3.7). No industrial remains were recovered. Sample C yielded 15.6 gm of charcoal; the corrected determination (GaK 2551) received was 4594 ± 680 years B.P.

TABLE 3.6
La Lloseta: Conchero Sample B, Faunal Inventory

Species	Absolute Frequency		Relative Frequency	
	Whole	Fragments	Whole	All
Patella spp.	136	27	0.531	0.471
Trochocochlea crassa	8	5	0.031	0.038
Mytilus edulis	108	46	0.422	0.445
Paracentrotus lividus		10		0.029
Helix nemoralis	4	2	0.016	0.017
Total	256	90	1.000	1.000
Other Faunal Remains				Number
Indeterminate bone fragments				19
Total				19

TABLE 3.7
La Lloseta: Conchero Sample C, Faunal Inventory

Species	Absolute Frequency		Relative Frequency	
	Whole	Fragments	Whole	All
Patella spp.	219	43	0.564	0.498
Patella vulg. sautuola	1		0.003	0.001
Trochocochlea crassa	12	4	0.031	0.030
Mytilus edulis	122	76	0.314	0.376
Ostrea edulis?		1		0.001
Indeterminate marine gastropods	23		0.059	0.044
Paracentrotus lividus		14		0.027
Helix nemoralis	11		0.028	0.021
Total	388	138	0.999	0.998
Other Faunal Remains				Number
Indeterminate bone fragments				21
Total				21

In view of the apparent similarity of the faunal inventories, Samples B and C were tested with a nonparametric technique called the Kolmogorov-Smirnov Two Sample Test (Siegel 1956: 127–136). This test assumes that if two samples are similar (drawn from the same or identically distributed populations), then the cumulative distributions of their relative frequencies may be expected to be fairly close to one another, showing only random deviation from the theoretical population distribution. Calculations were based for each group on the combined total of whole and fragmented specimens. It was assumed that equal proportions of shell were broken in both cases. The test determined that differences between the two samples were *not significant* at the 0.1 level. The Kolmogorov-Smirnov D statistic was 0.053, with $n_1 = 346$ and $n_2 = 502$. D was less than the critical value computed at the 0.01 level of significance (0.1138). Thus it is concluded that there are no significant differences between Samples B and C (for further discussion of this test, see Clark 1971a).

Conclusions

Considerable importance is attached to the changes in the numbers and relative frequencies of molluscan species exploited because of (1) their hypothetical paleoclimatic significance, and (2) their use as monitors of dietary stress over time. With respect to long-term paleoclimatic change, it has generally been argued that the transition from the large Pleistocene forms to the species characteristic of Asturian concheros coincided with the Post Glacial Climatic Optimum (the Atlantic period in modern schemes, 8150–5250 B.P.; Vega del Sella 1916, 1921, 1923). While available radiocarbon samples suggest that this transition probably began to take place considerably earlier than had previously been thought (probably at about the beginning of the Boreal, 9450–8150 B.P.), the absence or rarity of the edible periwinkle (*L. littorea*) in Asturian concheros is probably due to warmer climatic conditions. Cold temperatures (5–6° C) increase the survival of this species, while temperatures above 21° C reduce it (Newell, Pye, and Ahsanullah 1971). When exposed to air temperature above 32° C at low tide, *L. littorea* becomes comatose (Lewis 1964). Its reappearance on Cantabrian coasts today probably coincides with a post-Atlantic cooling trend, and the establishment of essentially modern climatic conditions.

The increase with time in the number of species exploited and the exploitation of more exposed coastal niches beginning later in the Magdalenian suggest that the prehistoric Cantabrians were undergoing a certain amount of long-term dietary stress, and they responded to this stress by expanding the number of zones from which marine resources were being taken. A long-term increase in population density, with a concomitant overexploitation of estuarine niches, has been proposed as the principal causal agent (see Chapter 6; Straus and others 1980, 1981; Clark and Straus 1982).

PORTUGUESE AND GALICIAN TERRACE SITES

Industries attributed to the Asturian but found outside Cantabria are located primarily in two areas along the Atlantic coast of Portugal, here designated (1) the Portuguese terrace sites, and (2) the Galician terrace sites (see Fig. 1.1). The Portuguese terrace sites are scattered along the Río Tejo (Tajo, Tage, Tagus) in the area around Santarém, capital of the province of Ribatejo, about 65 km northeast of Lisbon (Figs. 3.20–3.22). Cultural material occurs in three depositional contexts: (1) on the plateau surface above the present-day Tejo valley floodplain, (2) in and on top of river terraces, and (3) in Quaternary beach deposits. The chronological and stratigraphic implications of these discoveries have been analyzed by a large number of investigators (for example, Breuil and Zybszewski 1942; Viana 1956; Maury 1968, 1974, 1976, 1977; Aguirre 1964; Aguirre and Butzer 1967; and Jalhay and do Paço 1941; a complete bibliography is given in Clark 1976a: 363–370). The Galician terrace sites are located along the lower reaches of the Miño (Minho), Lima, and Douro rivers, and along the Atlantic coast in the provinces of Pontevedra (Spain), and Minho and Douro Litoral (Portugal) in the northwestern quadrant of the Iberian Peninsula (Fig. 3.23). The sites, numbering about 30, are found on top of river terraces (when situated inland) or on beach deposits and marine platforms of Quaternary age (when situated along the coast).

In both areas, "Asturian," "Pre-Asturian," "Proto-Asturian," and "Pseudo-Asturian" collections have been artificially "reconstituted" from collections of mixed and rolled terrace industries by the long-standing practice of using archaeological index fossils (*fossiles directeurs*) to identify and categorize assemblages. Two unwarranted assumptions underlie these classifications and the assertion that they are "related" in some way to the Asturian of Cantabria (Clark 1976a: 237–239). One assumption is that fossil directors are thought to be adequate to identify and discriminate among specific archaeological assemblages, especially when raw material, surface texture, degree of rolling, and patination are considered along with artifact morphology. The objective of this book has been to construct a more reliable and detailed synthesis of stratigraphic, industrial, and faunal criteria by which Cantabrian Asturian sites may be identified. No longer must reliance be placed on a single tool type, the Asturian pick, to identify Asturian cultural deposits.

The second and linked notion is the idea of progressive evolutionary development within "lineages" of stone tools. I refer to this concept as "tool type phylogeny," defined as the practice of assigning values to artifacts on the basis of their morphological characteristics and then drawing temporal and relational conclusions from them. The two values most commonly implied, if not explicitly stated, are the linked notions of chronological and progressive development. A large, technically unsophisticated handaxe, manufactured by direct percussion with a hard hammerstone or anvil, is considered older (on typological grounds) than a flat, symmetrical oval handaxe, produced with a soft hammerstone. The same argument has been applied to picks. While these assumptions may be valid for handaxes, although in terms so general as to be meaningless, it is quite unjustifiable to

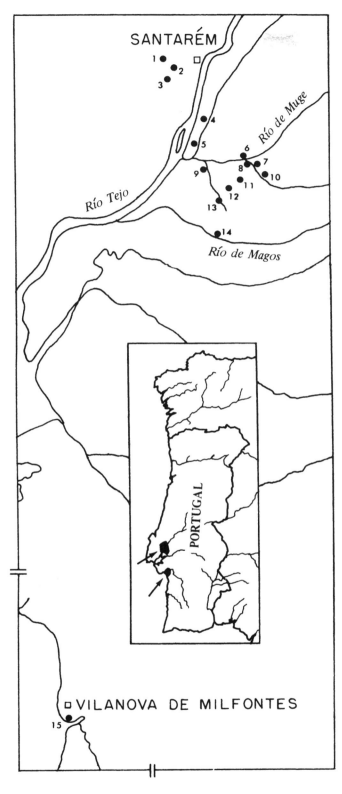

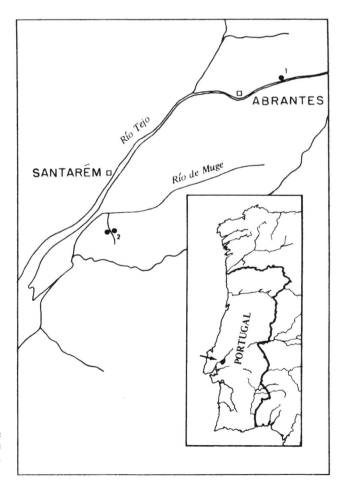

Figure 3.20. Location of Portuguese "Asturian" terrace sites in the provinces of Ribatejo and Baixo Alentejo:
 1. Quinta do Grainho
 2. Pero Filho
 3. Ponte do Celeiro
 4. Benfiça do Ribatejo
 5. Porto Sabugueiro
 6. Arneiro dos Pescadores
 7. João Boieiro
 8. Boa Vista
 9. Vale de Raposa
10. Cocharrinho
11. Grenho
12. Ponte do Coelheiro
13. Glória
14. Vale do Zebro
15. Vilanova de Milfontes
16. Casal do Monte (not shown)
17. Damaia (not shown)

Figure 3.21. Location of Portuguese "Paleolithic" terrace sites in the province of Ribatejo: 1, Urtiga; 2, Ponte do Coelheiro.

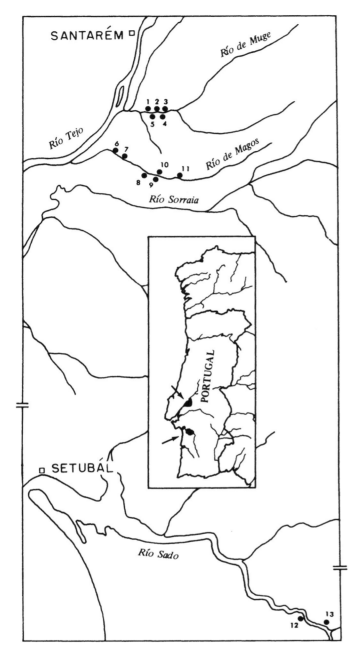

Figure 3.22. Location of Portuguese Mesolithic shell midden sites in the provinces of Ribatejo and Setubal:

 1. Fonte do Padre Pedro
 2. Flor da Beira
 3. Cabeço da Arruda
 4. Cabeço da Amoreira
 5. Moita do Sebastião
 6. Cova de Onça
 7. Monte dos Ossos
 8. Cabeço dos Morros
 9. Magos de Baixo
10. Magos de Cima
11. Barragem
12. Portancho
13. Quinta de Baixo

ence artifact morphology to a marked degree. More significant, however, are the unstated biases that underlie the phylogenetic approach, which limit potential explanations of patterns of variability to a very circumscribed set of factors. These biases are usually (1) the "culture-stratigraphic-units-equate-with-socially-conscious-groups" arguments so often espoused by the Bordes' (de Sonneville-Bordes 1963; Bordes 1968; Bordes and de Sonneville-Bordes 1970) and equally often attacked by the Binfords (Binford and Binford 1966, 1969; Binford 1972, 1973), and (2) the ill-defined notion that the passage of time, in and of itself, *causes* morphological change. By assuming that all change in artifact form can be identified exclusively with changes in the learned mental templates of the artifact producers over time, these approaches become circular and nonexplanatory; the "explanation" for patterned variation is embedded in the investigator's biases. The idea that a part of observed variability could be owed to the role of learning within a social context is, of course, a legitimate one, and one that can be tested against the archaeological record, but this is seldom if ever done in the context of European prehistory. By assuming that all change must reflect (or even be attributed to) the passage of time, other and potentially more powerful causal factors are ignored. These approaches present not only a biased impression of the range of industrial variability by restricting the monitors of industrial variability to a rigidly circumscribed set of types or morphological attributes, they also limit explanation to a small number of potential causal factors. These comments probably seem self-evident to most American readers. However, a thorough treatment of the Asturian demands that such arguments be dealt with simply because of the importance placed on them by some Spanish and Portuguese prehistorians.

apply the "tool type phylogeny" approach to *all* artifact types. Choppers and chopping-tools, for example, show no morphological progression through time. A chopper from an Asturian site is indistinguishable from one originating in a Lower Pleistocene Pebble Tool context in North Africa (Biberson and others 1960).

Undue emphasis on progressive, linear morphological change fails to take into account a host of other relevant variables (such as effects due to size and quality of raw material, implied functional differences) that must influ-

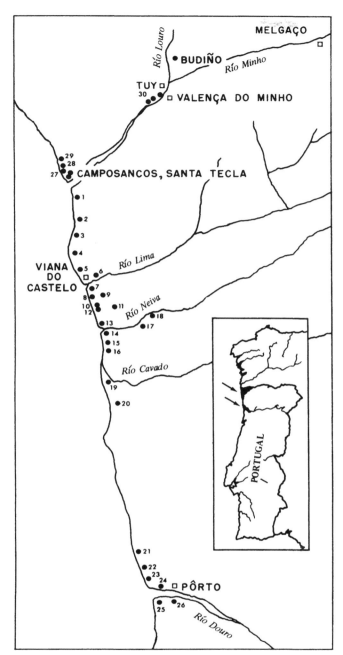

Figure 3.23. Location of Galician "Asturian" terrace sites in the provinces of Pontevedra in Spain and Minho and Douro Litoral in Portugal:

1. Moledo
2. Âncora
3. Afife
4. Carreço
5. Areosa Viana
6. Abelheira
7. Rodanho
8. Anha
9. Vila Fria
10. Alvarães
11. Vila de Punhe
12. São Romão do Neiva
13. Castelo do Neiva
14. São Paio do Antas
15. Belinho
16. São Bartolomeu do Mar
17. Aldreu
18. Durrães
19. Fão
20. Apúlia
21. São Braz
22. Boa Nova
23. Manhufe
24. Ervilha
25. Lavadores
26. Madalena
27. La Guardia
28. Arena Grande
29. Punta de los Picos
30. Sites recorded by Alvarez-Blasquez and Bouza-Brey in 1949

A review of the geological evidence and consideration of the factors determining group assignment (Clark 1976a: 237–266) clearly indicate that the "sites" in the Miño and Tejo valleys are both "heterogeneous and polygenetic" (Aguirre 1964: 6, 7). The distinction made between "Asturian" and Lower-Middle Paleolithic sites is strictly arbitrary, based on the presence of unifacial picks in some deposits (or, more accurately, collections) and their apparent absence in others. The implement is differentially distributed because of selective collecting or geological sorting. It is noteworthy that some of the "sites" (for example, Ponte do Coelheiro) have been classified both as Lower Paleolithic and as Asturian, depending on the predominance of tool types in the collection being studied (a fact noted by Jalhay and do Paço 1941: 76). Other sites such as Cocharrinho and Vale do Zebro are located in or immediately adjacent to present-day river channels, and still others (like Benfiça de Ribatejo) owe their classification as Asturian to the occurrence of a single unifacial pick among the pieces (usually handaxes) collected for the study. In no collection (except for Ponte do Coelheiro) are picks actually abundant, and in no case were any of the artifacts recovered from primary depositional contexts. Most of the pieces are moderately to heavily rolled and the geological contexts, when known, clearly indicate secondary deposition.

Most of the surface industries of the Tejo and Miño valleys are hopelessly mixed by geological agencies and probably do not merit further study. The predominant tool types indicate that the bulk of this material is probably of Lower and Middle Paleolithic date. Once a tool is liberated from its original depositional matrix, the degree of rolling so often used to classify an artifact is a function of the amount of time *and* the intensity with which the object has been tossed about in a river channel or a high-energy beach. Some of these objects actually may date to the Holocene, in which case they might have functioned like their Cantabrian analogues in the technology of strand-line shell gathering economies for which there is no archaeological trace. As local stream gradients, bedloads, velocity, and wave energy determine the extent of rolling for any particular area (these "sites" refer to expanses of beach and river terraces, not to single localities), and as these factors vary in any given place over time, the condition of these artifacts alone cannot serve to order them chronologically. The absence of an adequate geological sequence in the area is a severe drawback. Except for the formal coincidence in artifact morphology and the fact that both assemblages appear to occur in coastal contexts, there is no evidence whatever to link the Portuguese and Galician sites with the Asturian of Cantabria. I believe the morphological similarity between the Cantabrian picks and the unifacial implement of the Luso-Galician sites is fortuitous. Any efforts to establish chronological or "phylogenetic" relationships between the latter and the Cantabrian Asturian are not supported by present evidence.

In the Miño drainage, like that of Tejo, the presence of some open-air shell midden sites has caused confusion in the literature. One that has been dated by metal objects and pottery is located adjacent to the *castro* site of Santa Tecla and is probably contemporary with it (400–200 B.C., Iron Age II). There is also a conchero at Sáa near the famed "Chellean" site (Fontela 1925) that is probably also Iron Age. Both of these are coastal stations. There are no indications that these middens are related in any way to the terrace and beach "industries" under discussion, but they have not been studied in detail.

Finally, the Portuguese and Galician terrace sites should not be confused with the Tejo valley shell midden sites that are situated in the Muge valley on the south bank of the Tejo near the city of Muge. These sites, 11 in number, are Mesolithic shell middens characterized by a geometric microlithic industry reportedly of Tardenoisian affinity (Roche 1966). The middens contain multi-family structures and, in some cases, have cemeteries associated with them (Ferembach 1974). Other than the fact that they are midden sites, referred to as *concheiros* in the Portuguese literature, they bear no resemblance to the concheros of the Asturian of Cantabria. The lithic inventory is predominantly of flint and is almost completely microlithic. The faunal inventory is completely distinct from that of the Asturian. These sites have been dated by radiocarbon to about 7200 B.P. (average of C-14 dates).

It seems apparent that, in general, these "industries" are artificially constituted by various investigators on rather superficial morphological grounds. The question of identifying unmixed assemblages was never an important consideration with most Galician investigators (Jalhay 1925, 1928; Fontela 1925 excepted). For the most part, these men took for granted the fact that the collections were mixed and sought to isolate industrial entities on either morphological grounds (using criteria such as degree of rolling, patination) or "cultural" grounds (using a preconceived idea of the constituent tool types in given industrial assemblages defined elsewhere as a basis for comparison). It is clear that neither approach is successful to the extent that results can be duplicated independently, nor would the resultant collections be considered meaningful in behavioral terms even if replication were possible. Most Anglo-American scholars no longer consider this kind of typologically-oriented exercise to be of interest (but see Roe 1968a, b; 1970; Graham 1970; Collins 1969, 1970).

The discovery of the dated Late Pleistocene open-site of Budiño, near Pontevedra (Aguirre 1964; Aguirre and Butzer 1967); the work of Maury (1974, 1976, 1977) at Âncora and Carreço; and recently reported picks in stratigraphic contexts analogous to those of Âncora-Carreço at the strand-line sites of Bañugues, Aramar, and L'Atalaya near Gijón in Asturias (Blas Cortina and others 1978; Rodriguez Asensio 1978a, b) raise the interesting possibility that at least some of the artifacts found in surficial cobble and silt deposits on top of fossil beaches may date to the Late Pleistocene or even the Pleistocene-Holocene boundary. On the basis of pollen and sediment analyses, an early Holocene date is also implied for Liencres (see Chapter 4 and Appendix I). The possibility of a Pleistocene boundary date is not adequate, however, to account for the morphologically identical but heavily rolled "Asturian" and "Camposanquian" picks recovered from strand lines or in terraces of Middle Pleistocene date. The occurrence of picks in Acheulean deposits, unquestionably in situ, has been well documented at the stratified, open-air occupation site of Terra Amata near Nice (Lumley 1966: 41).

The locations that have yielded unrolled picks near Gijón tend to be situated in shallow, estuary margins like those in which most stratified Asturian midden sites are found (see Chapters 6 and 7; Blas Cortina and others 1978). This observation is also true of the isolated discovery at Luarca (Asturias) and may be true of some of the Portuguese and Galician sites just described. Whatever the relative age of these peculiar implements, and whatever their principal functions might have been, they are tightly associated with littoral or estuarine situations. Even the Acheulean site of Terra Amata, which has produced analogous artifacts, is a coastal site. In Iberia apparently no pick of any age is found more than a few kilometers inland, and it could be speculated that those sites containing fresh picks from Holocene geological contexts might be the disturbed functional equivalents of the Asturian of the caves.

In the case of completely fresh pieces from geological contexts of probably Late Pleistocene or Pleistocene-Holocene boundary date, it seems evident that their depositional contexts, in most cases, cannot be considered to be absolutely primary. This is true even of the relatively undisturbed and dated site of Budiño (Aguirre 1964; Aguirre and Butzer 1967). However, their pristine condition makes it equally likely that these pieces have not traveled far, which raises in turn the tantalizing prospect of the future discovery of more in situ open-air sites like

Liencres where the depositional context was demonstrably primary (Clark 1979b). The apparent absence of other cultural features in these strand-line open sites (for example, middens) could be due to factors of differential preservation. There are no caves along the granitic Luso-Galician littoral, and consequently few protected locales that might have favored preservation of these unconsolidated garbage heaps. However, while open-air shell middens have formed in the region in the relatively recent past (Santa Tecla, Sáa), fluvial and marine erosional processes and intentional human activity could conceivably have played significant roles in affecting the disappearance of more ancient concheros.

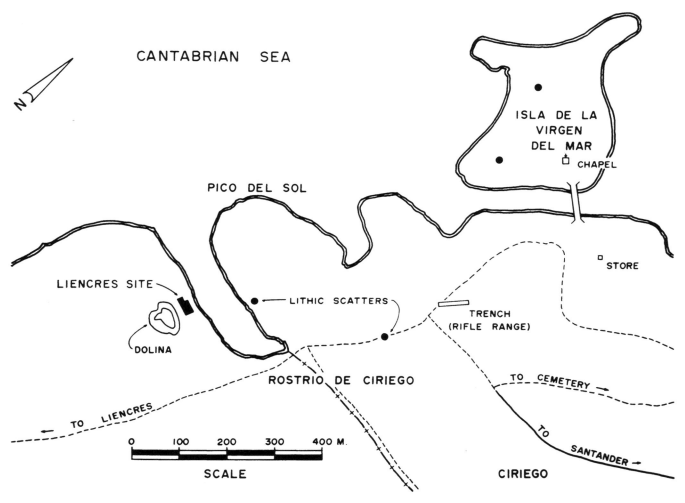

Figure 4.1. Location of the Liencres site in relation to coastal features west of the provincial capital of Santander.

4. ARCHAEOLOGICAL INVESTIGATIONS AT LIENCRES

Liencres is an open-air site located on the sea coast west of the provincial capital of Santander in northern Spain (see Figs. 3.1, 4.1). Until the discovery of Liencres in January, 1969, the Cantabrian Asturian was known only from cave and rock shelter contexts (see Chapter 3). Asturian assemblages from cave sites are characterized by crude quartzite industries found in low density in poorly stratified midden contexts (concheros), dated by radiocarbon to the late Boreal and early Atlantic phases (9000–7000 B.P.; Butzer 1971a: 531). Liencres is a different kind of site than the Asturian caves. It adds a new dimension to the expected range of variation of Asturian lithic assemblages because of the high probability of site functional distinctions between Liencres, on the one hand, and the conchero sites taken as a group, on the other (see Chapter 5).

The location and setting of Liencres are described in Chapter 3 (*Historical Review of Asturian Sites: Liencres*). Archaeological investigations at the site have been described in a Spanish monograph (Clark 1975a) and elsewhere (Clark 1979b). Aspects of the artifact distributions are treated in Clark (1979a), and an algorithm for the computerized, three-dimensional representation of artifact surface densities at Liencres is described in Scheitlin and Clark (1978).

Liencres was systematically collected and partially excavated from January through March in 1969, and during August, 1972. Unifacial quartzite picks characteristic of the Asturian were among the artifacts recovered. After preliminary description, analysis concentrated on assessing whether or not the lithic assemblage could be considered to pertain to the Cantabrian Asturian. Similarities in the relative frequencies of certain debitage and retouched tool classes were noted when the Liencres material was compared with that from the Asturian cave sites. A formal comparison of these lithic assemblages is presented in Chapter 5.

Considerable attention was paid to the distributional aspects of both surface and excavated samples at the site. After first determining that the context of deposition was undisturbed, the horizontal distribution of all artifacts from the surface collection was plotted by type to assess whether clustering of types—perhaps indicative of activity-specific areas—was present. These data were then subjected to a series of objective statistical tests to determine the nature and extent of clustering, dispersion, and association among the various artifact categories. The surface collection was also compared with the excavated sample using the Chi-square Test for Independent Samples. This statistic demonstrated that the two collections differed significantly with respect to debitage categories but were alike with respect to the kinds and frequencies of retouched tools.

The paucity of features and the relatively thin scatter of lithic debris indicated that occupation at the site was of short duration. That primary tool manufacturing activities were conducted was inferred from the scarcity of retouched pieces and the prevalence of debitage. No identifiable faunal remains were recovered, but the presence of a grinding slab, tiny shell and bone fragments, and phosphate concentrations (Butzer and Bowman 1979) suggest some food processing and consumption, and the accumulation of garbage. No substance suitable for radiometric dating was recovered. Pollen analysis (Appendix A) indicates a vegetational configuration similar to that of the present day.

SURFACE COLLECTION

A systematic surface collection was undertaken at Liencres in order to determine the horizontal distribution of artifactual debris. Maximum surface scatter covered an area about 9 m wide by 20 m long, altogether about 180 square meters. The area was small enough for a complete sample (approaching 100 percent) to be collected; thus sampling error was not a problem in the initial phase of the project. A grid of 663 squares, each 50 cm on a side, was erected over the site and material from the squares was systematically collected by the crew. A system of Cartesian coordinates was devised to permit simple and rapid designation of areas within the site. The positions of all artifacts were plotted, square by square, on a master sheet.

Artifacts also occurred sporadically and in low density in an arc 10 m wide extending along the east side of the main concentration (to the cliff edge above the inlet) and to the south of it. These artifacts were given a special designation, then collected and typed, but their positions were not plotted on the grid.

Each artifact was numbered in the field and subsequently renumbered with indelible ink in the laboratory so that the original position of any given piece could be reconstructed on the grid system. Retouched pieces were classified according to the typology developed for the European Upper Paleolithic by de Sonneville-Bordes and

Perrot (1954, 1955, 1956). Debitage and certain categories of large-stone tools were accommodated by the typologies developed by Bordes (1961) and Clark (1971a: 260–278), the latter specifically for the classification of Asturian assemblages.

When the classification was finished, the positions of all flint and quartzite artifacts were plotted again separately, resulting in two large distribution maps. From these maps, it was obvious that the scatter was not distributed at random over the surface of the site and that there were three definite areas of concentration within it. A preliminary analysis of the kinds of materials present in the surface collection suggests that the site is a workshop.

Composition of the Surface Sample

A total of 1046 artifacts was recovered from the surface of the site, including the areas peripheral to the main concentration (Table 4.1; see Appendix B for data from the 1972 season). Table 4.2 presents the data in the format advocated by de Sonneville-Bordes and Perrot (1954, 1955, 1956) for the construction of cumulative percentage graphs; for comparative purposes, only types recognized by those authors are tabulated. The resulting plot appears in Figure 4.2. Data are also presented in histograms (Figs. 4.3, 4.4).

The surface collection at Liencres shows most of the salient characteristics postulated for Asturian industries based on the few reliable samples available from cave sites (La Riera, Balmori; Clark 1971a: 281–317). I believe, however, that the Liencres data are more reliable than those from the cave sites because of the completeness of the systematic surface collection and because of improved excavation and recording techniques.

Debitage

Debitage consists of all unretouched pieces; unworked cobbles, unworked pebbles, split cobble segments, all nuclei, trimming flakes, plain flakes, primary and secondary decortication flakes, core renewal flakes, blades and bladelets are included (Table 4.1). Various categories of debitage account for no less than 92 percent of the surface total, a significant figure when it is noted that the proportion of debitage across all Asturian sites (taken together) is about 80 percent (Clark 1971a: 312). As at other sites, unaltered flakes, blades, and bladelets make up most of the debitage subtotal. Flakes exclusive of trimming flakes equal 74.5 percent of debitage; this figure exceeds the number of flakes (60 percent) in all the lithic material from Asturian cave sites. Trimming flakes at Liencres add another 13.6 percent of debitage, again significantly greater than the 8 percent characteristic of the Asturian cave sites. Blades and bladelets equal 6.1 percent of debitage, a figure less by half than the proportion characteristic of the cave sites (14 percent). The ratio of flint to quartzite (6.0:1.0) stands in marked contrast to that characteristic of the cave sites (1.0:2.7), but the proximity of a flint source may account for this reversal (Clark 1971a: 307). These statistics support the sug-

gestion that primary and secondary manufacturing activities were important at Liencres, and were conducted there more frequently than at the cave sites that typify the Asturian.

Nuclei (all types) are present in the surficial deposits at Liencres with a frequency of 3 percent of debitage; they occur in the cave sites with a frequency of about 8 percent (Clark 1971a: 307). While this figure seems inconsistent with the suggestion that the site is a knapping station, the high frequency of nucleiform endscrapers (see below) suggests reuse of cores as they approached the point of exhaustion. Nuclei that are regularized by consistent, undercutting "stepped" retouch around the circumference of the striking platform are classified as nucleiform endscrapers rather than cores. They are common at Liencres and compensate for a low frequency of unretouched cores. Flake cores and mixed bladelet-flake cores are most commonly found.

Heavy Duty Tools

Heavy duty tools (Clark 1971a: 267–272) consist of pebble and cobble hammerstones; typical and atypical Asturian picks; large, small, and double choppers; large, small, and double chopping tools; partial bifaces; handstones (manos); and grinding slabs (metates, undifferentiated grinding stone fragments, and all combinations of the above).

Heavy duty tools represent a scant one percent (nine specimens) of the surface total at Liencres. Due to this small sample size, relative frequencies for these types in the surface deposits are misleading and inflated if calculations are based on a heavy duty tool subtotal set equal to 100 percent. Except for the typical unifacial picks, heavy duty tools are scarce at Liencres; a few hammerstones occur.

Heavy duty tools show a strong association with the conchero sites, where they make up about 10 percent of the lithic inventory. Until recently the presence of unifacial quartzite picks has been the only certain criterion for the identification of an Asturian assemblage (Vega del Sella 1923, but see Clark 1971a). As a consequence, picks are grossly overrepresented in lithic collections from cave sites, reflecting the value placed on them as an index fossil. Aside from picks, the most numerous heavy duty tools in the cave sites are choppers and chopping tools. These simple objects have been manufactured for so long a period of human prehistory that they are worthless as industrial guide fossils. They have been used as such, however, to link the Asturian with the Lower Pleistocene pebble tool industries of the North African littoral (Crusafont 1963). Hammerstones are present in low but significant quantities in the conchero sites, along with a few partial bifaces.

Small Tools

Implements manufactured on flakes, blades, bladelets, or portions thereof are considered small tools. Nucleiform endscrapers are also included. Whereas the typological framework for heavy duty tools and debitage

TABLE 4.1
**Liencres: Surface Collection,
Inventory of Lithic Material**

Types	Quartzite	Flint	% Total
Unworked cobbles	3		0.003
Unworked pebbles	8		0.008
Split cobble segments	15		0.014
Nuclei (all types)	7	22	0.028
Flakes, plain	15	296	0.298
Flakes, primary decortication	2	35	0.035
Flakes, secondary decortication	63	299	0.347
Flakes, trimming	29	102	0.126
Flakes, core renewal		6	0.006
Pebble hammerstones	2		0.002
Picks, typical Asturian	4		0.004
Blades, bladelets	1	58	0.056
Denticulates		9	0.009
Chopping tools	1	1	0.002
Points		2	0.002
Knives, naturally backed		2	0.002
Perforators		7	0.007
Perforator-notch		1	0.001
Notches (including one inverse example)		6	0.006
Becs, typical		3	0.003
Becs, alternating burinating-typical sidescraper		1	0.001
Bladelets, backed		2	0.002
Bladelets, strangled		1	0.001
Bladelets, truncated		3	0.003
Burins, multiple		1	0.001
Burins, multiple and mixed		1	0.001
Burins, dihedral angle on a break (including one combined with a small denticulate)		6	0.006
Burins, flat		1	0.001
Burins, nucleiform		1	0.001
Sidescrapers, simple lateral straight		1	0.001
Sidescrapers, simple lateral convex	1	1	0.002
Endscrapers, nosed		1	0.001
Endscrapers, nucleiform (including one atypical example, one double nucleiform endscraper combined with two becs)		11	0.010
Pieces with continuous retouch on one or more edges		5	0.005
Various		2	0.002
Miscellaneous shell fragments		6	0.006
Total	151	893	1.003

Note: Artifacts not listed include two large quartzite boulders; one was a large grinding slab. Data from the 1972 season are in Appendix B.

TABLE 4.2
**Liencres: Surface Collection
Retouched Pieces Classified According to the de Sonneville-Bordes and Perrot Typology**

Category Number*	Type Name	Number	Percent Total	Cumulative Percent
14	Endscraper, flat nosed	1	0.014	0.014
15	Endscraper, nucleiform	11	0.151	0.165
23	Perforators	7	0.096	0.261
24	Perforators, atypical (becs)	4	0.055	0.316
25	Becs, multiple (perforator-notch)	1	0.014	0.330
30	Burins, dihedral angle on break	6	0.082	0.412
31	Burins, multiple	1	0.014	0.426
41	Burins, multiple mixed	1	0.014	0.440
43	Burins, nucleiform	1	0.014	0.454
44	Burins, flat	1	0.014	0.468
48	Point, gravette	1	0.014	0.482
65	Piece, continuously retouched on one side	4	0.055	0.537
66	Piece, continuously retouched on two sides	1	0.014	0.551
73	Picks	4	0.055	0.606
74	Notches	6	0.082	0.688
75	Denticulates	9	0.123	0.811
77	Sidescraper, simple lateral	3	0.041	0.852
84	Bladelets, truncated	3	0.041	0.893
85	Bladelets, backed	2	0.027	0.920
89	Bladelets, notched (strangled)	1	0.014	0.934
92	Various	5	0.069	1.003
Total		73	1.003	1.003

*Category numbers refer to the original type list (de Sonneville-Bordes and Perrot 1954, 1955, 1956).
Note: The category "various" includes the following tools that are not accommodated in this typology: chopping tools (2), pedunculate point (1), other (2).

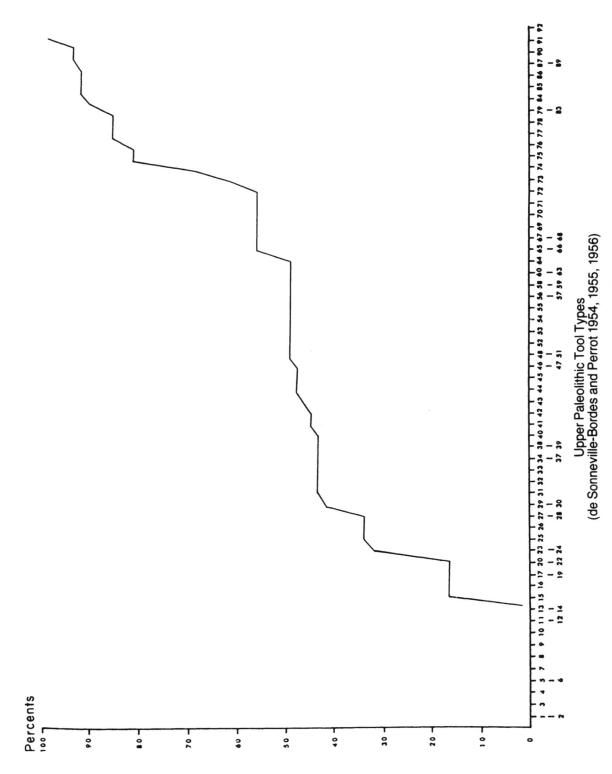

Figure 4.2. Cumulative percentage graph of the surface collection from Liencres.

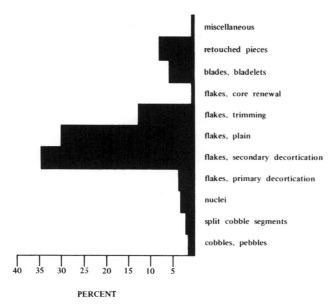

miscellaneous
retouched pieces
blades, bladelets
flakes, core renewal
flakes, trimming
flakes, plain
flakes, secondary decortication
flakes, primary decortication
nuclei
split cobble segments
cobbles, pebbles

40 35 30 25 20 15 10 5

PERCENT

Figure 4.3. Proportional representation of all artifact categories in the surface collection from Liencres.

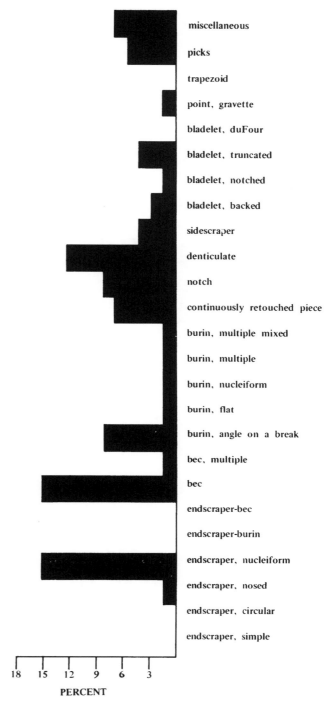

miscellaneous
picks
trapezoid
point, gravette
bladelet, duFour
bladelet, truncated
bladelet, notched
bladelet, backed
sidescraper
denticulate
notch
continuously retouched piece
burin, multiple mixed
burin, multiple
burin, nucleiform
burin, flat
burin, angle on a break
bec, multiple
bec
endscraper-bec
endscraper-burin
endscraper, nucleiform
endscraper, nosed
endscraper, circular
endscraper, simple

18 15 12 9 6 3

PERCENT

Figure 4.4. Proportional representation of retouched pieces in the surface collection from Liencres.

was devised specifically for this study, the de Sonneville-Bordes and Perrot (1954, 1955, 1956) typology accommodates most of the small tools found in Asturian assemblages.

Small tools constitute 7.1 percent of the surface total at Liencres, compared with about 9 percent for the Asturian cave sites. Endscrapers are the most numerous, equaling 17.4 percent of small tools. Liencres and the group of Asturian cave sites show remarkably little variation in the relative frequency of endscrapers; the most prevalent single type, nucleiform endscrapers, is the same in both cases.

Continuously retouched pieces and sidescrapers exhibit the same kind of intergroup consistency. Continuously retouched pieces make up 7.2 percent of small tools for the surface level at Liencres. Their frequency in the cave sites is about 8 percent. The corresponding figures for sidescrapers are 4.5 percent (Liencres, surface) and 5.4 percent (cave sites). Straight and convex simple sidescrapers (Bordes 1961: 25–27) are most commonly found, but all sidescraper frequencies are low.

Burins, on the other hand, show little intergroup consistency, although angle burins made on breaks are the most numerous in both the cave site group (4 percent) and in the surface deposits at Liencres (8.7 percent). Other types are present (see Table 4.1), but rare. Burins account for 11.6 percent of the small tool total in the surface deposits at Liencres.

Flake denticulates equal 13 percent of the small tools at Liencres (surface), contrasted with a frequency of about 19 percent for the cave site group. Flake notches are common in both groups. The relative frequency of notches at Liencres (surface) is 8.7 percent; the corresponding figure for the cave sites is 9 percent.

Perforators, like burins, show little intergroup consistency. Atypical perforators (becs) are the most prevalent form both in the cave sites and at Liencres, but relative frequencies range from 17.4 percent (Liencres, surface) to less than 2 percent (cave sites). Perforators in general are much more common at Liencres (12.5 percent for the site as a whole) than in the cave sites.

Retouched bladelets account for 7 percent of small tools in the cave sites; the figure for the surface deposits at Liencres is 8.7 percent. Individual bladelet type frequencies are low, however. Prior to recent excavations in unquestionably Asturian levels at La Riera (Clark and Richards 1978), no retouched bladelets (in fact, no bladelets at all) had ever been reported from an Asturian site. The assemblage can be demonstrated to succeed the Azilian in time, so the occurrence of bladelets in the assemblage is not particularly surprising. Bladelet production appears to have been confined mainly to siliceous materials, although quartzite bladelets (and even backed bladelets) do occur, principally at the cave site of La Riera.

The surface collection at Liencres shows all the salient characteristics of Asturian industries so far tentatively postulated on the basis of the few good samples available (La Riera, Balmori), including substantial numbers of nucleiform endscrapers, small denticulated flakes, becs, perforators, notches, and angle burins (Figs. 4.5–4.8). Retouched bladelets are also relatively common (Fig. 4.8). Four of the characteristic picks were recovered from the surface of the site (Fig. 4.5). The high proportion of debitage (flakes, nuclei, and, significantly, small blades and bladelets) suggests that the site was primarily a workshop area, occupied on but a single occasion or sporadically for short periods of time. The low frequency of retouched pieces supports that idea. The presence of a quartzite grinding slab indicates that activities related to food preparation may also have been carried out at the site.

Distribution of Artifact Types in the Surface Sample

To define activity areas within the site, lateral dispersion of common artifact types across the surface was mapped (Figs. 4.9–4.12). Frequencies were recorded by squares; artifact types that occurred in extremely low quantity were not included. Various statistical measures were applied to the artifact dispersions in order to distinguish significant from nonsignificant artifact clusters. A method for measuring the degree of clustering objectively was also developed.

As Figures 4.9 and 4.10a indicate, quartzite debris is most heavily concentrated in two areas within the site. There is a marked cluster of debris due west of and adjacent to the only objects that can be called features: two massive quartzite boulders, one of which is an inverted grinding slab. There is a secondary concentration about 3 m east of the first, and a hint of a third cluster in the westernmost part of the site.

The clusters are best defined by the distributions of primary and secondary decortication flakes; trimming and plain flakes appear to be distributed in the same way. Curiously, few flakes occur north of the boulders. There are no microtopographical reasons (such as microerosional patterns, breaks in slope) why this should be the case. If the individual or individuals responsible for knapping sat on one of the boulders facing almost due west, with his back to the inlet, his position might explain the location of the most marked scatter of debris, which would have accumulated at his feet and for some distance in front of him. From inspection of the maps there appear to be no significant differences in the dispersion of flake types, which would have been expected had decortication, roughing out, and secondary retouch been carried on in spatially discrete areas within the site.

The distribution of nuclei and split cobbles (Fig. 4.9c) is more general, and the two clusters defined by flake dispersion are not present. Instead, an east-west trending elipse coinciding in distribution with the most marked flake cluster is apparent. Again, the scatter of nuclei and split cobble segments is centered around the quartzite boulders.

Picks, unmodified pebbles, and unmodified cobbles (Fig. 4.10a) appear to have the most general distributions of all artifacts. Except for the east-west trending in most of the distribution maps from Liencres, there is little evidence for any clear-cut clustering effect.

Flint artifacts (Figs. 4.10b, c–4.12) do not cluster as distinctly as quartzite artifacts. Considerably more numerous, they have a much more widely dispersed distribution throughout the site. There is a marked concentration centered on the quartzite boulders, however. Again, debris is most dense west of the boulders, although there is also considerable scatter east of that feature. There is a spatially discrete secondary concentration in the northwest corner of the site, much better defined than the analogous quartzite cluster. These distributional patterns are evident for primary and secondary decortication flakes and plain flakes.

Trimming flakes, small blades, and bladelets have a much more restricted distribution. These artifacts are essentially confined to the main scatter, especially trimming flakes.

Nuclei, and all retouched tool categories, show few discernible patterns, although there is an ill-defined tendency to cluster about the boulders. The distribution of denticulates and notches is much more dispersed than that of other types.

Casting these data into a hypothetical interpretative framework, it can be suggested, first, that the knapping of flint and quartzite was conducted in spatially congruent, or at least heavily overlapping, areas (with the possible exception of the flint cluster in the northwest corner of the site). I do not believe the site has been extensively disturbed. Had geological forces sorted these objects, it is likely the quartzite and flint would have been redeposited in more or less discrete areas because of the marked differences in density of raw material and in flake size.

Second, the preparation of raw material prior to the removal of flakes (decortication) does not appear to have been important at Liencres. There is scant need to remove the exterior surface of a quartzite cobble unless the outermost surface of that cobble has been badly fractured by geological agencies. The chert at Liencres occurs as small nodules, irregular in shape and often heavily corroded. If all cortical material were removed, little usable chert would have remained for manufacturing purposes.

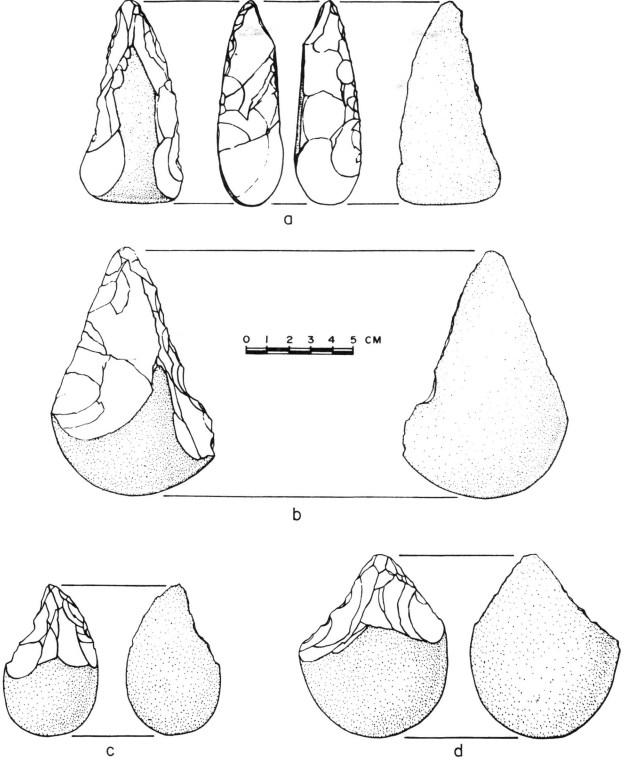

Figure 4.5. Surface collection of Asturian picks, Liencres. All picks are in mint condition, made on fine-grained, brown quartzite cobbles. Thickness of *a* is 3.0 cm; *b,* 3.7 cm; *c,* 1.8 cm; and *d,* 3.3 cm.

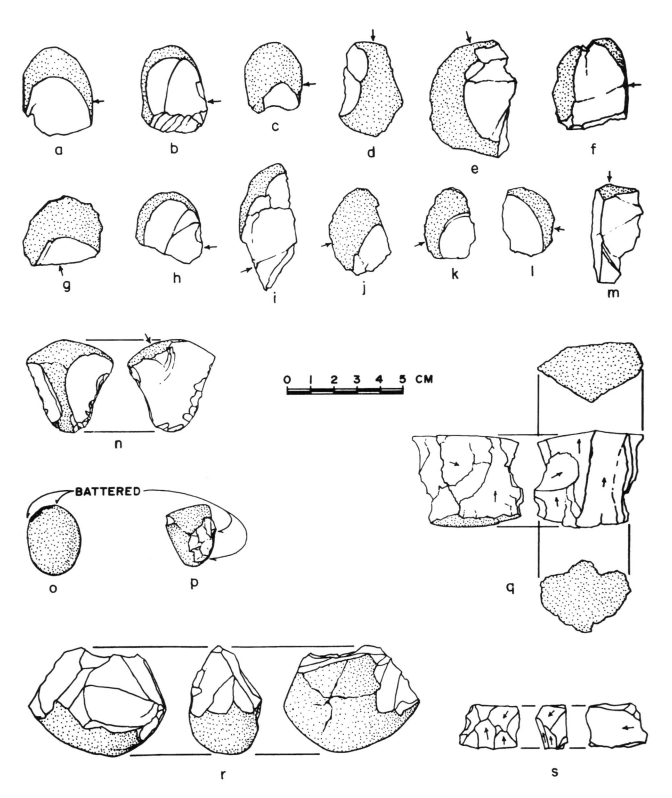

Figure 4.6. Surface collection of quartzite decortication flakes and nuclei, Liencres: *a–m*, flakes; *n*, sidescraper (from periphery of site); *o, p*, pebble hammerstones; *q, s*, nuclei; *r*, chopping tool.

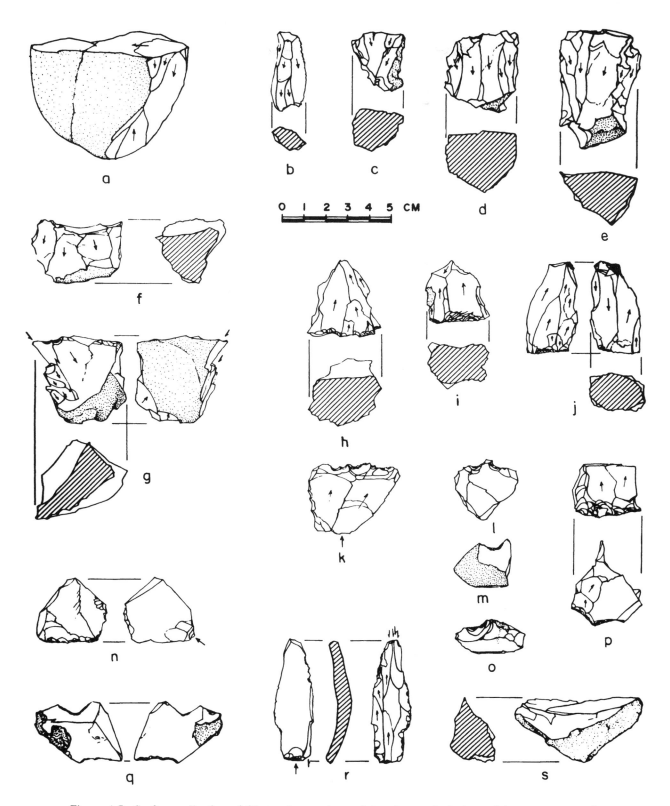

Figure 4.7. Surface collection of flint and quartzite nuclei and retouched pieces, Liencres: *a*, quartzite nucleus; *b–f*, flint nuclei; *g*, nucleiform burin; *h–j, p*, nucleiform endscrapers (*j* is double); *k*, denticulate (from periphery of site); *l*, bec; *m, o*, notches; *n*, piece continuously retouched on one edge; *q*, notch-denticulate; *r*, multiple burin; *s*, naturally backed knife.

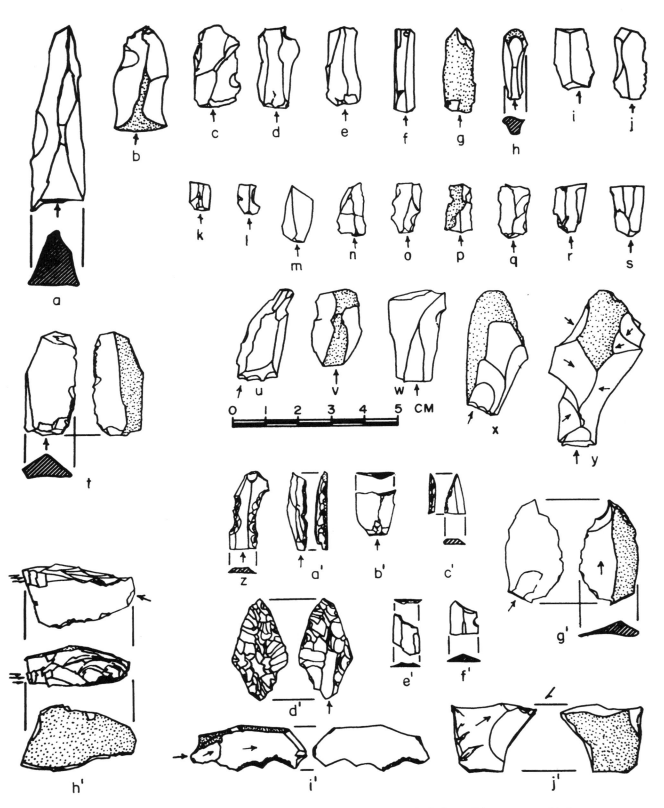

Figure 4.8. Surface collection of flint blades, bladelets, and retouched pieces, Liencres: *a–s*, blades and bladelets; *t*, piece continuously retouched on two edges, with inverse retouch; *u–y*, bladelike flakes; *z*, strangled bladelet; *a'*, backed bladelet; *b'*, *e'*, *f'*, truncated bladelets; *c'*, gravette point fragment(?); *d'*, projectile point (may postdate the main occupation); *g'*, perforator; *h'*, sidescraper-multiple burin; *i'*, denticulate, with inverse retouch; *j'*, angle burin on a break.

Had these considerations been important to the occupants of the site, these activities might have occurred in spatially discrete areas, resulting in discernible clustering of debris categories.

Third, there is some evidence for the utilization of discrete areas for specific activities at Liencres. The secondary retouching of flint artifacts (resulting in tiny trimming flakes) and, to a lesser extent, the production of blades and bladelets appear to be activities confined to the central cluster. The dispersion of cores and retouched pieces shows no such clustering. No associational clues are provided that might shed some light on the function of picks. Their tips, however, are often discernibly abraded on the bottom side, suggesting that the points were used most heavily. The extensively retouched sides of the picks were simply a function of the production of a point on the end of an oval cobble; the sides themselves show no macroscopic signs of utilization or wear.

Finally, the density of debris at Liencres and the apparent lack of features (except for the quartzite boulders) suggest an occupation of short duration, possibly of only a few days and probably for the specific purpose of exploiting the rare deposits of flint nearby. There is no stratigraphic evidence to indicate that the site was reoccupied.

Nearest Neighbor Analysis

Although the preceding description gives an impression of the distribution of the principal artifact categories over the site surface, it is useful to apply a technique that simultaneously (1) permits the objective measurement of the *degree* of artifact aggregation, and (2) provides a statistical assessment of the significance of any measure so obtained. The technique adopted here is called Nearest Neighbor analysis (P. J. Clark and Evans 1954; Haggett 1965: 231–233).

Nearest Neighbor analysis is an outgrowth of research conducted initially by plant and animal ecologists and expanded on by mathematically inclined population demographers. The classic study by P. J. Clark and Evans (1954) dealt with the distribution and spacing of forest and grassland plant species. The method has since been applied to the analysis of prehistoric (Plog 1968) and contemporary settlement patterns (King 1962; Dacey 1960). The method is based on:

"... the measurement of...the straight line distance separating a point and the closest [analogous] point, and the comparison of these distances with that which might be expected if the points were distributed randomly in [some given area]" (Haggett 1965: 231, 232).

Points are dispersed over a two-dimensional plane surface.

The Nearest Neighbor statistic (R_n) is given by the formula:

$$R_n = \frac{\sum_{i=1}^{r} r/N}{\frac{1}{2\sqrt{\rho}}}$$

where r is the distance measure to the nearest neighbor; Σ is a summation symbol; N specifies the number of measurements taken in the observed population (that is, it corresponds to the number of artifacts of type x); ρ (rho) is the density function in the observed distribution, given by N/A; and A is the area in units squared comparable to those used to compute ΣR_i. Possible values for R_n range from 0 to 2.15; three values specify particular distribution patterns. If $R_n = 0$, all N points are clustered together in a single spot within A, or, alternatively, occur as pairs, triplets, and so on. If $R_n = 1.00$, the points are randomly distributed within A. If $R_n = 2.15$, the points form a regular hexagonal pattern. The implication of a hexagonal distribution is that the points are located as far as possible from one another.

For obvious reasons, it is important to be able to assess the significance of intermediate values of R_n. The test of significance is given by the formula:

$$c = \frac{\bar{r}_a - \bar{r}_e}{\sigma_{\bar{r}_e}}$$

where $\bar{r}_a = \Sigma r/N$, or the mean of the series of distances to nearest neighbor; $\bar{r}_e = 1/2 \sqrt{\rho}$, which is the mean distance to nearest neighbor expected in an infinitely large random distribution of density ρ; and $\sigma_{\bar{r}_e} = 0.26136/\sqrt{N\rho}$, the standard error of the mean distance to nearest neighbor in a randomly distributed population of density ρ. The test statistic c is a standard normal deviate with zero mean and unit variance. Probabilities associated with values of the standard normal variable have been extensively tabulated (for example, see Goodman and Ratti 1971: 438, 439). Under given $\bar{r}_a$ and $\bar{r}_e$, the probability of c indicates the extent of departure of R_n from 1.00, the value expected if the points are randomly distributed.

The Nearest Neighbor statistic, with observed and expected mean distances, standard deviation by density, standard normal variable, and its associated probability are given in Table 4.3. Probabilities are for a two-tailed test (P. J. Clark and Evans 1954: 447, 448). Data consisted of artifact types commonly found in the Liencres surface collection. Discrepancies in frequency between Tables 4.1 and 4.3 are due to artifacts located in the peripheral areas of the site that were recorded and typed but not plotted on the grid; no Nearest Neighbor statistic could be computed to include them. If a p(c) less than or equal to 0.005 is arbitrarily regarded as significant, the implication is that the associated statistic could occur through chance alone only once in two hundred times in a sample of a randomly distributed population of density ρ. Inspection of Table 4.3 shows that flint and quartzite decortication flakes, flint plain flakes, and flint and quartzite trimming flakes exhibit the highest degree of clustering. Flint burins and bladelets are also concentrated in restricted areas on the site surface; unmodified quartzite cobbles, split cobble segments, and flint nuclei are clustered to a lesser extent. The remaining artifact types do not show statistically significant degrees of clustering. Examination of Figures 4.9 through 4.12, however, reveals that gross artifact frequency may influence

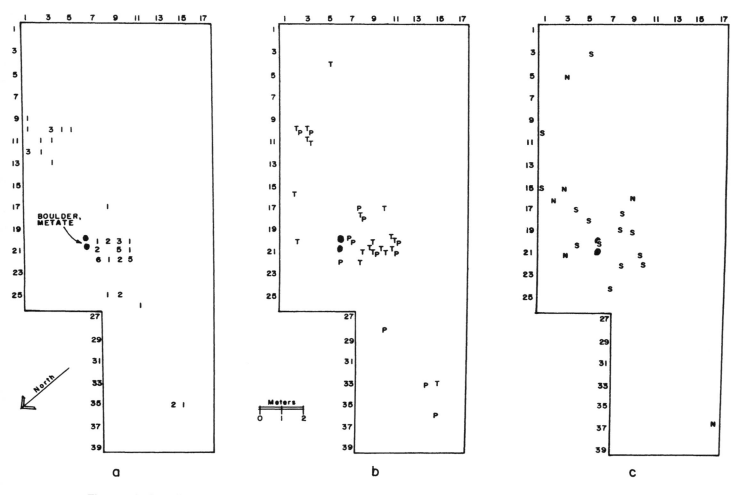

Figure 4.9. Distribution of artifacts in the surface collection, Liencres: *a,* primary and secondary quartzite decortication flakes; *b,* quartzite trimming (T) and plain (P) flakes; *c,* quartzite nuclei (N) and split cobble segments (S). Note: point proveniences are available for these data (see Nearest Neighbor analysis). For display purposes, they are recorded here as quadrat counts.

TABLE 4.3

Liencres: Surface Collection
Nearest Neighbor Statistic (R_n) For Common Artifact Types
Observed ($\bar{r}_a$) And Expected ($\bar{r}_e$) Mean Distances, With Standard Deviation By Density ρ ($\sigma_{\bar{r}_e}$),
Standard Normal Variable (c), And Its Associated Probability, p(c).

Artifact Type	N	R_n	$\sum r/N(=\bar{r}_a)$	$1/2\sqrt{\rho}(=\bar{r}_e)$	$0.26136/\sqrt{N\rho}\ (=\sigma_{\bar{r}_e})$	c	p(c)
Pebbles, cobbles: unmod., quartzite	11	0.551	52.971	91.592	14.436	−2.67	0.0076
Nuclei: flint	18	0.648	47.727	71.597	8.821	−2.70	0.0058
Nuclei: quartzite	6	0.919	124.849	124.038	26.469	+0.03	0.9760
Split cobble segments: quartzite	14	0.681	57.346	81.186	11.342	−2.10	0.0358
Flakes, decortication: flint	267	0.598	11.146	18.589	0.595	−12.51	<0.0002
Flakes, decortication: quartzite	54	0.432	18.009	41.336	2.940	−6.12	<0.0002
Flakes, plain: flint	194	0.595	13.001	21.809	0.818	−10.76	<0.0002
Flakes, plain: quartzite	14	0.777	65.429	81.221	11.342	−1.39	0.1646
Flakes, trimming: flint	91	0.691	22.117	31.841	1.745	−5.57	<0.0002
Flakes, trimming: quartzite	19	0.508	36.399	69.687	8.357	−3.98	≅0.0002
Flakes, core renewal: flint	5	0.533	80.942	135.888	31.764	−1.73	0.0836
Bladelets: flint	43	0.757	35.489	46.322	3.692	−2.93	0.0034
Perforators, becs: flint	11	1.125	108.023	91.600	14.436	+1.14	0.2542
Notches, denticulates: flint	11	1.269	121.880	91.600	14.436	+2.10	0.0358
Retouched bladelets: flint	6	0.452	61.457	124.039	26.469	−2.36	0.0182
Burins: flint	8	0.381	43.750	107.411	19.851	−3.21	0.0014
Endscrapers, nucleiform: flint	8	1.135	130.328	107.411	19.851	+1.15	0.2502

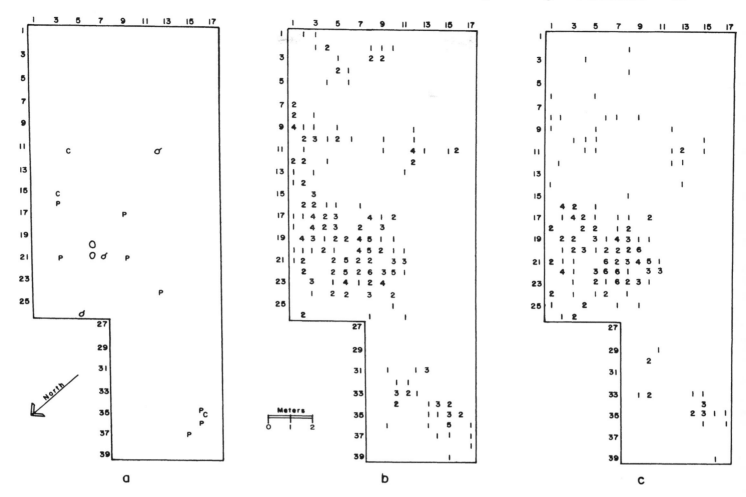

Figure 4.10. Distribution of artifacts in the surface collection, Liencres: *a,* quartzite pebbles (P), cobbles (C), and picks (symbol); *b,* primary and secondary flint decortication flakes; *c,* flint plain flakes.

the reliability of the statistic if N is small. Most visually satisfactory results are associated with large N and with probabilities less than or equal to 0.0002 (see Table 4.3); examples are decortication, plain, and trimming flakes. P. J. Clark and Evans (1954: 448) discuss the problem of small N, and suggest that the Pearson Type III distribution be used in place of the normal curve for N less than 100.

Computation of the Nearest Neighbor statistic is tedious and time consuming for large N. A computer program has been written for the purpose of calculating the Nearest Neighbor statistic (Johnstone and others 1977). The program locates Cartesian coordinates on a grid, measures the distance of each point to every other point, determines the mean distance among points of like type, and performs additional mathematical operations.

TEST EXCAVATIONS

Although the analysis of the surface collection produced significant information about distributional patterning with respect to artifact categories, it was ap-

parent that the cultural materials studied were weathering out of the grayish sandy loam due to the process of deflation. Because of the certainty of finding buried material in situ, limited test excavations were undertaken. A comparison of the distribution of artifacts on the site surface, or portions of the site surface, with the distribution of one or more subsurface samples was the original objective.

Because it was impossible to excavate the entire area covered by surface debris, a sampling problem arose. Ideally, a random sampling design should have been implemented to select squares from the surface grid. These squares would have had a known surface composition (because the surface sample approached 100 percent) and could have been excavated to determine the composition of the subsurface sample on an exactly comparable basis. Although a 10 percent random sample of the population of grid squares was drawn, using a table of random digits (Arkin and Colton 1967: 26, 27, 159), I was not able to excavate in all of the sample squares because of time limitations on my excavation permit. I concentrated instead on the four areas indicated on Figure 4.13 (Cuts 1, 2, 4, and 6).

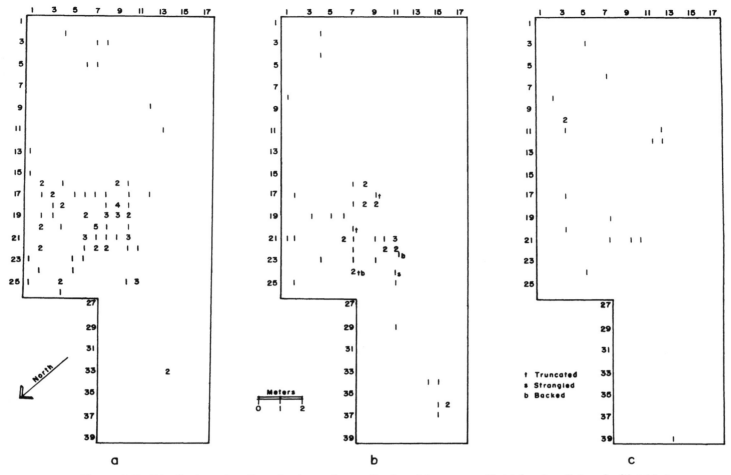

Figure 4.11. Distribution of artifacts in the surface collection, Liencres: *a,* flint trimming flakes; *b,* flint blades, bladelets, and retouched bladelets; *c,* flint nuclei.

Cut 1, on the northeast side of the site, was a stratigraphic section designed to determine the depth of stratified levels and to obtain geological samples for analysis in the laboratory. Cut 2 was excavated because it was in an area of high concentration of both flint and quartzite debris. Cut 4 corresponded to the highest concentration of flint and quartzite artifacts recorded in the surface collection at Liencres. This concentration was associated with two large quartzite boulders, partially buried, one of which was a quartzite grinding slab. Cut 4 was in an area where I encountered pieces that could be fitted together, suggesting that the site, although probably exposed to the elements for a long period of time, had only been slightly disturbed. Cut 6, linking the site with the dolina, was placed along the southwestern edge of the main concentration of artifacts. The dolina was covered with dense, low-lying matorral, precluding the collection of a surface sample. I wanted to determine if there were cultural deposits within the dolina. I also sought to link the strata there with those exposed in Cuts 1, 2, and 4. Excavation was done according to the grid units established for the surface collection. Two major strata were defined

across the site as a whole. Initially encountered was a dark brownish-grayish loam, Level 1. It extended rather uniformly to a depth of about 35 cm below the surface, where it graded into a brown, then a yellowish-brown loam designated Level 2. Level 2 directly overlay bedrock, an irregular limestone encountered at depths from 47 to 65 cm below the surface (Butzer and Bowman 1979).

Composition of the Excavated Sample

A total of 556 artifacts was recovered from the excavated areas of the site. All the artifacts from the excavated sample pertain to a single cultural level, contiguous with the surface, and here designated Level 1.

The artifacts recovered from Level 1 are listed in Table 4.4. The relative frequency of each type was computed; Table 4.5 casts the data into the format designed by de Sonneville-Bordes and Perrot for the construction of cumulative percentage graphs. For comparative purposes, only types recognized by those authors are tabulated. Category numbers refer to the original type lists (de Sonneville-Bordes and Perrot 1954, 1955, 1956).

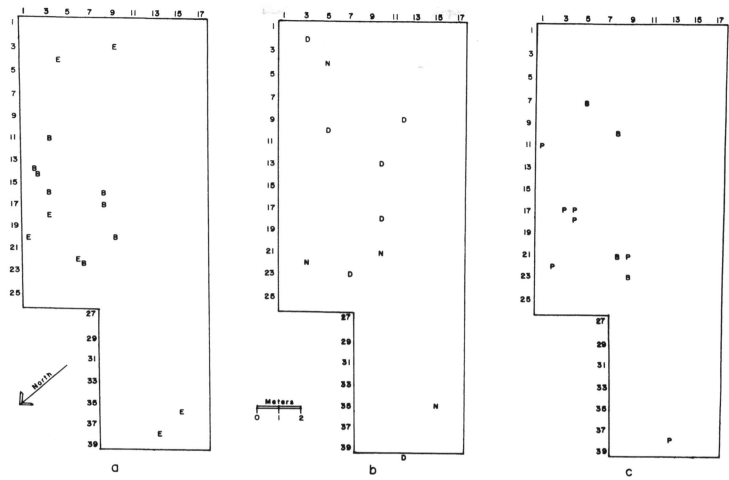

Figure 4.12. Distribution of artifacts in the surface collection, Liencres: *a*, flint burins (B) and endscrapers (E); *b*, flint denticulates (D) and notches (N); *c*, flint perforators (P) and becs (B).

Types are identified in Table 4.5 and the resulting plot appears in Figure 4.14. Figure 4.15 shows the proportional representation of *all* artifact categories recovered from Level 1, and Figure 4.16 indicates relative frequencies of types in the retouched tool category.

Chi-square Test for Two Independent Samples

The excavated sample closely parallels the surface sample in composition. To demonstrate whether or not the two samples can be considered to have been drawn from the same population, the chi-square test for two independent samples (Siegel 1956: 104–111) was applied to the data. The null hypothesis (H_o) is that the samples are drawn from the same or from identically distributed populations; the alternative hypothesis is that they are different. The level of significance selected for rejection of H_o was $\alpha = 0.001$. Sample size differences are compensated for by converting raw counts into relative frequencies based on the respective table totals.

The null hypothesis may be tested by the equation:

$$\chi^2 = \sum_{i=1}^{r} \sum_{j=1}^{k} \frac{(O_{ij} - E_{ij})^2}{E_{ij}}$$

where O_{ij} equals the observed number of cases in the ith row of the jth column; E_{ij} specifies the number of cases expected under H_o to occur in the ith row of the jth column, and where $\sum_{i=1}^{r} \sum_{j=1}^{k}$ directs one to sum over all r rows and all k columns (that is, to sum over all cells; modified slightly from Siegel 1956: 104). Values for chi-square given by the preceding formula approximate the chi-square distribution with $(r-1)$ $(k-1)$ degrees of freedom (df). Expected cell frequencies (E_{ij}) are obtained by multiplying marginal totals cellwise, and then dividing this product by the total number of cases, N. Data are presented in Table 4.6. Major types compared are given, with observed and expected cell frequencies. The chi-square statistic obtained was 58.0, with 13 degrees of freedom. If the chi-square statistic is equal to or greater than the tabulated value for a particular level of significance, at a particular df, then H_o may be rejected at that level of significance (Siegel 1956: 106). Consultation of a table of critical values for chi-square (Siegel 1956: 249; Arkin and Colton 1967: 126) indicates that the statistic obtained is significant beyond the 0.001 level. The condi-

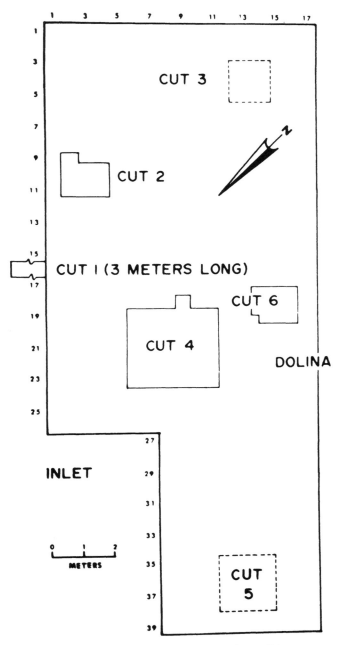

Figure 4.13. Areas tested by excavation at Liencres.

collapsing evident in the table stems from two constraints that limit the usefulness of chi-square: (1) no more than 20 percent of the cells in the contingency table can have expected frequencies less than 5.0, and (2) no cell can have an expected frequency less than 1.0. The null and alternative hypotheses, and the level of significance for rejection of H_o, remained the same. The chi-square statistic obtained was 2.498, with five degrees of freedom. Consultation of a table of critical values for chi-square indicates that this value for chi-square is not significant beyond the 0.001 level (probability under H_o that $\chi^2 \geq$ chi-square $\cong$ .75). The conditions for acceptance are met in this case. Therefore, the null hypothesis is accepted with respect to the retouched tool inventory at α = .001. While there are significant differences between the two samples with respect to debitage, there are no significant differences between the surface sample and Level 1 with respect to the category "retouched tools."

Distribution of Artifact Types in Level 1

The excavated sample is derived from the four areas shown in Figure 4.13. Two additional tests (3 and 5) were planned but not completed. The positions of pieces recovered from the peripheral tests were not plotted because of scarcity (Cut 1), and because of limited horizontal exposure (Cut 6). Distributions for Level 1 are known precisely for Cuts 2 and 4, and approximately for Cut 6. The dispersion of flint and quartzite artifacts in the main exposure (Cut 4) is given in Figures 4.17 and 4.18. Cut 2 is shown in Figure 4.19.

Obviously, it is not permissible to compare the distribution of Level 1 artifacts with that of the surface collection; the two are not coextensive, nor is Level 1 a random sample of excavation units based on the area defined by the surface collection. I can only compare analogous units of area. Most of the artifacts are concentrated in Cut 4.

Quartzite debris in Cut 4 is sparse and shows no marked patterning. There is a slight tendency for concentration in the southwest quadrant of the unit. Decortication and trimming flakes are the most prevalent types represented. Two nuclei and two unmodified cobbles were also recovered. This particular concentration coincides in distribution with an analogous cluster of quartzite artifacts in the same area in the surface collection. The quartzite boulder and grinding slab are depicted on the upper left of Figure 4.9.

Flint remains were much more prevalent; they are also concentrated in the southwestern quadrant of Cut 4. Decortication, plain, and trimming flakes show a dispersion roughly congruent with that defined by the same types for the same area in the surface collection. The density of nuclei, small blades and bladelets, nucleiform endscrapers, notches, and denticulates is much greater than would be expected from the surface array. A secondary cluster of bladelets occurs southeast of the quartzite boulders.

These data suggest the possibility that Cut 4 exposed a knapping area. There is abundant evidence for primary manufacturing processes, as shown by the prevalence of

tions for acceptance are not met. The null hypothesis is rejected and it is concluded that there are significant differences between the surface and the excavated samples.

An examination of Tables 4.1–4.2 and 4.4–4.5, however, shows that the major difference between the two samples is in the debitage categories. Most assessments of interindustrial differences are based on categories of retouched tools. In order to assess the significance of differences in the retouched tool inventory, I performed the test again using the types listed in Table 4.7. The

TABLE 4.4
Liencres: Level 1
Inventory of Lithic Material

Types	Quartzite	Flint	% Total
Unworked cobbles	8		0.014
Unworked pebbles	4		0.007
Split cobble segments	1		0.002
Nuclei (all types)	9	18	0.050
Flakes, plain (*including two in quartz)	4*	110	0.205
Flakes, primary decortication	1	13	0.025
Flakes, secondary decortication	25	134	0.286
Flakes, trimming	14	83	0.174
Flakes, core renewal		4	0.007
Pebble hammerstones	2		0.004
Picks, typical Asturian	1		0.002
Blades, bladelets	1	58	0.106
Denticulates	1	4	0.010
Choppers	1		0.002
Compressor(?)	1		0.002
Perforator, multiple		3	0.005
Becs (atypical perforators)		8	0.014
Notches (*including one in quartz)	2*	7	0.016
Bladelets, backed		1	0.002
Bladelets, truncated		1	0.002
Bladelets, notched		1	0.002
Bladelets, Dufour		1	0.002
Geometrics, trapezoid		1	0.002
Burin, angle on a break		6	0.011
Sidescrapers, simple lateral		3	0.005
Endscraper, simple		1	0.002
Endscraper, circular		1	0.002
Endscraper, nosed thick		3	0.005
Endscraper, nosed flat		1	0.002
Endscraper, nucleiform		11	0.020
Endscraper-burin		1	0.002
Endscraper-bec		1	0.002
Pieces with continuous retouch on one or more edges	—	6	0.011
Total	75	481	1.003

TABLE 4.5
Liencres: Level 1
Retouched Pieces Classified According to the
de Sonneville-Bordes and Perrot Typology

Category Number	Type Name	Number	Percent Total	Cumulative Percent
1	Endscraper, simple	1	0.014	0.014
9	Endscraper, circular	1	0.014	0.028
13	Endscraper, nosed thick	3	0.043	0.071
14	Endscraper, nosed flat	1	0.014	0.085
15	Endscraper, nucleiform	11	0.157	0.242
17	Endscraper-burin	1	0.014	0.256
21	Endscraper-perforator	1	0.014	0.270
24	Perforator, atypical (bec)	8	0.114	0.384
25	Perforator, multiple	3	0.043	0.427
30	Burin, angle on a break	6	0.086	0.513
65	Piece, continuously retouched on one side	5	0.071	0.584
66	Piece, continuously retouched on two sides	1	0.014	0.598
73	Picks	1	0.014	0.612
74	Notches	9	0.129	0.741
75	Denticulates	5	0.071	0.812
77	Sidescrapers, simple lateral	3	0.043	0.855
81	Geometrics, trapezoids	1	0.014	0.869
84	Bladelets, truncated	1	0.014	0.883
85	Bladelets, backed	1	0.014	0.897
89	Bladelets, notched	1	0.014	0.911
90	Bladelets, Dufour	1	0.014	0.925
92	Various	4	0.057	0.982
Total		69	0.982	0.982

Note: The category "various" includes the following tools that are not accommodated in this typology: large chopper (1), pebble hammerstones (2), compressor? (1).

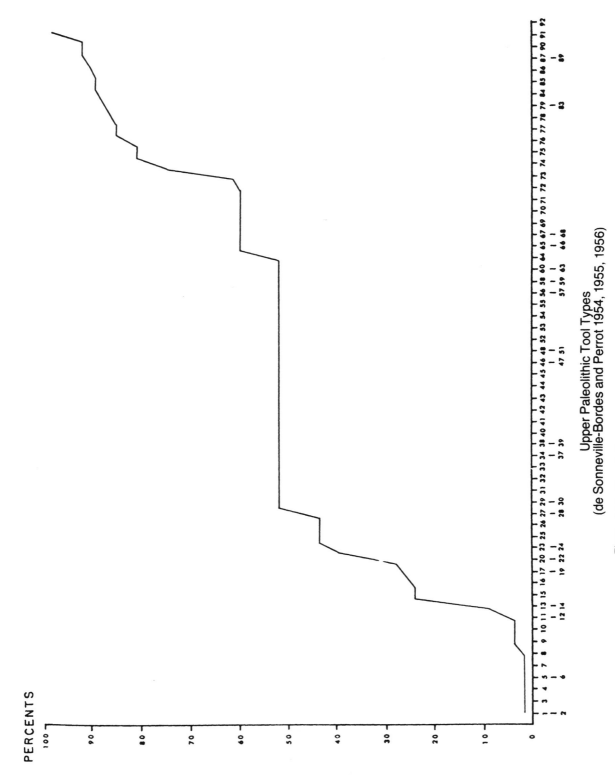

PERCENTS

Upper Paleolithic Tool Types
(de Sonneville-Bordes and Perrot 1954, 1955, 1956)

Figure 4.14. Cumulative percentage graph for Level 1, Liencres.

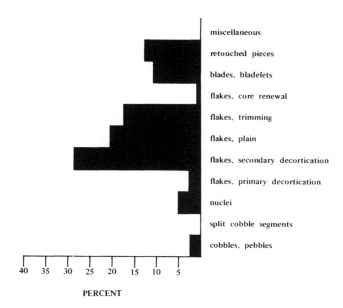

Figure 4.15. Proportional representation of all artifact categories in Level 1, Liencres.

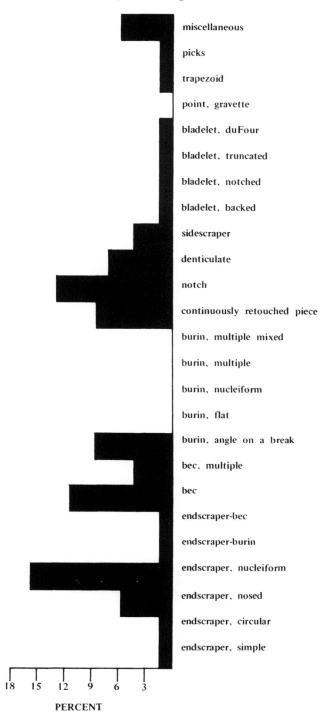

Figure 4.16. Proportional representation of all retouched pieces in Level 1, Liencres.

primary and secondary decortication flakes, plain flakes, blades, bladelets, cores, and core renewal flakes. Most of these artifacts are concentrated in the southwest quadrant of the test.

The presence of numerous trimming flakes suggests that some secondary retouching was also carried on in the area of concentration. The fact that the endscrapers present are nucleiform endscrapers (cores modified by retouch) leads to speculation that the conversion of nuclei to endscrapers might have been one of the principal activities conducted here. Activities involving the use of notched and denticulated flakes also seem indicated by the evidence in Cut 4. What those activities might have been remains conjectural, however, as wear pattern studies have not been conducted. Perhaps the area was allotted to the manufacture of the tools themselves.

Other types do not occur with sufficient frequency to permit any conclusion from their distributions. Similarly, Cut 2 contained only a few artifacts. Types commonly found in the Level 1 lithic inventory, together with debitage categories, are depicted in Figures 4.20 through 4.24.

CONCLUSIONS

Liencres is a unique site; there are no other Asturian open-air sites with which it can be compared, nor are there Upper Magdalenian or Azilian open-air sites on the Cantabrian coast that might contain similar industries. The case for assigning Liencres to the Asturian must rest on the presence of the characteristic unifacial pick, so far recovered in situ and in mint condition only from the Asturian of the caves, and on similarities in the relative

frequencies of certain common tool types (flakes; flake and mixed cores; endscrapers, especially nucleiform; continuously retouched pieces; retouched bladelets; certain sidescraper categories; and flake notches).

TABLE 4.6
**Liencres: Chi-square Analysis of Lithic Artifacts
from the Site Surface and from Level 1
(Combination tools excluded)**

Type	Surface		Level 1		
	E_{ij}	O_{ij}	E_{ij}	O_{ij}	Total
Unworked cobbles, pebbles	15.0	11	8.0	12	23
Split cobble segments	10.5	15	5.5	1	16
Nuclei (all types)	36.6	29	19.4	27	56
Flakes, plain	277.8	311	147.2	114	425
Flakes, decortication	373.9	399	198.1	173	572
Flakes, trimming	149.0	131	79.0	97	228
Flakes, core renewal	6.5	6	3.5	4	10
Blades, bladelets	77.1	59	40.9	59	118
Endscraper, nucleiform	14.4	11	7.6	11	22
Perforators, becs (all)	13.7	10	7.3	11	21
Notches, denticulates	18.9	15	10.0	14	29
Bladelets, retouched	6.5	6	3.5	4	10
Burins (all)	9.8	9	5.2	6	15
Continuously retouched pieces	7.2	5	3.8	6	11
Total		1017		539	1556

Note: $\chi^2 = 58.0$, df = 13; χ^2 significant at $\alpha = 0.001$, so H_o rejected, with the probability of Type I error = 0.001.

TABLE 4.7
**Liencres: Chi-square Analysis of Retouched Pieces
from the Site Surface and from Level 1
(Combination tools excluded)**

Type	Surface		Level 1		
	E_{ij}	O_{ij}	E_{ij}	O_{ij}	Total
Endscrapers (all)	14.6	12	14.4	17	29
Perforators, becs	11.6	12	11.4	11	23
Burins (all)	8.1	10	7.9	6	16
Denticulates, notches	15.1	15	14.9	15	30
Retouched bladelets	5.0	6	5.0	4	10
Continuously retouched pieces	5.6	5	5.5	6	11
Total		60		59	119

Note: $\chi^2 = 2.498$, df = 5; χ^2 not significant at $\alpha = 0.001$, so H_o accepted, with the probability of Type I error = 0.001. The probability under H_o that $\chi^2 \geq$ chi square is approximately 0.75. Discrepancies between Tables 4.6 and 4.7 are due to collapsing in Table 4.7 and the inclusion of retouched pieces that occur as parts of combination tools. Collapsing was necessary in Table 4.7 because of low E_{ij}. A constraint of this test is that no more than 20 percent of the cells can contain $E_{ij} < 5$, no $E_{ij} < 1.0$.

With the radiocarbon determinations now available, and the stratigraphic evidence from La Riera (Clark and Richards 1978), Balmori (Clark 1974a), and Coberizas (Clark and Cartledge 1973a, b), it is logical to suppose that the Asturian developed in situ from the Cantabrian Azilian. It is impossible to demonstrate this assertion, of course, because of the absence of comparable material. To at least attempt to hold constant facies variation, the Liencres data should be compared with data from an Azilian, coastal, open-air station. No such site has been reported.

The most comparable material available to compare the Asturian at Liencres with the Santander Azilian comes from the Azilian Level 1 at Cueva Morín, near Villanueva, Santander (González Echegaray and Freeman 1971: 267–275). Such a comparison is not valid in any rigorous sense, however, because it remains to be demonstrated that variation due to facies differences within industries is no greater than variation due to differences among industries themselves. Figure 4.25 presents a comparison of cumulative percentage graphs using the Liencres data (Surface, Level 1) and that from the Azilian Level 1 at Morín. All that can be concluded from the graphs is that both collections show relatively high frequencies in the notch, denticulate, continuously retouched piece, and retouched bladelet categories. The graphs deviate most with respect to nucleiform endscrapers and various kinds of perforators, both common in the Asturian at Liencres and rare in the Azilian at Morín. Statistically speaking, the two samples do not pertain to the same or similar underlying populations.

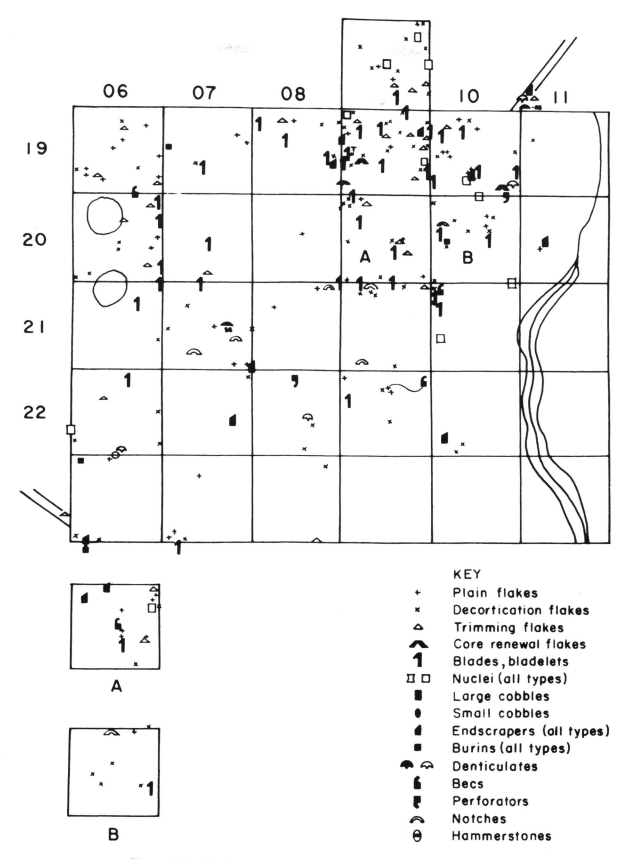

Figure 4.17. Distribution of flint artifacts in Cut 4, Level 1, Liencres.

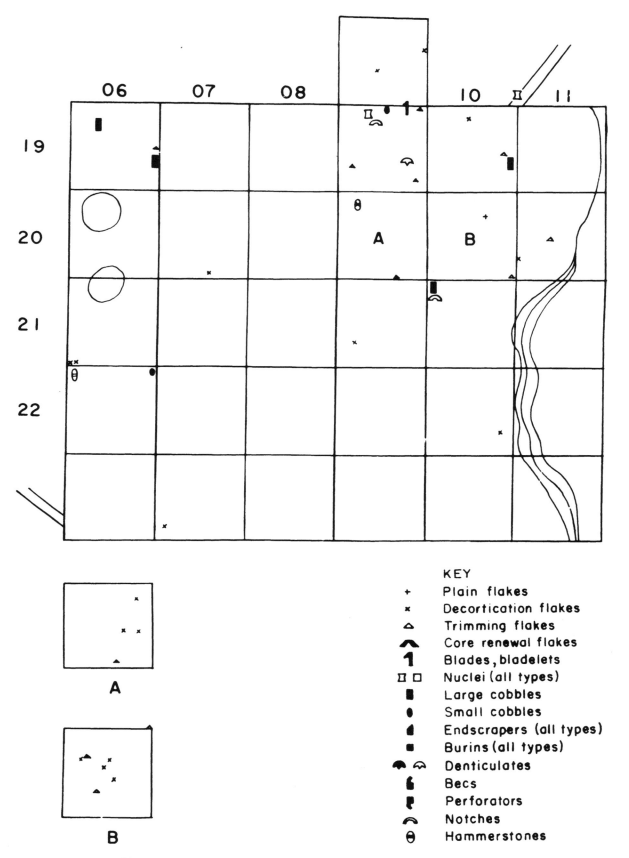

Figure 4.18. Distribution of quartzite artifacts in Cut 4, Level 1, Liencres.

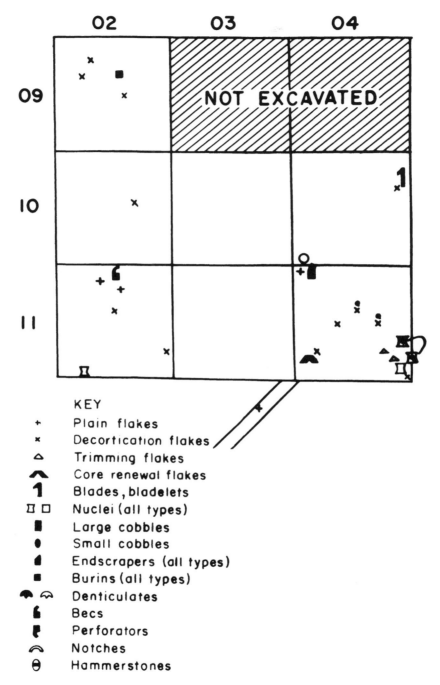

KEY

+	Plain flakes
×	Decortication flakes
△	Trimming flakes
︿	Core renewal flakes
1	Blades, bladelets
⊓ ▢	Nuclei (all types)
▮	Large cobbles
●	Small cobbles
◢	Endscrapers (all types)
▪	Burins (all types)
☂ ︵	Denticulates
▙	Becs
▜	Perforators
⌢	Notches
⊖	Hammerstones

Figure 4.19. Distribution of flint and quartzite
artifacts in Cut 2, Level 1, Liencres.

[73]

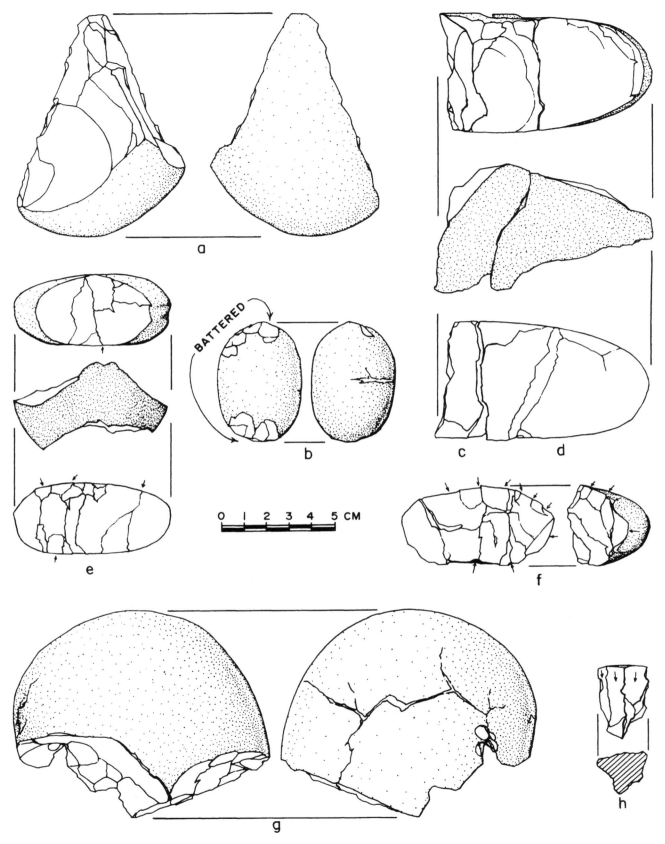

Figure 4.20. Quartzite nuclei and heavy duty tools in Level 1, Liencres: *a*, Asturian pick (3.8 cm thick); *b*, pebble hammerstone; *c–f*, *h*, nuclei; *g*, chopper.

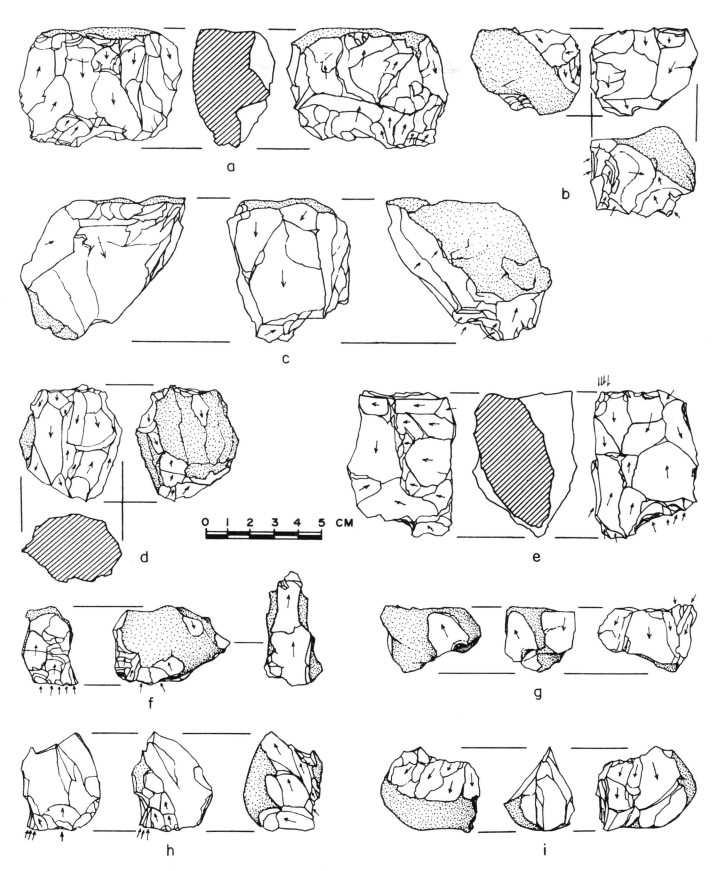

Figure 4.21. Flint nuclei and nucleiform endscrapers in Level 1, Liencres: *a–e, g, i,* nuclei; *f, h,* nucleiform endscrapers.

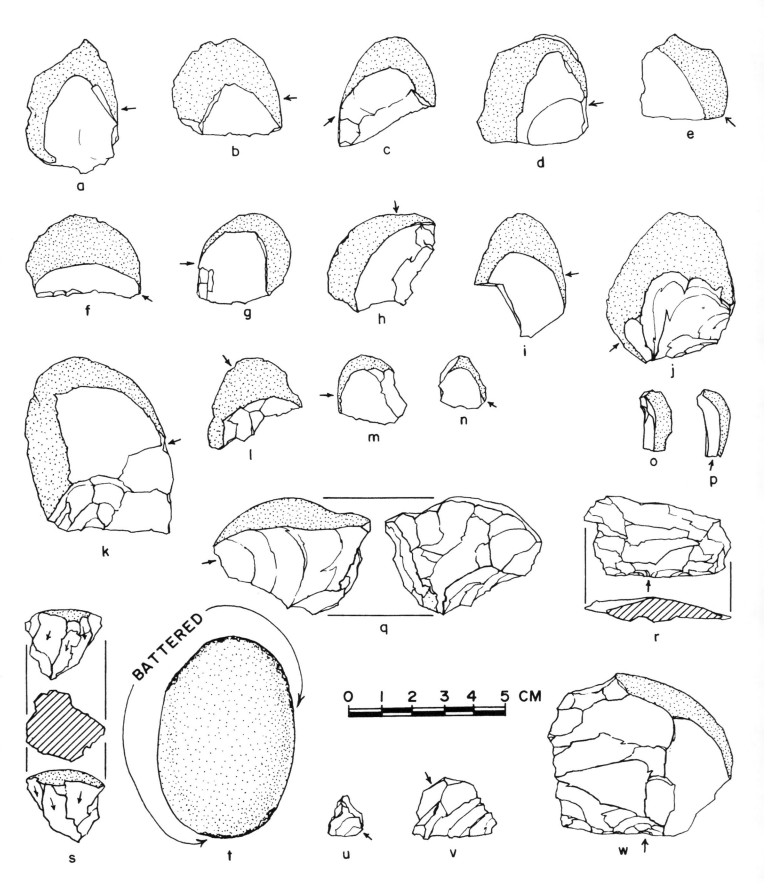

Figure 4.22. Quartzite nuclei, decortication flakes, and plain flakes in Level 1, Liencres: *a–n, q,* flakes; *o, p,* bladelike flakes; *r, w,* flakes with heavy scalar retouch on one edge, perhaps detached from the sides of picks; *s,* nucleus; *t,* pebble hammerstone; *u, v,* trimming flakes.

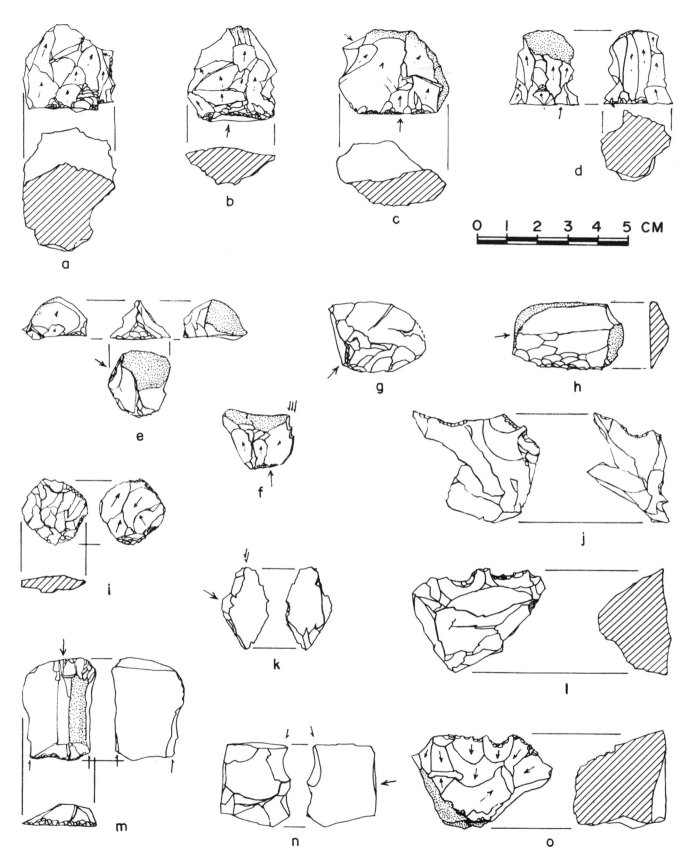

Figure 4.23. Flint retouched pieces in Level 1, Liencres: *a−d*, nucleiform endscrapers (*b, c*, fragments); *e*, endscraper made on a thick flake; *f, k, n*, burins on breaks; *g, h*, sidescrapers; *i*, atypical circular endscraper; *j*, notch-bec; *l*, bec; *m*, endscraper-burin; *o*, denticulate. (*j, l, o*, made on nucleus fragments.)

[77]

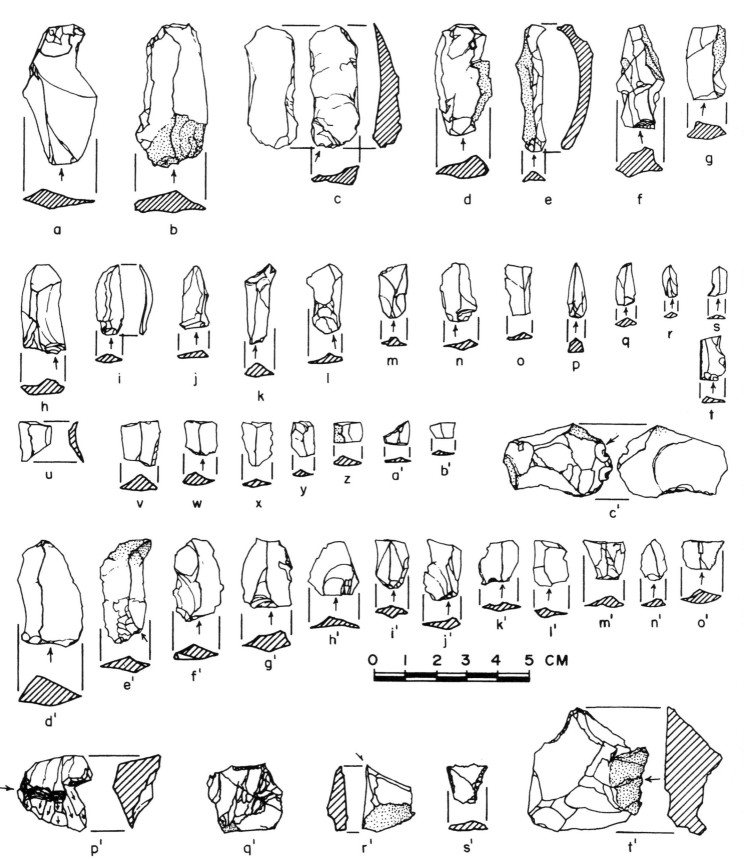

Figure 4.24. Flint blades, bladelets, and retouched pieces in Level 1, Liencres: *a–r*, blades and bladelets; *s*, notched bladelet; *t*, Dufour bladelet; *u–b'*, bladelet fragments; *c'*, piece continuously retouched on two edges, with inverse retouch; *d'–o'*, flakes; *p'*, platform renewal flake; *q'*, perforator; *r'*, burin on a break; *s'*, truncated element; *t'*, notch-atypical nosed endscraper.

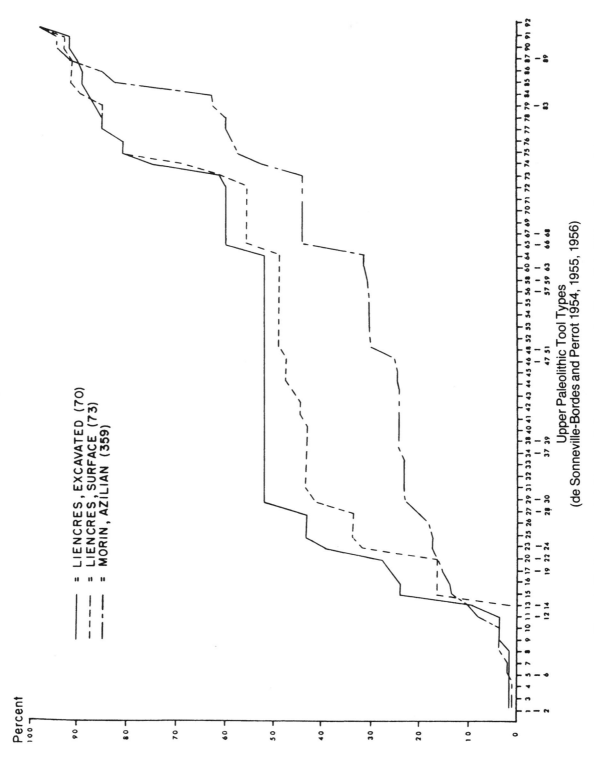

Percent

Figure 4.25. Asturian and Azilian cumulative percentage graphs (Upper Paleolithic tool types only).

Upper Paleolithic Tool Types
(de Sonneville-Bordes and Perrot 1954, 1955, 1956)

= LIENCRES, EXCAVATED (70)
= LIENCRES, SURFACE (73)
= MORIN, AZILIAN (359)

5. INDUSTRIAL REMAINS

LITHICS

The typology described below has been constructed to accommodate the range of industrial debris found in Asturian sites so far reviewed. An internally consistent classificatory framework for Asturian industrial remains has not been attempted previously. Although the purpose of such a typology is descriptive, it also presents a more comprehensive picture of the assemblage than can be gleaned from the literature. The typology facilitates comparison of Asturian assemblages with other European "macro" assemblages, and reliance on a fossil director to identify the assemblage is eliminated. Finally, the typology can be used to determine variation among sites within the Asturian as a whole.

The typology adopted here is a morphological one. Type names that imply function (for example, endscraper, chopper) are enshrined in the literature and are retained for comparative purposes; the artifacts themselves may or may not have been used in the way that their names imply.

An artifact is defined as any object that exhibits signs of modification by man. Most of the objects included in the typology are artifacts. A few that indicate man's presence but are not altered from their natural states are not, by this definition, artifacts.

Artifacts were first sorted by two raw materials: stone and bone or antler. Although present by the millions in Asturian sites, no objects manufactured from marine shells were found in the samples examined (more than 11,000 shells). No worked pieces of wood were recovered.

Lithics were further sorted by material: quartzite, flint (including chert), quartz, sandstone, limestone, and miscellaneous. Cross-tabulated against raw material were categories designed to facilitate site comparison and permit the identification of "functionally specific" areas within sites: debitage (16 types), heavy duty tools (17 types), and small tools (48 types).

Debitage

Debitage (D), the waste products of the primary and secondary manufacturing processes, by definition excludes any pieces that exhibit secondary retouch, but includes unmodified natural resources brought into the site as raw material for tool manufacture.

Unmodified Debris

1. Unmodified pebbles. Rolled, water-rounded pebbles less than 6 cm along the longest axis; usually ovoid in plan and cross section. In Asturian assemblages, the type so far occurs only in quartz and quartzite.

2. Unmodified cobbles. Rolled, water-rounded cobbles more than 6 cm long. The type occurs in quartzite only. Unmodified quartzite cobbles were the raw materials for the manufacture of picks, choppers, and chopping tools in Asturian assemblages.

3. Unmodified nodules. Natural flint nodules, generally small (less than 6 cm), irregular in plan and cross section, usually characterized by well developed cortices; rare in Asturian sites (noted only at Fonfría, Liencres, and La Riera). These objects are the only source of flint commonly available in Cantabria, which probably accounts for the intensive use of quartzite in the area and for the small size of Cantabrian flint industries in general.

Nuclei

4. Split cobble segments. Oval cobbles of quartz, quartzite, or sandstone split by percussion across their long axes to form pieces D-shaped in plan and oval in cross section. Regarded as a preliminary phase in core manufacture, they show no signs of flake removal.

5. Nucleus, flake. Any pebble or cobble of flint, quartzite, quartz, or sandstone showing evidence of the intentional removal of at least one flake. Evidence of flake removal consists necessarily of a flake scar, and optionally of a negative bulb of percussion. A flake scar is defined by its dimensions, less than twice as long as it is wide (Bordes 1968: 27). No blade scars (that is, scars more than twice as long as wide) should be present on the nucleus (see also D: Types 9, 14).

6. Nucleus, blade. Any pebble or cobble of flint or quartzite showing evidence of the removal of at least one blade. Evidence of blade removal consists minimally of at least one blade scar and optionally of a negative bulb of percussion. A blade scar is defined by its dimensions, at least twice as long as it is wide when measured along the axis of percussion, and it must exceed 4 cm in length.

7. Nucleus, bladelet. Any pebble or cobble of flint showing evidence of the removal of at least one bladelet. Evidence of bladelet removal consists necessarily of a bladelet scar, and optionally of a negative bulb of percussion. A bladelet scar is defined by its dimensions, at least twice as long as it is wide, and it must *not* exceed 4 cm in length.

8. Nucleus, mixed. Any nucleus of flint or quartzite showing evidence of the removal of both flakes and blades-bladelets, defined according to D: Types 5 through 7.

Debitage types 5 through 8 are ideal categories. In practice it was not always possible to adhere strictly to the typological criteria presented above. For instance, a nucleus exhibiting flake scars over most of its surface area, with only a few blade scars present, was classified as a flake nucleus. Mixed nuclei are truly mixed, with the proportion of flake to blade scars approaching one-to-one. In the case of the Asturian, core shape appears to have been determined more by the shape of the raw material than by preconceived notions in the mind of the artificer. Most nuclei are described as amorphous or roughly prismatic.

Flakes

9. Flakes, plain. Any piece of flint, quartzite, quartz, sandstone, or limestone exhibiting a cone and a conchoid (bulb) of percussion, and optionally splinters, striations, and ondulations on its ventral surface (Bordes 1968: 26). Flakes are also defined by their dimensions, length must not exceed twice the width of the piece, as measured along its axis (Bordes 1961, 1968: 27). The axis of a flake is "an imaginary line which prolongs the axis of percussion and passes through the point of impact, separating the cone and the conchoid into two more or less equal parts" (Bordes 1961: 7). Plain flakes are further defined by the absence of cortical material on their dorsal surfaces. With quartzite, the unaltered surface is considered as cortex for classificatory purposes.

Shatter flakes are a subcategory of plain flakes that are by-products of the manufacturing process. They are small, sharply angular, blocky fragments of flint or quartzite produced by percussion flaking that do not exhibit any of the characteristics of flakes defined above.

10. Flakes, primary decortication. This type of flake exhibits cortex over the entire dorsal surface (that is, it does not show evidence of prior flake removal). It would be among the first detached in the preparation of a nucleus.

Shatter flakes, as defined in D: Type 9, that show cortex covering one surface and show no evidence of prior flake removal from that surface are counted as primary decortication flakes.

11. Flakes, secondary decortication. These flakes exhibit cortical material on their dorsal surface but also show evidence of the prior removal of flakes from that surface.

Shatter flakes exhibiting these characteristics are counted as secondary decortication flakes.

12. Flakes, core renewal. Flakes detached from a nucleus to regularize it are divided into two subtypes.

Platform renewal flakes are detached from the striking platform of a nucleus by a blow directed at the side of the core immediately below the surface of the striking platform. They must show evidence of a core edge, characterized by the proximal ends of flake or blade scars and by the minute crescentic flake scars indicative of battering. Platform renewal flakes tend to be roughly polygonal in plan. The intent, as the name implies, seems to have been to remove entirely the old striking platform.

Cores, due to the nature of rocks with conchoidal fracture, tend to become undercut at the edges of the striking platform after the successive removal of a number of flakes or especially blades. To straighten future blades, it is desirable to remove the overhanging edge of the striking platform. This procedure is accomplished by a blow directed at the edge of the overhang, immediately below the surface of the striking platform. The blow, struck from one side, results in the removal of a thick flake or blade. The flake has a triangular cross section, preserving on one of its faces a piece of the striking platform and on the other a series of facets that are the proximal ends of flake-blade scars. (The third surface is the ventral surface of the flake or blade.) This kind of core renewal flake is designated an edge renewal flake. It is commonly referred to in the Spanish literature as an *hoja (hojita) del borde del nucleo,* blade (bladelet) from the edge of a nucleus.

13. Flakes, trimming. Flakes produced by secondary retouch are divided into two subtypes.

Minute flakes (less than 0.3 cm), usually of flint, represent the by-product of pressure retouch. They are plain flakes, flat, very thin, and often as wide (or wider) than they are long, with tiny but distinct conchoids. Lamellar retouch is not common in the Asturian, but rare bladelets, the by-products of such retouch, are also classified as trimming flakes.

The second subtype occurs only in quartzite. These thin, flat flakes, less than 1.5 cm long (measured along the flake axis), seem to represent the waste products from the secondary retouch characteristic of the margins of Asturian picks. No other tool type in the Asturian inventory regularly exhibits the kind of retouch necessary to produce flakes of this dimension. Pick trimming flakes were recovered in quantity only at Liencres. A mean length for 14 specimens was 0.86 cm.

Blades and Bladelets

14. Blades. Blades are arbitrarily defined here to equal or exceed 4 cm in length, and the dimension of length is equal to or exceeds twice that of the width. Fragments of "true blades" less than 4 cm long are also included in D: Type 14. True blades have dorsal surfaces characterized by parallel facets caused by the prior removal of other blades (Bordes 1961: 6). Blades are not common in Asturian industries, due to the paucity of raw material of sufficient size and homogeneity to permit their removal.

15. Bladelets. Blades, as defined in Type 14, with a length less than 4 cm are classified as bladelets. Blades and bladelets form a continuum in Asturian industries, and any distinction based on length is arbitrary.

Various

16. Various, debitage. This category includes any object that adheres to the definition of debitage but is not covered by D: Types 1 through 15.

Heavy Duty Tools

All objects classified as heavy duty tools (HDT) show either extensive battering or primary retouch, the minimal criteria adopted to define the term "tool." Heavy duty tools include artifacts classified by earlier writers as "core tools." These large pieces are made almost invariably on quartzite cobbles, although a few are manufactured on large flakes. With the exception of the Asturian pick, most types show minimal secondary retouch.

Hammerstones

1. Pebble hammerstones. Pebbles (D: Type 1) that show intentional battering on either one or both extremities, around the entire circumference of the piece, or on a delimited portion of either or both surfaces.

2. Cobble hammerstones. Cobbles (D: Type 2) that conform to the definition of HDT: Type 1; battering tends to be restricted to one or both ends.

Picks

3. Asturian picks, typical. A unifacial tool, invariably manufactured on a flattened and rounded quartzite cobble, oval in plan and cross section. Primary retouch consists of detaching flakes with a cobble hammerstone around three-quarters of the circumference of the cobble, producing a long, narrow point at one extremity (Vega del Sella 1923: 14). Secondary retouch consists of edge regularization, probably also by percussion, producing as a by-product pick trimming flakes (D: Type 13).

The tool is long and pointed, with straight or concave sides (rarely convex) in plan view. The extremity opposite the point preserves the natural, rounded end of the cobble. The piece is oval in cross section at its base, quadrilateral in section at the midpoint on the axis and trihedral near the tip where flake removal from both edges coalesces to form a central ridge.

Asturian picks show little lateral wear. When abrasion does occur, it is found almost exclusively at the tip and takes the form of beveling on the unworked side. Not all picks show this wear pattern. Some picks show battering at the base (end opposite the point), suggesting that the tool was hammered or was itself used as a hammerstone. No alteration suggestive of hafting has ever been recorded.

Asturian picks had a tendency to break at the base of the point either during manufacture or in use. A broken pick resembles a chopper (HDT: Types 5, 6), but can usually be distinguished from it by a quadrilateral or trihedral cross section at the point of breakage.

4. Asturian picks, atypical. A tool manufactured as HDT: Type 3, but is (a) poorly made (lacking in symmetry, secondary retouch), (b) unusually small (less than 5 cm long), (c) partially bifacial, or (d) characterized by convex sides in plan view.

Choppers and Chopping Tools

This group is united by the common characteristic of minimal, often simple primary retouch; the tools were manufactured with the apparent objective of forming a crude, usually convex, sometimes sinuous cutting edge. Straight, retouched, or unretouched cutting edges perpendicular to the axis of the piece (*hachereaux*, cleavers) are uncommon in the industry.

5. Choppers, large. A chopper is defined as a unifacial tool, manufactured by percussion retouch on one extremity of a flint nodule, quartzite cobble, or cobble fragment (rarely, in the Asturian, on a large flake). The end opposed to the cutting edge almost invariably preserves unaltered the end of the cobble. On a flake chopper, the cutting edge is lateral or transverse to the butt of the flake. The cutting edge tends to be convex and irregular, rarely concave or straight. Secondary retouch may or may not be present.

Large choppers are distinguished from small choppers arbitrarily by their dimensions. Width must not exceed 6 cm. Width is maximal width measured on any line perpendicular to the axis. The axis is defined as a line that bisects the tool along the plane of maximum symmetry (Bordes 1961: 7).

6. Choppers, small. Similar to HDT: Type 5, except that maximum width must not equal or exceed 6 cm.

7. Choppers, double. Similar to HDT: Type 5, except that the piece is manufactured on an elongated cobble that has been unifacially retouched on both extremities.

8. Chopping tools, large. A bidirectionally retouched tool manufactured by percussion retouch on one extremity of a quartzite cobble or cobble fragment (rarely on a large flake). Chopping tools fabricated obliquely to the cobble axis, or on the lateral edge of a cobble, are rare. The type is "bifacial" only in the sense that the cutting edge has been worked from both surfaces of the cobble (Bordes 1961: 48). In the Asturian, the cobble surfaces themselves are never altered. As with choppers, the cutting edge tends to be convex or sinuous, rarely concave or perfectly straight. Recognizable secondary retouch is extremely rare. The end opposed to the cutting edge invariably preserves the unaltered end of the cobble. Large chopping tools must equal or exceed 6 cm in width.

9. Chopping tools, small. Similar to HDT: Type 8, except that maximum width must not equal or exceed 6 cm.

10. Chopping tools, double. Similar to HDT: Type 8, except that the piece is manufactured on an elongated cobble that has been bidirectionally retouched on both extremities.

Bifaces

11. Bifaces, partial. The term "biface" is reserved for pieces with both surfaces showing modification by flaking. True bifaces, retouched entirely over both surfaces, do not exist in the Asturian.

Partial bifaces are made on elongated, flattened, oval quartzite cobbles. Primary retouch consists of the removal of thin, broad flakes from the edges of both faces to produce strong, sharp, and relatively regular cutting edges. One extremity of the cobble is invariably fashioned into a blunt point. The other end, and a narrow central spine, preserve the natural cobble surface. Secondary retouch may or may not be present.

Partial bifaces are known from only three Asturian sites: Cuartamentero (where the pieces are crude, bifacial picks), Lledías, and La Riera.

Milling Stones

12. Manos. These objects are cobbles or cobble fragments of sandstone or coarse quartzite with one or more flat or slightly convex surfaces characterized by smoothing and striations due to abrasion from use by man. Called handstones or manos in Southwestern archaeology, they tend to be roughly rectangular in plan and cross section, although in the Asturian sample little effort was made to regularize the edges by battering or flaking. Handstones exhibiting a single grinding surface are termed unifacial; those showing artificial grinding on both surfaces are termed bifacial. Manos are rare in Asturian sites.

13. Metates. The fixed, nether stone in the quern complex, metates are defined as sandstone or coarse quartzite boulders that exhibit a single, artificial flat or slightly concave surface, characterized by smoothing and striations due to abrasion. Only a single unquestionable metate has been found in situ in an Asturian site (Liencres), although fragments of grinding stones with concave sections occur in rare instances in other sites.

14. Milling stone fragments, undifferentiated. This category includes small and irregular pieces of sandstone or quartzite with smoothing and striations due to artificial abrasion that cannot be assigned to either HDT: Types 12 or 13.

Combination Tools

15. Hammerstone-choppers. Implements manufactured on quartzite cobbles combining extensive battering on one extremity (HDT: Type 2) with a unifacial chopper (HDT: Types 5, 6) on the other.

16. Hammerstone-chopping tools. Implements manufactured on quartzite cobbles combining extensive battering on one extremity (HDT: Type 2) with a bifacial chopping tool (HDT: Types 8, 9) on the other.

Various

17. Various, heavy duty tools. This category includes any object fitting the definition of heavy duty tools that is not defined by HDT: Types 1 through 16.

Small Tools

Implements manufactured on flakes, blades, and bladelets are called small tools (ST). Whereas the typological framework for debitage and heavy duty tools was devised specifically for this research, the typology devised for the European Upper Paleolithic (de Sonneville-Bordes and Perrot 1953, 1954, 1955, 1956) accommodated most of the small tool types found in the Asturian. Because of wide acceptance by Old World prehistorians, it was adopted for classification of the Asturian flake tools to make assemblage description more readily comparable with that of other European assemblages.

The de Sonneville-Bordes and Perrot classification contains a total of 92 tool types; 33 (36 percent) of them occur in excavated Asturian sites. These types are listed with the appropriate citation rather than described. Ten types not included in the typology are defined. Small tools are numbered consecutively with types already defined; the de Sonneville-Bordes and Perrot numbering system is not used.

Endscrapers

1. Endscrapers, simple (de Sonneville-Bordes and Perrot 1954: 328).

2. Endscrapers on flakes (de Sonneville-Bordes and Perrot 1954: 330).

3. Endscrapers, circular (de Sonneville-Bordes and Perrot 1954: 330).

4. Endscrapers, carinate or keeled (de Sonneville-Bordes and Perrot 1954: 332).

5. Endscrapers, nucleiform (de Sonneville-Bordes and Perrot 1954: 332).

6. Endscrapers, thick shouldered (de Sonneville-Bordes and Perrot 1954: 332).

7. Endscrapers, flat shouldered (de Sonneville-Bordes and Perrot 1954: 332).

8. Endscrapers, atypical (de Sonneville-Bordes and Perrot 1954: 328).

Continuously Retouched Pieces

9. Continuously retouched on one edge (de Sonneville-Bordes and Perrot 1956: 550).

10. Continuously retouched on two edges (de Sonneville-Bordes and Perrot 1956: 550).

Sidescrapers

11. Sidescrapers, simple straight (de Sonneville-Bordes and Perrot 1956: 552; Bordes 1961: 25).

12. Sidescrapers, simple convex (de Sonneville-Bordes and Perrot 1956: 552; Bordes 1961: 26).

13. Sidescrapers, convex convergent (Bordes 1961: 27).

Burins

14. Burins, straight dihedral (de Sonneville-Bordes and Perrot 1956: 408).

15. Burins, angle dihedral (de Sonneville-Bordes and Perrot 1956: 408).

16. Burins, angle on a break (de Sonneville-Bordes and Perrot 1956: 408).

17. Burins, multiple dihedral (de Sonneville-Bordes and Perrot 1956: 410).

18. Burins, multiple mixed (de Sonneville-Bordes and Perrot 1956: 410).

19. Burins, flat (de Sonneville-Bordes and Perrot 1956: 410).

20. Burins, nucleiform (de Sonneville-Bordes and Perrot 1956: 410).

Denticulates

21. Denticulates, on flakes (de Sonneville-Bordes and Perrot 1956: 552).

22. Denticulates, on blades (de Sonneville-Bordes and Perrot 1956: 552).

Notches

23. Notches, on flakes (de Sonneville-Bordes and Perrot 1956: 552).

Wedges

24. Wedges. A wedge is defined as a thick flake (usually) or a thick, short blade (rarely), *any* side (not necessarily the distal side) of which has been retouched bifacially by percussion to form a short but straight and regular cutting edge. Often, although not exclusively, they are rectanguloid in plan and section. Wedges are difficult to distinguish from flakes produced by the bipolar method (Clark 1976a: 144). Wedges may be considered a subtype within splintered pieces (*pièces esquillées*; de Sonneville-Bordes and Perrot 1956: 522).

Points

25. Points, Mousterian (Bordes 1961: 21, 22).

26. Points, Azilian (de Sonneville-Bordes and Perrot 1956: 556).

27. Point, pedunculate. This point, made on a small flake, is rhomboidal or lozenge-shaped in plan and biconvex in cross section. Both surfaces show thinning by pressure retouch. Secondary retouch, tending toward lamellar scars, has been applied to all margins. The base exhibits an ill-defined stem or tang, produced by flat and invasive pressure flaking. The only specimen of this type so far recovered is from Liencres.

28. Points, microgravette (de Sonneville-Bordes and Perrot 1956: 547).

Perforators

29. Perforators, typical (de Sonneville-Bordes and Perrot 1955: 78).

30. Perforators, atypical (bec) (de Sonneville-Bordes and Perrot 1955: 78).

31. Becs, multiple (de Sonneville-Bordes and Perrot 1955: 78).

32. Becs, alternate burinating. A bec, as defined in ST: Type 30, is characterized by a straight, chisellike cutting edge produced when a flake or blade margin is retouched first dorsally (to form a notch), then ventrally (to form a second notch). The notches, adjacent to one another, place in relief a small segment of the unaltered flake or blade edge that projects above them (the notches) and constitutes the bec.

Knives

33. Knives, naturally backed. A flake roughly semicircular in plan and triangular in (vertical) cross section (cutting edge oriented down) is termed a knife. The cutting edge may be either transverse or lateral to the axis of the flake and must show sporadic flaking due to use, but no intentional retouch. The side opposed to the cutting edge is naturally blunt (backed), generally arcuate, and more or less perpendicular to the vertical axis of the piece. It may or may not exhibit a cortical surface but is *not,* in any case, *retouched* to produce backing.

Truncated Pieces

34. Truncated pieces, oblique concave (de Sonneville-Bordes and Perrot 1956: 548, 550).

35. Truncated pieces, oblique convex (de Sonneville-Bordes and Perrot 1956: 548, 550).

36. Truncated pieces, straight concave (de Sonneville-Bordes and Perrot 1956: 548, 550).

Retouched Bladelets

37. Bladelets, backed (de Sonneville-Bordes and Perrot 1956: 554).

38. Bladelets, partially backed. Similar to ST: Type 37, but with backing extending over only a portion of the edge opposed to the cutting edge.

39. Bladelets, notched or strangled (de Sonneville-Bordes and Perrot 1956: 554).

40. Bladelets, denticulated (de Sonneville-Bordes and Perrot 1956: 554).

41. Bladelets, truncated (de Sonneville-Bordes and Perrot 1956: 554).

42. Bladelets, Dufour (de Sonneville-Bordes and Perrot 1956: 554).

Combination Tools

43. Endscraper-burins (de Sonneville-Bordes and Perrot 1955: 76).

44. Endscraper-becs. Flakes or blades on which both an endscraper (ST: Types 1–8) and a bec (ST: Type 30) have been manufactured.

45. Notch-denticulates. Flakes or blades on which both a notch (ST: Type 23) and a denticulate (ST: Types 21, 22) have been manufactured. The two areas of retouch must not be contiguous with one another.

46. Perforator-notches. Flakes or blades on which both a perforator (ST: Types 29–32) and a notch (ST: Type 23) have been manufactured.

47. Perforator-denticulates. Flakes or blades on which both a perforator (ST: Types 29–32) and a denticulate (ST: Types 21, 22) have been manufactured.

Various

48. Various, small tools. This category includes any object that adheres to the definition of small tools but is not defined by ST: Types 1–47.

BONE AND ANTLER

Implements worked in bone and antler are extremely rare in Asturian sites (Vega del Sella 1930: 15–18). Eight types have been defined so far, all but one of them represented by only one or two examples (see Table 5.1). Continued excavation may increase the number of types and specimen frequency within types, but the near absence of worked bone in the Asturian is striking, especially considering the plethora of bone and antler objects found in Cantabrian Magdalenian and Azilian sites. As the Boreal-Atlantic environment became more densely wooded, it is possible that wood was increasingly substituted for implements made previously of bone and antler.

Points

1. Points, oval cross section. Antler or bone fragments, rectangular in plan, oval in cross section; all surfaces show smoothing and striations due to intentional grinding and polishing. One extremity may exhibit a well-defined point, produced by grinding and polishing. Oval-sectioned shaft segments are counted as points. No complete specimens exist and the base of the piece cannot be described. About a half dozen examples, from three sites, have been recovered.

2. Points, rectangular cross sections. Similar to Bone (B): Type 1, but with a rectangular cross section. Only a single example, from La Meaza, has been recovered.

Perforating Tools

3. Punches, awls, perforators. This group of objects is divided into two subtypes.

One subtype is made on large fragments of long bone and is characterized by minimal modification of the natural bone surface, except at the point. The point shows polishing and striations due to at least perfunctory sharpening and use. The extremity opposed to the point is unmodified and usually exhibits a ragged broken surface. Transverse sections tend to be concave-convex, reflecting the curvature of the exterior portion of the bone.

The second subtype is manufactured on the proximal segments of ungulate long bones or metatarsals. A crude point is produced, by flaking or simple breakage, on the broken (distal) end opposed to the epiphysis. The point must show smoothing due to use. The articular (proximal) end of the bone fragment may or may not be preserved; it is never modified.

4. Sharpened splinters, needle fragments. Objects manufactured on bone splinters; oval, circular, or concave-convex in cross section; one or both ends may exhibit points produced by grinding and polishing; surfaces or portions thereof may or may not show smoothing and striae due to polishing and use. Bases are variable; most exhibit unmodified breaks. Bipointed pieces are extremely rare.

Antler Tips

5. Antler tips, use modified. Broken antler tips, the distal ends of which exhibit faceting, battering or polishing due to use; otherwise unmodified. Artifacts characterized by distal faceting and battering called "antler flakers" in the literature comprise this type.

Perforated Batons

6. Perforated batons (*bastones de mando*, Spanish; *bâtons de commandement*, French). Distal segments of cervid antler exhibiting a large, oval perforation, biconical in section, near the center (Vega del Sella 1923: 23–25, 28; 1930: 16, 17). The tip (distal end) invariably presents smoothing and striations due either to use or to intentional modification. The surface of the shaft may or may not show intentional smoothing; when smoothing is present, the objective seems to have been to remove the roughened antler exterior. The base (proximal end) exhibits the irregular, roughened surface characteristic of an unmodified break. Artifacts analogous to these have been recovered from Magdalenian levels throughout Cantabria and, because of striae on the interior margins

of the perforation, are usually considered to be elements of straightening devices for wooden spear, dart, or arrow shafts.

Bone with Cutting Marks

7. Bone with cutting marks. Bone or antler fragments with short, linear, parallel or subparallel incisions that are sharply defined and V-shaped in cross section.

Engraved Bone Fragments

8. Bone fragments, engraved. Bone or antler fragments with shallow and irregular, nonparallel or subparallel incisions that are W-shaped in cross section, often meandering in plan.

Various

9. Various, worked bone. Any object of worked or modified bone or antler not defined by B: Types 1 through 8.

SUMMARY STATISTICS

Tables 5.1 through 5.10 record the distribution of tool types and debitage across the 23 Asturian sites that have produced industrial remains, excluding the dubious find at Luarca (González 1965). The 3089 artifacts recorded constitute all Asturian industrial remains that could be located in 1971.

Lithic material is presented in Tables 5.1 through 5.7 and the data are summarized in Table 5.8; Figures 5.1 through 5.4 illustrate some of these artifacts. Extreme variation in collection size made site-by-site comparison of type-specific raw frequency counts uninformative. Conversion to relative frequencies is equally misleading, again due to low counts and sample selectivity. The data can be stratified on logical grounds, however, into two roughly comparable groups.

The 22 sites cited in the literature form a homogeneous entity, perhaps not because they were originally so, but because most have been subjected to the same kinds of postexcavation selection. The sites share industries manufactured almost exclusively in quartzite, probably partly due to a scarcity of suitable flint in eastern Asturias during the Asturian period. Flint becomes more prevalent as sample size and excavation techniques are improved. Within this group, only the samples from La Riera and Balmori are large enough to be at least potentially (if not demonstrably) representative. Complete inventories are available from the small test exposures I made at those sites in 1969. Upper Paleolithic levels were exposed at La Riera, Balmori, and Coberizas, but only the Asturian levels are recorded in these tables.

The lithics from Liencres form a second group. Liencres contrasts sharply with the traditional sites. First, it is situated within 500 m of a flint (chert) source, and the proportion of flint artifacts is relatively much greater than at any other site. Second, a virtually complete surface collection (more than 95 percent of site surface area) was made at the site, supplemented by an excavated sample. As a result, a much more complete

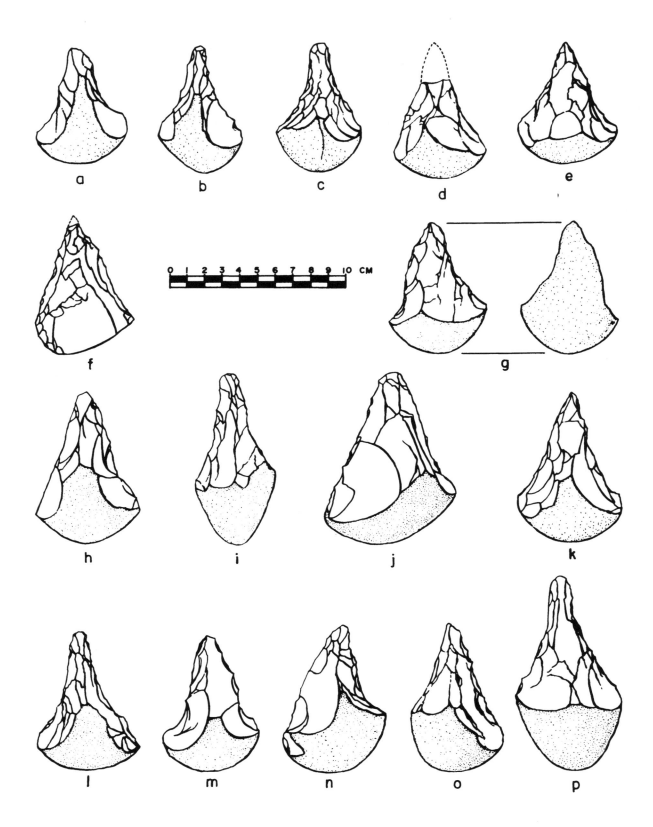

a   b   c   d   e

f   g

0 1 2 3 4 5 6 7 8 9 10 CM

h   i   j   k

l   m   n   o   p

TABLE 5.1
Quartzite Debitage Distribution Across All Sites

Sites	(Type No.)	Cobbles, unmodified (2)	Pebbles, unmodified (1)	Split cobble segments (4)	Nucleus, flakes (5)	Nucleus, blades (6)	Nucleus, mixed (8)	Flakes, plain (9)	Flakes, 1 dc (10)	Flakes, 2 dc (11)	Flakes, trimming (13)	Blades (14)	Bladelets (15)	Various (16)	Total
Arnero		+						4							4
Balmori		2	4	2	5			80	+	+	24	5	11		133
Bricia		+	+		1			6				2	1		10
Ciriego		+						+							
Coberizas		+	1					7							8
Colombres		1	1					+	1	1		1			5
Cuartamentero[a]		22+	+	15	6			47	+	+					90
Cueto de la Mina		+	2	1				+						1	4
Cueva del Río								2							2
Fonfría		1[b]		1				2				1			5
Infierno								+							
La Franca				1			1	1	1						4
La Cuevona		+	1				1	+							2
La Lloseta		1+		1	8	1		9				2			22
La Loja		+	1	+	+			29	+			6			36
La Meaza		+	+	+	+		+	+	+					+	
La Riera		2	7	7	11	2	3	149			27	9	29	1	247
Liencres, Surface		3	8	15	6		1	15	2	63	29	1			143
Liencres, Level 1		9	4	1	8			2	1	25	14	1			65
Llanes															
Lledías[c]		+	1		1			+							2
Penicial		3	1		6	1		3							14
Tres Calabres						1									1
Vidiago								1							1
No provenience			4					4							8
Total		44	35	42	54	5	6	361	5	89	94	28	41	2	806

+ = Item present but frequency not specified or unknown.
a.   Includes pieces at site and in landlord's home.
b.   Small cobble with ochre stains on one face.
c.   Mixed collection. Only the ceramic phallus, unmodified pebble, flake nucleus, nucleiform endscraper, and two of the picks are from Level 1; other objects are from the certainly Asturian Level 2. Reportedly, Level 1 also contained potsherds and two ground stone axes (Uría-Riú 1941), suggesting that the level postdates the Asturian. The picks, however, never occur in Neolithic levels in Cantabria.

Figure 5.1. Unifacial quartzite picks, guide fossils for the Asturian lithic industry. Site locations: *a*, Arnero; *b*, Fonfría; *c*, Colombres; *d*, Cueto de la Mina; *e*, La Loja; *f*, Bricia; *g*, Coberizas; *h*, Balmori; *i*, Penicial; *j*, Liencres; *k*, Lledías; *l*, *m*, La Riera; *n*, Cuartamentero; *o*, Tres Calabres; *p*, Infierno. All specimens are from conchero contexts and are in mint condition. (Excavator and storage location of specimens are listed in Appendix C.)

The Asturian pick is described as a unifacial tool, invariably manufactured on a flattened and rounded quartzite cobble, oval in plan and cross section. Primary retouch consists of detaching flakes with a cobble hammerstone around three-quarters of the circumference of the cobble, producing a long, narrow point at one end (Vega del Sella 1923: 14). Secondary retouch consists of edge regularization, probably also by percussion, producing as a by-product the pick trimming flakes described in Clark (1971a: 266–268).

The resultant tool is long and pointed, with straight or concave sides (rarely convex) when seen in plan view. The end opposite the point preserves the natural, rounded end of the cobble. The piece is oval in cross section at its base, quadrilateral in section at the midpoint on the axis of the piece, and trihedral near the tip where flake removal from both edges coalesces to form a central ridge.

Asturian picks show little lateral wear. When abrasion does occur, it is found almost exclusively at the tip and takes the form of beveling on the unworked side of the piece. Not all picks show this wear pattern. Some picks show battering at the butt (end opposite the point), suggesting that the tool was hammered or was itself used as a hammerstone. No alteration suggestive of hafting has ever been recorded.

Asturian picks had a tendency to break at the base of the point either during manufacture or in use. A broken pick resembles a chopper (Clark 1971a: 269, 270), but can usually be distinguished from it by a quadrilateral or trihedral cross section at the point of breakage.

TABLE 5.2
Quartzite Tool Distribution Across All Sites

Retouched Pieces

Sites (Type No.)	Cobble hammerstones (2)	Pebble hammerstones (1)	Picks, typical (3)	Picks, atypical (4)	Choppers, large (5)	Choppers, small (6)	Choppers, double (7)	Chopping tools, large (8)	Chopping tools, small (9)	Chopping tools, double (10)	Bifaces, partial (11)	Manos (12)	Metates (13)	Hammerstone chopper (15)	Hammerstone chopping tool (16)	Endscraper on a flake (2)	Endscraper, circular (3)	Endscraper, nucleiform (5)
Arnero			14	1	1	1		2						1				
Balmori	+		4	1	3	2			3					1				1
Bricia			1													1		
Ciriego				1														
Coberizas			11							1								
Colombres	2[c]	3	4+[d]	1	1	1												
Cuartamentero			8		6[e]	4	2				2							
Cueto de la Mina			7	1														
Cueva del Río			2															
Fonfría	5[g]		9	2[h]	2	2[i]					1	1[j]		1				1
Infierno			2		1													
La Franca		1	1		4	3												
La Cuevona		1[l]			1													
La Lloseta	1		1		1			1										2
La Loja			14	2[n]		1		2	1									1
La Meaza																		
La Riera	2		37		1		1		2		1				1			3
Liencres, Surface		2	4						1				1					
Liencres, Level 1		2	1		1													
Llanes			1															
Lledías			13	1[p]				1			4						1	1
Penicial	1		10	1	3			1								1		
Tres Calabres			2	1[s]														
Vidiago																		
No provenience	2	1	22		3	1		1				1[j]			1			
Total	13	10	168	12	28	15	3	9	6	2	7	2	1	3	2	2	1	9

+ = Item present but frequency not specified or unknown.

a. A simple endscraper, made on a blade.

b. Polishing stone, large quartzite cobble with polishing on both faces.

c. Both pieces are cylindrical, resembling pestles; battered on both extremities (1), on one extremity (1).

d. Carballo (1926: 12) noted that three or four additional picks were found in the levels overlying the burial.

e. Two are made on massive flakes; one flake is "side-struck."

f. A disk core or partial biface made on a secondary decortication flake; a small unifacial point on a secondary decortication flake; and an atypical elongated chopper (single) with a circular depression in the center of one face produced by battering.

g. Oval flattened cobbles; three battered on one end, two on both ends.

h. One is a partially bifacial pick.

i. One shows battering along the unretouched edge.

j. Bifacial manos.

Retouched Pieces

Endscraper, atypical	Cont. ret. piece-1	Sidescraper, simple, straight	Sidescraper, simple, convex	Sidescraper, double convex-converging	Burin, straight dihedral	Burin, multiple	Denticulate on flake	Denticulated blade	Denticulated bladelet	Notch on a flake	Wedges	Point, Mousterian	Perforator-notch	Perforator-denticulate	Various	Retouched Pieces Total	Quartzite Grand Total
(8)	(9)	(11)	(12)	(13)	(14)	(17)	(21)	(22)	(40)	(23)	(24)	(25)	(46)	(47)			
													1			21	25
1[a]	2	1	2		1		1			2					1[b]	26	160
1						1										4	14
																1	1
	1															13	21
																12	17
	2			1			1	1							3[f]	25	115
																13	17
																2	4
															2[k]	27	32
																3	3
			1													9	13
																2	4
							2								2[m]	10	33
							5	1		1		1	1			30	65
							7	1	1	6	1			1		64	311
																9	152
							1			2					1[o]	8	73
																1	1
1															1[q]	22	24
			1												2[r]	20	34
																4	5
																	1
															2	34	42
3	5	1	4	1	1	1	17	3	1	11	1	1	2	1	14	361	1167

k. Cobble beveled on two surfaces to form a point, and a shallow mortar made on a roughly spherical cobble battered over all surfaces except on a small concave platform showing striae due to grinding.

l. Battered on both ends, one surface highly polished.

m. A shallow mortar made on a quartzite cobble, with a shallow depression in one face defined by and covered with battering; and a huge limace.

n. One piece appears to have been heavily rolled—the lateral flake scars are almost obliterated; its tip, however, shows a fresh break, suggesting reuse of a piece from an earlier terrace(?) industry. The second partially bifacial piece is atypical.

o. A compressor—an oval quartzite pebble with localized battering on one surface.

p. Atypical (small).

q. A circular endscraper made on a large flake (possibly a "jar stopper").

r. A circular endscraper, and a quartzite anvil (a flattened subrectangular chunk of coarse quartzite exhibiting a shallow subrectangular depression caused by battering on one of its surfaces, otherwise unmodified).

s. Atypical (short and pointed).

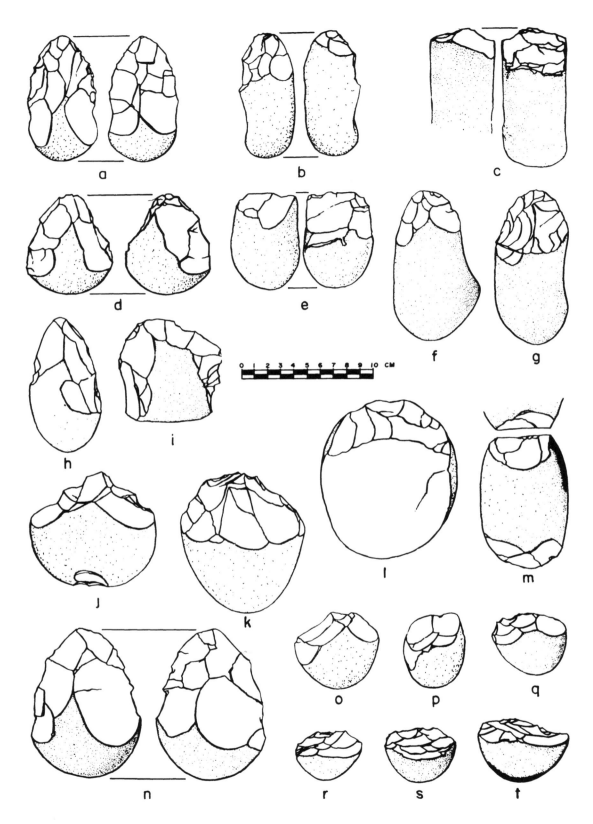

Figure 5.2. Asturian heavy duty tools from Cantabria: *a, d, n,* partial bifaces; *b, c,* chopping tools on elongated pebbles; *e,* chopping tool; *f, g,* choppers on elongated pebbles; *h,* partial uniface; *i,* chopper; *j, k,* large choppers; *l,* large chopper made on a flake; *m,* chopper-chopping tool, battered along the right edge; *o–t,* small choppers. All specimens are made of fine to medium grained quartzite and are in mint condition. (Excavator and storage location of specimens are listed in Appendix C.)

TABLE 5.3
Flint Debitage Distribution Across All Sites

	Flint Debitage													
Sites	Nodules, unmodified	Nucleus, flakes	Nucleus, blades	Nucleus, bladelets	Nucleus, mixed	Flakes, plain	Flakes, 1 dc	Flakes, 2 dc	Flakes, trimming	Flakes, core renewal	Blades	Bladelets	Various	Total
(Type No.)	(3)	(5)	(6)	(7)	(8)	(9)	(10)	(11)	(13)	(12)	(14)	(15)	(16)	
Arnero														
Balmori		1	1			27			9		4	13		55
Bricia						2					1	1		4
Ciriego														
Coberizas		1				6						2		9
Colombres														
Cuartamentero						4[a]								4
Cueto de la Mina														
Cueva del Río														
Fonfría	1	2		2		1						+		6
Infierno														
La Franca														
La Cuevona														
La Lloseta		3		1		2					1			7
La Loja					4	23				1	5	11		44
La Meaza		+	+	+	+	+					+	+		
La Riera		2	1	1	2	103			19	2	6	24	1[b]	161
Liencres, Surface	+	10	1[c]	3	8	296	35	299	102	6	10[d]	48		818
Liencres, Level 1	+	9	1	2	6	110	13	134	83	4	13[d]	45		420
Llanes														
Lledías														
Penicial						2								2
Tres Calabres														
Vidiago														
No provenience														
Total	1	28	4	9	20	576	48	433	213	13	40	144	1	1530

+ = Items present but frequency not specified or unknown.
a. Pieces in collection in landlord's home.
b. All small blades, approaching bladelets.
c. One burin spall.
d. All blades are small, grading into bladelets; none of the nuclei were large enough to have permitted the removal of large blades.

TABLE 5.4
Flint Tool Distribution Across All Sites

Sites	Chopping tool, small	Endscraper, simple	Endscraper on a flake	Endscraper, circular	Endscraper, keeled	Endscraper, thick-shouldered	Endscraper, flat-shouldered	Endscraper, nucleiform	Perforator, typical	Perforator, atypical	Bec, multiple	Bec, alternating-burinating	Burin, straight-dihedral	Burin, angle-dihedral	Burin, angle on break	Burin, multiple-dihedral	Burin, multiple-mixed	Burin, nucleiform	Burin, flat	Knives, naturally backed	Point, microgravette	Point, pedunculate
(Type No.)	(9)	(1)	(2)	(3)	(4)	(6)	(7)	(5)	(29)	(30)	(31)	(32)	(14)	(15)	(16)	(17)	(18)	(20)	(19)	(33)	(28)	(27)
Arnero																						
Balmori		1	1					2				1			2	1					1	
Bricia																						
Ciriego																						
Coberizas																						
Colombres																						
Cuartamentero																						
Cueto de la Mina																						
Cueva del Río																						
Fonfría					1ᶜ			1ᶜ														
Infierno																						
La Franca																						
La Cuevona																						
La Lloseta							1						1									
La Loja														1	1							
La Meaza									+	+												
La Riera			1					3		2					2	2		1				
Liencres, Surface	1						1	11	2	9	1				6	1	1	1	1	2	1	1
Liencres, Level 1		1		1		3	1	11		8	3				6							
Llanes																						
Lledías																						
Penicial																						
Tres Calabres																						
Vidiago																						
No provenience																						
Total	1	2	2	1	1	3	3	28	2	19	4	1	1	1	17	4	1	2	1	2	2	1

+ = Items present but frequency not specified or unknown.
a.   Bladelet with flat inverse retouch.
b.   Blade, poorly truncated with scalar retouch along one edge.
c.   On small bladelet core.
d.   There may be some flint points, of undetermined type, made on blades.
e.   Atypical sidescraper—alternating burinating bec.
f.   Geometrics: one trapezoid.

Retouched Pieces

Point, Azilian	Truncated piece, oblique-concave	Truncated piece, oblique-convex	Truncated piece, straight-concave	Cont. ret. piece - 1	Cont. ret. piece - 2	Notch, flake	Denticulate, flake	Wedge	Sidescraper, simple straight	Sidescraper, simple convex	Bladelets, backed	Bladelets, partially backed	Bladelets, strangled	Bladelets, truncated	Bladelets, Dufour	Endscraper-burin	Endscraper-bec	Notch-denticulate	Perforator-notch	Various	Retouched Pieces Total	Flint, Grand Total
(26)	(34)	(35)	(36)	(9)	(10)	(23)	(21)	(24)	(11)	(12)	(37)	(38)	(39)	(41)	(42)	(43)	(44)	(45)	(46)			
1												1									2	2
			1	1		2	1	1			1			1						1[a]	18	73
							1				1									1[b]	3	7
																						9
																						4
				1																	1	1
			1																		3	9
																					2	9
					1																3	47
	1	1					5		2	1	1	3						1		+[d]	26	187
				4	1	6	9		1	1	2		1	3					1	3[e]	71	889
				5	1	7	4		1	2	1		1	1	1	1	1			1[f]	61	481
																						2
					1																1	1
1	1	1	2	11	4	15	20	1	4	4	6	4	2	5	1	1	1	1	1	6	191	1721

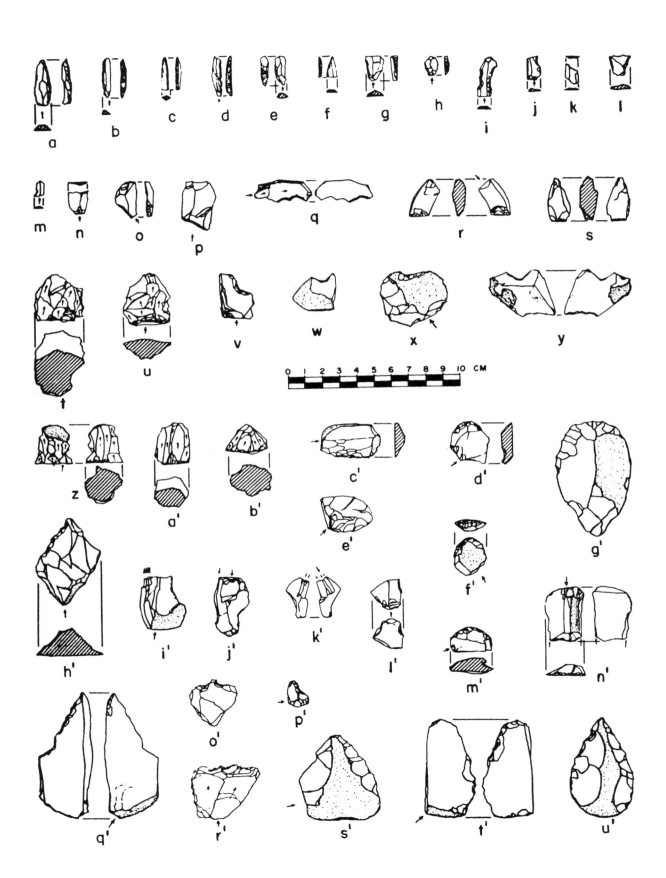

TABLE 5.5

Quartz Debitage and Tool Distribution Across All Sites

Sites	Debitage							Retouched Pieces							Grand Total
	Pebbles, unmodified	Crystals	Nucleus, flakes	Chunks	Flakes	Bladelets	Total	Endscraper, thick-shouldered	Cont. ret. piece-1	Notch	Wedge	Denticulate	Various	Total	
(Type No.)	(1)		(5)		(9)	(15)		(6)	(9)	(23)	(24)	(21)			
Arnero															
Balmori			1		3		4								4
Bricia															
Ciriego															
Coberizas					1		1								1
Colombres					2		2		2					2	4
Cuartamentero															
Cueto de la Mina															
Cueva del Río															
Fonfría			1	1			2								2
Infierno															
La Franca															
La Cuevona															
La Lloseta															
La Loja				3	1	1	5								5
La Meaza															
La Riera	1	32			26	2	61	1		1	1	1	1ᵃ	5	66
Liencres, Surface		1		1	3		5								5
Liencres, Level 1					2		2			1				1	3
Llanes															
Lledías															
Penicial															
Tres Calabres															
Vidiago															
No provenience	—	—	—	—	—	—	—	—	—	—	—	—	—	—	—
Total	1	33	2	5	38	3	82	1	2	2	1	1	1	8	90

+ = Items present but frequency not specified or unknown.
a.   Fragment of ground quartz.

Figure 5.3. Asturian small tools from Cantabria: *a*, backed bladelet resembling an Azilian point; *b, d*, backed bladelets; *c, f*, backed and pointed bladelet fragments; *e*, partially backed bladelet; *g*, backed bladelet fragment; *h*, atypical backed bladelet; *i*, strangled or notched bladelet; *j*, Dufour bladelet; *k*, truncated bladelet; *l*, truncated element; *m*, notched bladelet; *n*, partially truncated bladelet; *o, p*, truncated flakes; *q*, denticulated bladelet with inverse retouch; *r, s*, wedges; *t, u, z−b'*, nucleiform endscrapers; *v−x*, notched flakes; *y*, notched flake-denticulate; *c', e'*, sidescrapers; *d', f', g', m'*, flake end-scrapers; *h', r', s', t'*, denticulated flakes; *i'−k'*, multiple dihedral burins; *l'*, bec formed by inverse retouch; *n'*, multiple dihedral burin-atypical endscraper made on a blade; *o'*, bec; *p'*, thick-shouldered microendscraper; *q'*, denticulate with perforator formed by inverse retouch; *u'*, sidescraper-denticulate. Material: *a−r, t, u, w, y−f', i'−n', o', r'* are of flint or chert; *s, v, x, g', h', q', s'−u'* are of fine-grained quartzite, and *p'* is of quartz. (Excavator and storage location of specimens are listed in Appendix C.)

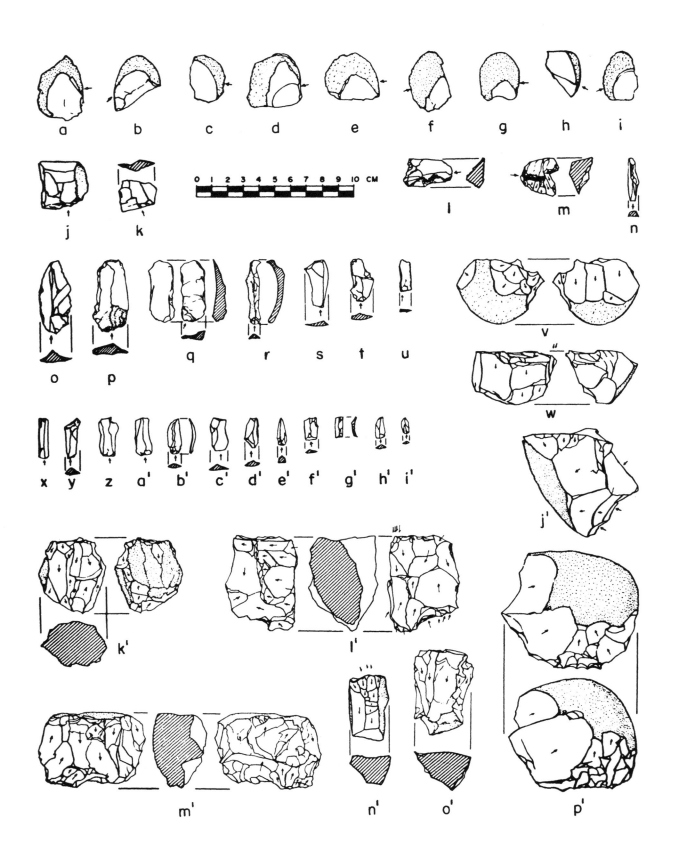

0 1 2 3 4 5 6 7 8 9 10 CM

TABLE 5.6 Sandstone Debitage and Tool Distribution Across All Sites

	Debitage and Tools					
Sites	Chunks	Split cobble segment	Nucleus, flake	Flakes, plain	Mano	Metate	Total
(Type No.)		(4)	(5)	(9)	(12)	(13)	
Arnero							
Balmori							
Bricia							
Ciriego							
Coberizas							
Colombres	+[a]				1[b]		1
Cuartamentero							
Cueto de la Mina							
Cueva del Río							
Fonfría							
Infierno							
La Franca							
La Cuevona							
La Lloseta							
La Loja		1		2	1[c]	1	5
La Meaza							
La Riera	2		2				4
Liencres, Surface							
Liencres, Level 1							
Llanes							
Lledías							
Penicial							
Tres Calabres							
Vidiago							
No provenience							
Total	2	1	2	2	2	1	10

+ = Items present but frequency not specified or unknown.
a. A considerable quantity of fire-cracked and blackened sandstone chunks was recovered.
b. Bifacial
c. Unifacial

TABLE 5.7 Limestone Debitage and Tool Distribution Across All Sites

	Limestone Debitage and Tools					
Sites	Stalactite fragments	Cobble hammerstone	Chunks	Flakes	Blades	Picks, atypical	Total
(Type No.)		(18)		(9)	(14)	(4)	
Arnero							
Balmori	1						1
Bricia							
Ciriego							
Coberizas							
Colombres							
Cuartamentero							
Cueto de la Mina							
Cueva del Río							
Fonfría		1					1
Infierno							
La Franca							
La Cuevona							
La Lloseta							
La Loja			1	4			5
La Meaza						2[a]	2
La Riera	2			8	1		11
Liencres, Surface				1			1
Liencres, Level 1							
Llanes							
Lledías	1						1
Penicial					1		1
Tres Calabres							
Vidiago							
No provenience							
Total	4	1	1	13	2	2	23

+ = Item present but frequency not specified or unknown.
a. Of coarse limestone, pick classification debatable.

Figure 5.4. Asturian debitage from Cantabria: *a—i,* secondary decortication flakes; *j, k,* pick trimming flakes; *l, m,* platform renewal flakes; *n, hojita del borde de nucleo; o—u,* small blades; *v,* mixed flake-bladelet nucleus; *w, j',* flake nuclei; *x—i',* bladelets; *k'—m', o',* mixed flake-bladelet nuclei; *n',* bladelet nucleus; *p',* flake nucleus with some retouch on the edge of the striking platform. Material: *a—k, o, s—w, j', p'* are of quartzite; *l—n, p—r, x—i', k'—o'* are of chert or flint. (Excavator and storage location of specimens are listed in Appendix C.)

TABLE 5.8

Lithic Material: Summary Statistics

Categories	All Sites		Liencres		Other Sites	
	No.	%	No.	%	No.	%
Raw Material						
Quartzite	1167	0.387	225	0.140	942	0.669
Flint	1721	0.571	1370	0.854	351	0.249
Quartz	90	0.029	8	0.005	82	0.058
Sandstone	10	0.003			10	0.007
Limestone	23	0.008	1	0.001	22	0.016
Total	3011	0.998	1604	1.000	1407	0.999
Debitage						
Unmodified pebbles	36	0.015	12	0.008	24	0.025
Unmodified cobbles	44	0.018	12	0.008	32	0.034
Unmodified nodules	1				1	0.001
Split cobble segments	43	0.018	16	0.011	27	0.028
Nucleus flake	86	0.036	33	0.023	53	0.056
Nucleus blade	9	0.004	2	0.001	7	0.007
Nucleus bladelet	9	0.004	5	0.003	4	0.004
Nucleus mixed	26	0.011	15	0.010	11	0.012
Flakes, plain	990	0.412	429	0.296	561	0.592
Flakes, primary decort.	53	0.022	51	0.035	2	0.002
Flakes, secondary decort.	522	0.217	521	0.359	1	0.001
Flakes, core renewal	13	0.005	10	0.007	3	0.003
Flakes, trimming	307	0.128	228	0.157	79	0.083
Blades	70	0.029	25	0.017	45	0.047
Bladelets	188	0.078	93	0.064	95	0.100
Various, debitage	3	0.001			3	0.003
Total	2400	0.998	1452	0.999	948	0.998

Debitage accounted for 0.797 of all lithics.

Categories	All Sites		Liencres		Other Sites	
Heavy Duty Tools						
Pebble hammerstones	10	0.033	4	0.286	6	0.021
Cobble hammerstones	14	0.046			14	0.049
Asturian Pick, typical	168	0.556	5	0.357	163	0.566
Asturian Pick, atypical	14	0.046			14	0.049
Chopper, large	28	0.093	1	0.071	27	0.094
Chopper, small	15	0.050			15	0.052
Chopper, double	3	0.010			3	0.010
Chopping tool, large	9	0.030			9	0.031
Chopping tool, small	7	0.023	2	0.143	5	0.017
Chopping tool, double	2	0.007			2	0.007
Biface, partial	7	0.023			7	0.024
Manos	4	0.013			4	0.014
Metates	2	0.007	1	0.071	1	0.003
Hammerstone—chopper	3	0.010			3	0.010
Hammerstone—chopping tool	2	0.007			2	0.007
Various, heavy duty tools	14	0.046	1	0.071	13	0.045
Total	302	1.000	14	0.999	288	0.999

Heavy duty tools accounted for 0.101 of all lithics.

TABLE 5.8
(continued)

Categories	All Sites		Liencres		Other Sites	
	No.	%	No.	%	No.	%
Small Tools						
Endscraper, simple	2	0.008	1	0.007	1	0.008
Endscraper, on a flake	4	0.015			4	0.031
Endscraper, circular	2	0.008	1	0.007	1	0.008
Endscraper, keeled	1	0.004			1	0.008
Endscraper, nucleiform	38	0.144	22	0.162	16	0.125
Endscraper, thick shouldered	4	0.015	3	0.022	1	0.008
Endscraper, flat	3	0.011	2	0.015	1	0.008
Endscraper, atypical	3	0.011			3	0.023
Cont. ret. piece-1 edge	18	0.068	9	0.066	9	0.070
Cont. ret. piece-2 edges	4	0.015	2	0.015	2	0.016
Sidescraper, simple straight	5	0.019	2	0.015	3	0.023
Sidescraper, simple convex	8	0.030	4	0.029	4	0.031
Sidescraper, double convex-converging	1	0.004			1	0.008
Burin, straight dihedral	2	0.008			2	0.016
Burin, angle dihedral	1	0.004			1	0.008
Burin, angle on a break	17	0.064	12	0.088	5	0.039
Burin, multiple dihedral	5	0.019	1	0.007	4	0.031
Burin, multiple mixed	1	0.004	1	0.007		
Burin, flat	1	0.004	1	0.007		
Burin, nucleiform	2	0.008	1	0.007	1	0.008
Denticulate, flake	38	0.144	14	0.103	24	0.188
Denticulate, blade	3	0.011			3	0.023
Notch, flake	28	0.106	16	0.118	12	0.094
Wedge	3	0.011			3	0.023
Point, Mousterian	1	0.004			1	0.008
Point, Azilian	1	0.004			1	0.008
Point, pedunculate	1	0.004	1	0.007		
Point, microgravette	2	0.008	1	0.007	1	0.008
Perforator, typical	2	0.008	2	0.015		
Perforator, atypical	19	0.072	17	0.125	2	0.016
Bec, multiple	4	0.015	4	0.029		
Bec, alternating burin	1	0.004			1	0.008
Knives, naturally backed	2	0.008	2	0.015		
Truncated piece, oblique concave	1	0.004			1	0.008
Truncated piece, convex	1	0.004			1	0.008
Truncated piece, straight concave	2	0.008			2	0.016
Bladelets, backed	6	0.023	3	0.022	3	0.023
Bladelets, partially backed	4	0.015			4	0.031
Bladelets, notched	2	0.008	2	0.015		
Bladelets, denticulated	1	0.004			1	0.008
Bladelets, truncated	5	0.019	4	0.029	1	0.008
Bladelets, Dufour	1	0.004	1	0.007		
Endscraper-burin	1	0.004	1	0.007		
Endscraper-bec	1	0.004	1	0.007		
Notch-denticulate	1	0.004			1	0.008
Perforator-notch	3	0.011	1	0.007	2	0.016
Perforator-denticulate	1	0.004			1	0.008
Various, small tools	7	0.026	4	0.029	3	0.023
Total	264	1.004	136	0.996	128	1.002

Small tools accounted for 0.088 of all lithics.

range of tool types can be defined at Liencres than is recorded for any other single site. Imputed site function is a third source of variation. Liencres is an open-air site, where flint and quartzite knapping appear to have been the principal activities (Clark 1979a, b). By contrast, the cave sites of eastern Asturias and western Santander were located near occupation sites, although there is no good evidence that they were occupation centers themselves. Because of these essential differences, two sets of summary statistics are presented. One includes all sites; the second set excludes Liencres.

The data permit a generalized description of the industry as a whole, but other factors introduced by the unreliable nature of the sample suggest extreme caution. The fact that Liencres is overrepresented in the sample must be taken into consideration. Nonrepresentative samples from the cave sites and imputed functional differences between sites may introduce variation that can be neither adequately controlled nor explained.

For all sites taken together, debitage amounts to almost 80 percent of all lithic material. As elsewhere, unaltered flakes and blades make up most of the debitage. Because decortication flakes were distinguished only at the sites tested, plain, primary, and secondary decortication flakes are added together; flakes in general equal from 60 percent to 69 percent of total debitage. The larger figure from Liencres lends support to the suggestion made in Chapter 4 that the site is a knapping station, a hypothesis further reinforced by the relatively greater frequency (16 percent) of trimming flakes there, compared with other sites (8 percent). Bladelet frequencies oscillate between 6 percent and 10 percent; blade frequency does not exceed 5 percent. As noted, the distinction between blades and bladelets is an artificial one.

Across all sites, nuclei make up from 4 percent to 9 percent of the debitage total. The 4 percent figure at Liencres seems inconsistent with the suggestion that the site is a knapping station, but the high frequency of nucleiform endscrapers there suggests reuse of cores as they approached the point of exhaustion. Nuclei that are regularized by consistent, undercutting "stepped" retouch around the circumference of the striking platform are classified as nucleiform endscrapers rather than cores. They are common at Liencres and compensate for a low frequency of unretouched cores. For all sites, flake cores (2 to 5 percent) and mixed cores (approximately 1 percent) are most commonly found.

Heavy duty tools represent 10 percent of all lithics. Relative frequencies for Liencres are misleading and inflated because of the small sample size (14 specimens). Although relative frequencies for Liencres must be viewed with caution, heavy duty tools do show a high association with the conchero sites; except for picks, they are extremely rare in Liencres.

For the cave sites, picks are greatly overrepresented in the sample, a reflection of the value placed on them as an archaeological guide fossil. Picks were always saved for museum collections while other material might be discarded. Hammerstones are present in low but significant quantities (2 to 5 percent), along with a few partial bi-

faces (less than 2.5 percent). Picks again excepted, choppers and chopping tools are the most numerous single subcategory; as a group they equal about 21 percent of the heavy duty tools. Large choppers are most prevalent (9 percent), but small choppers are also common (5 percent). Large (3 percent) and small (approximately 2 percent) chopping tools are present but in lower frequencies. Double forms are rare (less than 1 percent).

Small tools constitute almost 9 percent of the lithic total. Endscrapers are the most important single tool group; they make up between 21.3 percent and 21.9 percent of the total. Liencres (21.3 percent) and the group consisting of the rest of the sites (21.9 percent) show remarkably little variation in the relative frequency of endscrapers, and nucleiform endscrapers form the most prevalent type in both cases. At Liencres, nucleiform endscrapers account for 16 percent of the small tool total; in the other sites, the figure is 12.5 percent. Simple, circular, and flat-shouldered endscrapers are also comparable between the two groups, although the three types occur in low frequencies. The cave sites show a significantly higher frequency of flake (3 percent) and atypical (2 percent) endscrapers, whereas Liencres contains a relatively greater number of thick-shouldered forms (more than 2 percent; cave sites, less than 1 percent).

Continuously retouched pieces and sidescrapers exhibit the same kind of intergroup consistency. Pieces continuously retouched on one side make up between 6.6 percent (Liencres) and 7 percent (cave sites) of the total. Pieces continuously retouched on two sides are rare (less than 2 percent) in both groups. Simple straight sidescrapers account for 1.5 percent at Liencres, 2.3 percent in the cave sites. The simple convex form varies even less (2.9 percent at Liencres, 3.1 percent at cave sites), but all sidescraper frequencies are low.

Burins, on the other hand, show little intergroup consistency. Angle burins made on breaks constitute the most numerous type in both the cave site group (4 percent) and at Liencres (9 percent). Multiple dihedral burins equal 3 percent of the small tool subtotal in the cave sites, less than 1 percent at Liencres. The other types are rare.

Flake denticulates make up from 10 percent (Liencres) to 19 percent (cave sites) of the small tool total. Flake notches are also common in both groups, with frequencies varying between 9 percent (cave sites) and 12 percent (Liencres).

Perforators show little intergroup consistency. Atypical perforators (or becs) are most prevalent both in the cave sites and at Liencres, but relative frequencies range from less than 2 percent (cave sites) to 12.5 percent (Liencres). Perforators in general are much more common at Liencres than in the cave sites.

Retouched bladelets equal 7 percent (cave sites) and 7.3 percent (Liencres) of the total number of small tools in the two groups. Prior to the excavations in unquestionably Asturian levels in La Riera and Balmori in 1969, no bladelets had been reported from an Asturian site. Because the assemblage perhaps overlaps with, and in any event can be demonstrated to succeed, the Azilian, the

TABLE 5.9
Bone and Antler Tool Distribution Across All Sites

Sites	Worked Bone									
	Points, oval cross section	Points, rectangular cross section	Punches, awls, perforators	Sharpened splinter needle fragments	Antler tips	Perforated batons	Bone with cutting marks	Engraved fragments	Various	Total
(Type No.)	(1)	(2)	(3)	(4)	(5)	(6)	(7)	(8)	(9)	
Arnero			1						1	2
Balmori	3		1				11		1[a]	16
Bricia	1				2[b]					3
Ciriego										
Coberizas				1[c]						1
Colombres										
Cuartamentero										
Cueto de la Mina										
Cueva del Río										
Fonfría[d]						1			1[e]	2
Infierno										
La Franca										
La Cuevona										
La Lloseta										
La Loja					1		2			3
La Meaza		1					2			3
La Riera	2		1	3			26			32
Liencres, Surface										
Liencres, Level 1										
Llanes										
Lledías										
Penicial										
Tres Calabres						1				1
Vidiago					1[f]					1
No provenience										
Total	6	1	3	4	4	2	37	4	3	64

a. Bone compressors.
b. An antler tip, much used, showing polishing and smoothing at tip; and an antler tip encrusted with calcium carbonate, showing some signs of battering through possible use as an antler flaker.
c. A needle or fine awl fragment; the polished bone cylinder is broken and burned at both ends and all surfaces show smoothing and striae from polishing and use.
d. Some human bone is mixed in with this collection, including four parietal fragments and one piece of an ulna.
e. Fragment of a rectangular sectioned piece.
f. Antler tip, heavily polished, no battering; deeply incised at base, which is broken.

occurrence of bladelets is not particularly surprising.

Although bladelets occur both at Liencres and in the cave sites, except for backed bladelets, the subtypes have different relative frequencies in the two groups. The backed bladelets make up 2.2 percent of the small tools at Liencres and 2.3 percent of the small tool total in the cave site group. Partially backed bladelets occur in some frequency (3 percent) in the cave sites; they are absent at Liencres. The reverse is true for notched bladelets (1.5 percent at Liencres). Truncated bladelets occur in both groups, but are much more prevalent at Liencres (3 percent) than in the cave sites (less than 1 percent).

Table 5.9 summarizes the few bone tools recovered. The prevalence of bone fragments with cutting marks at those sites where adequate samples were available suggests that at least secondary butchering was done at or near the cave sites, a conclusion borne out by preliminary analysis of fauna from the 1976–1978 seasons at La Riera (Straus and others 1981). No faunal material was preserved at Liencres.

Asturian concheros are not entirely devoid of ceramic material (Table 5.10). Pottery occurs at five sites (Bricia, Lledías, La Lloseta, La Riera, Las Cáscaras), but associational evidence is questionable in three of them. One of the sherds from Bricia is a fragment of incised ware from the Iron Age Castro period (500–100 B.C.), suggesting some disturbance in the Asturian deposits there. Like most objects from that site, the phallus from Lledías is suspect. There is no detailed provenience data for the La Lloseta material. Carballo (1924: 138–141) supposedly found pottery in the Las Cáscaras concheros, but no details are given. The remaining sherds, which appear to be in situ finds, are remnants of crude, handturned, brown ware vessels, devoid of ornamentation.

Picks

Because they were invariably salvaged by excavators and museum curators alike, picks are numerically the

TABLE 5.10
**Miscellaneous Artifact
Distribution Across All Sites**

Sites	Potsherd, hand-turned	Pottery object	Hematite nodules	Ochre nodules	Ground shale or slate fragments	Total
			Artifacts			
Arnero						
Balmori					1	1
Bricia	2[a]					2
Ciriego						
Coberizas						
Colombres			1			1
Cuartamentero						
Cueto de la Mina						
Cueva del Río						
Fonfría						
Infierno						
La Franca						
La Cuevona				1[b]		1
La Lloseta	3					3
La Loja						
La Meaza						
La Riera	4			1		5
Liencres Surface						
Liencres Level 1						
Llanes						
Lledías		1[c]				1
Penicial				1		1
Tres Calabres						
Vidiago						
No provenience						
Total	9	1	1	2	2	15

a. Both hand turned; one is the common crude brownware, the other is an Iron Age Castro Period sherd (500–100 B.C.) with an incised design, almost certainly intrusive.
b. Battered on both ends, one surface is highly polished.
c. Lightly fired pottery phallus.

most abundant tool type in Asturian collections today; that frequency, however, does not reflect the proportional occurrence of picks in Asturian assemblages. The measurable attributes of picks can be treated statistically to determine if significant size and shape modes existed within the pick sample, and if so, whether these correspond to particular sites or groups of sites. Such subgroups might be expected to occur if picks were manufactured with different (albeit general) functions in mind (Clark 1976c). Four attributes were selected for analysis; they were computed in centimeters using the axis of symmetry (axis of the piece) as a basis for calculation. Orientation for measurement is shown in Figure 5.5.

Pick length is defined as the maximum vertical dimension of the piece, measured from the base along its axis of symmetry. Width is the maximum horizontal dimension measured at any point perpendicular to the axis of symmetry. Thickness is maximum thickness, measured at any point along the axis of symmetry. Distance from base determines the maximum vertical extent of cortex (unflaked surface, in this case) preserved along the central spine of the pick when measured from its base along the axis of symmetry. Formulae used in the calculation of summary statistics appear in Table 5.11 and summary statistics for picks are given in Table 5.12. Observations on length (x_l), width (x_w), and distance from base (x_d)

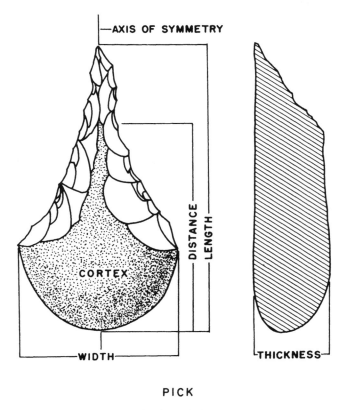

Figure 5.5. Definition of pick measurements.

were taken on a sample of 141 picks; observations on thickness (x_θ) were taken on a sample of 118 picks. A total of 168 typical picks was recorded for the Asturian as a whole (see Table 5.2). Discrepancies appear because a number of specimens were embedded in blocks of conchero; their proveniences could be established with reasonable certainty, but they could not be removed for cleaning and measurement. Picks shown in scaled photographs or drawings in various monographs, but which could not be located in 1969, were also included. They amounted to fewer than a dozen pieces.

Figure 5.6 indicates the frequency distributions of the four attributes selected for analysis, plotted on a scale graduated in centimeters. Only those observations utilized in the Kruskal-Wallis H Test are given. Sites containing fewer than three observations are omitted. Inspection suggests that width and thickness measurements are approximately normally distributed across sites. The graph for length is ambiguous. Distance seems to deviate from the normal curve to a considerable degree.

In a normal distribution, the interval $(\bar{x} \pm s)$ contains 68.3 percent of the observations in the total distribution. This statistic can be used as a guide to determine whether a distribution is normal or not.

Ignoring site provenience and combining all samples, the mean sample length of picks is 8.21 cm and the standard deviation is 1.726 cm. It is to be expected then, that approximately 68.3 percent of the observations on length will be between 6.48 cm to 9.94 cm, if the population is

TABLE 5.11
Formulae and Notation Used in Statistical Calculations of Lithic Data

Mean:

$$\bar{x} = \frac{\sum_{i=1}^{n} X_i}{n}$$

where: $\bar{x}$ is the sample mean
    n is the number of observations
    i is the index of summation
    Σ is a summation symbol

Variance:

$$s^2 = \frac{\sum_{i=1}^{n} (x_i - \bar{x}_i)^2}{n - 1}$$

where: s^2 is the sample variance

Note: s^2 is an unbiased estimator of the population parameter σ^2
s, the positive square root of s^2, is the sample standard deviation
x is an unbiased estimator of the population parameter μ
x_{med} is the median; the median is any number which neither exceeds nor is exceeded by more than half of the observations

Kruskal-Wallis H Test:

$$H = \frac{\frac{12}{N(N+1)} \sum_{i=1}^{k} \left(\frac{R_i^2}{n_i} \right) - 3(N+1)}{C}$$

where: C is a correction term for ties, and:

$$C = \frac{1 - \Sigma T_1}{N^3 - N}$$

where: $T = t^3 - t$, T is the number of ties per set. Summation is over all sets of ties; if no ties, C = 1.

N is the total sample size
k is the number of groups
R_i are the ranks, summed by sample, then squared

Note: H has a chi-square distribution, on k − 1 degrees of freedom.

TABLE 5.11
(continued)

Nearest Neighbor Statistic:

$$R_n = \frac{\Sigma r / N}{.5\sqrt{\rho}}$$

where: r = measurements of distance to nearest neighbor: the sum of all of them

N = the number of measurements taken in the observed population (the number of sites)

A = area in units comparable to units of measurement used in r

ρ = density of the observed distribution as given by A/N

Range of R:
Max R_n = 2.15: points are as far as possible from one another, forming a regular, hexagonal distribution

Min R_n = 0: points are all clustered together in one single spot within A or occur in pairs, triplets, and so on

If R_n = 1.00: points are randomly distributed

Test of Significance: $c = \dfrac{\bar{r}_A - \bar{r}_E}{\sigma_{\bar{r}_E}}$, where:

$\bar{r}_A = \dfrac{\Sigma r}{N}$, the mean of the series of distances to nearest neighbor

$\bar{r}_E = \dfrac{1}{2\sqrt{\rho}}$, the mean distance to nearest neighbor expected in an infinitely large random distribution of density ρ

$\sigma_{\bar{r}_E} = \dfrac{0.26136}{\sqrt{N\rho}}$, the standard error of the mean distance to nearest neighbor in a randomly distributed population of density ρ

c is normally distributed with mean 0 and variance 1, a standard normal deviate
Note: This is a test of nonrandomness.

Kolmogorov-Smirnov Two Sample Test:

$$C \sqrt{\frac{n_1 + n_2}{n_1 n_2}}$$

where formula gives critical value of D: if Kolmogorov-Smirnov D statistic (greatest observed difference: $n_1 - n_2$) is greater than the critical value, reject H_o at the level of significance indicated

where n_1 and n_2 are the sample sizes, and
C = 1.63 for α (Probability of Type I error) = 0.01
C = 1.95 for α (Probability of Type I error) = 0.001

TABLE 5.12
Picks: Summary Statistics

$\bar{x} = \sum_{i=1}^{n} x_i/n$ Sites	n	Σn_l	$\bar{x}_l$	Σn_w	$\bar{x}_w$	Σn_θ	$\bar{x}_\theta$	Σn_d	$\bar{x}_d$
Arnero	13	92.7	7.1	71.6	5.5	45.0	3.5	56.7	4.4
Balmori	2	18.2	9.1	11.9	5.9			12.4	6.2
Bricia	1	7.9	7.9	5.7	5.7	3.1	3.1	0.0	0.0
Ciriego	1	8.8	8.8	4.8	4.8			4.8	4.8
Coberizas	10	79.0	7.9	57.8	5.8	31.3	3.1	33.6	3.4
Colombres	3	25.6	8.5	16.2	5.4			11.5	3.8
Cuartamentero	8	73.7	9.2	49.5	6.2	21.6	2.7	37.6	4.7
Cueto de la Mina	6	44.1	7.4	30.6	5.1	18.2	3.0	30.1	5.0
Fonfría	11	83.7	7.6	61.4	5.6	31.1	2.8	48.4	4.4
Infierno	2	22.7	11.35	12.1	6.05	6.6	3.3	7.6	3.8
La Franca	1	10.7	10.7	5.8	5.8	2.7	2.7	7.3	7.3
La Loja	17	125.7	7.4	95.3	5.6			59.0	3.5
La Riera	36	301.9	8.4	202.5	5.7	109.2	3.0	146.6	4.1
La Lloseta	1	11.2	11.2	5.9	5.9	3.4	3.4	8.1	8.1
Liencres	5	47.6	9.5	30.3	6.1	15.7	3.1	26.9	5.4
Lledías	11	83.3	7.6	56.9	5.2	28.3	2.6	34.0	3.1
Tres Calabres	2	14.2	7.1	11.5	5.75	6.1	3.05	9.0	4.5
Penicial	11	106.5	9.7	61.7	5.6	41.5	3.8	54.9	5.0
	141	1157.5	8.21	791.5	5.61	363.8	3.08	588.5	4.17
	N	ΣN_l	μ_l	ΣN_w	μ_w	ΣN_θ	μ_θ	ΣN_d	μ_d

σ_l = 1.726 σ_l^2 = 2.98
σ_w = 0.863 σ_w^2 = 0.745
σ_θ = 0.530 σ_θ^2 = 0.281
σ_d = 1.711 σ_d^2 = 2.928

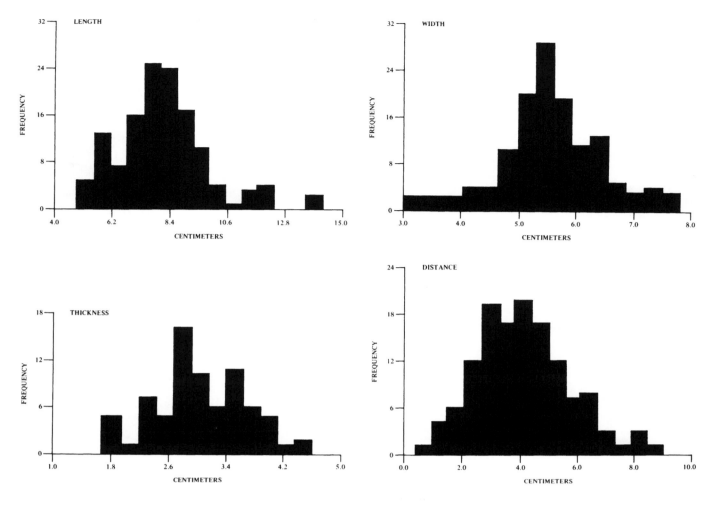

Figure 5.6. Frequency distribution of pick measurements: *a,* length; *b,* width; *c,* thickness; *d,* distance.

normally distributed. By inspection, 72.3 percent of the observations are within the stated interval. Mean sample distance is 4.17 cm; the standard deviation is 1.711 cm. The interval ($\bar{x} \pm s$) is 2.46 cm to 5.88 cm, and 73.1 percent of the observations are within the stated interval. The mean sample width for picks is 5.61 cm; the standard deviation from that mean is only 0.863 cm. The interval ($\bar{x} \pm s$) is 4.75 cm to 6.47 cm and 77.3 percent of the observations are within those limits. Data for thickness are even more tightly clustered about the mean (3.08 cm). The standard deviation is only 0.530 cm, giving an interval ($\bar{x} \pm s$) of 2.55 cm to 3.61 cm, and 74.6 percent of the observations are within the stated limits.

Width and thickness are less variable than either length or distance, as indicated by the size of their standard deviations. The information in Figure 5.6 suggests that width and thickness are approximately normally distributed across sites, although the mode is more pronounced and the tails shorter than would be expected of a normal curve. Skewing is apparently absent in both cases; the graphs are symmetrical. Ranges are relatively

tightly defined, compared with those of length and distance, and standard deviations are correspondingly small.

Length and distance are characterized by curves that deviate from normality, in spite of their normal-appearing interval values. Both graphs are unimodal but there is apparent skewing to the left in each case. Skewing is marked for distance. Ranges are much wider than those of width and thickness, and standard deviations are comparatively large.

In order to compare variables with different mean values, I measured variability relative to the mean (rather than in absolute units). Here the coefficient of variation, or the relative standard deviation from the mean ($s/\bar{x}$) is used (Wallis and Roberts 1967: 256). This statistic was calculated for all four attributes. Length (21 percent), width (15 percent), and thickness (17 percent) form an internally consistent group with respect to variation about the mean. Distance (41 percent), however, has a much larger coefficient of variation, almost double that of length.

These data apparently reflect general selection for oval, flattened, quartzite cobbles from the range of raw material available in Cantabria. Length appears to be more variable (less important) within the stated limits than does either width or thickness. Extent of cortex, as measured along the axis of symmetry, may be simply a function of length and possibly should be discarded as a variable.

Kruskal-Wallis Test

With respect to picks, it has been assumed that all Asturian sites constitute samples drawn from a single population. If modalities do exist within the population of picks, as defined by their metrical attributes, they may show correlations with geographically restricted areas within the Cantabrian region. Internal variation may reflect units of more intensive interaction within the area defined by *all* Asturian sites. (It is preferable to use attributes from whole ranges of artifacts to assess internal variation, but sampling problems preclude that approach for Asturian remains.)

The statistical method most amenable to testing this kind of variance is an extension of the Wilcoxon Two-Sample test, called the Kruskal-Wallis H test; it uses a nonparametric one-way analysis of variance model (Wallis and Roberts 1967: 599–601; Siegel 1956: 184–193). The Kruskal-Wallis test analyzes the amount of variance among ranked series of observations for a single variable (for example, length). It tests the null hypothesis (H_o) that k samples come from the *same* population or from identical populations with respect to the *median* of the original observations. The alternative hypothesis (H_1) is that they do not. The resulting statistic (H) has a chi-square distribution with k−1 degrees of freedom. Alternatively, the normal approximation $J = \sqrt{2H} - \sqrt{2k-3}$ can be used with reasonable accuracy if chi-square tables are not available (Wallis and Roberts 1967: 599).

The Kruskal-Wallis test has few constraints, making it suitable for the data available here. No assumptions are made regarding the shape of the underlying distribution. There are no restrictions with respect to the number of samples, although special tables are used for k = 3 (where k is the number of groups); calculations become tedious for large k, and ranking is arduous for large total sample size. All samples should contain at least three observations for the chi-square distribution, however, to give a high degree of confidence in the answer. At least ordinal measurement is required. Samples need not be of equal size. When compared with the most powerful parametric test appropriate to the problem (assuming an underlying normal distribution), the F test, the Kruskal-Wallis one-way analysis of variance has a power-efficiency level of 95.5 percent (Andrews 1954; Siegel 1956: 192, 193).

All observations from k samples are ranked, ignoring individual samples, from 1 to N. Tied observations are given the mean of the ranks for which they are tied. Ranks for each sample are summed (ΣR_i) and H is calculated from the formula given in Table 5.11. If many observations are tied, H is divided by a correction term, C ($0 < C \leqslant 1$).

The results of the test confirmed earlier observations based on the measures of central tendency discussed above. For length, N = 131 and k = 11. Samples containing fewer than three observations (sites with fewer than three picks on which measurements were taken) were omitted because of constraints in the test. For this and the other variables, the level of significance for rejection of H_o was arbitrarily set at $\alpha = 0.01$. The test *rejected* the null hypothesis (that all lengths were drawn from the same population). H = 25.83, with ten degrees of freedom. The probability of a Type I error (rejecting H_o when, in fact, it is true) was very small; the alternative hypothesis (H_1) is thus accepted—there are significant differences between sites in the population of pick lengths.

For widths, N = 131 and k = 11, and for this variable the test *accepted* the null hypothesis—there are no significant differences in the population of pick widths. H = 8.829, with 10 degrees of freedom.

For thickness, N = 75 (due to some measurements inadvertently omitted or unobtainable in the field) and k = 8. Predictably, given the summary statistics discussed above, the test *accepted* the null hypothesis—there are *no* significant differences in the population of pick thicknesses. H = 17.57, with 7 degrees of freedom.

For distance I expected a result paralleling that of length, because distance may be considered as a function of length. Length and distance are dimensions that reflect human modification of the original cobble, while width and thickness probably record the unaltered dimensions of the raw material selected for pick manufacturing. For distance, N = 131 and k = 11. If distance did vary with pick length, the test should have rejected the null hypothesis, but it did not do so. H = 2.90, with ten degrees of freedom. Reference to a chi-square table indicates that the value tabulated has a probability of $\alpha = 0.99$ of Type I error. These figures indicate that the null hypothesis is accepted—there are no significant differences in the population of distances.

This result, which I am inclined to reject for the following reasons, may be due to marked differences in the site variances for distance. Although the test makes no assumptions with respect to the shapes of the underlying distributions, it does assume those distributions are the same, or similar, for each group (site), which implies that the sample variances are approximately equal. It is usual procedure to assume that these two conditions are met, although the possibility exists that they may not be. Small sample sizes within sites preclude reliable estimation of these conditions in the present case. The ranges for each site, however, provide grounds for suspicion that site variances are not equal for distance. To support this suggestion, the means, medians, minima, and maxima were plotted for all sites used in the Kruskal-Wallis test. These plots, which show the range by site for all four variables, are reproduced in Figures 5.7 and 5.8. Both length and distance exhibit considerable variation, so that the results of this test must be regarded as inconclusive. However, if 10th and 90th percentile points are plotted (not shown), the ranges become more regular because outliers are excluded. Site specific ranges for distance are the broadest of the four attributes plotted; in other

SITES

Liencres
Penicial
Cuartamentero
Colombres
La Riera
Coberizas
Fonfría
Lledías
La Loja
Cueto de la Mina
Arnero

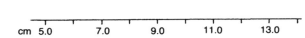

LENGTH

cm 5.0   7.0   9.0   11.0   13.0

SITES

Penicial
Arnero
Liencres
Coberizas
Cueto de la Mina
La Riera
Fonfría
Lledías

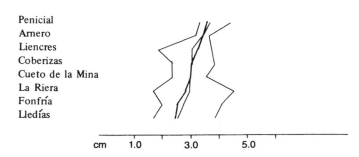

cm 1.0   3.0   5.0

THICKNESS

Liencres
Cuartamentero
La Riera
La Loja
Penicial
Fonfría
Colombres
Coberizas
Arnero
Lledías
Cueto de la Mina

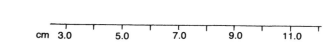

WIDTH

cm 3.0   5.0   7.0   9.0   11.0

Figure 5.7. Picks: length and width ordered by medians, with mean and range indicated.

Cueto de la Mina
Liencres
Cuartamentero
Fonfría
Arnero
Penicial
La Riera
La Loja
Colombres
Coberizas
Lledías

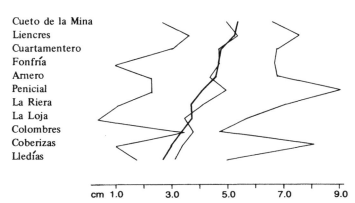

cm 1.0   3.0   5.0   7.0   9.0

DISTANCE

Figure 5.8. Picks: thickness and distance ordered by medians, with mean and range indicated.

words, a masking effect is present. It is conceivable that the two measures of central tendency (median, mean) are similar for all samples (sites), but that the variances of each site are not the same. It is possible that this factor may be influencing the outcome of the test.

If it is postulated, either because of human interaction or the availability of raw material for tool manufacture, that geographical location is the determining factor in the variation of any given attribute, then pick lengths should be a function of geographical proximity among sites. Under the first condition, human interaction, picks from sites close to one another should have lengths that vary little, compared with sites or site groups situated farther away (ignoring temporal variation). Under the second condition, similarity of raw material, temporal variation is irrelevant, assuming that a single source or similar sources were exploited during the period of site occupancy. Picks from sites located distant from one another should be dissimilar.

The Kruskal-Wallis test indicated that pick lengths are not the same across all sites. By looking at actual values of length for each site, sites may be grouped together impressionistically. This was done by using means and, secondarily, medians as ordering criteria (Fig. 5.9). It is interesting to note that geographical relationship was preserved in that the sites are more or less linearly oriented along an east-west axis. Arnero was arbitrarily picked as the center.

Nearest Neighbor Analysis

Another approach that allows for the objective assessment of site groupings is Nearest Neighbor analysis (P. J. Clark and Evans 1954). This method determines whether or not objects (sites in this case) are clustered geographically and, within limits, indicates the degree and type of clustering. The area was defined as the coastal strip containing these sites. The unit of measurement used was centimeters. Spanish and German Army maps (1:50,000) were used as a basis for calculation. The width of the coastal strip was set equal to 12.5 km. I believe this to be a conservative estimation; the figure usually given is

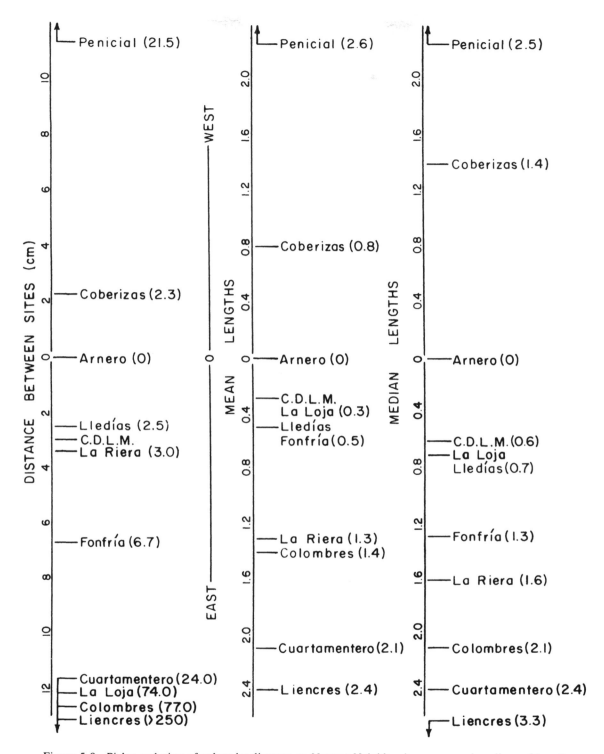

Figure 5.9. Picks: ordering of values by distance to Nearest Neighbor by means and medians of length.

about 15 km. The length of the area was determined by the distance between the westernmost site (of those used in the Kruskal-Wallis test, Penicial) and that situated farthest east (La Loja). Liencres, an obvious geographical outlier, was excluded. The sites show a considerable degree of clustering with $R_n = 0.673$ ($\Sigma_r = 54.5$ cm, A = 2642.2 cm^2, N = 10 and $\rho = 264.2$). The standard normal deviate, c, was calculated to determine the significance of the departure of the value obtained for R_n (0.673) from that expected if the sites were randomly distributed ($R_n = 1.00$, see Table 5.11). The value for c obtained was 2.0. There is only a 0.023 probability that this calculated value of R_n comes from a distribution with $R_n = 1$. Thus if the true value of R_n is 1, then R_n would equal or be less than 0.673 only about 2.3 percent of the time due to chance alone. The alternative hypothesis is accepted: the value is significantly different from that which would be expected if the sites were randomly distributed (1.00), tolerating a probability of Type I error (α) equal to 0.023.

Making use of the fact that the sites are not randomly distributed along the coast, sites can be grouped together based on geographical proximity; this grouping can be compared with the two previous groupings based on the mean and median lengths. Figure 5.9 shows the relationship obtained between the three orderings noted above. Correspondence between them is not complete, which is what would be expected if variation among pick lengths were simply a function of geographical proximity among sites. In particular, the (dubious) site of La Loja is out of sequence. Despite this, however, the general patterns of order and clustering are in high agreement.

Sites to the west of Arnero (Penicial, Coberizas) show the isolation that would be expected, given their geographical distance from the central group. The central group itself (Arnero, Cueto de la Mina, Lledías, Fonfría) is reasonably well reduplicated in all three orderings, although there is greater dispersion (note the position of La Riera) for the measures of central tendency than would be expected from the geographical ordering. Sites to the east of Arnero (Colombres, Cuartamentero, Liencres) show the metrical isolation expected, considering their geographical isolation from the other sites. The exception, as noted, is La Loja, which should have been grouped with Colombres. The position of La Loja in the central group is anomalous. The picks attributed to that site probably come from Balmori or one of the Posada area sites, in which case the fit would be considerably better. Provenience is a problem with the La Loja material (see Chapter 3). The general increase in pick length also noted both to the east and west of the central group (Fig. 5.9) is possibly due to increases in the length of available raw material (quartzite cobbles).

Choppers and Chopping Tools

In addition to picks, choppers and chopping tools also occur frequently in the collections studied. An attempt was made to assess the range of variability among all choppers and chopping tools for which data could be recorded. Only two attributes were used in the analysis, length and width, and they are defined the same as pick

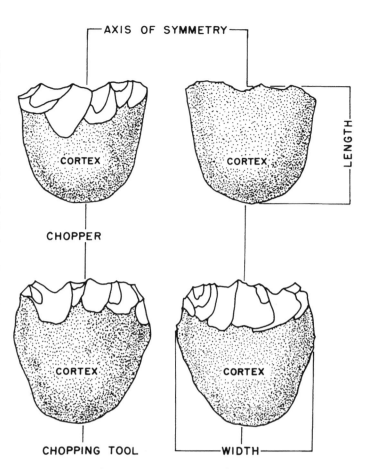

Figure 5.10. Definition of chopper and chopping tool measurements.

length and width. Pieces were oriented for measurement with the base down (Fig. 5.10). All measurements were taken in centimeters, using the axis of symmetry as the basis for calculations.

Sites are regarded as samples of n_i observations, drawn from a population consisting of k sites, with a total of N_i observations on any given variable. The summary statistics for both choppers and chopping tools are given in Table 5.13. Length (x_l) and width (x_w) were computed on samples drawn from a population of 36 choppers and 15 chopping tools.

For choppers across all sites, computation of population standard deviations suggests that length is more variable than width. Mean length is 8.16 cm, with a standard deviation equal to 3.46 cm. If the population of lengths is normally distributed, about 68 percent of the observations should be within the interval 4.70 cm to 11.62 cm; actually 64 percent are within the stated interval. It is concluded that the population of lengths is normally distributed, but samples are small and caution must be exercised in interpretation.

Mean width for choppers is 7.44 cm, with a standard deviation equal to 2.36 cm. If chopper widths are normally distributed, 68.3 percent of the observations should be within the range of 5.08 cm to 9.80 cm; actually no less than 83 percent are within the stated interval. The results suggest that chopper widths are not normally

TABLE 5.13
Choppers and Chopping Tools: Summary Statistics

$\bar{x} = \sum_{i=1}^{n} x_i/n$ Sites	Means									
	Choppers					Chopping Tools				
	n	Σn_l	$\bar{x}_l$	Σn_w	$\bar{x}_w$	n	Σn_l	$\bar{x}_l$	Σn_w	$\bar{x}_w$
Arnero	2	17.5	8.75	16.8	8.4	1	7.4	7.4	5.1	5.1
Balmori	3	26.1	8.7	21.8	7.3	3	22.6	7.5	19.7	6.6
Coberizas						1	10.5	10.5	6.7	6.7
Colombres	2	16.4	8.2	14.9	7.5					
Cuartamentero	10	88.5	8.85	78.9	7.9					
Fonfría	4	27.9	7.0	24.0	6.0	1	10.5	10.5	6.5	6.5
Infierno	1	15.1	15.1	9.5	9.5					
La Franca	7	44.9	6.4	43.9	6.3					
La Cuevona	1	8.5	8.5	7.4	7.4					
La Lloseta						1	7.0	7.0	9.1	9.1
La Loja	1	5.1	5.1	5.6	5.6	3	23.0	7.7	20.6	6.9
La Riera	1	7.9	7.9	12.6	12.6	2	20.5	10.25	9.2	4.6
Lledías						1	7.4	7.4	6.5	6.5
Liencres, Surface						1	4.8	4.8	5.8	5.8
Liencres, Level 1	1	11.1	11.1	9.3	9.3					
Penicial	3	24.8	8.3	23.0	7.7	1	5.7	5.7	6.2	6.2
	36	293.8	8.16	267.7	7.44	15	119.4	7.96	95.4	6.36
	N	ΣN_l	μ_l	ΣN_w	μ_w	N	ΣN_l	μ_l	ΣN_w	μ_w

$$\sigma_l = 3.46 \qquad \sigma_w = 2.36 \qquad \sigma_l = 2.26 \qquad \sigma_w = 1.44$$
$$\sigma_l^2 = 12.0 \qquad \sigma_w^2 = 5.57 \qquad \sigma_l^2 = 5.10 \qquad \sigma_w^2 = 2.08$$

distributed but, again, this may be due to small sample size. The Kruskal-Wallis H test was applied to the observations on chopper length from the sites of Balmori, Cuartamentero, Fonfría, La Franca, and Penicial (where n_l was greater than or equal to 3). Other sites were excluded because of their small sample size. As with picks, the objective was to determine whether the series of seemingly disparate sample medians could have been drawn from the same population. Total sample size was 27, from five sites. The level of significance for rejection of H_o was set at $\alpha = 0.01$. The test *accepted* the null hypothesis—all lengths were drawn from the same population. H = 2.07, with 4 degrees of freedom. There are *no* significant differences in the population of chopper lengths across the five sites evaluated.

For width, total sample size was again 27, with five groups. The test *accepted* the null hypothesis—all widths were drawn from the same population. H = 4.91, with 4 degrees of freedom. There are *no* significant differences in the population of chopper widths.

Chopping tools numbered only 15 specimens. Mean length was 7.96 cm, with a standard deviation of 2.26 cm. For a normal distribution about 68 percent of the observations on length should be within the interval 5.70 cm to 10.22 cm; actually only 54 percent of the observations are within the specified limits, but the departure from the expected value is probably due to small sample size.

For the width of chopping tools, the mean was equal to 6.36 cm, with a standard deviation of 1.44 cm. If the population is normally distributed, the 68 percent interval is 4.92 cm to 7.80 cm; actually 74 percent of the observations are within the stated limits. The population is probably normally distributed, but sample size is very

small, precluding a more definite statement on distribution. Data are not sufficient to permit calculation of the Kruskal-Wallis H statistic.

CONCLUSIONS

Asturian lithics clearly leave much to be desired in terms of their analytical potential, not only because of the likelihood of severe sampling problems but also because of the generally impoverished nature of the industry. What is available from the old and poorly-provenienced museum collections is highly selected, but nonetheless prompts the suggestion that lithic debris appears to have been relatively scarce in *all* Asturian sites so far known, with the exception of Liencres. Even recent tests by me at La Riera, Balmori, Coberizas, and Penicial, and by González Morales at La Franca (Mazaculos II)—all of which were conducted with the current concern for sample representativeness firmly in mind—have failed to produce industrial debris in appreciable quantities. Lithic debris is not a common component of these midden sites in general, implying (Liencres excepted) that the Asturian cave and rock shelter sites are the tangible remnants of a set of basically similar activities—perhaps dumps. Differences in lithic inventories do not throw into sharp relief possible functional distinctions among Asturian sites. The artifact inventories are sparse and monotonous, and are derived from sites located in similar microenvironmental circumstances (Chapter 7). Although clearly associated with sites used for habitation, as demonstrated by the discovery of an in situ floor at La Franca (González Morales 1978; González Morales and Marquez 1978), conchero deposits themselves do not necessarily indicate cave habitation.

6. FAUNAL REMAINS

Faunal material has been reported from all the 31 recorded sites except Liencres, the open-air site. Qualitative data pertinent to species exploited, however, exist for only 18 of these sites, and quantitative information is available for 10 sites. These data are used to specify resources exploited by Asturian groups, and to compare typically Asturian faunal spectra with those from concheros bracketing the Asturian in time. A microenvironmentally oriented evaluation of the principal species collected sheds light on the range and nature of extractive techniques, which are developed into a comprehensive model of subsistence and settlement in Chapter 7. The only Asturian pollen sample of reasonable adequacy is from Liencres (see Appendix A). The general picture is one of a long-standing and successful adaptation, based on intensive exploitation of a restricted spectrum of terrestrial and aquatic (principally estuarine) resources.

Data were drawn from site reports, conchero samples, excavated tests, and museum collections, and were variable in quality. Only approximations of species frequencies were provided in the literature, but some detailed quantitative information resulted from the conchero samples and tests. Museum collections were generally sparse and selective. Counts of individual animals represented and age and sex data are lacking in most cases for the mammals, and little information specifying body parts recovered is available. Faunal samples were judged too small to be meaningfully investigated for these variables by Dr. Jesús Altuna, vertebrate paleontologist at the Museo de San Telmo, San Sebastián, Guipúzcoa.

THE SUBSISTENCE BASE

Terrestrial Fauna

Table 6.1 summarizes the qualitative data available for the evaluation of the mammalian spectrum, and Table 6.2 presents more restricted quantitative information (Clark 1971b). The predominance of woodland species and species adapted to the forest margins is marked. Red deer (*Cervus elaphus*) are by far most common, both numerically and in terms of estimated meat yields. Roe deer (*Capreolus capreolus*) and wild boar (*Sus scrofa*) are prevalent but occur in lower frequencies. A secondary concentration of chamois (*Rupicapra rupicapra*) and ibex

(*Capra ibex*) is also indicated. The last are alpine species adapted to the rocky montane uplands found in the vicinity of most Asturian sites (Chapter 7). The only truly open country form, the horse (*Equus caballus*), occurs in low frequency.

This deer-dominated configuration first appears in the Upper Solutrean (Altuna 1972, Straus 1977) and becomes marked during the Cantabrian Lower Magdalenian (Freeman 1973). To date, it cannot be neatly correlated with a particular set of paleoclimatic conditions, nor with a particular site type, nor with a particular paleogeographic setting. What is significant is that basically similar faunal spectra can be identified with quite distinct culture-stratigraphic units when monitored in terms of their artifact contents. These varying associations suggest that adaptational shifts might not necessarily correspond to changes in the composition of artifact assemblages, although a case can be made for some marked similarities in the composition of the lithic components of at least some Upper Solutrean and Lower Magdalenian sites (Clark 1974b; Straus 1975b). It is naive, though, to expect a direct relationship between activity spectra and their artifactual residues, as Binford (1978a, b) has observed with respect to extant Eskimo campsites.

It is unfortunate that age and sex information is lacking and that the number of individual animals taken could not be calculated. Most of the structural characteristics of animal populations exploited can be reconstructed from the archaeological record if adequate samples are available. A sophisticated evaluation of faunal sample composition can generate testable hypotheses that have bearing on the extractive strategies employed by prehistoric men (Clark 1971a: 434–437). A great deal is known, for example, about the social behavior of red and roe deer (Darling 1963, Prior 1968). Group composition varies markedly throughout the annual cycle, according to age, sex, and locational parameters. Extractive strategies formulated on the basis of current behavioral patterns can be made quite explicit, and can be tailored to fit particular sets of well-defined environmental circumstances. Perhaps more important, they can take into account a wide variety of different hunting practices.

As a case in point, expected group compositions for red deer under natural conditions are given in Table 6.3. Data pertain to detailed studies of herds located on large tracts of open and forested land in Wester Ross, northwestern coastal Scotland (Darling 1963). Comparably detailed data are not available for Cantabria, although the regions are similar in certain respects. Patterns vary from area to area, of course, due to local topographical circumstances and climatic factors.

The data in Table 6.3 indicate that what might best be exploited by the archaeologist for the purposes of hypothesis evaluation are the seasonal fluctuations in the age and sex composition of the herds. Tooth eruption, abrasion, and variation in antler form are useful criteria for aging red deer populations and for determining, within limits, the seasons during which kills were made. Comparable data are available for some of the other large ungulates (Prior 1968; Kurt 1968).

Most of the structural characteristics of the major economic species, at least, can be extracted from the literature of animal ethology and be incorporated into tests of hypotheses about procurement and processing stratagems if adequate archaeological samples are available. Unfortunately, sufficiently precise data are not available for the Asturian, and only a crude reconstruction of the faunal aspects of the Asturian ecosphere can be attempted.

Environmental Reconstruction: Mammalian Fauna

The mammalian faunal spectrum suggests an environmental situation like that known historically for Cantabria prior to extensive deforestation during and after the Middle Ages. Red deer (*Cervus elaphus*) are found most commonly in microenvironmental zones characterized by open, temperate, mixed deciduous-coniferous woodlands, at low to moderate elevations (0–500 m) in areas with adequate moisture regimes (Darling 1963; Walker and others 1968; Van den Brink 1967: 164, 165). They occur in lower frequency in mixed woods where conifers predominate. The lowland forests of post-Pleistocene Cantabria have favored deciduous species.

The habitat of roe deer (*Capreolus capreolus*) is more restrictive. Young deciduous woodlands are preferred in microenvironmental zones where dense undergrowth is present. Roe deer have a tendency to occupy copses near more extensive woodlands; when in fully wooded country, they favor the forest edge. Stands of birch (*Betula vulgaris*), if present, are said to be preferred over other deciduous species (Corbet 1966: 162). Roe deer are more tolerant than red deer of areas where no surface water is present (Prior 1968: 67).

Wild boar (*Sus scrofa*) occupy similar habitats, although they prefer marshy country characterized by small lakes and streams (Van den Brink 1967: 152, 155). Dense undergrowth is a prerequisite (Morris 1965: 369). Rocky areas are preferred lairs, but fallen trees and dense thickets suffice (Walker and others 1968).

The literature on red and roe deer, and on the wild boar, contains much information on diet. A dietary table compiled by Darling (1963: 149–153) lists over 135 species of plants eaten by red deer on a regular or sporadic basis, cross-indexed by relative frequency of consumption and by macro- and microenvironmental proveniences. Diet varies markedly between geographical regions, however. Within regions, plant associations are distributed differentially according to microenvironmental zones. It is risky, therefore, to use food preferences to flesh out paleoenvironmental reconstructions, especially if pollen spectra are not available for comparison. The woodland species most prevalent in Asturian deposits, though catholic in their tastes, exhibit tendencies to eat the following general kinds of plants.

Red and roe deer are silvan browsers; the mainstays of their diets include deciduous foliage, twigs, and berries such as cottonwood (*Populus* spp.), willow (*Salix* spp.), birch (*Betula* spp.), alder (*Alnus* spp.), and oak (*Quercus* spp.). Conifers are usually spurned. During the fall, mosses and lichens of various kinds are consumed in quantity. Evergreen gorse (*Ulex* spp.), heather (*Calluna* spp., *Erica* spp.), sedges (*Carex* spp.) and broom (*Genista* spp.), all locally available along the coast and on high ground, are eaten during the winter months. Grasses (*Agrostis* spp.) and fungi are also consumed occasionally. Genera cited are those that occur in Cantabria today (Guinea Lopez 1953; Mapa Forestal de España 1966).

Wild boar consume various roots, tubers, bulbs, nuts, acorns (*Quercus* spp.), fruit, and beechmast (*Fagus* spp.), but are more carnivorous in their habits than are the cervids. Flesh foods include occasional carrion, insect larvae, rodents, young rabbits (*Oryctolagus cuniculus*), snails (*Helix* spp.) and birds' eggs.

The presence of the pyrenean ibex (*Capra ibex*) and chamois (*Rupicapra rupicapra*) suggests exploitation of the alpine zones located a few kilometers inland from the forested coastal plain. Ibex are a species adapted to the open, rocky country of montane regions. During most of the year they are found on barren ground at, or substantially above, the tree line (variable today in the Cantabrian Mountains, but usually at about 1600 m). During the winter months, adverse weather conditions and the lack of food drive them from these high elevations into the broken, forested transitional zone below the tree line. These seasonal migrations are a characteristic of the species. It is likely that the ibex occurring in Asturian sites were taken during the winter months when the animals were most accessible to predation from the coast.

Chamois are more confined to montane woodlands than to open ground; their range extends downslope into deciduous as well as coniferous forests (Van den Brink 1967: 165, 166; Morris 1965: 424). They also occur on rocky slopes at elevations above the tree line, especially during the summer months. Heather, sedge, gorse, broom, lichens, and grasses are consumed by both species. The vegetational configuration is termed "alpine" or "true" matorral by Spanish geographers (Mapa Forestal de España 1966).

Marine Fauna

Marine shellfish constitute the second major element in the Asturian faunal inventory. Tables 6.4 and 6.5 indi-

TABLE 6.1
**Asturian Faunas: Mammal Distribution
Across All Sites**

	Sites Cuts and Levels						
Species	**Penicial all**	**Cueto de la Mina A**	**La Franca B**	**Coberizas B – 1**	**Rio A**	**Tres Calabres B**	**Balmori E – 1, C – 1**
Bos sp.	P	P	P				P
Bos primigenius							
Sus scrofa	P	P		A			P
Cervus elaphus	P	P	A	A	?	P	A
Capreolus capreolus	P	P	P	P			
Vulpes vulpes		P					
Ursus arctos							
Felis sylvestris	P	P					
Erinaceus europaeus							
Equus caballus	P	P					S
Rupicapra rupicapra		P	P				P
Capra ibex	P	P					P
Microtus arvalis							S
Lepus sp.							S
Lepus europaeus		P					
Sylvaemus spp.							S
Glis glis							
Arvicola amphibius							
Arvicola terrestris				P			P
Crocidura sp.							S
Mustela nivalis				P			
Putorius putorius		P					
Meles meles		P		P			
Lutra lutra		P					
Indet. rodents			S				A

A = abundant; P = present in unknown frequency or less than abundant; S = scarce; ? = possibly present

TABLE 6.2
Asturian Faunas: Mammals, Quantitative Data

	Sites Cuts and Levels							
Species	**Balmori E – 1, C – 1**	**La Riera A – 1, 1/2, 2, 3**	**La Riera B**	**Coberizas B – 1**	**Bricia A**	**Penicial Conchero**	**La Meaza Loc. 1 – 2, 5 – 2**	**Total**
Bos sp.	6							6
Bos primigenius							2	2
Sus scrofa	5			5[a]		2	2	14
Cervus elaphus	27	23[b]	28	5[a]	1			84
Capreolus capreolus			4	1		3		8
Ursus arctos							1	1
Felis sylvestris						1		1
Equus caballus	1	1						2
Rupicapra rupicapra	4							4
Capra ibex	5	2[c]						7
Microtus arvalis	1							1
Lepus sp.	1							1
Sylvaemus spp.	1				1			2
Glis glis			1					1
Arvicola terrestris	5			1				6
Crocidura sp.	1							1
Mustela nivalis				1				1
Meles meles				1			1	2
Indeterminant rodents	137	—	—	25	—	—	—	162
Total	194	26	33	39	2	6	6	306

a. At least 2 individuals.
b. At least 4 individuals.
c. At least 2 individuals.

		Sites Cuts and Levels					
La Riera A – 1, 1/2, 2, 3	**La Riera B**	**Colombres all**	**La Meaza 1 – 2, 5 – 2**	**Lledías B**	**Bricia A**	**Valdedíos Conchero**	**Fonfría' B**
			A			?	
		A	A				
A	A	A	A	?	P	A	P
	P					?	
		S					
		S	S				
			S				
S			P				
P		P				?	
						?	
					P		
	S						
			P				
			S				
	P				P		

TABLE 6.3

Cervus Elaphus: **Herd Composition Through Time by Age, Sex, and Provenience Within Range**

Month	Group Composition	Provenience Within Range	Cyclical Events
January	Ffm/M	Lower hillslopes between sea level and 500 m	
February	Ffm/M	Lower hillslopes between sea level and 500 m	Regrowth of antlers in velvet (Mm)
March	Ffm/M	Lower hillslopes between sea level and 500 m	Deer begin to wander
April	Ffm/M	Deer wandering Herds move from low to high country	
May	Ffm/M	Deer wandering Herds move from low to high country	
June	Ffm;/M/M Ffm/M/M	Hilltops above 500 m	Calving season peaks (mid-June). Maturing males (2–3 yrs.) break away from the hind group
July	Ffm;/M/M Ffm/M/M	Hilltops above 500 m	Velvet shed, antlers harden (Mm)
August	Ffm/M M Ffm/M	Hilltops above 500 m	
September	Ffm;/M	Hilltops above 500 m	
October	FfMm	Hilltops above 500 m Herds begin to move from higher to lower country	Herd together as a whole, harems begin to form Rut occurs in hinds' territory, lasts approximately six weeks (Sept. 15 – Nov. 1)
November	Ffm;/M Ffm;/F/M	Lower hillslopes between sea level and 500 m	3 – year hinds form groups
December	Ffm/M		Antlers shed (Mm)

F = Females, adult.   / = Sexes apart, each maintaining separate territories.
M = Males, adult.   ;/ = Temporary splitting according to age sets, sex.
f = Females, immature.   Sex ratio approximates 6(M):4(F). Density approximates 1 deer:30 – 50 acres.
m = Males, immature.

TABLE 6.4
Asturian Faunas: Marine Molluscs, Echinoderms, Crustacea, Terrestrial Molluscs, Amphibians, Osseous Fishes, and Birds Distribution Across All Sites

	Sites Cuts and Levels									
Species	Penicial all	Penicial Conchero	Cueto de la Mina A	Arnero A	Alloró Conchero	Fonfría B	La Franca B	Coberizas Conchero Sample A	Coberizas Conchero Sample B	Coberizas B−1
Patella spp.	P	A	A	A	A	A	A	A	A	A
Trochocochlea crassa	?	A	A	A	A	A	A	A	A	A
Mytilus edulis		S	S			S	S	P		P
Cardium edulis			?			A	S			
Ostrea edulis			?				P			
Tapes decussata										
Nassa reticulata		S	S							
Tuberculata atlantica			S							
Triton nodiferus			S			?	S			
Halyotis tuberculata								S		
Astralium rugosus										
Tellina tenuis										
Oricium sp.										
Gibbula umbilicalis		S								
Indeterminate marine gastropods								A	P	P
Solea spp.						P				
Indeterminate Teleostomi		A		S					P	S
Paracentrotus lividus		A	P	A		P	S	P	S	P
Cancer pagurus			P			P	P			
Portunus puber			P			P				
Indeterminate crustaceans								S		
P. vulgata sautuola	?	?								S
Littorina littorea	P			?						S
Helix nemoralis		P	P	S		P	S	A	A	A
Helix arbustorum		S		S				P	P	S
Indeterminate terrestrial gastropods										S
Indeterminate Anura								P		S
Indeterminate Aves										S

A = abundant, P = present in unknown frequency or less than abundant, S = scarce, ? = possibly present.

cate intensive selection for limpets (*Patella vulgata* and *P. intermedia*; also *P. aspera, P. lusitanica*) and the topshell (*Trochocochlea crassa*). Both groups consist of littoral species, most prevalent in the intertidal zone. In Table 6.5, categories of quantitative data are directly comparable for most species. Counts represent individual animals. Exceptions are sea urchins (*Paracentrotus lividus*), unidentified boney fishes (Teleostomi), and terrestrial gastropods (*Helix nemoralis, H. arbustorum*). These species occur only as fragments so the figures are inflated; counts of individuals could not be computed.

Patella spp. are found on rocks in tidal pools and on the walls of inlets from the high water mark of neap tides to the low water level of ordinary spring tides. They select areas well exposed to light, but will not tolerate rocks subjected to too much movement. Due to their extraordinary powers of adhesion, exposure to the direct impact of waves is not an important factor; exposures vary from as high as 90 percent to as low as 5 percent. Salinities as low as three parts per thousand can be withstood, so that the genus thrives near river mouths under

estuarine conditions (Fretter and Graham 1962: 680). Limpets occasionally colonize other environments (for example, consolidated sands, sheltered pebbly areas), but always in lower density than that found on fixed rocky surfaces. In Cantabria, they occur almost exclusively on the limestones into which the coastal inlets are cut. Water temperatures vary between 10° C (50° F) and 21° C (70° F); salinities vary between 3.5 and 3.6 parts per thousand (figures based on Madariaga 1967). Limpets rarely occur below 5 m beneath the water surface, although they may be found high on inlet walls, up to 3 m above the low tide mark (Madariaga 1967: 363, 371; Fretter and Graham 1962: 680). They are exposed twice daily by the action of the tides and can be collected in great numbers by anyone with a minimal expense of energy; of course the caloric return per individual is very low (approximately 6.5 calories).

The topshell (*Trochocochlea crassa*) was a secondary element in the Asturian diet; it occurs in the samples, as it does in nature, in consistently lower frequencies than the limpets. Topshells occupy similar habitats but never

Río A	Mar Concheros	Colombres all	La Meaza Loc. 1–2, 5–2	Lledías B	Bricia A	Valdedíos Conchero	La Cuevona Conchero	Elefante Conchero	Balmori E–1, C–1	La Riera A–1, 1/2, 2, 3	La Riera B
							Sites Cuts and Levels				
A	A	A	A	A	A	A	A	A	A	A	A
A	A	A	A	P	A	?	A	A	A	A	A
		S	A								S
		S			S					S	P
P		S	S								
			S								S
											S
		S									S
			S		S						S
					S						
					A				P	P	P
					S				S		S
											P
			P		P				S		P
									S		S
					S				S	S	?
					S				S	S	
			P		P				P	S	P
					P				S	S	P
									S	?	S
									P		
					S					S	S

extend so high as *Patella* because they are less able to withstand prolonged periods without water. Exposure to direct wave action varies from 60 percent to 50 percent, due to a comparative lack of adhesive power. The species select sunny areas on horizontal or vertical surfaces; the latter are occupied in relatively low frequency (Fretter and Graham 1962: 527, 623). The present distribution of the topshell extends from the British Isles to the Iberian Peninsula. It occurs sporadically, but when found, is locally abundant (Fretter and Graham 1962: 673).

Environment and Exploitation

Locations of ten Asturian sites with respect to the topographical features characteristic of the area surrounding Posada de Llanes, Asturias, are shown in Figure 6.1. The sites are optimally situated to enable their occupants to exploit coastal, forest, and montane resources with a minimal expenditure of effort. In spite of intensive survey in this region, no sites have been recorded inland of Lledías, about 3 km from the coast. Perhaps the interior

woodland and montane zones were deliberately left unoccupied on a permanent or semipermanent basis in an effort to preserve those areas as undisturbed hunting territories. At best, one might expect to find ephemeral food processing stations in these areas. Intense occupation appears to have been centered on the coast where red deer provided the basis for daily subsistence. Exploitation of roe deer and ibex were more opportunistic, perhaps, with the latter possibly taken on a seasonal basis. The role of shellfoods in the Asturian diet is difficult to assess. In the short-term shellfish are a stable resource and one relatively insensitive to man's presence. Despite the visually impressive remains of what must have been large shell middens, however, the dietary contributions of limpets and topshells must have been minimal compared with that of the ungulates. It is probably most reasonable to regard shellfish as a perennial dietary supplement or as an insurance resource, most intensively exploited in times or seasons when game was relatively scarce. According to Nicholas Shackleton, limpets were apparently collected mainly during the winter months at

TABLE 6.5
**Asturian Faunas: Marine Molluscs, Echinoderms, Crustacea,
Terrestrial Molluscs, Amphibians, Osseous Fishes, and Birds,
Quantitative Data**

Species	Penicial Conchero	Coberizas B–1	Balmori E–1, C–1	La Riera A–1, 1/2, 2, 3	La Riera B	Arnero A	Bricia A	Fonfría[a] B	La Franca[b] B	Vidiago Conchero	Lledías B
Patella spp.	1494	2205	2113	556	2299	163	1237	5	60	92	420
Trochocochlea crassa	117	775	1066	132	751	91	280	8	20	31	82
Mytilus edulis	6	69			1			1			
Cardium edulis		12		3	4		6	5		1	
Ostrea edulis		2						2			
Nassa reticulata	2	1			8						
Halyotis tuberculata		1									
Oricium sp.							1				
Gibbula umbilicalis	2				1		2				
Indeterminate marine gastropods	42[c]	119[c]	128[c]	80[c]	72[c]	40[c]	237[c]				1[d]
Solea spp.					1			2			
Indeterminate Teleostomi	28	6	11		62	2	5				
Paracentrotus lividus	138	70	39	1	90	144	32	7			
Cancer pagurus			1		1						
Indeterminate crustaceans		1						2			
P. vulgata sautuola		2	19	3			1				
Littorina littorea		3[e]	10	2		1[f]	3				
Helix nemoralis	24	184	85	4	107	6	57	5		15	37
Helix arbustorum	5	40	10	7	44	2	30			2	6
Indeterminate terrestrial gastropods		8	1	3	8						

a = Small sample, Museo Arqueológico Nacional (Madrid).
b = Small sample, Museo Municipal (Madrid).
c = Fragmentary specimens or with diagnostic characteristics obscured by CaCO₃; probably mostly *Trochocochlea crassa*.
d = *Tapes decussata*.
e = All small, modern sized specimens.
f = Fragmentary, identification questionable.

La Riera. Although there is evidence of some exploitation of anadromous (and marine) fish in many Asturian levels, and some bird bones, there are no indications that these resources were taken systematically or intensively. That they were exploited at all during the Asturian represents a departure from patterns of resource exploitation characteristic of Late Pleistocene assemblages.

Faunal Evidence for Post-Pleistocene Climatic Shifts

If analysis of terrestrial resources exploited shows a stable pattern from the Late Pleistocene through the Asturian, analysis of marine fauna reveals a marked shift in species collected, due to climatic and possibly demographic factors, and a quantitative increase in the amount of shellfish remains present in the sites and in the number of species collected. Evidence for climatic change is most apparent in the near-total replacement of the cold-adapted winkle (*Littorina littorea*) by the topshell (*Trochocochlea crassa*), a shift first reported by the Conde (Vega del Sella 1916: 82–89). He believed the change corresponded with the onset of the postglacial climatic optimum (about 8000 to 5000 B.P.), a period marked by conditions warmer and wetter than those of the present day (Butzer 1964: 406, 407). Radiocarbon

determinations indicate that the Conde was remarkably accurate in his estimate of the duration of the postglacial optimum.

The "sautuola" variety of *Patella vulgata*, first described by the Marqués de Sautuola (1880) over a century ago, also is extremely rare in Asturian middens. This limpet (*P. vulgata*, varieties *mayor, aurea*), which is common in the Cantabrian Upper Paleolithic middens, is much larger than the commonly represented Asturian varieties (*P. vulgata, P. intermedia*), and can be readily distinguished from them by surface texture and color. The exterior is characterized by smooth, concentric circles rather than by the sharp radial spines of contemporary species, and, in the case of the *aurea* variety, by uniform gold interior coloration. Some specimens measure 70 mm in diameter, against a mean of about 38 mm for the modern variants. The shells of the Pleistocene form may weigh as much as 15 gm (Madariaga 1967: 364, 365). The disappearance of the "sautuola" variety in Asturian concheros is probably due to an increase in water temperature, which may have provided less than optimal conditions for growth (see below), and to overexploitation of estuarine habitats by human groups beginning late in the Pleistocene. It is interesting to note that these large limpet varieties still exist along Cantabrian coasts, al-

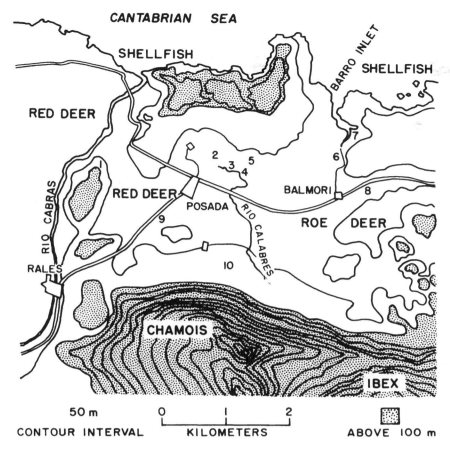

Figure 6.1. Topography of the Posada de Llanes area, showing the location of Asturian sites in relation to features of the landscape and major resources exploited prehistorically (from Clark 1971b: 1253):

1. Coberizas
2. Bricia
3. Cueto de la Mina
4. La Riera
5. Tres Calabres
6. Balmori
7. Fonfría
8. Allorú
9. Arnero
10. Lledías

though they are quite rare. Like most limpets, they are estuary-adapted forms; the *mayor* variety is found presently in estuaries and ports where water pollution inhibits their collection for human consumption.

The edible mussel (*Mytilus edulis*) reappears in the post-Pleistocene and increases in size and frequency during the postglacial optimum. *Mytilus edulis* is a relatively thermophile species; rapid declines in sea water temperature destroy the beds. Mussels favor brackish water in estuarine situations, but they also occur attached to rocks on tidal flats and on stable, pebbly, or muddy bottoms (Rogers 1920: 288). The species is not commonly found in Asturian sites, again an observation first made by the Conde (Vega del Sella 1916: 82–89). It was extensively exploited subsequent to 6000 B.P., however, as indicated by radiocarbon dated concheros at Les Pedroses and La Lloseta B.

Figure 6.2 summarizes some of the results of the 1969 conchero testing program. Sample size exceeded 10,000 specimens; sites with small or selective samples were omitted from the study. Nine radiocarbon determinations from several levels at eight sites (two Upper Paleolithic, five Asturian, and two post-Asturian) provide, for the first time, a moderately accurate scale against which to make the following conclusions. The set of radiocarbon dates is given in Table 6.6. The calculation of ages is based on the Libby half-life for carbon–14 (5570 years), and the indicated error factors are the standard devia-

tions for each sample calculated from the statistical errors in the beta ray counting number. Dates corrected for the new half-life (5730 ± 40) are also presented.

The Cut E Sequence at Balmori

The best sequence for examining changes in shellfish frequencies is from the cave site of Balmori (Cut E), although it is duplicated, at least partially, at El Cierro, La Riera, Coberizas, and Les Pedroses. The sequence at Balmori spans a period of at least 7000 years from the Lower Magdalenian until the Asturian (Clark 1974a; Clark and Clark 1975).

The Upper Paleolithic levels show the decline through time of the "sautuola" limpet (*Patella vulgata*, varieties *aurea, mayor*) and the corresponding increase in frequency of its modern analogues (*P. vulgata, P. intermedia*). Winkles (*Littorina littorea*), never present at frequencies greater than 10 percent, drop off by the Level 2-3 contact to less than 3 percent. Topshells (*Trochocochlea crassa*) first appear in Level 4 and increase in frequency to 8 percent at the Level 2-3 contact. Mussels are absent throughout.

Asturian levels, from four dated sites, show considerable variability due to local factors (microenvironmental differences, differences in intensity of exploitation). The overall configuration, however, reflects the systematic collection of limpets, which make up from 60 percent to

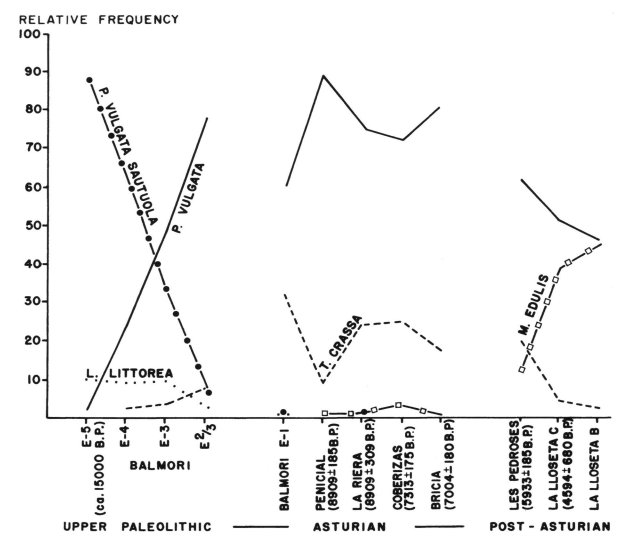

Figure 6.2. Major shellfish species exploited from 15,000 to 4600 B.P. (Clark 1971b: 1254).

TABLE 6.6
**Radiocarbon Determinations from Late and Post-
Pleistocene Concheros in Eastern Asturias
B.P. dates are number of years before 1950**

Site	Period	Sample No.	Determination (New Half-life)	Determination (Libby Half-life)	Range at 1σ (Libby Half-life)
LA LLOSETA (SAMPLE A)	LOWER MAGDALENIAN	GaK 2549	15,656 ± 412	15,200 ± 400	14,800 – 15,600
EL CIERRO	UPPER MAGDALENIAN-AZILIAN	GaK 2548	10,712 ± 515	10,400 ± 500	9900 – 10,900
LA FRANCA	ASTURIAN	GaK 6884	9568 ± 453	9290 ± 440	8850 – 9730
PENICIAL	ASTURIAN	GaK 2906	8909 ± 185	8650 ± 180	8470 – 8830
LA RIERA (CUT B)	ASTURIAN	GaK 2909	8909 ± 309	8650 ± 300	8350 – 8950
COBERIZAS (CUT B)	ASTURIAN	GaK 2907	7313 ± 175	7100 ± 170	6930 – 7270
BRICIA (CUT A)	ASTURIAN	GaK 2908	7004 ± 165	6800 ± 160	6640 – 6980
LES PEDROSES	POST-ASTURIAN	GaK 2547	5933 ± 185	5760 ± 180	5580 – 5940
LA LLOSETA (SAMPLE B)	POST-ASTURIAN	GaK 2551	4594 ± 680	4460 ± 660	3800 – 5120

Note: All samples are wood charcoal.

92 percent of the shellfish inventory, and topshells, which vary from 32 percent to 10 percent. Mussels first occur in the concheros around 8900 B.P., but they never exceed 3 percent of the sample collected. Pleistocene limpets and winkles are extremely rare (less than 1 percent). The absence or low frequency of the winkle (*Littorina littorea*) suggests a climatic regimen somewhat warmer than that of the present day.

The post-Asturian pattern is most distinctive because of the steady increase in the frequency of mussels, which are present, although rare, in the late Asturian conchero at Coberizas and which attain a high of 47 percent at La Lloseta. Limpets, always numerous, appear to decline slightly; they make up from 63 percent to 47 percent of the inventory. Topshells are also present in lower frequency.

Limpets, winkles, topshells, and mussels all occur on the Cantabrian coast today, suggesting a slight and gradual decrease in sea water temperature since the postglacial optimum. A decrease sufficient to permit the reappearance of the cool-water winkle, yet not drastic enough to destroy the beds of thermophile mussel, is a necessary postulate in order to explain present-day observations. All four species are eaten the year round. They are gathered from inlets where they are not subject to the ingestion of the poisonous planktonic organisms that affect shellfish occupying exposed coastal niches during the summer months (Ricketts and Calvin 1948: 119, 120), a fact suggesting that the Asturian coastal sites could have been occupied year round, or at least that the Asturians could have exploited shellfoods from protected estuarine niches on a perennial basis. Other data are required to substantiate or disprove the question of permanency of occupation.

The general sequence of Late and post-Pleistocene faunal replacements that the Conde first defined on the basis of the molluscan data (Vega del Sella 1916: 77–89; 1923: 38–41) tends to be confirmed by the results of the present investigations. The replacement of *L. littorea* by *T. crassa,* the disappearance of the "sautuola" variety of *P. vulgata* from concheros of Asturian date, and the reappearance of *M. edulis* in post-Asturian concheros are clearly marked in the sequences discussed above. Combined with radiocarbon determinations from Asturian, and from pre- and post-Asturian middens (see Table 6.6), the faunal data do much to refute claims for a pre-Mousterian chronological position for the assemblage so prevalent in the literature of recent years (Jordá 1957, 1958, 1959, 1963, 1975; Crusafont 1963; González 1965; Llopis-Lladó in Hernández-Pacheco and others 1957: 24, 25).

7. CATCHMENT ANALYSIS
OF ASTURIAN SITES

Geoffrey A. Clark and Shereen Lerner

Resources available to the prehistoric occupants of 28 Asturian cave and rock shelter sites located in the coastal provinces of Asturias and Santander may be used to construct an ecological model based on concepts developed in archaeological site catchment analysis (Vita-Finzi and Higgs 1970; Jarman 1972). It is assumed initially that the Asturian settlements in Cantabria are the remains of permanent or semipermanent "base camps" with fairly continuous occupation by either an entire local group or a major portion of it. Supporting this hypothesis is the observation that the sites are optimally situated to facilitate exploitation of coastal, estuarine, forest, and montane resources with a minimal expenditure of energy; weak negative evidence is provided by the fact that no inland, montane Asturian sites have been recognized to date. Two other hypotheses are evaluated. They specify (1) a bilocal model, with two strategically located base camps and a series of limited activity sites located in intervening resource zones; and (2) a no base-camp model, which describes a completely transhumant population engaged in the cyclical exploitation of plant and animal resources within a circumscribed territory (specifically, a river basin).

Like most such studies, statements about human economic and decision-making behavior are incorporated into this study. So-called "least-cost" principles are basic assumptions (that is, a group will economically or efficiently utilize exploitable resources in its territory). It is further assumed that easily exploitable resources known to have been present in the past were unlikely to have been ignored prehistorically. Seasonal availability of resources is an additional consideration in the definition of exploitation patterns, and the concept is used whenever there is reason to believe that a differential in availability may have been operative prehistorically in regard to a particular species. Distance measures combined with a realistic stratification of environmental zones permit assessments of "ease-of-access" factors that were probably operative and likely important in prehistoric decision-making about resource priorities. Both marine and terrestrial resources are analyzed; both are known archaeologically and can be ranked in terms of probable prehistoric economic importance. Fauna are studied in conjunction with sparse archaeological remains, and in relation to a series of distance and access variables, to try to determine whether the sites are representative of the Asturian settlement-subsistence system as a whole (the null hypothesis stated above), or whether they simply formed part of a larger and more extensive system, inland components of which are not known archaeologically.

A variety of nonparametric and multivariate statistical procedures are used in both an inductive-generalizing and a deductive analytical mode to form and correlate groups of sites with particular faunal, lithic, and environmental variables. Empirically derived patterns of resource exploitation are then compared with expectations under various permutations of the model derived from the null hypothesis (that is, that the sites are all functional equivalents).

SITE CATCHMENT ANALYSIS: BASIC CONCEPTS AND ASSUMPTIONS

Archaeological site catchment analysis has been defined by Vita-Finzi and Higgs (1970: 36) as the determination of the "total area from which the contents of a site have been derived." It is assumed that human groups are basically territorial, and that a group will make use of those resources in its territory that can be readily identified and easily exploited. It has been shown empirically that the region habitually exploited by a group tends to be relatively restricted in extent, and lies within fairly well-defined limits. These generalizations are particularly appropriate to hunter-gatherers, although there is enormous variation in the actual extent of ethnographically defined hunter-gatherer site catchment areas. The approach, of course, has been applied successfully to more complex societies characterized by whole or partial dependence on domesticates, but as social complexity increases, factors that determine "the total area" from whence site contents are derived become so numerous and difficult to control that the approach breaks down as a unified format of analysis. On the state and chiefdom levels of sociocultural integration (Service 1962), site catchment analysis tends to be replaced by more systemic approaches that monitor interaction between and among different kinds of sites and in regard to different kinds of commodity and "information" flow (for example, central place and locational analysis, various economic exchange models; Smith 1976a, b; Hodder and Orton 1976; Johnson 1977). At the level of hunter-gatherers, however, some confidence may be placed in the site catchment approach, precisely because the range of site contents is usually fairly restricted and probable source areas can often be identified with some degree of specificity.

The notion of the site catchment area can be juxtaposed with that of the site territory. A site territory is defined as "the territory surrounding a site which is exploited habitually by the inhabitants of a site; hunter-gatherer groups limit themselves to within two hours walking distance from the site" (Vita-Finzi and Higgs 1970: 30). The dubious generalization about walking distance aside, the point is that site catchment areas may be larger than site territories because site contents may include rare or unusual items derived from afar. While conceptually important for more complex societies characterized by regional exchange networks, the distinction is perhaps less germane to the hunter-gatherer case; site catchment areas and site territories are probably coextensive in many, although certainly not all, hunting and gathering situations.

Resource accessibility is customarily measured in terms of site-to-resource distance. That distance is usually measured in other than linear map distance, however, and is similarly qualified here in terms of local topography; the operative factors are estimates of the time and effort involved in traveling the distance itself (Jarman and others 1972: 63). It is further assumed that the more distant a resource is from a site, the less likely it is to be exploited. The counter implication is that easily exploited resources are unlikely to have remained untouched for long.

In stating this and the previous assumptions, it is recognized that many counter examples exist that challenge the universal generality of these statements. As they are themselves empirical generalizations of wide, albeit not universal, validity, they are necessary to provide a justification for various site catchment methodologies that depend on operationalizing distance and access factors.

MINIMAX, LEAST EFFORT, AND SATISFICER PRINCIPLES

In considering various economic principles that might be appropriate to an investigation of Early Holocene Cantabrian hunter-gatherer subsistence and settlement location, minimax, least effort, and satisficer models were examined briefly. The minimax principle states that economic man attempts to maximize the harvest of the "most efficient" resource available at any particular point in time (Thomas and others 1975). Criticisms leveled at the minimax approach have recently been summarized by Sullivan and Schiffer (1977), who suggest that a minimax perspective is perhaps more typical of intensively specialized agrarian societies than it is of primitive agriculturalists practicing a mixed economy, or of most hunter-gatherers (see also Bailey 1981a). They also observe that minimax models tend to be overly rigid and simplified to the extent that they are unrealistic. It is unlikely, for example, that any human group develops extractive strategies in either near ignorance of, or complete knowledge of, the nature of environmental variability. Either one or the other must be taken into account from a "classic" minimax perspective.

The principle of least effort is based on the assumption that people seek to minimize work involved in resource procurement and processing such that the individual is constantly striving toward a compromise between "adequate" returns and effort minimization (Zipf 1949). The principle can be applied to groups as well as individuals. As was the case with minimax, these behavioral idealizations conflict with the empirical fact that all human societies use a variety of alternative strategies in the extraction of resources from the environment (Bailey 1981b; Davidson 1981). In order for these two principles to adequately model human behavior, it must be assumed that groups (1) formulate and evaluate probabilities of success entailed in the adoption of alternative strategies; (2) select a potentially "best" strategy; and (3) minimize miscalculation, thereby maximizing the probability of selecting the "best" strategy. We almost envision a naked trog, with furrowed brow and Hewlett-Packard in hand, sitting on a rock calculating a probability function that will enable him to decide whether he ought to go after some venison or be content with yet another meal of rubber-eraser-like limpets. The major problem stems from inherent constraints on conceptual and temporal variables that limit the effectiveness of decision-making performances in any "real-world" situation. Still more tenuous is our ability to accurately evaluate such variables in the distant past.

The so-called "satisficer" model was first developed by Herbert Simon in 1945; it assumes that man seeks to satisfy some predetermined but submaximal aspiration level. Whereas economic man selects the best alternative from those available, satisficing man pursues what is "good enough," and so can choose without calculating probabilities. Jochim (1976) has termed the satisficer model "descriptive" (that is, it describes how people actually behave) as opposed to "normative" (for example, minimax models, which describe how people should act). In some ways, satisficer models are regarded as most realistic because they more closely approximate actual decision-making processes in all of their nebulous complexity (Jochim 1976: 7; Bailey 1981b). At any rate, there seem to be fewer unrealistic assumptions involved because economic goals remain suitably vague; minimization of effort or the maintenance of its expenditure within predetermined limits are both acceptable. Jochim (1976: 9) has argued that there is an inherent tendency to limit effort that underlies all economic decisions, and that maximization (in the exploitation of any particular resource) is the exception, rather than the rule.

ECONOMIC ACTIVITY: SETTLEMENT LOCATIONS AND THE RELATIVE VALUE OF RESOURCES

The primary objectives of all economic activity are (1) the attainment of the caloric needs of the population concerned, whether directly or indirectly; and (2) the acquisition of those nonfood items of technology needed to obtain food and deemed necessary for other, culturally-defined aspects of human existence. Resource procurement depends on the linked factors of (1) ease or difficulty of exploitation, which in turn may be influenced by seasonal variation in resource availability (in the case of plants) and location (in the case of mobile game animals), and (2) distance traveled (Jochim 1976: 16). Distance minimization may play an important role in settlement location, a fact long recognized by economic geographers. Haggett (1965) has stated that uneven resource distributions and their effect on settlement configurations are important considerations in any locational study.

Most previous work on archaeological catchment analysis has emphasized the location of sites with respect to one another and compared with various resource categories. For example, Jarman (1972: 707) views archaeological sites as occupying strategic positions within exploitation territories and attempts to analyze the economic possibilities offered by particular site location in relation to theoretically available resources. He views distance as being a common variable in the exploitation of territories, in that humans impose limitations on themselves to the extent that they make decisions about where exploitation ceases to be profitable and so is no longer likely to take place. Examination of Asturian site locations in Cantabrian Spain tends to support this statement; the cost of exploiting a particular kind of resource located at a given distance from a site is apparently a major factor influencing site location.

Less emphasized have been attempts to arrive at operational statements about the relative value of different kinds of plant and animal resources. Obviously, all food resources are not equally nutritious, available, or easily exploited, so it is important to try to establish criteria that will permit ranking of potentially available resources. Ranked potential resources may then be compared statistically with evidence for resources actually exploited prehistorically, thus enabling statements about relative extractive efficiency to be made. There are a number of criteria that can be used as a basis for ranking. They include, but are not restricted to, (1) relative nutritive value, (2) reliability, (3) procurement efficiency, (4) yield per unit weight, (5) seasonal variation in availability, and (6) relative transport costs (Thomas and others 1975: 35–90).

Following Thomas and his colleagues, it is assumed that the most nutritious resource will give the greatest number of calories per gram. In this sense, collection of sessile shellfish is a more "reliable" activity than is the hunting of mobile game. The most easily procured foods are those requiring a minimum input of energy balanced against caloric yield per unit weight or time. However, because terrestrial resources are characterized by higher caloric yields per unit weight than are shellfish, and are much larger, fewer are needed to fulfill the caloric needs of a population. Procurement efficiency, then, refers to the amount of food obtained during each procurement activity. The resources with the optimal combination of the above four factors are expected to be the dominant subsistence resources for any nonagricultural group (Thomas and others 1975: 55).

The most efficient hunted species should be that which returns the largest amount of usable meat per kill, yet still satisfies the requirements of ease in procurement and reliability (for example, roe deer are high in caloric yield, found in forest margin habitats, and are available on a year-round basis).

Seasonally abundant or seasonally available resources may be procured intensively at their proper season to the temporary exclusion of, or deemphasis on, resources that are present the year round (for example, red deer have a high caloric yield per unit weight, a relatively high 50 percent of the body weight is usable meat, and they are concentrated in herds five months out of the year). Gathered resources are chosen over hunted resources, provided the above constraints are not violated (for example, limpets over wild boar). In cases of overlapping priorities among potential resources, two corollaries are used to predict dominant subsistence activities:

1. Seasonally available gathered resources (plants, some shellfish) should be chosen over seasonally available hunted resources.
2. Seasonally available hunted resources should be chosen over gathered resources that are available year round (Thomas and others 1975: 57).

Consideration of these decision priorities should permit the establishment of a ranked series of resources available at any particular locus in a region, given knowledge of, or well-grounded assumptions about, permanency or periodicity of occupation at that locus. If it is granted that these kinds of decision priorities were operative prehistorically, some predictions may also be made about site location. Sites, for example, should be located in a "good gathered resource area," to permit optimum utilization. Moreover, the time expended getting to and from the resource should be minimal. Clark (1971b: 1252, 1253) has pointed out that many Asturian sites are located in excellent resource availability locales, almost always in close proximity to "good gathered resource areas" (estuaries rich in shellfish and adjacent to forest-grassland mosaics).

The exploitation of shellfish requires that large quantities be obtained due to minimal individual caloric yield; a heavy load is needed to collect enough to be worth the effort. The quantity of shellfish that can be transported with primitive technology is small, however, so that a number of trips are required. Therefore, we would expect the location of sites with shell middens to be fairly close to the source of supply (Bailey 1978). Because shellfood spoils quickly, inland sites should contain little shell. Given tectonic stability, for the time ranges considered here (9000 to 7000 B.P.) it is assumed that the coastline was at its present location, so that distance and access factors may be monitored with some degree of accuracy. Moreover, direct palynological evidence of Asturian paleoclimatic conditions from the open-air site of Liencres in Santander (Clark and Menéndez-Amor 1975) and from La Riera in Asturias (according to Leroi-Gourhan in 1977) permits us to conclude that the vegetational associations during the Preboreal-Atlantic interval were not markedly different from climax vegetation in Cantabria prior to the Middle Ages, a time when extensive deforestation began to result in the formation of the artificial grasslands (*prados*) that are so prevalent a feature of the contemporary landscape. These scanty pollen records, in conjunction with topographical variables, provide a basis for environmental stratification with respect to major resource zones present prehistorically.

THE CANTABRIAN LANDSCAPE

The model we propose is based in part on a human ecological perspective. The culture of a group is defined as that part of the behavioral repertoire by which the group maintains itself in the ecosystem of which it is a part (Rappaport 1969: 185). Priority is given to an examination of exploitative activities and their relation to settlement location and resource distribution. This approach permits the study of interaction between human populations and the environment.

In central Cantabria, archaeological residues of hunter-gatherer groups living between 8900 and 7000 B.P. are concentrated in the mouths of caves and are usually assigned to the Asturian culture-stratigraphic unit, first defined by the Count of Vega del Sella (1914, 1916, 1923, 1930). The 28 known Asturian sites are confined to the adjacent provinces of Asturias and Santander, and are especially dense in the area of Llanes, in eastern Asturias (see Fig. 3.1). Although not apparent from Figure 3.1, there is a tendency for sites with similar or overlapping catchment areas to proliferate in clustered groupings, so that site territory may have been capable of supporting a larger population than could be accommodated within the confines of a single cave or rock shelter (Bailey 1978). The most intensive occupations appear to have been centered on or near the coast where shellfish were readily available that, along with red deer (*Cervus elaphus*), probably provided the protein base for daily subsistence (see Fig. 6.1). Nothing is known of plant resources collected prehistorically, although oak (acorns), beech (beechnuts), hazel (hazelnuts), juniper, and a variety of cereal grasses are known to have been present in the region during the early Holocene.

As noted in Chapter 2, the landscape in eastern Asturias consists of four major structural components, created by Mesozoic orogeny and subsequent folding and faulting of Carboniferous date, that ultimately produced the Cordillera Cantabrica mountain chain. These components, distributed from north to south, consist of (1) a series of low (50 m to 100 m) ridges and platforms that parallel the coast and that often occur within a kilometer of the present shoreline; (2) a narrow coastal plain, perhaps extending at most some 15 km inland of the present strand; (3) low (100 m to 300 m) ranges of foothills distributed in broken east-west trending chains parallel to the coast; and (4) the intermontane valleys and summits of the Cordillera, which attain a maximum elevation of 2500 m in the majestic Picos de Europa, a scant 27 km from the sea (Clark 1971a; 1976a; Martínez Alvárez 1965). Superimposed on these structural elements are a variety of life zones, the distributions of which are dependent on variations in the moisture and temperature regimes, vegetation, and the proximity of watercourses

and the sea. The major topographic features along a north-south transect in the vicinity of Llanes are presented in Figure 7.1.

The region is drained by a regular lattice of north-south flowing rivers, which have their headwaters in the Cordillera and which transect the east-west trending ranges of mountains and hills, and the coastal plain. Spaced at intervals of 10 km to 15 km, these watercourses provide natural avenues of north-south transit in a region that is quite rugged topographically and difficult of access. Straus (1975a: 41–58) has suggested that the Cantabrian river valleys were sheltered locales during the rigorous climatic conditions of pleniglacial times, and provided natural routes of north-south migration, presumably utilized seasonally by both men and animals as part of a seasonal round. Karst topography, produced by the channeling of surface waters into preexisting depressions and by subsequent dissolution of the Carboniferous and Devonian limestone bedrock, is a common feature of the area. This is particularly true of the eastern coastal plain, which is dotted with linear depressions, sinkholes, caves, rock shelters, chimneys, and other karstic phenomena, producing a jagged, cratered landscape muted today by the accumulation of a thick (2 m to 4 m) mantle of Holocene soil (Clark 1976a: 23, 24).

The landscape has been much altered by man. Natural vegetation cover apparently consisted of a mosaic of mixed deciduous-coniferous forest and open grassland in the first century B.C. at the time of initial Roman colonization (González 1976). Predominant arboreal species included several kinds of oak and pine, with chestnut, beech, and birch in association (Guinea Lopez 1953: 220–228). Systematic deforestation beginning in Roman times became much accelerated during the Middle Ages, so that the predominant cover today is artificial grassland (*prado*) with isolated, but occasionally quite extensive, plantations of eucalyptus and Monterrey pine that were introduced during the last century as part of an extensive reforestation program. Only in comparatively isolated intermontane valleys (those of the Ríos Dobra, Cares, and Dujé) do vestiges of the original climax vegetation remain (Clark 1976a: 27–31).

ARCHAEOLOGICAL DATA

As demonstrated in Chapters 3 and 6, Asturian sites have been identified with the formation of a particular kind of shell midden in cave mouths dated to the period 9000 to 7000 B.P. These conchero accumulations are artificial deposits composed of variable quantities of sediment (usually scarce), bone fragments, and thousands of marine shells. Concheros have formed since Solutrean times in Cantabria, and they may be more or less cemented into breccialike deposits depending on the extent of percolation by carbonate-charged waters and on subsequent microclimatic conditions in the area of accumulation (Butzer and Bowman 1979). Normally, little discernible stratigraphy is present in them and artifact density, unfortunately, is low (see Chapter 5). Concheros probably represent nothing more than big garbage heaps. They are not interpreted as habitation sites, which were

BLOCK DIAGRAM

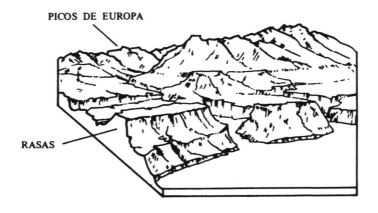

PICOS DE EUROPA

RASAS

Figure 7.1. Surface morphology and geological substrate in the vicinity of Llanes in eastern Asturias (Houston 1967: 181, 182).

SECTION

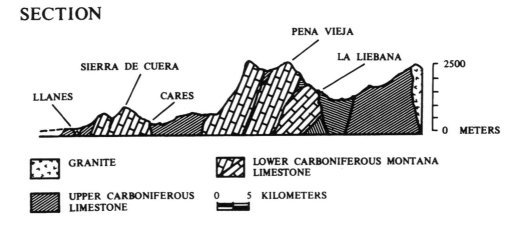

PENA VIEJA

LA LIEBANA

SIERRA DE CUERA

LLANES   CARES

2500

0   METERS

▢ GRANITE

▨ LOWER CARBONIFEROUS MONTANA LIMESTONE

▨ UPPER CARBONIFEROUS LIMESTONE

0   5 KILOMETERS

probably located in the open air in close proximity to the caves.

Sites are classified as Asturian if they (1) contain concheros, with or without substantial industrial remains, in which modern variants of limpet (*Patella* spp.) and topshell (*Trochocochlea crassa*) predominate, and in which the so-called Pleistocene limpet variant (*Patella vulgata sautuola*) and the winkle (*Littorina littorea*) are absent, and (2) if the deposits contain the characteristic Asturian stone pick in primary depositional context.

An effort has been made to use as much information about the environment as possible, while attempting to avoid unrealistic assumptions about the location and importance of particular resources based on extrapolation from present day conditions (Francis and Clark 1979). The variables can be divided into four major groups that reflect (1) gross biotopes probably present prehistorically in the vicinity of each site, (2) distance and access measures, (3) faunal resources potentially available and actually recovered, and (4) archaeological remains present (Table 7.1). It is reasoned that a settlement-subsistence model derived from knowledge of present local ecology

TABLE 7.1
Settlement-subsistence Model Variables

1. BIOTOPES PROBABLY PRESENT PREHISTORICALLY:

Alpine	Marshes
Forest-Forest Margin	Open Country
Estuarine	Sea

2. PERCENT OF BIOTOPES PROBABLY PRESENT PREHISTORICALLY

3. RANKED PERCENTS OF BIOTOPES PRESENT PREHISTORICALLY

4. MEAN LINEAR DISTANCE TO EACH BIOTOPE IN CATCHMENT AREA

5. RANKED MEAN DISTANCES TO EACH BIOTOPE IN CATCHMENT AREA

6. FAUNA:

Terrestrial Fauna Theoretically Present by Biotope
Terrestrial Fauna Actually Represented Archaeologically
Percent of Usable Meat-Species
Marine Fauna Theoretically Present by Biotope
Marine Fauna Actually Represented Archaeologically

7. ARCHAEOLOGICAL REMAINS PRESENT:

Debitage
Small Tools
Heavy Duty Tools

TABLE 7.2
**Conversion of Present-day Environments
into a Reduced Series of Early Holocene Environments**

PRESENT-DAY ENVIRONMENTS	PREHISTORIC ENVIRONMENTS
ALPINE	ALPINE: Elevation 200 m or greater than 100 m with steep gradient (greater than 40°).
FOREST-FOREST MARGIN	FOREST-FOREST MARGIN: Land less than 100 m elevation, excluding marshes, estuaries, sand, and open coast; unforested areas may also be included.
ESTUARINE	First 500 m of river flood-plain
RIVER VALLEY FLOOD PLAIN	FOREST-FOREST MARGIN: Mixed deciduous-coniferous woodland; deciduous species dominant.
MARSH	MARSH
OPEN COUNTRY	FOREST-FOREST MARGIN OR OPEN COUNTRY: Open Country if above 100 m, relatively flat, no higher than 200 m (see below).
PASTURE LAND (prado)	FOREST-FOREST MARGIN: Between 0–100 m; more than 500 m back from shoreline and not anything else (see below).
AGRICULTURAL LAND	FOREST-FOREST MARGIN or OPEN COUNTRY (see below).
MONTE BAJO	FOREST-FOREST MARGIN if 0–100 m in elevation and at least 100 m from coast. OPEN COUNTRY if between 100–200 m and relatively flat.
MONTE ALTO	FOREST-FOREST MARGIN if 0–100 m in elevation and at least 100 m from coast; otherwise OPEN COUNTRY.
OPEN COASTLINE	OPEN COASTLINE: 0–100 m from shoreline.
SEA	SEA: It is assumed that the coastline has not fluctuated significantly since the Boreal period.

may enable us to suggest a settlement-subsistence system that would have been efficient in the past. Before such a model can be constructed, however, it is necessary to transform contemporary classifications of environmental life zones into one that might have been present prehistorically (Table 7.2). There are 12 contemporary life zones that can be identified on a scale gross enough to be transformed into one that is applicable prehistorically. Mainly they reflect modern vegetation cover and land usage. Obviously much finer distinctions may be made, but they would be so far removed from any demonstrable connection with past environments as to be worthless for our purposes. The resulting conversion produces the seven zones listed in Table 7.1. It is noteworthy that only four of these zones appear to have been important prehistorically (alpine, forest-forest margin, estuarine, open country). There is, for example, little systematic evidence for exploitation of open coastal or deep sea resources. The algorithm for conversion presented in Table 7.2 is a reasonable one, considering the present knowledge of early Holocene paleoenvironments and a realistic appreciation of the scale at which it is defensible to operate; a one-to-one equivalence is not provided in every case. If we believe that much early Holocene topography in Cantabria consisted of a forest-open country mosaic, as certainly seems to have been the case, then a means must be found for making unambiguous "on the ground" assignments of present zones that could have been either forested or grassland to one or the other category. This can only be done on a random basis, using knowledge of present ratios of forest to open country biotopes. A procedure for making relatively unambiguous assignments of this kind is presented below.

METHODOLOGICAL CONSIDERATIONS

It is crucial that estimates be made of what the early Holocene environment was like in eastern Asturias because radical, man-made alterations of the environment have taken place in the region since the Mesolithic period. Macroclimatic changes probably have also occurred, but we know nothing in detail of them and must assume that the early Holocene climate was not significantly different from that of today. What shreds of pollen evidence we do have tend to support this assumption (Clark and Menéndez-Amor 1975).

A circular catchment area was imposed around each of the 28 sites. The catchment circles were designed with a 3 km radius that, considering the zonal compression and the rugged terrain characteristic of this portion of the north Spanish coast, was considered to be an adequate estimate of the distance the members of a group would be willing to travel in one day to attain a particular resource without the need for transient camp sites. As a preliminary step, the 12-part classification of present-day biotopes given in Table 7.2 was used to make a record of the distributions of life-zones surrounding each site today. The areal proportion of each biotope in the catchment circle was also computed. These biotopes were subsequently transformed into the simplified seven-part classification also presented in Table 7.2, a fairly straightforward procedure except for the ambiguity inherent in the realization that a mosaic of forest and open country was present in the early Holocene, just as it is today. We had no way of distinguishing those areas that were forested from those that were covered with open scrub and grassland vegetation.

If it is legitimate to assume that the ratio of grassland to woodland biotopes has remained fixed for the region as a whole since the early Holocene, even if distributions of biotopes have changed, then a conversion can be accomplished using the eastern half of Asturias as a basis for computation. This part of the province was examined, and the ratio of present day open country to woodland was determined to be approximately 38:62. After transformation according to the rules given in Table 7.2, the area of combined wooded-open country was determined for each circle, and areas designated open country were located using a random selection process within those portions of the circle assigned to the combined biotopes. This procedure was followed until a 4:6 ratio of open country to woodland was achieved. This process causes the circular character of some open country biotopes in Figures 7.2 and 7.3; the locations of open country biotopes are randomly assigned at a fixed ratio of 4:6. Catchment circles "transformed" in this manner provided the basic data for the remainder of the analysis. A number of access and distance variables were then computed.

Prehistoric resource potential was monitored by computing the proportional representation of each biotope in the site catchment area (Figs. 7.2, 7.3), using a dot counter overlay on the transformed catchment circles. Area was computed by a simple algorithm, and then converted to a percent of total area within the catchment circle (Area = πr^2), which was fixed for each site (Clark and Lerner 1980: 91).

Resource accessibility was monitored by computing the mean distance from each site to each biotope class. A mean distance had to be used because biotopes were often irregular in shape and discontinuous in distribution. We wanted some overall measure of accessibility for each site catchment area as a whole, so the linear distance to each patch of a given biotope class was taken; the distances were summed and divided by the number of distances taken. The process was repeated for each biotope class in each of the 28 site catchment circles, providing at least a relative measure of resource accessibility. Both mean distances to resources and ranked mean distances were analyzed using a battery of nonparametric statistics.

Next, potential and actual resources themselves were considered. This aspect of the analysis was confined to fauna; both marine and terrestrial fauna figure in the archaeological records from Asturian sites. It was necessary to obtain an index of species available within each site catchment area that could then be compared with species actually found archaeologically. The larger species of terrestrial mammals are generally mobile and flexible in their habitat requirements and, as such, typically cross-cut several biotopes (Thomas and others 1975: 7). Thus, it is difficult to assess their subsistence importance solely in terms of the relative frequencies of preferred habitats in a site catchment area. In Table 7.3 the principal game species potentially available to Holocene hunters are listed, along with live weights derived from northern Spanish data (Noval 1976: 13–28, 43–59) and the proportion of usable meat-species. Although 13

species are potentially important, there is archaeological evidence for the systematic exploitation of only six of them (red deer, roe deer, chamois, ibex, and to a much lesser extent, boar and horse). The species predominating in Asturian sites are listed below, along with a brief description of their habitat requirements (from Clark 1976a; Jochim 1976; Corbet 1966; Noval 1976; Van den Brink 1967; Morris 1965; Walker 1964; Freeman 1973).

Red deer (*Cervus elaphus*): in Asturias found in open, temperate, mixed deciduous-coniferous woodlands at low to moderate elevations (0–500 m), also in *monte bajo*, matorrals (especially in winter). Densities for western Europe range from about 1 to 16 per square kilometer, with an average of about 4 per square kilometer; densities lower in mixed woods where conifers predominate (lowland forests in post-Pleistocene Cantabria have favored deciduous species). Antlers shed in March or April. From November to February, they frequent brush-covered hillslopes at lower elevations (0–300 m); March-May, female and young separate from males, tend to wander to higher country; June-October, deer remain in separate herds at higher elevations; October-November, males rejoin females, the combined herds begin to move from higher to lower country. The rut occurs from mid-September to mid-October, with the young born in June or July. A crepuscular species, they are also active at night. Abundant in Asturias.

Roe deer (*Capreolus capreolus*): occur in young, deciduous woodlands where dense undergrowth (*monte alto*) is present; favor forest margin when in heavily wooded country; also in open fields with good cover; stands of birch preferred; require adequate moisture, though more tolerant than red deer of areas where no surface water is present; not found at high elevations in Asturias. Western European densities range from 1 to 40 per square kilometer, with an average of 12 per square kilometer. Frequently solitary, they may also occur in small groups composed of monogamous pairs and young; rut occurs in August; young are born in May or June; crepuscular and nocturnal, they are generally inactive during the day. Abundant in Asturias.

Wild boar (*Sus scrofa*): found in marshy country with small lakes, streams; dense undergrowth a prerequisite; rocky areas preferred for lairs, but fallen trees, dense thickets suffice. Intolerant of snow or extremely dry conditions. Density figures variable, with extremely high densities, 40 to 190 per square kilometer, reported by Fleming (1972) for Medieval Europe; present-day average for Germany is 12 per square kilometer. Males solitary except during gestation period (December-June); rut occurs from November to January; young born March-June; nocturnal and crepuscular. The wild boar is a large, unpredictable, and dangerous animal, which may account for its scant representation in Late Pleistocene—Early Holocene Cantabrian sites.

Chamois (*Rupicapra rupicapra*): an alpine species with a tendency for seasonal movement along an altitudinal gradient; found in montane woodlands (winter), above tree line in steep, rocky areas (summer). Alpine matorrals preferred habitat, open deciduous and coniferous woodland margins tolerated. In Cantabria, confined to high elevations on the Cordillera Cantabrica in south central and eastern Asturias, southwestern and central Santander; tolerant of snow. Form small herds composed of females and young, or of adult males; rut occurs November-December; young born May-June. A diurnal species, relatively rare in Cantabria today.

TABLE 7.3
**Mammals Potentially Available
As Game Animals to Early Holocene Hunters in Cantabrian Spain**

Order Genus and Species	Common Name	Average Live Weight Range in Kilos (Sexes combined)	Percent Usable Meat	Preferred Habitat
ARTIODACTYLA				
Cervus elaphus	red deer	180 – 330	50	Open deciduous woodland, woodland margins; matorrals, parklands
Capreolus capreolus	roe deer	15 – 32	50	Deciduous woodland, woodland margins; *monte alto*
Capra ibex	ibex	80 – 110	50	Alpine zones above tree line (summer); rocky areas with matorrals
Rupicapra rupicapra	chamois	22 – 35	50	Alpine zones above tree line (summer); rocky areas with matorrals; forest
Sus scrofa	boar	100 – 275	60	*Monte bajo, monte alto;* open montane woodlands and forest margins
Bos primigenius	auroch	625 – 750	60	Open parklands, grasslands; open deciduous woodland
PERISSODACTYLA				
Equus caballus	horse	275 – 300	60	Open woodland, woodland margins (browser); heathland, grassland (grazer)
CARNIVORA				
Ursus arctos	brown bear	105 – 155	70	Woodland margins, open deciduous woodland; mixed deciduous-coniferous woodland
Lutra lutra	otter	6.8 – 10.7	70	River banks, lakeshores, estuaries
LAGOMORPHA				
Oryctolagus cuniculus	rabbit	1.2 – 1.5	50	*Monte bajo;* woodland margins
Lepus europaeus	brown hare	2.3 – 3.8	50	*Monte bajo,* open grasslands; woodland margins
PINNEPEDIA				
Phoca vitulina	harbor seal	80 – 140	70	Coastline, rocky coastal cliffs; estuaries
Halichoerus grypus	Atlantic gray seal	125 – 360	‑ 70	Coastline, rocky coastal cliffs; estuaries

Ibex (*Capra ibex*): alpine species found on open, rocky terrain above tree line; may descend to tree line in winter due to lack of forage and adverse weather conditions, but rarely found below it. Occurs in herds of 5 to 20 individuals (occasionally up to 50) during breeding period (October-December); males solitary, confined to higher peaks (January-September). A crepuscular-nocturnal form, active mostly at night (Hainard 1949: 157); extinct in Asturias but survives in Vascongadas.

Horse (*Equus caballus*): species present in two ecotypes, one local variety (the so-called *caballo Asturcón*); Pleistocene-Holocene boundary forms (and 17th to 18th century survivals) include open country, steppe-adapted grazers, forest and forest—margin browsers (Zeuner 1963: 310; Cornwall 1968: 48). In herds from 3 to over 100 individuals of all ages, both sexes; breeding seasonality not well defined; active both at night and during the day. Late Pleistocene Cantabrian faunas include both "normal-sized" and smaller, stocky, deep-chested, short-nosed varieties, the latter similar in size and shape to the Asturian forms described by the Romans in the first century B.C. Wild horses of mixed ancestry occur today in the Cordillera del Sueve in eastern Asturias; some resemble the forest-margin browsers of antiquity.

Of the species listed, two prefer deciduous forest and forest-margin habitats (red and roe deer), two are alpine creatures, principally found on rocky, treeless terrain (ibex and chamois), and one (boar) is rather tightly restricted to matorral vegetation (dense, thorny undergrowth) near flowing water. Red deer are by far the most important species prehistorically in Cantabria, both in

terms of numbers of individuals represented and in terms of meat yield. This is true not only for the Asturian culture-stratigraphic unit (Clark 1971b), but for the Magdalenian and Solutrean periods as well (Freeman 1973: 3–44; Straus 1975a: 381–420).

When Cantabrian microfauna and noneconomic species are considered, a clearer picture of the kinds of animals present in the pristine Holocene environment emerges (Table 7.4). Some 47 terrestrial mammalian species are indigenous to eastern Asturias (Noval 1976: 80–83); 23 of them are known from Asturian archaeological contexts (Clark 1971a: 430–432; 1971b: 1246). Apart from the marked selectivity evident in the archaeological sample, the microfauna, which tend to be relatively nonmobile and restricted at times to quite specific habitats, provide a good deal of information about vegetation cover and microenvironments in general in the immediate vicinity of archaeological sites. Archaeological representation of terrestrial mammalian fauna is summarized for Asturian sites in Table 6.1. Bird, amphibian, freshwater fish, and saltwater fish remains also occur, but in quantities so small that they suggest only sporadic, infrequent exploitation of these resources, probably on an opportunistic basis.

The other major component in the Asturian diet, for which there is archaeological evidence, was shellfood. There are no less than 140 species of shellfish on the Asturian coast today, but only about a dozen occur in archaeological contexts assigned to the Asturian period.

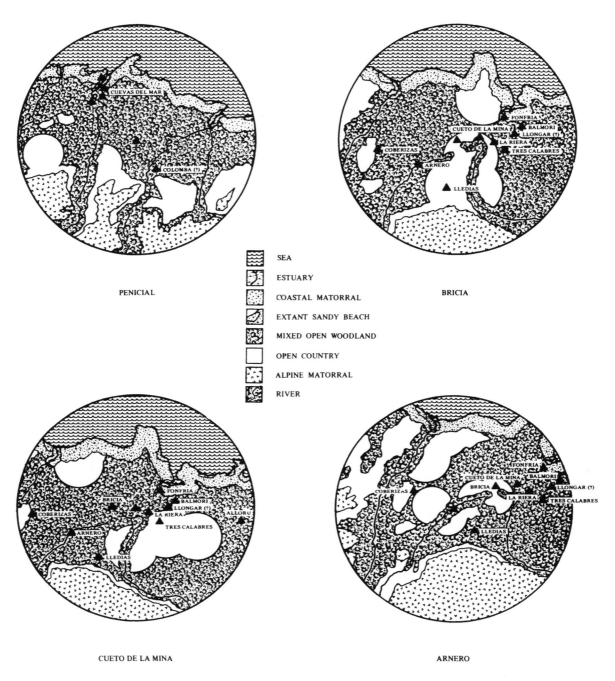

SEA

ESTUARY

COASTAL MATORRAL

EXTANT SANDY BEACH

MIXED OPEN WOODLAND

OPEN COUNTRY

ALPINE MATORRAL

RIVER

PENICIAL

BRICIA

CUETO DE LA MINA

ARNERO

Figure 7.2. Site catchment circles for the Asturian sites of Penicial, Bricia, Cueto de la Mina, and Arnero.

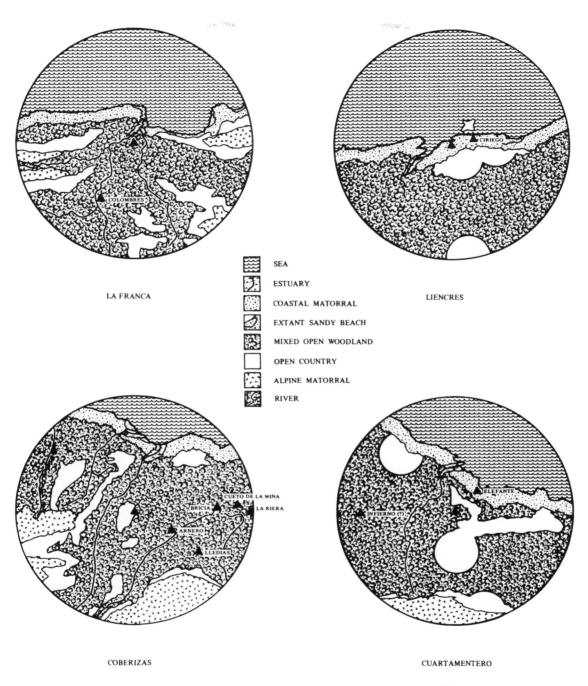

LA FRANCA

LIENCRES

COBERIZAS

CUARTAMENTERO

SEA
ESTUARY
COASTAL MATORRAL
EXTANT SANDY BEACH
MIXED OPEN WOODLAND
OPEN COUNTRY
ALPINE MATORRAL
RIVER

Figure 7.3. Site catchment circles for the Asturian sites of La
Franca, Liencres, Coberizas, and Cuartamentero.

TABLE 7.4
Contemporary Mammalian Fauna of Asturias
(after Noval 1976: 80−83; Clark 1971a: 535−553)

ORDER
  FAMILY
    Genus and Species
	English Common Name	Spanish Common Name

INSECTIVORA		
SORICIDAE (shrews)		
Suncus etruscus Savi	Etruscan shrew	Musarañita
Crocidura sauveolens Pallas	Lesser white-toothed shrew	Musaraña campesina
Crocidura russula Hermann	European white-toothed shrew	Musaraña común
Sorex araneus L.	Common shrew	Musaraña de cola cuadrada
Sorex minutus L.		Musaraña enana
Neomys anomalus Cabrera	Miller's water shrew	Musgaño de Cabrera
Neomys fodiens Pennant	Northern water shrew	Musgaño patiblanco
TALPIDAE (moles)		
Desmana pyrenaica Geoffroy St. H.	Pyrenean desman	Topo de agua
Talpa europaea L.	Eurasian mole	Topo comun
Talpa caeca Savi	Blind mole	Topo ciego
ERINACEIDAE (hedgehogs)		
Erinaceus europaeus L.	European hedgehog	Erizo común
RODENTIA		
MICROTIDAE (voles)		
Clethrionomys glareolus Schreber		Topillo rojo
Pitymys mariae F. Major		Topillo oscuro
Arvicola amphibius L.	Water vole	Rata de agua
Arvicola terrestris S.-Longchamps		Rata de agua norteña
Microtus arvalis Miller	Common vole	Ratilla asturiana
Microtus agrestis L.		Ratilla agreste
Microtus nivalis Martins	Guenther's vole	Ratilla nival
MURIDAE (rats, mice)		
Rattus rattus L.	Black rat	Rata campestre
Rattus norvegicus Berk.	Brown rat	Rata común
Apodemus sylvaticus Cabrera	Wood mouse	Ratón de campo
Apodemus flavicolis Melchior		Ratón leonado
Mus musculus L.	House mouse, field mouse	Ratón casero
Micromys minutus Pallas		Ratón espiguero
GLIRIDAE (dormice)		
Eliomys quercinus L.	Garden dormouse	Lirón común
Glis glis L.	Edible dormouse, fat dormouse	Lirón gris
SCIURIDAE (squirrels)		
Sciuris vulgaris L.	Red squirrel	Ardilla común
CARNIVORA		
MUSTELIDAE (martens)		
Mustela erminea L.	Ermine, stoat	Armiño
Mustela nivalis L.	Weasel	Comadreja
Martes foina Erxlben	Beech marten, stone marten	Garduña
Martes martes L.	Pine marten	Marta
Lutra lutra L.	Otter	Nutria
Meles meles L.	Badger	Tejón
Putorius putorius L.	European polecat, skunk	Turón
Lutreola lutreola L.		Visón europeo
FELIDAE (cats)		
Felis sylvestris Schreber	European wild cat	Gato montés
VIVERRIDAE (genets)		
Genetta genetta L.	Small spotted genet	Gineta
CANIDAE (canids)		
Vulpes vulpes L.	Red fox	Zorro común
Canis lupus L.	Wolf, European wolf	Lobo
URSIDAE (bears)		
Ursus arctos L.	Brown bear	Oso
ARTIODACTYLA		
CERVIDAE (deer)		
Cervus elaphus L.	Red deer	Ciervo común
Capreolus capreolus L.	Roe deer	Corzo
Dama dama L.	Fallow deer (introduced)	Gamo
BOVIDAE (bovids)		
Rupicapra rupicapra L.	Chamois	Rebeco
SUIDAE (suids)		
Sus scrofa L.	Boar	Jabalí
LAGOMORPHA		
LEPORIDAE (rabbits, hares)		
Oryctolagus cuniculus	Rabbit	Conejo de monte
Lepus europaeus L.	Brown hare, European hare	Liebre común

Only three are commonly found in great numbers: the European topshell *Trochocochlea crassa* (= *Trochus lineatus*) and two limpets (*Patella vulgata, Patella intermedia*); together they account for about 90 percent of identified shell.

Patella vulgata: noted at many beaches and inlets along the coasts of Asturias, Santander (such as Bahía de Santander, Playa de Ciriego, San Vicente de la Barquera, Barro, and Niembro inlets); occurs on rocks and in pools on rocky shores from high water neap tide to low water spring tide, 90 to 5 percent exposure; also on pebbles not subjected to too much movement; extends onto bare rocks to 6 m above mean sea level; rarely found below 5 m in depth; in sheltered and polluted waters; withstands salinities less than or equal to 3 parts per thousand (estuarine); extremely abundant; often sympatric with *P. intermedia* (Madariaga 1967).

Patella intermedia: on rocks and in pools on rocky shores from HWNT to LWST; extends onto bare rock; avoids sheltered and polluted locales; able to withstand the direct impact of waves (100 percent exposure); often sympatric with *P. vulgata* (Madariaga 1967).

Trochocochlea crassa: occurs on rocks exposed to the sun in intertidal pools just below HWNT; 60 to 50 percent exposure; very localized in distribution but common where found; noted at Playa de Sardinero, Santoña, Suances, San Vicente de la Barquera, Niembro, and Barro inlets, and Playa de La Franca; lower density per unit area than *Patella* spp., with comparatively reduced adhesive power; cannot withstand long periods without water (Clark 1971a: 602).

All are estuarine and intertidal species, exposed twice daily by the action of the tides. The limpets in particular are often found concentrated in great numbers (12 to 30 per square meter) and can be collected by anyone with comparative ease. While these species were of undoubted economic importance, just how important they were as a staple is difficult to assess. Certainly their combined dietary contribution compared with red deer was minimal. Bailey (1973: 74) has estimated that a single red deer provides the caloric equivalent of about 20,000 shellfish. The shellfish must represent either (1) dietary supplements accumulated over the long term either seasonally or perennially, or (2) an insurance resource exploited intensively only when other staples were unavailable. A seasonal pattern of collection is suggested by preliminary analysis of oxygen isotope ratios from Asturian shell samples from the La Riera cave that indicate collection during the winter months.

The co-occurrence of limpets and topshells in shell middens is a phenomenon peculiar to the early Holocene in Cantabrian Spain; other midden deposits that pre- and postdate the Asturian are composed of different but equally distinctive spectra of molluscan species. Reasons for these systematic changes over time have been discussed in Chapter 6 and elsewhere (Clark 1971a: 428–460; 1971b: 1253–1256). They involve both long term macroclimatic change (mean annual sea water temperature increased during the Asturian period, and declined somewhat after about 6000 B.P.) and a concentration on the estuarine and intertidal zones for exploitative purposes. Human predation on these zones had become so

intensive by the end of the Pleistocene that mean limpet size within species declines significantly during and after the Azilian as a consequence of over-exploitation, according to Ortea. The archaeological representation of shellfish species in Asturian deposits is given in Table 6.4.

Fauna known archaeologically were compared, on a site-by-site basis, with estimates of faunal resources potentially available by using the relative frequency of life zones. If, for example, woodland zones accounted for a significant proportion of a particular site's catchment area, it would be expected that those species adapted to forest-margin and forest habitats would account for most of the remains present archaeologically. The proportion of the various reconstructed life zones in each catchment circle were then used to rank resources potentially available. If the life zone typology is a reasonably accurate representation of gross life zones present prehistorically, then strong correlations between faunal resources potentially available and those represented archaeologically would be expected to occur. Marine fauna were treated in a similar fashion. The objective was to isolate groups of sites similar to one another (1) with respect to the percentage composition of zones in their catchment areas, and (2) with respect to marine and terrestrial fauna present archaeologically. Strong correlations did emerge.

Finally, a tabulation by site of artifactual material was attempted to determine whether or not Asturian sites were similar to one another with respect to categories of remains. Artifacts are rare in these midden deposits, and the problem of coping with artifact variation within the Asturian is exacerbated by the variable quality of the preserved collections. Consequently, only a crude typology of lithic and bone artifacts was attempted, as a more refined effort could not be justified by the scarce and heavily selected material available for study. Lithic artifacts were divided into (1) debitage, (2) heavy duty tools, and (3) small tools. It was assumed that such general divisions would have at least some functional referents (a site in which heavy tools predominated probably reflects a different spectrum of activities from one in which, for example, debitage is mainly represented). Debitage was defined as "the waste products of the primary manufacturing process.... [and] excludes any pieces which exhibit secondary retouch" (Clark 1971a: 262). Small tools are implements manufactured on flakes, blades, and bladelets, characterized by secondary retouch. They include most of the formal morphological types defined in the de Sonneville-Bordes and Perrot typology for the European Upper Paleolithic. Heavy duty tools are large items manufactured on nodules, cobbles, or large flakes that exhibit either extensive battering (hammerstones) or primary, percussion retouch (picks, choppers). There are also some categories of worked bone and antler attributed to the Asturian, but they are rare (Clark 1971a); examples include points (probably weapon tips), so-called "bastones de mando" (perforated shaft straighteners), and a variety of worked splinters. Owing to scarcity and the likelihood of extensive postexcavation selection, artifact variables were scored as present or absent (Table 7.5).

TABLE 7.5
Archaeological Remains Found in Asturian Sites

Site	Debitage	Heavy Duty Tools	Small Tools	Bone
Allorú				
Arnero	x	x	x	x
Balmori	x	x	x	x
Bricia	x	x	x	x
Ciriego		x		
Coberizas	x	x	x	x
Colombres	x	x	x	
Cuartamentero	x	x	x	
Cueto de la Mina	x	x	x	
Cuevas del Mar				
Cueva del Río	x	x		
Elefante				
Fonfría	x	x	x	x
Infierno	x			
La Colomba	x	x	x	
La Cuevona(?)	x	x		
La Franca (Mazaculos I)	x	x	x	
La Llongar(?)				
La Meaza(?)				x
La Riera	x	x	x	x
Las Cascaras(?)				
Liencres	x	x	x	
Lledías(?)				
Mésé(?)				
Penicial	x	x	x	
Tres Calabres	x	x		x
Vidiago	x	x		x

x = Category represented in preserved museum collections at Museo Arqueológico Provincial (Oviedo); Museo Arqueológico Provincial (Barcelona); Museo Provincial de Prehistoria (Santander); Museo Municipal (Madrid); Museo Arqueológico Nacional (Madrid); Museo Nacional de Ciencias Naturales (Madrid).

? = Classified as an Asturian site on the basis of typical conchero deposits only (no artifactual remains, or only a few, represented).

SETTLEMENT-SUBSISTENCE SYSTEM MODELS

Hypothetical settlement-subsistence system models should take into account (1) particulars of regional topography, (2) probable resource distribution (in part a function of regional topograpy), and (3) cyclical or periodic variation in resource availability and in the use-occupation of a particular locus in the site system. An imperfect knowledge of early Holocene vegetation and climate restricts us to the three alternatives outlined below, designated models A, B, and C (Figure 7.4).

Model A proposes the existence of two base camps, one located near or on the coast and the other more inland, perhaps in one of the valleys of the east-west trending foothill ranges that parallel the Cordillera. Assuming significant seasonal movement along the north-south trending river valleys that transect the coastal plain, it would have been advantageous to have a bipolar system, entailing a fall-winter encampment in close proximity to seasonally available montane resources like ibex and chamois, yet situated at a low enough elevation (and in a sheltered valley) so that the occupants themselves would not suffer from the effects of the altitudinal gradient. The other base camp would have been occupied in the spring and summer, situated on or near an estuary, and orientated toward the exploitation of lowland cervids and shellfish. In support of this model are the observations that some Asturian sites are more inland than others (see Fig. 3.1); remains of alpine species are commonly found, indicating systematic exploitation of that life zone; and alpine caprids do descend to lower elevations during the

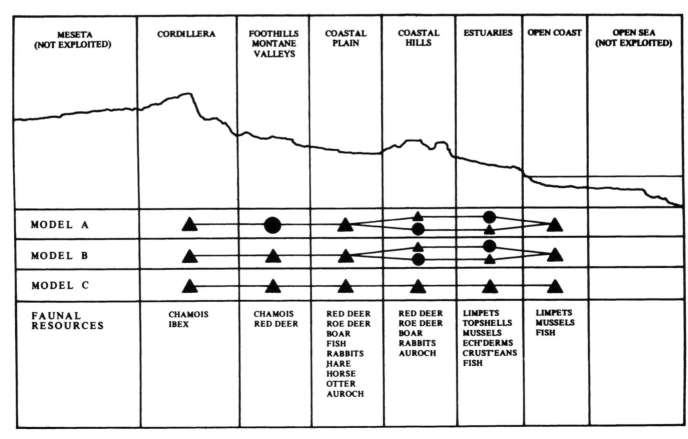

winter months and they would have been more accessible to human predation at that time. Test implications for Model A entail demonstration of a bimodal pattern of life zone distributions and of species present and potentially available. It is also reasonable to expect that artifact spectra would be distinct in this situation, but artifact data are of such poor quality that this distinction might be obscured. Limited activity sites located in intervening areas may be identified in statistical comparisons of site catchment areas and resources.

Model B proposes a single base camp located on the coastal plain or in the east-west trending valleys of the coastal hill range adjacent to it. Presumably occupied by at least a portion of a local group on a perennial basis, such a camp would have been strategically located to take advantage of the demonstrated mainstays of the Asturian diet: red deer and shellfish, both concentrated the year round on the wooded lowlands and in the coastal estuaries that cut across them. Resources located at some distance from the camp would have been obtained by hunting and gathering parties sent out from the home site on a periodic basis. Life zones in eastern Asturias are defined by altitudinal differences and are compressed from north to south into a narrow band from 7 to 12 km wide. Thus a hypothetical single base camp located near the coast is a viable alternative to the bipolar model discussed above. Distances are not so great, nor movement so difficult, nor alpine resources so important that they could not have been obtained by hunting parties detached from a perennially occupied home site. Test implications for Model B entail demonstration of an essentially unimodal pattern of life zone distributions and of species present and potentially available. If limited activity sites are present, they should be recognizable by distinctive faunal and perhaps lithic components (for example, a high incidence of chamois, ibex) and by distributions inland of presumed base camps, following north-south trending river courses (such as R ío Bedón-Cabras).

Model C is a no base-camp model. It proposes movement, in the course of an annual round, by an entire local group, up and down the major river courses with transhumance confined in each case to a single drainage system. It is difficult to generate test implications for this model. It assumes that the only differences among sites will be in terms of the resources found in them; in other words, no base camp-limited activity site distinction is to be made. Also, in order to reach any conclusions about whether a single group, or several groups, are involved, it is necessary first to be able to control for stylistic variation and to be able to compare stylistic variables within and between river systems. Unfortunately, there is nothing in the restricted spectrum of Asturian artifacts that is both sufficiently numerous and also likely to be a good indicator of stylistic variability. We cannot demonstrate that a single group is involved in any case, which thrusts us back on the more general Models A and B.

While the notion of extended family bands moving up and down the major valley systems exploiting resources as they become available has a certain intrinsic appeal, it is impossible to demonstrate one way or the other with the data presently available. Confirmation of a Model C type situation depends almost entirely on the degree of distinctiveness of the different resources to be derived from each of the six life zones shown in Figure 7.4. As there is an evident and considerable degree of overlap in resource distributions, the probable result is likely to be confounded with the test implications for Model B: namely, a unimodal pattern of life zone distributions, species present, and species potentially available.

ANALYSIS AND RESULTS

The preliminary analysis consisted of tests for homogeneity over (1) the proportional representation of life zones and (2) the ranks of the proportional representation of life zones across all sites listed in Tables 7.5 and 7.6. Statistical tests are summarized in Table 7.7. Proportional representation is given by the percentage of total area per catchment circle of each life zone represented in that circle. Both percentages and ranks were used because percentage representation gives a more accurate picture of overall life zone similarity across sites than does the simple rank of the various life zones. However, the ranks provide an additional measure of difference-similarity that is perhaps not as sensitive to random variation in the actual area represented. The number of sites is small, and, because the catchment areas themselves are small, it is expected that they would vary considerably among themselves (Table 7.6).

Homogeneity Tests

Data from Table 7.6 were used to plot the percentage representation of life zones for each site catchment circle, and the resulting graphs were first compared visually. Although it was possible to group sites impressionistically by overlaying pairs of cumulative percentage graphs that appeared to be similar to one another, when all of the sites were examined together, no clear subgroup definition was evident. A Kolmogorov-Smirnov test was then performed on the percentage data from all possible pairs of sites (Siegel 1956: 127–136; Blalock 1972: 262–265). A Kruskal-Wallis H test, a nonparametric approach analogous to the one-way analysis of variance model, was used to evaluate the ranks (Siegel 1956: 184–193; Blalock 1972: 349, 350). In both cases, the null hypotheses (H_0) are nondirectional:

H_0 Kolmogorov-Smirnov Test: the proportional representation of environmental zones is the same or similar across all (pairs of) sites.

H_0 Kruskal-Wallis H Test: the ranks of the proportional representation of environmental zones are the same or similar across all sites.

Figure 7.4. Schematic representation of three alternative settlement-subsistence models for the Asturian of Cantabria.

TABLE 7.6
Asturian Site Catchment Area Data
Proportional Representation of Transformed Zones by Site,
Mean Distance to Each Site from Each Zone, Other Sites in Catchment Circle,
and Site Elevation

Data	Bricia	Cueto de la Mina	La Riera	Tres Calabres	Coberizas	Alloru	Vidiago	Balmori	Lledias	Fonfria	Arnero	Penicial	Colomba	Cuevas del Mar
PERCENT ZONE BY SITE														
Woodland	46.0	45.0	45.7	49.7	52.0	48.6	16.8	45.0	43.9	40.5	34.0	35.6	48.0	32.9
Open Country	13.7	13.8	10.5	9.5	15.4	14.1	10.9	11.1	17.9	13.3	25.9	15.9	11.0	5.7
Alpine	8.8	7.1	6.7	13.0	14.8	1.3	7.4	2.1	31.0	1.4	20.1	11.3	17.4	7.0
Coastline	11.5	13.2	16.2	11.5	8.1	9.2	11.7	14.6	4.3	13.5	9.1	16.0	9.3	11.2
Sea	19.0	19.7	20.4	16.4	6.9	25.2	37.1	27.2	1.4	30.3	7.3	18.1	10.4	41.6
Estuarine	0.9	1.3	0.7		2.8	1.3	2.8		1.4	0.9	3.8	2.8	2.5	1.5
DISTANCE FROM SITE IN KILOMETERS														
Woodland	0.05	w/in	0.5	w/in	w/in	w/in	w/in	0.7	w/in	w/in	w/in	w/in	w/in	w/in
Open Country	w/in	0.7	w/in	1.6	1.5	0.9	1.5	w/in	1.3	0.8	1.1	1.1	1.16	1.5
Alpine	2.0	2.2	2.0	2.5	1.6	2.5	1.8	2.8	0.6	2.6	1.8	2.5	1.3	2.0
Coastline	1.0	0.8	1.0	0.7	1.5	0.5	w/in	w/in	2.3	0.1	2.0	1.0	1.6	w/in
Sea	1.8	1.5	1.5	1.3	1.8	1.3	0.5	0.8	2.6	0.5	2.5	1.4	2.1	0.5
Estuarine	2.0	2.2	2.2		1.6	2.2	1.1		2.3	2.6	1.5	1.7	2.3	along
River	1.3	1.4	1.1	1.8	0.5	2.2	1.0	2.0	1.2	1.5	1.4	0.8	1.5	1.5
Beach	2.0	1.9	1.4	1.6		1.4						1.8		0.2
SITES IN CATCHMENT CIRCLE	Sites 1–11 and 28 are all in similar catchment circles											13	12	12
												14	13	13
ELEVATION IN METERS	65	65	65	55	55	55	15	40	55	15	65	10	35	10

The corresponding alternative hypotheses (H_1) are that the areal percentages and their ranks are not the same (that they deviate by an order of magnitude greater than that attributable to chance variation alone). Acceptance of the null hypothesis in either case would indicate that the sites are all basically similar so far as their locations are concerned, which would tend to support Model B. Rejection of H_0 would tend to support Models A and C.

The Kolmogorov-Smirnov test indicated that the sites formed a homogeneous set with respect to life zone composition, with individual differences in site catchment areas falling within the range expectable due to chance variation. The Kruskal-Wallis test over the ranked life zone data produced similar results. The H statistic was 21.27, with k-1, or 27 degrees of freedom. The probability associated with a value for H greater than or equal to 21.27 is approximately 75 percent. In both cases the null hypothesis is accepted, and it is concluded that Asturian site catchment areas are not significantly different among themselves with respect to life zone representation.

The distance to the various life zones across sites is also regarded as an important measure, principally of resource accessibility. An overall index of accessibility is derived by ranking the mean distances to resource zones by site, and then comparing the ranks across all sites using a rank-order statistic (the Kruskal-Wallis test). The null hypothesis is again nondirectional:

H_0: The ranks of the mean distances to resource zones is the same or similar across all sites.

H_1: The ranks of the mean distances to resource zones are not the same across all sites (they deviate by an order of magnitude greater than that attributable to chance variation).

Again, homogeneity implies similarity of location compared with different life zones, and, by extension, functional equivalence among the sites evaluated. The H statistic in this case was 25.87, with 27 degrees of freedom. The probability associated with a value for H greater than or equal to 25.87 lies between 50 percent and 70 percent, and by interpolation is approximately 53 percent. The null hypothesis is consequently accepted, with a probability of Type I error equal to 0.05.

In sum, the results of the tests for homogeneity are quite consistent; they support the notion that Asturian sites are generally located in similar environmental circumstances with comparable resource zone accessibility indices. As noted, this tends to support Model B, which postulates the existence of coastally situated base camps, although Model C is not conclusively refuted. Model A, a bipolar hypothesis with inland and coastal base camps, seems to be rather unlikely, although it should be kept in mind that inland Asturian sites may exist but have simply not yet been identified. It should also be noted that little information is provided by the homogeneity tests about what particular variables are important in determining

Data	\multicolumn{14}{c}{Sites}												
	La Franca	Colombres	Infierno	Cuartamentero	Elefante	Cueva del Río	La Cuevona	La Lloseta	Liencres	Ciriego	Las Cáscaras	La Meaza	Mésé	Llongar
PERCENT ZONE BY SITE														
Woodland	34.0	38.8	45.0	51.8	39.7	56.4	40.6	∖42.8	38.2	32.3	31.5	57.8	38.5	46.4
Open Country	12.7	29.6	23.3	10.5	14.5	6.5	8.3	17.4	6.4	7.3	21.9	25.4	2.4	10.8
Alpine	6.3	14.2	10.4	5.3	1.7	2.1	1.7	6.0			14.2	7.4	59.0	3.0
Coastline	11.0	12.3	11.7	9.5	8.9	14.8	11.7	11.8	13.4	11.4	14.6	5.3		11.4
Sea	34.0	3.8	7.4	21.6	34.3	16.9	33.5	19.8	40.9	47.8	14.8	1.7		28.0
Estuarine	1.6	0.8	2.3	1.2	1.0	3.2	4.4	2.2	1.1	1.2	3.0	1.4		
DISTANCE FROM SITE IN KILOMETERS														
Woodland	w/in	w/in	0.6	0.8	0.8	w/in	w/in	w/in	0.9	0.9	w/in	w/in	w/in	w/in
Open Country	1.2	1.1	w/in	1.8	1.5	2.1	1.7	1.2	1.3	1.14	0.4	0.7	0.1	0.8
Alpine	1.5	2.0	2.0	2.2	2.8	2.5	2.6	2.5			1.0	2.2	2.2	2.5
Coastline	0.3	1.8	2.0	0.4	w/in	0.2	0.2	0.8	w/in	w/in	1.3	2.4		0.1
Sea	0.8	2.4	2.5	0.9	0.01	0.6	0.7	1.25	along	0.1	1.8	2.8		0.5
Estuarine	0.3	2.0	2.3	1.0	1.0	0.7	0.3	1.2	1.2	1.7	2.2	2.5	2.5	
River	0.3	0.6	1.2	0.8	0.8	0.8	0.2	0.9			1.1	3.0	3.0	1.5
Beach						1.3	0.6	1.0			2.8	2.7	2.7	1.6
SITES IN CATCHMENT CIRCLE	16	15	18	17	17	21	20	20	24	23				1–11
			19	19	18	22	22	21						
ELEVATION IN METERS	40	85	65	45	55	10	1	12	13	13	115	137	100	50

site location; all that has been shown so far is that site location is reasonably consistent.

Cluster Analysis

In order to be able to refine the examination of possible differences among Asturian sites, and ultimately to be able to identify those variables that are important in the determination of site location, a q-mode (case-type) cluster analysis was performed on the data, using as variables (1) mean distances from sites to life zones, (2) percentage representation of life zones in site catchment circles, (3) potentially available and archaeologically documented fauna, and (4) stone artifacts. In this kind of cluster analysis, the 28 sites are the cases, and the four major variables are divided into the 30 categories listed in Table 7.8. Cluster analysis makes use of a matrix of case x case correlation coefficients to partition a group of units (here sites) into smaller and more homogeneous subgroups. The coefficients summarize a series of scores on all variables for each case in the array. These new classes of data may be more amenable to interpretation than the original unsorted array (Hodson 1970). In this application, the H-CLUS program package (Wood 1974) was selected because it generates a similarity matrix and then analyzes it sequentially according to eight different clustering algorithms. The version used here (H-CLUS II, modified by A. Olshan), is an "agglomerative" one; it measures the degree of similarity between each pair of

cases by computing a Euclidean distance matrix and joining those cases most similar to one another into the same group. At each step in the procedure, the union of every possible pair of clusters is reconsidered and the two clusters whose fusion results in the minimum increase in the error sum of squares are combined (Everitt 1974). The most similar sites, then, are placed into groups one at a time until all are joined in a single cluster. Ward's method (Everitt 1974: 7–15) was chosen subjectively as the algorithm resulting in the best cluster definition. It is interesting to note, however, that in five of eight cases nearly identical groups were formed despite rather marked differences in computational routines.

Figure 7.5 displays the results of the cluster analysis in the form of a dendrogram. The sites are listed in the column on the right and a scaled similarity coefficient is given across the top of the figure. Sites joined at the higher levels indicated on the right side of the scale are most similar to one another; those joined at lower levels of similarity represented on the left are least alike. Values listed adjacent to site names are merge levels that, when ordered from smallest to largest, reproduce the sequence of cluster formation. The sites are divided, somewhat arbitrarily and at about the 50 percent level of similarity, into five groups. The fact that group formation is not an objective and easily replicable procedure underscores the observation made earlier on the basis of the homogeneity tests—really marked differences among

TABLE 7.7
Basic Statistics, Statistical Tests, and Notation Used in the Site Catchment Analysis

Mean:

$$\bar{x} = \sum_{i=1}^{n} / n,$$

where: $\bar{x}$ is the sample mean
n is the number of observations
i is the index of summation

Standard Deviation:

$$s = \sqrt{\sum_{i=1}^{n} (x_i - \bar{x}_i)^2 / n - 1}$$

where: s is the sample standard deviation, an unbiased estimator of the population standard deviation σ

$\bar{x}$ is an unbiased estimator of the population parameter μ

x_i is any unspecified observation

Kolmogorov-Smirnov Two Sample Test:

$$D = c \sqrt{n_1 + n_2 / n_1 n_2}$$

where: the formula gives the critical value for D.
If the Kolmogorov-Smirnov D statistic (maximum $| S_{n_1}(X) - S_{n_2}(X) |$) is greater than the critical value, reject H_0 at the level of significance (*a*) indicated.

n_1 and n_2 are the sample sizes

c = 1.36 for *a* (probability Type I error) = 0.05

Kruskal-Wallis H Test:

$$H = \frac{\dfrac{12}{N(N+1)} \sum_{i=1}^{k} \left(\dfrac{R_i^2}{n_i} \right) - 3(N+1)}{C}$$

where: C is a correction term for ties:
$C = 1 - \Sigma T_i / N^3 - N,$

where: $T = t^3 - t$, and T is the number of ties per set. Summation is over all sets of ties; if no ties occur, C = 1

N is the total sample size (all samples combined)

k is the number of groups

R_i are the ranks, summed by sample, then squared

NOTE: The Kruskal-Wallis H statistic has a chi-square distribution on k − 1 degrees of freedom.

Ward's Method: Ward's method is a hierarchical, agglomerative algorithm for clustering cases or variables. At any stage of the analysis, the loss of information that results from the grouping of individual (cases) into clusters can be measured by the total sum of squared deviations at every point from the mean of the cluster to which that point belongs. At each step in the analysis, union of every possible pair of clusters is considered, and the two clusters whose fusion results in the minimum increase in the error sum of squares (E.S.S.) are combined. These results can be summarized as a dendrogram (from Everitt 1974: 7–15).

Error Sum of Squares:

$$E.S.S. = \sum_{i=1}^{n} x_i^2 - \frac{1}{n} (\Sigma x_i)^2$$

where: x_i = the score of the ith individual (case)
n = the number of cases

Fisher's Discriminant Function:

$$Z = \sum_{i=1}^{x} \lambda_i x_i$$

where: x_i = the score on the ith variable
λ_i = a weighting factor for the ith variable

TABLE 7.8
Major and Minor Variables Used in the Cluster and Discriminant Function Analyses

1. Mean Distance from Site to Life Zone for 8 Life Zones:
   $\bar{x}$ distance to open country
   $\bar{x}$ distance to mixed open woodland
   $\bar{x}$ distance to alpine matorral
   $\bar{x}$ distance to coastal matorral
   $\bar{x}$ distance to estuaries
   $\bar{x}$ distance to all rivers
   $\bar{x}$ distance to sea
   $\bar{x}$ distance to (sandy) beaches

2. Percentage Representation of 8 Life Zones in Site Catchment Circles:
   % open country
   % mixed open woodland
   % alpine matorral
   % coastal matorral
   % estuaries
   % river valleys
   % (sandy) beaches

3. Economically Important Faunal Resources:

Oryctolagus cuniculus	Hare
Lepus europaeus	Rabbit
Sus scrofa	Boar
Cervus elaphus	Red deer
Capreolus capreolus	Roe deer
Equus caballus	Horse
Rupicapra rupicapra	Chamois
Capra ibex	Ibex
Lutra lutra	Otter
Phoca vitulina	Seal
Patella vulgata	Limpet
Trochocochlea crassa	Topshell

4. Stone Artifacts:
   Debitage
   Heavy duty tools
   Small tools

the sites are not apparent. Only a few pairs of sites are really similar (for example, Ciriego and Liencres, Cueto de la Mina and La Riera), and these, not surprisingly, are generally located near one another in closely similar if not identical environmental settings. Although the Posada de Llanes site cluster is reasonably well replicated in Groups 2 and 3, there is no hint of *marked* differentiation in resources available to site occupants, nor in accessibility to those resources. Only in the case of the Santander strand line knapping stations (Liencres, Ciriego) can a strong case be made for functional differentiation, and that case could have been made on the basis of unrelated prior knowledge (Clark 1975a, 1979; Clark and others 1977; Johnstone and others 1977; Scheitlin and Clark 1978). In general, Model B continues to be supported; Asturian sites appear to be basically similar in terms of locational setting.

Discriminant Function Analysis

In order to isolate variables that are important in the determination of site location, groups defined by the cluster analysis were tested for group integrity and subjected to further analysis using a discriminant function. A discriminant analysis is a multivariate statistical pro-

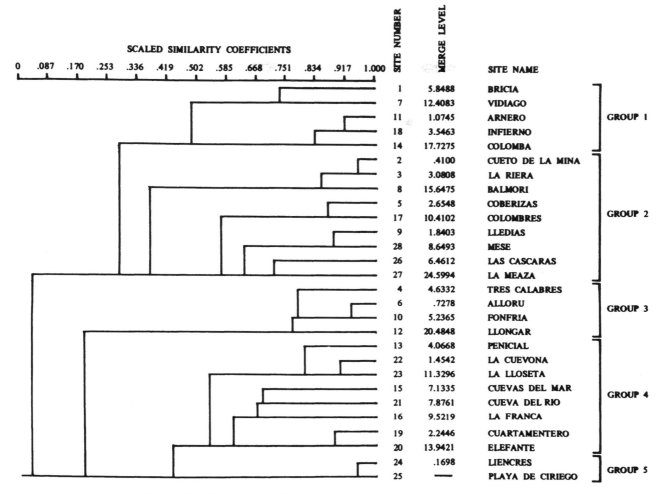

Figure 7.5. Dendrogram of cluster analysis of 28 Asturian sites, with scaled similarity coefficients and merge levels indicated.

cedure originally developed to assign cases of unknown group affiliation to one of a series of groups of known statistical composition on the basis of a linear combination of observations taken over a series of variables (Table 7.7). Discriminant function analysis computes a new variable, Z, a linear function of the general type $Z = \lambda_1 x_1 + \lambda_2 x_2 + \lambda_3 x_3 + \ldots$, which describes a line or a plane cutting across an intermixed cluster of points representing observations taken on a series of variables from two or more groups. The function is so constructed that as many as possible of the members of one group will have high values for Z and as many as possible of the members of the others will have low values, so that Z serves as a much better discriminant of the groups than does any single variable or pair of variables (Sokal and Rohlf 1969: 488, 489). The particular discriminant analysis program used here (BMDP7M) is a stepwise version: variables are entered one at a time according to their decreasing capacity to discriminate the criterion groups. Variables are entered until a stopping criterion (a user-specified F statistic) is encountered. Group membership is assumed, and, at each step, a group x group classifica-

tion matrix is printed from which the incidence of misclassification can be computed. When the run is completed (up to 15 "steps" are permitted), a table summarizing the variable entry sequence is printed, along with the associated F and U statistics (the latter, Wilk's λ, is used to test for equality of group means). A final group x group classification matrix identifies misclassified cases individually, and gives the Mahalanobis D^2-based posterior probabilities for case-specific group assignments (Dixon 1975). Usually four or five functions are derived that can be ordered in terms of their discriminating power by inspection of associated eigenvalues and canonical correlations; these in turn denote the *relative* ability of each function to separate the groups. All of the functions are not required for group separation, and usually only the first one or two are really good discriminators. While the sum of the eigenvalues is a measure of the total variance existing in the discriminating variables, no rule exists as to when an eigenvalue is to be regarded as too small. In this study, four canonical correlates were generated but the first two account for about 98 percent of the variance, and by themselves result in adequate

TABLE 7.9
Jackknifed Mahalanobis D-square Distance
From Group Means and Posterior Probability
of Group Membership for Each Case

	1		2		3		4		5		Incorrect Classifications
GROUP 1											
Case											
1	17.6	1.000	82.3	0.000	550.4	0.000	746.6	0.000	179.8	0.000	
7	117.9	1.000	163.9	0.000	553.1	0.000	741.8	0.000	156.5	0.000	
11	98.3	1.000	555.1	0.000	1885.5	0.000	2666.6	0.000	709.9	0.000	
14	59.0	1.000	121.2	0.000	590.7	0.000	772.2	0.000	323.6	0.000	
18	161.7	0.000	82.1	1.000	551.0	0.000	751.6	0.000	188.6	0.000	INFIERNO
GROUP 2											
Case											
2	97.1	0.000	24.6	1.000	222.1	0.000	385.6	0.000	186.2	0.000	
3	92.0	0.000	20.8	1.000	335.9	0.000	422.5	0.000	117.9	0.000	
5	115.4	0.000	99.3	0.999	422.8	0.000	477.6	0.000	116.2	0.000	
8	100.5	0.000	12.6	1.000	274.1	0.000	366.1	0.000	118.5	0.000	
9	205.9	0.000	46.2	1.000	253.1	0.000	331.3	0.000	191.2	0.000	
17	242.7	0.000	65.4	1.000	219.1	0.000	330.6	0.000	354.2	0.000	
26	136.9	0.000	75.9	1.000	258.4	0.000	395.5	0.000	164.1	0.000	
27	97.4	0.000	16.4	1.000	263.3	0.000	403.5	0.000	131.6	0.000	
28		0.000		1.000		0.000		0.000		0.000	
GROUP 3											
Case											
4	712.3	0.000	394.7	0.000	108.4	1.000	267.4	0.000	665.2	0.000	
6	1063.5	0.000	517.0	0.000	85.7	0.004	74.9	0.996	796.1	0.000	ALLORÚ
10	561.1	0.000	230.0	0.000	5.9	1.000	96.2	0.000	417.8	0.000	
12	575.9	0.000	223.4	0.000	18.9	1.000	133.3	0.000	430.6	0.000	
GROUP 4											
Case											
13	1192.5	0.000	512.0	0.000	86.6	0.274	84.6	0.726	977.4	0.000	
15	1127.0	0.000	629.2	0.000	169.3	0.000	110.5	1.000	621.5	0.000	
16	771.3	0.000	326.7	0.000	243.4	0.000	98.9	1.000	533.0	0.000	
19	748.6	0.000	359.6	0.000	74.2	1.000	110.5	0.000	532.9	0.000	CUARTAMENTERO
20	832.3	0.000	478.4	0.000	340.5	0.000	157.9	1.000	787.2	0.000	
21		0.000		0.000		0.000		0.000	528.8	1.000	CUEVA DEL RÍO
22	923.5	0.000	461.6	0.000	124.2	0.000	20.2	1.000	769.4	0.000	
23	741.4	0.000	327.0	0.000	170.4	0.000	49.6	1.000	535.7	0.000	
GROUP 5											
Case											
24	179.6	0.000	122.7	0.000	417.6	0.000	537.4	0.000	12.5	1.000	
25	168.9	0.000	135.1	0.000	455.3	0.000	602.2	0.000	12.5	1.000	

group discrimination. The program also plots both individual case and group mean coordinates on the first and second canonical variables.

Discriminant function analyses cannot fail to separate cases into groups; that is what discriminant functions are designed to do and they do it remarkably well. When the groups defined subjectively by inspection of the cluster analysis dendrogram (Fig. 7.5) were tested for integrity using discriminant functions, reasonably good replication was attained, with only four instances (14.34 percent) of misclassification (Table 7.9). This implies that the cluster groups are distinctive in terms of subtle differences in life zone and resource representation, but, except for Group 5 (Liencres, Ciriego), what those differences mean in behavioral terms is not at all clear. Certainly such differences are not apparent on the basis of the homogeneity tests discussed above.

Inspection of the variable entry sequence, however, does reveal those variables that are probably significant determinants of site location (Table 7.10). Variables are ordered by their F statistics from most to least important; only the first 15 are given, as the program is limited to 15 steps. Variables that enter the equation after Step 7 are negligible in terms of their contribution to the discriminatory power of the equation. What is immediately evident from an inspection of Table 7.10 is that three of the first four variables consist of, or are related to, the exploitation of alpine resources (ibex, ranked first; chamois, third; percentage of alpine zone present, fourth). Woodland adapted roe deer (ranked second) are a principal secondary contributor to the resource base, but one that is not uniformly found in Asturian sites (see Table 6.1). Mean distance to and areal percentage of estuarine life zones (ranked fifth and seventh, respectively) are also variables of some significance, underscoring the importance of accessibility to shellfish gathering zones, and parenthetically the importance of shellfoods themselves in the Asturian diet. The other distance measures,

TABLE 7.10
Variable Entry Sequence

Variable Code Number	Rank	Variable Name	F Statistic to Enter
22	1	Ibex	17.0689
19	2	Roe deer	9.4679
21	3	Chamois	7.6447
11	4	% alpine zones	6.7208
5	5	$\bar{x}$ distance to estuaries	6.3285
23	6	Otter	5.6298
13	7	% estuarine zones	4.2469
15	8	Hare	3.1206
10	9	% woodland zones	3.0021
7	10	$\bar{x}$ distance to sea	2.7173
2	11	$\bar{x}$ distance to woodland	2.1188
3	12	$\bar{x}$ distance to alpine	1.6540
14	13	% sea	1.5938
26	14	Heavy duty tools	1.4060
24	15	Harbor seal	1.3571

however, are of comparatively minor significance—an observation due to (1) the proximity of alpine zones (ranked 12th) to the coast, (2) an absence of evidence for the exploitation of marine resources (ranked 10th), and (3) the ubiquity of forested patches (ranked 11th) in the reconstructed early Holocene environment. It is significant that the Asturian dietary staples (red deer, limpets, and topshells) do not figure at all in the list of site location determinants. This underscores the fact that these resources are found in all Asturian sites, and so presumably would have little or no discriminatory value for differentiating among them.

CONCLUSIONS

These results are most consistent with Model B, which postulated that Asturian sites are the remains of base camps situated among the hills and along the estuaries near the coast. In support of this contention, we cite (1) the apparent near homogeneity of Asturian sites with respect to proportional, distance, and access measures of life zone categories, which in turn implies that the Asturian sites so far known are functional equivalents; (2) the overall similarity in resources potentially available in those life zones, and in resources represented archaeologically; (3) the absence of any Asturian sites situated in the foothills and intermontane valleys of the Cordillera that might represent the inland base camps postulated by Model A; and (4) the apparent absence of inland limited activity sites postulated by Model C. We recognize that the detection of limited activity sites is a major problem with the analysis, considering the kinds of data on hand or likely to become available in the near future. At the same time, it is gratifying to observe that the only two functionally distinct limited activity sites known and recognized beforehand—the coastal knapping stations at Ciriego and Liencres—were, in fact, isolated by both cluster and discriminant function analyses.

8. EARLY HOLOCENE ADAPTATIONS

This monograph has integrated artifactual, faunal, and locational data pertinent to the Early Holocene adaptation called the Asturian of Cantabria. The bias is a broadly-defined systemic ecological one, in that economic variables are regarded as primary (and perhaps most visible archaeologically), and prehistoric economies are considered to be intimately adjusted to, although not determined by, the distributions of available and perceived natural resources. The study is diachronic in that an effort has been made to define a distinctive Asturian configuration, and to examine it in relationship to adaptations that bracket it in time. Much more behavioral information can be extracted from the archaeological record if a systemic and diachronic perspective is adopted than if archaeological evidence is "simply regarded as a means for identifying groups of people or periods of time," as is so often the case in Old World prehistoric research (J. G. D. Clark 1975: 7). It is a "broadly-defined" study because archaeological monitors of subsystem components (technology, economy, habitats, and the like) are not, in the present case, adequate to permit a more sophisticated, quantitatively oriented investigation. Overall, the data are quite bad, for reasons discussed in Chapter 2. Only in isolated cases (such as La Riera, La Franca, El Juyo, Los Azules) are they likely to improve in the foreseeable future. Although it is recognized that in *any* systemic model, the relationships among the various component subsystems are multiple, reciprocal, and complex, and that in this case only a first approximation has been made toward limning in the outlines of a peculiarly Asturian adaptation, it is nevertheless possible to suggest a principal, if not a single, determining factor for the subsistence and settlement transformations observable at the Pleistocene-Holocene boundary in the Cantabrian archaeological record. That principal factor is long-term regional population growth.

In what follows, I first attempt to summarize the major findings of this research. In addition to the extended review of Asturian sites (Chapters 3 and 4), four major topics were presented, corresponding to Chapters 2 and 5 through 7. Wherever possible, these research conclusions are put in the broader regional and diachronic perspective of the La Riera Paleoecological Project (1976–1980) and of other recent work in the area. Second, I outline the major tenets of Cohen's (1977) demographic stress model. Archaeological indicators of demographic stress are identified and compared with the Late

Pleistocene-Early Holocene Cantabrian data presented here. Because alternative causal factors can probably be ruled out, at least for the present, it is concluded that the Cohen model provides the most adequate, parsimonious explanation of patterns in Cantabrian mesolithic archaeological data available to date.

GEOGRAPHIC SETTING

Chapter 2 describes present-day geological, geomorphological, faunal, and floral characteristics of the provinces of Asturias and Santander. A description of the geographical setting is justified because it has changed little (except for extensive deforestation) since Asturian times. All evidence available points to floral and faunal communities similar in composition and in gross distribution to those of the present day.

The Holocene pattern stands in marked contrast to geomorphological evidence from the Late Pleistocene, especially that portion of it corresponding to the last part of the Würm glaciation. While it has been recognized for a long time that the crests of the Cantabrian Mountains were glaciated (Obermaier 1914, Hernández Pacheco 1944), Butzer (1970: 1, 2), Laville (Straus and others 1981) and others report the presence of periglacial features (polygenetic screes, consisting mainly of frost-weathered rubble, alluvial terraces, rare cryoturbations) at low elevations along the coastal plain (for example, Morín, La Riera).

The geomorphological evidence, which "attests to cold, glacial age climates with accelerated frost-weathering and denudation from the coast to the edge of the glaciers" (Butzer 1970: 3) is clearly at odds with faunal spectra from Cantabrian sites. From the Cantabrian Upper Solutrean (about 20,000 B.P.) until the Azilian (about 10,200 B.P.), faunal remains suggest that forested biotopes predominated at low elevations, although the presence of species characteristic of alpine and more open country is also clearly indicated (Freeman 1973: 3–44). Moreover, forest dwellers are commonly represented throughout the Mousterian and early Upper Paleolithic sequence.

Extrapolating from the long sequence at Cueva Morín (González Echegaray and Freeman 1971, 1973), Butzer (1970: 9, 10) contends that the Late Pleistocene was characterized by a series of oscillating cold and temperate environments, sedimentological differences at that site and at others in western and central Santander apparently reflecting variations in the intensity of cold. Alluvial terraces attest to depositional-erosional sequences that may ultimately be correlated witth Würm interstadial-stadial fluctuations. By contrast, the salient geomorphological characteristic of post-Pleistocene Cantabria has been a marked increase in erosion. Prior to the early Aurignacian (about 30,500 B.P.) and extending as far back as Mousterian times (more than 45,000 B.P.), the dominant geological process appears to have been deposition, coinciding with the mid-Würm interstadial complex (Butzer 1970: 10). By the Upper Perigordian (about 25,000 B.P.), cold conditions prevail and the cycle of cold-temperate oscillations alluded to above becomes the dominant pattern. Although Azilian levels at Cueva Morín and at Piélago (also in Santander) are cold (Butzer 1970: 8, 10), there is no evidence for cold oscillations subsequent to 9000 B.P.

The contradiction between the faunal and sedimentological data can perhaps be explained by (1) ungulate plasticity—large mammals are poor indicators of climatic change and most of the ungulates that provided the bulk of the calories consumed prehistorically are mobile and capable of adaptation to a wide variety of habitats; and (2) the effect of the sea on the narrow Cantabrian coastal plain. A stable maritime climate probably ameliorated conditions along the coast to some (perhaps considerable) extent, sparing coastal hunter-gatherers most of the effects of the more marked climatic shifts characteristic of the Last Glacial in regions farther inland or at greater elevations.

EVALUATION OF THE LITERATURE

Chapter 3 was devoted primarily to prior research. The discussion of that literature concerned the major problems of statigraphy and chronology. As prosaic as such considerations might seem in better investigated areas, the chronological position of the Asturian has been placed in grave doubt by some recent Spanish authors (Jordá 1957, 1958, 1959; Crusafont 1963). Discussion of prior research contained in published accounts presented evidence treating stratigraphic sequences and faunal inventories. It became clear that at those sites where unequivocal stratigraphic superpositioning was available, the Asturian directly overlies Magdalenian and Azilian deposits. This chronological succession was first demonstrated by Vega del Sella (1923, 1930) and is, of course, suggestive of a post-Pleistocene date.

An alternative interpretation of the stratigraphy emphasizing sites where the stratigraphic succession is not continuous (that is, where concheros are suspended as cornices from cave walls) was also presented. This theory, developed by Jordá (1957, 1958, 1959, 1963, 1975) and by Llopis-Lladó, holds the Asturian to be of Middle Paleolithic date (more than or equal to 37,000 B.P.). Supposedly concheros accumulated in the cave mouths subsequent to the deposition of the Mousterian sequence, were indurated by calcium carbonates, then dissolved

and removed by a cycle of karstic rejuvenation leaving only remnants of conchero cornices on the cave walls. The caves, emptied of post-Mousterian cultural deposits, were then filled with Upper Paleolithic remains.

At La Riera, Balmori, and Coberizas, typical Asturian concheros were uncovered atop either Azilian or Magdalenian levels. Charcoal samples from Asturian concheros at La Riera, Coberizas, and Penicial yielded determinations ranging between 7000 and 8900 B.P. Sediment samples from two Upper Paleolithic, three Asturian, and one post-Asturian site are interpreted as recording sequences of internal deposition, largely unrelated to paleoclimatic regimes outside of the caves. There is, however, no Holocene evidence for either extremely warm or extremely cold climatic conditions. Abundant faunal evidence is completely consistent with the assignation of a post-Pleistocene date. Virtually all species present are found today (or have been extinguished in the recent past) in the Cantabrian zone.

DESCRIPTION OF THE LITHIC INDUSTRY

Chapter 5 dealt with Asturian lithic industries in general. An effort was made to visit and examine all collections of lithic artifacts from Asturian sites housed in Spanish museums. The sparse collections for which provenience data were available proved to be highly selective and probably not representative of the industry as a whole.

The testing program yielded a small, but more representative, corpus of Asturian lithic material. These artifacts and the salvageable museum pieces were cast into a single typological format, one devised for the European Upper Paleolithic by Denise de Sonneville-Bordes and Jean Perrot (1953, 1954, 1955, 1956). For the first time data from an Asturian site, converted to cumulative frequency graphs, could be compared directly with data from other European sites.

A synthesis incorporating data from the newly discovered open-air site of Liencres and describing Asturian industries as a group was attempted. It does much to alter the illusion of primitiveness so often associated with the industry. In particular, small quantities of Upper Paleolithic tools, small blades, and bladelets appear to be present, the existence of which was not previously reported. The industry as a whole is characterized by a heavy duty tool component consisting of unifacial picks, choppers, chopping tools, partial bifaces, milling stones and hammerstones (together about 10 percent). Small tools made on flakes and blades constitute about 9 percent of the lithic total; endscrapers (including nucleiform endscrapers) are the most important small tool type. Various debitage categories account for the remaining 80 percent. The number of tool types attributed to the Asturian was increased from about a dozen to over 35, excluding composite types. Small, nonrepresentative samples from the cave sites precluded more detailed evaluation of intersite variation.

The study also defined the existence of two subgroups within the Asturian that probably reflect different activity spectra. These are (1) a facies containing all or most of the cave sites, and (2) a facies consisting of the open-air site of Liencres. It is suggested that the middens represent dumps associated with occupation sites. The almost complete absence of discernible features and the low incidence of artifacts tend to confirm this interpretation. It is argued that the groups responsible for the accumulation of the concheros might have lived in the open air in front of the caves. Post-Pleistocene erosion probably would have destroyed most of these sites as they are often found near river or estuary margins, which presumably would have fluctuated somewhat through time.

As it stands now, the Asturian can be placed in time but little is known of its direct antecedents and still less of its successors. It is logical to suppose that the industry developed out of the Cantabrian Azilian, but that supposition cannot yet be demonstrated. Comparison of cumulative percentage graphs from Liencres (an open-air site) and the Azilian level at nearby Cueva Morín (a cave site) shows some similarities in the frequency of certain lithic components (notches, denticulates, continuously retouched pieces, retouched bladelets), but there are equally marked differences (nucleiform endscrapers, perforators). A comparison of this nature cannot expect to hold facies differences constant. What is required for a more satisfactory comparison is either a coastally-located, open-air Azilian site or an Asturian cave site with an adequate lithic sample. Neither has been recorded as yet. The radiocarbon date from the inland Azilian cave site of Los Azules II in the upper Sella drainage indicates partial contemporaneity between some late Azilian and the earliest Asturian assemblages (Tresguerres 1976a). This, of course, suggests the possibility of seasonal or structural "poses" being represented by these artifactually distinctive assemblages (Straus and others 1978; Straus 1979b).

The lithic industry provides few clues about the activities conducted at Asturian sites, although its fundamental redundancy implies a certain functional equivalence, as noted in Chapter 5. Asturian industries are technologically primitve, casually made, and have a substantial "heavy duty" component. There is nothing in them to suggest the existence of a "curation technology" (Binford 1972, 1976). Even the most elaborate artifact—the Asturian pick—can be fabricated from abundant and easily procured raw material by a competent knapper in a few minutes with a minimal expenditure of effort. Formal tools are few, lending a markedly "expedient" character to these assemblages. Most cutting edges were probably simply unmodified flakes such as could have produced the cutting marks found in some frequency on bone fragments from Asturian middens (see Table 5.9). Picks, choppers, and chopping tools are considered multipurpose bashers, whackers, and pounders, which undoubtedly functioned in a wide variety of contexts; they were readily manufactured and as readily discarded when the task at hand was finished. One of those contexts, however, was probably the comminution of bone to extract the marrow; faunal remains from Asturian middens were uniformly heavily triturated in antiquity. It is tempting to imagine that these large and heavy implements also functioned in various woodworking contexts, but there is no direct evidence for this beyond the knowledge that the Boreal-Atlantic environment on the Cantabrian coast was, in fact, heavily forested. The near absence of milling stone fragments is striking, and perhaps implies a comparative de-emphasis on the processing of plant foods when these assemblages are compared with those of Early Bronze Age date when milling stones are present in some frequency (González 1976).

The little retouched flake and blade tools, which are never common in the assemblage, are thought to be (1) the durable components in composite weapon tips and edges (retouched bladelets in general, "Azilian" points, microgravettes, truncated elements, continuously-retouched pieces), and (2) objects used in a broad spectrum of cutting-slicing-shaving activities (the relatively common notches and denticulates, burins and endscrapers in general, sidescrapers). Although microwear analyses might demonstrate the latter suggestion, there is only a low probability that such analyses could be successfully undertaken here because of a low incidence of wear traces on many common materials worked experimentally (Stafford 1977, 1979), and a high incidence of extremely hard quartzite tools and debitage in Asturian lithic assemblages. It is nevertheless suggestive that areas within Liencres can be identified that may have had functional equivalents related to these broadly-defined activity sets. The problem of identifying activity-specific areas within Asturian sites is discussed in general terms by González Morales (1978) and in regard to Liencres by Clark (1979a, b; Clark and others 1977).

FAUNAL REMAINS

Chapter 6 evaluated the faunal evidence. Much information was available in the literature, although most of it was qualitative in nature and therefore of limited utility. The combined results of a literature search and the testing program permitted the description of some of the major elements peculiar to Asturian adaptations. A faunal configuration characteristic of Asturian concheros was defined, using the literature as a base and expanding on it with fresh evidence from test excavations at La Riera, Balmori, Coberizas, and Penicial, and with more limited faunal samples from other conchero sites. Subsistence was shown to be dependent on the exploitation of red and roe deer, with a secondary concentration on alpine caprids. Shellfish were also collected in considerable quantities. Two species of limpet (*P. vulgata, P. intermedia*) and the topshell (*T. crassa*) were shown to be the main constituents in Asturian concheros, although some dozen other molluscs were also represented. Gathering, which might have been a seasonal activity at La Riera, appears to have been restricted to the intertidal zone in estuary and moderately open coastal contexts.

There is no morphological evidence for animal domestication in *any* Asturian site so far known, nor any suggestion as yet of the kind of animal husbandry allegedly found, for example, at Chateauneuf-lez-Martigues, in the

Rhone Valley, where intensive and selective culling of young caprids is present (Escalon de Fonton 1966). Many cervids, however, were apparently killed in their first year, and there is a suggestion of an overrepresentation of hinds. When viewed in the context of the 12,000 year sequence at La Riera cave, it is evident that proportionately more young cervids were taken over time (that is, they are relatively more common in the latter part of the sequence, Upper Magdalenian to Asturian, than they are in the earlier part, Upper Solutrean to Lower Magdalenian). This pattern may indicate preferential killing of females and their young, which form discrete herds during much of the year.

Faunal data were also used to place the Asturian adaptation in perspective with respect to adaptations both preceding and succeeding it in time. It is significant that these apparent adaptational shifts do not neatly correspond with, and, in fact, vary independently of, the culture-stratigraphic units that are commonly used in southwestern France and northern Spain to organize archaeological data. Faunal samples were taken from concheros antedating (El Cierro, Balmori, La Lloseta) and postdating (Les Pedroses, San Antonio, La Lloseta) the Asturian. The literature also provided essential qualitative information with respect to the Cantabrian Upper Paleolithic. These data permitted a description of change through time in the frequencies of species exploited, especially shellfish species.

Analysis of terrestrial resources shows a generally stable pattern from the Late Pleistocene through the Asturian. Although data are scanty for the earlier (pre-Solutrean) part of the Upper Paleolithic time range, red deer (*C. elaphus*) are apparently numerically most common from Aurignacian times on, both in terms of "minimum number of individual" (MNI) estimates and in terms of raw bone counts. The contribution of this species to subsistence, as measured by usable meat provided, is variable, however, when compared with that of open country ungulates (horses, bovids; Freeman 1973). As noted in Chapter 6, red deer became extremely prevalent in Cantabrian Upper Solutrean levels, suggesting the adoption, perhaps for the first time, of specialized and intensive extractive strategies concentrating on the exploitation of woodland resources (Straus 1975a, 1977). Freeman (1973) has argued that the Azilian sees a return to primary dependence on open-country forms, but the extent of this generalization is presently open to question (Straus and others 1981). Asturian deposits are clearly characterized by a reappearance of the Solutrean-Magdalenian configuration. Open country adapted species are extremely rare in Asturian sites. Red deer are overwhelmingly predominant; roe deer and boar are also relatively common.

Analysis of marine fauna reveals a marked shift in species collected due to climatic and demographic factors, and a quantitative increase in the amount of shellfish remains present in the sites and in the number of species collected. Evidence for climatic change is most apparent in the replacement of the coolwater adapted winkle (*L. littorea*) by the topshell (*T. crassa*). The change is believed to have corresponded with the onset of the postglacial climatic optimum (about 9000-6000 B.P.), a period marked by conditions somewhat warmer and wetter than those of the present (Butzer 1964: 406, 407). The edible mussel (*M. edulis*), present in the Upper Paleolithic, reappeared in the post-Pleistocene and increased in size and frequency during the postglacial optimum. Never commonly found in Asturian sites, it was extensively exploited subsequent to 5000 B.P. Limpets, winkles, and topshells all occur on the Cantabrian coast today, suggesting a slight and gradual decrease in seawater temperature since the postglacial optimum.

Perhaps more important than paleoclimatic and chronological implications, however, are inferences that can be made about the Asturian adaptation when it is viewed from the broader perspective of research on marine and terrestrial faunas. Investigations in La Riera cave by members of the La Riera Paleoecological Project (1976–1980) have shown that the limpet varieties represented throughout the 12,000-year site sequence are derived from two different types of gathering zones. These are (1) the rocky, moderately wave-beaten littoral, defined by the presence of *P. intermedia, T. crassa,* and sea urchins (*Paracentrotus lividus*); and (2) a more sheltered zone, probably the rocky estuary shore, defined by the presence of *P. vulgata* and *L. littorea*. During the earlier occupations at La Riera, which pertain to Upper Solutrean and Lower Magdalenian culture-stratigraphic units (see Chapter 3), gathering took place only in sheltered zones (estuaries) where large specimens of *P. vulgata* (varieties *aurea* and *mayor*) and *L. littorea* were collected. After about Level 20 (a Lower Magdalenian stratum estimated to date to about 15,000 B.P.), and possibly because of an increase in human population density requiring the exploitation of new food sources, gathering extended onto the open, moderately wave-beaten shore, beyond the estuarine zone. *P. intermedia, T. crassa,* and a few mussels (*M. edulis*) were added in the Asturian. Limpet size tended to be constant (46 mm to 35 mm) in Upper Paleolithic Levels 1 through 20, with only slight oscillations probably due to episodes of overexploitation and subsequent recovery of limpet populations. Above Level 20, and perhaps due to increased food requirements and a constant expansion of the coastal areas exploited, the average size of limpets decreased, because the large estuarine *P. vulgata* specimens became mixed with smaller ones from the more open littoral and with specimens of *P. intermedia*, a species that is always smaller. It is generally true that the smaller the average size of the limpets, the less the relative importance of estuarine collection and the greater the use of the open littoral (Ortea in Straus and others 1981). The absence of *P. rustica* and *P. ulyssiponensis* at La Riera indicates that human exploitation of marine mollusca did not extend beyond the moderately wave-beaten littoral zone; both of these species are typical of open, heavily wave-beaten coasts. The absence of edible barnacles (*Polliceps cornucopia*), found today on the high-energy shore of nearby Llanes, tends to confirm this observation (Ortea in Straus and others 1981).

There is also some evidence for marine coastal fishing late in the use-occupation of La Riera cave. Sparse remains of anadromous salmonid species (*S. trutta, S.*

salar) are present throughout the sequence, and indicate casual fishing in estuarine or riverine waters; all present salmonids in Asturias are adapted to both salt and fresh water. Marine fish first appear in Level 24 (Upper Magdalenian, dated at 10,890 ± 430 B.P.), indicating the inception of coastal fishing. Along with remains of Sparidae (sea bream family) and other, as yet unidentified, marine species, the presence of echinoderms in the uppermost levels confirms the beginning of exploitation of the open littoral, again possibly as a response to increased population density (de la Hoz in Straus and others 1981). Although fish bones are useful indicators of this apparent expansion of the resource base late in the La Riera sequence, they are not, in themselves, sufficiently numerous to suggest that fish were ever intensively exploited.

La Riera Level 20 is also a significant stratum with respect to apparent shifts in the exploitation of avifauna, and it signals important changes in the intensity and variety of ungulate species exploited. Beginning around Level 20 there is evidence of (1) an increase in the taking of birds (especially in Level 24); (2) the appearance of boar (and, momentarily, reindeer); (3) an increase in the intensity of roe deer hunting, and (4) an increase in the killing of newborn red deer. These trends parallel those observed in the analyses of the molluscan and fish remains (specifically, increased exploitation of shellfish and initial utilization of marine fish). Starting with Level 25 there is a marked increase in the shell-to-bone weight ratios, sometimes exceeding one-to-one in the uppermost levels (26–30). All this evidence indicates an intensification of wild resource exploitation in the Late Pleistocene and Early Holocene, and an inferred degree of subsistence pressure on human populations in the region, which may in turn be due to a long-term increase in regional population density (Straus and others 1980, 1981; Clark 1982; Clark and Straus 1982).

SITE CATCHMENT ANALYSIS

Resources available to the prehistoric occupants of 28 Asturian sites were used in Chapter 7 to develop and evaluate alternative settlement-subsistence models based on concepts developed in site catchment analysis (Vita-Finzi and Higgs 1970; Jarman 1972). Distance measures combined with a realistic stratification of environmental zones permitted the assessment of "ease of access" factors, which were probably important prehistorically in making decisions about resource priorities. Both marine and terrestrial faunal resources were analyzed to try to determine whether the sites were representative of the Asturian settlement-subsistence system as a whole, or whether they simply formed part of a larger and more extensive system, inland components of which are not known archaeologically.

The results of these analyses were most consistent with Model B, which postulated that Asturian sites are the remains of base camps situated among the hills and along the estuaries near the coast. In support of this contention were (1) the apparent near homogeneity of Asturian sites with respect to proportional, distance, and access measures of life zone categories, which in turn implied that the Asturian sites so far known were functional equivalents; (2) the overall similarity in resources potentially available in those life zones, and in resources represented archaeologically; (3) the absence of any Asturian sites situated in the foothills and intermontane valleys of the Cordillera that might represent the inland base camps postulated by bipolar Model A; and (4) the apparent absence of inland limited activity sites postulated by Model C.

A pattern like that postulated by Model B makes sense in terms of resource accessibility and efficiency in the expenditure of energy, given the topography of the region and the north-south compression of environmental zonation. Sites located near the coast are ideally situated (1) to exploit both forest and forest-margin staples (red and roe deer) and high-yield parkland-grassland ungulates (auroch, horse); (2) to take advantage of seasonally available alpine resources (ibex, chamois); and (3) to exploit estuarine limpets and topshells either as permanent dietary supplements or as "emergency" foods in times (or seasons) of relative scarcity. While it is argued that Asturian sites so far known are most compatible with base camp components in a Model B type situation, it is important to stress that movement up and down the north-south trending watercourses by task groups of variable size and composition (Freeman 1968) and with various objectives is certainly not precluded. It is rather a question of archaeological visibility, and the collection of the right kinds and quantities of data, which makes detection of these camps so difficult. Ephemeral hunting and collecting stations, occupied for a few days at most, would be nearly invisible archaeologically, even if deposition took place in cave or rock shelter contexts. If encampments were in the open air, only fortuitous geological circumstances (like blowouts or stream erosion) or the massive excavations associated with large-scale public works would lead to their discovery and excavation.

The discussion presented in Chapter 7 was based on a study of exploitation activities and their theoretical relationship to settlement location. It was assumed throughout the chapter that the spatial distribution of human activity reflects an ordered adjustment to the linked factors of distance and accessibility, and that locational decisions are made, in general, so as to minimize the frictional effects of distance (Garner 1967: 304, 305). Resource procurement is regarded as an element—perhaps the most archaeologically visible element—in a systemic conception of hunter-gatherer social organization. Procurement of faunal resources in Cantabria was assumed to have a transient aspect, entailing a dichotomy of site types (base camps, limited activity sites). Faunal resources known to have been exploited were found to be amenable to ranking in terms of nutritional potential and procurement efficiency. A desire to limit the expenditure of energy was believed to underlie all economic decisions, so that economic behavior in our view corresponds most closely to the satisficer model proposed by Simon (1945). As such, the objective of much economic behavior may be the maintenance of the expenditure of effort within a predetermined range. If this is true, given regional topographic and resource zone distribution factors, it seems more plausible to postulate a single base camp model with satellite limited activity stations (Model B), than to argue for the existence of a bipolar configuration (Model A), or movement by a local group within a recognized territory through a seasonal round (Model C). While much of the evidence in Chapter 7 supports this hypothesis either directly or by implication, there is a long-recognized and obvious need for better data pertinent to both seasonality and the exploitation of plant resources. Determinations of seasonality in the exploitation of mammalian and marine faunas may be made by studying eruption patterns on juvenile cervid dentitions and on the dentitions of other commonly represented economic species, and by examining oxygen isotope ratios in the growth rings of marine shells. Bailey (1978, 1981a, b) has made a number of interesting observations about seasonal behavior with respect to Asturian settlement-subsistence systems that can only be resolved by the acquisition of these kinds of data (Was coastal occupation associated with the summer exploitation of inland resources? Was wide-ranging exploitation of terrestrial mammals linked to seasonal herd aggregation-dispersion patterns?). Straus (1979b) has suggested that some late Azilian (Urtiaga, Los Azules) and early Asturian (La Riera, Penicial) sites might be contemporaneous and functionally-complementary parts of a single kind of pan-Cantabrian mesolithic settlement-subsistence system. It is hoped that conclusive answers to some of these important questions may be forthcoming in the relatively near future.

PORTUGUESE AND GALICIAN TERRACE SITES

Surface finds of quartzite tools in Galicia and in the Tejo Basin (Portugal) frequently have been alleged to be related to the Cantabrian Asturian. Evidence on which these claims are based was examined in Chapter 3. Claims of relationship were shown to depend on the co-occurrence in all three areas of the unifacial pick characteristic of the Cantabrian Asturian. Literature referring to the geological contexts from which these pieces were recovered was examined in some detail.

It was shown that, in general, the "industries" so defined were artificially constituted by various investigators on the most impressionistic of morphological grounds, with scant attention paid to geological contexts. The assemblages termed Camposanquian, Languedocian, and Asturian appeared to have no meaning with respect to referent assemblages defined elsewhere, and it was concluded that the bulk of these artifacts should probably be assigned to mixed and, therefore, undifferentiated Lower-Middle Paleolithic culture-stratigraphic units.

The discovery of Budiño, the work of Maury at Âncora and Carreço, and recent discoveries at Bañugues, Aramar, and L'Atalaya near Gijón (Blas Cortina and others 1978; Rodríguez Asensio 1978a, b) raise the interesting possibility that some, at least, of the artifacts found in

surficial cobble and silt deposits on top of fossil beaches may, in fact, date to the Late Pleistocene or even the Pleistocene-Holocene boundary. An early Holocene date is also implied for Liencres on the basis of pollen and sediment analyses (see Chapter 4, Appendix A), and for Asturian-like industries stratified in dune sands and lignites above the Mouligna beach at Biarritz (Passemard 1924; Ferrier 1948, 1950).

RESOURCE STRESS—A POSSIBLE EXPLANATION

The Asturian appears to represent the culmination of a number of trends that are most evident in the faunal data and that began at different points in the late Pleistocene. These show up most clearly in the long-term, diachronic study of subsistence change at La Riera, although they are also manifest to varying degrees at other sites with shorter sequences. They include (1) a diversified molluscan assemblage, representing exploitation of both protected estuarine and exposed, moderately wave-beaten coastal habitats; (2) a sharp increase in shell-to-bone weight ratios in Asturian sites, indicating relatively greater emphasis on shellfish gathering than previously; (3) a decline in the size of limpets, suggesting overexploitation and culling earlier in the growth cycle; (4) the earliest intensive exploitation of echinoderms in the local archaeological record; and (5) the continued presence of scarce marine fish and birds, which first appear in Upper Magdalenian contexts around 11,000 B.P. When viewed from a regional perspective over time, these diverse lines of evidence converge to indicate intensified use of traditional resources and expansion of the resource base to include new economic species. The differences between the Asturian and Upper Paleolithic configurations can thus be "explained" as due to stress on the resource base—stress that compelled human groups in Cantabria to diversify their means of subsistence, and stress that at present cannot be attributed to any other factor than a long-term increase in regional population density.

The general model most compatible with the Asturian data appears to be one developed by Mark Cohen (1975, 1977) in order to explain the near-simultaneous appearance of agricultural economies at widely dispersed places in both the Old and New worlds. While we are not directly concerned here with the origins of agriculture, it is significant that many elements of Cohen's model fit the Asturian data remarkably well, and they can be incorporated into attempts to explain economic transformations of far reaching consequences in general. There is clear-cut evidence for such economic transformations from Cantabrian archaeological contexts that date from 15,000 to 7000 B.P. (Straus and others 1980, 1981; Clark and Yi 1982).

By adopting a demographic stress model borrowed from Ester Boserup (1965) and modified by Lewis Binford (1968), Cohen contends that (1) population growth has been a continuous factor throughout human history; (2) that it is intrinsic to the species, and (3) that regional population pressure resultant from that growth has been a major determinant not only of the emergence of domestication economies, but also of the gradual evolution of subsistence strategies in general. He argues that when simple colonization of unoccupied lands and environments no longer sufficed, as it had throughout most of the Pleistocene, and when local mechanisms for the redistribution of populations within hunting groups became inadequate to balance pressure from region to region, human groups responded to population growth by adjustments in their diets. These adjustments emphasized the exploitation of plentiful and nutritious but less palatable foods—resources that would not have been considered primary for a variety of reasons under conditions of lower population density. The emergence of domestication economies is viewed as a particular instance, albeit the most far reaching one in evolutionary terms, of this general case.

Population pressure is defined by Cohen as "...nothing more than an imbalance between a population, its choice of foods, and its work standards, which forces the population either to change its eating habits or to work harder" (Cohen 1977: 50). Defined like this, population pressure may be viewed both as a stimulus for technological change and as a causal factor necessitating the rearticulation of component subsystems of the overall subsistence system of any particular group. It is in the latter sense that the definition is most appropriate, for, as we have seen, there is little evidence for significant technological change in Asturian assemblages. Rather, it is an expansion of the resource base, implying the exploitation of a wider range of environments than is characteristic of Late Pleistocene assemblages, that makes the Asturian distinctive from Cantabrian Solutrean or Magdalenian adaptations.

If population growth is a significant causal factor in bringing about systemic change, it is reasonable to ask how it can be recognized archaeologically (Cohen 1975: 471–474). One of the most direct monitors of population growth is simply the number of sites that can reasonably be assigned to a particular culture-stratigraphic unit of known temporal duration. While it has commonly been argued that the European Mesolithic represents a decline in the number of sites compared with the Upper Paleolithic as a whole, Butzer (1971: 563–568) has suggested that it is doubtful whether the number is substantially less than that for any Upper Paleolithic period *of equivalent length* (about 3000 years). The apparent decline in the number of open-air sites is probably due to (1) active downcutting of streams dating from the Pleistocene-Holocene boundary, which would have tended to bury riverine sites under post-Pleistocene alluvium, (2) the rapid and continuing rise of sea level from about 9000 to 5000 B.P., which would have submerged coastally-situated sites located in regions characterized by shallow continental shelves, and (3) the absence of massive loess sedimentation on upland surfaces after the end of the Pleistocene, which would have deprived post-Pleistocene sites of an excellent depositional medium conducive to good preservation (Cohen

TABLE 8.1
Incidence of Cantabrian Sites Adjusted for Time

Culture Stratigraphic Unit	Number of Sites	Approximate Temporal Duration	Number of Sites Per Millennium
Iron Age[1]	259[2]	1,500	172.67
Neolithic/ Bronze Age[3]	(88)[4]	2,500	35.20
Mesolithic[5]	110	5,000	22.00
Upper Magdalenian	36	3,000	12.00
Lower Magdalenian	35	3,000	11.67
Solutrean	33	4,000	8.25
Aurignacian/ Perigordian	18	15,000	1.20
Mousterian/ Châtelperronian	14	65,000	0.21
Acheulean	3	100,000	0.03

1. Includes the Vasco-Roman Iron Age and the 'Romanization'; approximate dates 1100 BC–500 AD (Apellaniz 1974, 1975).
2. A minimum figure; 259 *castro* sites are reported by González (1976) for Asturias alone. *Castros* are fortified habitation sites with domestic architecture supposedly occupied by small groups of families (1976: 54). Although permanent occupation of all *castros* has not been demonstrated (some might have been occupied only in times of stress), they are nevertheless a good index of population because they are believed to correspond in a lineal fashion to other (as yet unidentified) hamlets and towns.
3. Includes a late and very ephemeral 'neolithic' and 'eneolithic'; approximate dates 3600–1100 BC (Apellaniz 1975).
4. An extrapolation based on Apellaniz (1974); 180 sites are reported for the Neolithic-Bronze Age of the Basque Provinces alone (Guipúzcoa, Vizcaya, Alava), but of these only 20 (11 percent) contain occupation levels. The remainder are dolmens and other megalithic constructions, tumuli, art sites, and sepulchral caves which lack evidence of habitation. In Santander and Asturias, the number of sites assigned to the Bronze Age exceeds 800, but no distinction is made between habitation sites and other Bronze Age constructions (Jordá 1977).
5. Includes sites assigned to the Azilian, Asturian, and Tardenoisian. Gavelas (1980) reports the discovery of 49 Asturian concheros since 1977, bringing the Asturian total to 77 (see also Clark and Straus 1982).

1977: 129, after Butzer 1971: 563–568). It is worth remarking that (1) Butzer has specifically identified deposition as the principal geological agency operative in Early Holocene Cantabrian Spain (see Chapter 6), and that (2) Asturian sites are at least as numerous as those assigned to the Upper Magdalenian, and are as common as those assigned to *any* Cantabrian culture-stratigraphic unit (Table 8.1). The relatively large number of Asturian sites may be attributed to the fact that the Cantabrian shelf is a comparatively deep one (CLIMAP 1976), so that proportionately fewer sites located on Early Holocene strand lines would have been lost to the progressive encroachment of the sea equated with the postglacial optimum. As noted in Chapter 1, there is considerable evidence for relatively dense and growing mesolithic populations from at least some other western European localities (Newell 1973, Piggott 1965, Brothwell 1972, Jacobi 1973). The Asturian site density data would, then, tend to support a model for long-term population growth.

In addition to the gross number of sites adjusted for time, Cohen (1977: 78–83) has spelled out other stress indicators that might monitor population pressure in archaeological contexts. Again, the basic assumption is that changes in the subsistence economy may be viewed as evidence of population pressure so long as other, more viable competing explanations are ruled out and certain conditions are met. These conditions are (1) that the change in the subsistence economy must be in the direction of increasing the total caloric productivity of the region in question, (2) that they should occur in the absence of significant technological change (such as might have increased the productivity of the resource base) or the appearance of new resources in the environment, and (3) that the resources involved can be shown to be "secondary" (that is, less palatable or desirable, more labor intensive than those exploited previously). It is apparent that many of Cohen's archaeological stress indicators are relevant to the Asturian situation. Given the vagaries of preservation in the archaeological record in general, and inconsistencies in data collection, it is unrealistic to expect that all of these criteria would be met in any particular situation.

1. When it is possible to isolate the exploitative cycle of a single group making its annual round, evidence that the range covered is increasing (through time) should indicate population pressure (Cohen 1977: 78).

In the Asturian case, we are not yet in a position to isolate the exploitative cycle of a single group, except in theoretical terms (see Chapter 7). However, a relative monitor of this stress indicator could be a series of comparative catchment analyses of sites ordered in time by the major Upper and post-Paleolithic culture-stratigraphic units. The marked zonal compression characteristic of Cantabria on a north-south transect seems likely to have inhibited the archaeological visibility of changes in the extent of the exploitation cycle. What seems to have happened impressionistically is that the areal extent of the exploitative cycle remained fairly constant through time, but that various parts of it were exploited differentially. Coastal resources, in particular, become more heavily stressed beginning in the Late Magdalenian. Only in exceptional cases would recoverable archaeological data be of sufficient precision to put this criterion of stress to an empirical test, although it might theoretically be done.

2. When a group expands into new ecological zones, population pressure may be assumed if expansion takes place into areas which present new adaptive difficulties such as extreme heat, cold, high altitude, disease or danger of predators (Cohen 1977: 78).

There is nothing in the Cantabrian situation that is relevant to this criterion, or at least nothing likely to be detected archaeologically. Cantabria is located far enough south of areas affected by continental glaciation to have been spared most, although evidently not all (see Chapter 6), of the macroclimatic changes that might have caused adaptive difficulties in middle latitude Europe.

While there is evidence for montane glaciation in the Cordillera Cantábrica, and for sporadic periglacial phenomena at low elevations in Santander and Asturias, it is suggested that these macroclimatic changes were ameliorated throughout the Late Pleistocene by the maritime climate enjoyed by the Cantabrian coastal plain.

3. When the inhabitants of a region become more eclectic in their exploitation of microniches, utilizing portions of the environment (forests, deserts, coastal areas) previously ignored, while continuing to exploit the old niches, demographic pressure can be assumed (Cohen 1977: 79).

4. When human populations show a shift toward more eclectic food gathering patterns, shown by reduced selectivity in the foods eaten, it can be argued that they are demonstrating the need to obtain more calories from the same territory in order to feed denser populations (Cohen 1977: 79).

5. When a group increases its concentration on water-based resources relative to its use of land-based resources, especially when the resources are shellfish whose exploitation is independent of the invention of any new technology, this shift may be viewed as arising from demographic necessity rather than choice (Cohen 1977: 79).

These three stress indicators are considered together because they monitor essentially the same phenomenon—an expansion of the subsistence base into areas and foods previously unexploited. As noted in Chapters 6 and 7, there is abundant evidence to support this kind of an expansion for the Asturian when Asturian faunas are compared with those of the Upper Paleolithic. For these time intervals, the Asturian configuration is viewed as the culmination of a long-term trend beginning in the Upper Magdalenian, best documented by excavations at La Riera. This trend is evident not only in an increase in the number of shellfish species exploited, but also in the gross relative importance of shellfoods in the regional economy over time. Although the bone-to-shell weight ratios fluctuate considerably during the Upper Paleolithic sequence at La Riera, the only genuine midden deposits (those in which shell weights exceed bone) are dated after about 9000 B.P. Increased exploitation of shellfoods is also accompanied by greater emphasis on fishing, as marine species are taken for the first time late in the sequence. Also occurring are the initial exploitation of birds and indications of maximum utilization of the cervids and caprids—species that were, and continued to be, the dietary mainstays (Clark and Yi 1982). As Parmalee and Klippel (1974) have observed, fish and shellfish remain secondary resources, despite the visually impressive vestiges of concheros that have led to suggestions that these foods become staples during the mesolithic. Cohen (1977: 79) points out that shellfoods are evidently low-prestige resources for many, although not all, human groups, so that *any* increase in their utilization may be considered as an indicator of significant dietary stress. Whether or not they were "low prestige" is not, of course, knowable. What is significant about shellfish is that they are "expensive," *low-yield* resources—resources that would only be exploited in quantity if nothing better (that is, a higher-yield, lower-cost resource) was available.

6. When a group shifts from eating large huntable land mammals to eating smaller mammals, birds, reptiles, and land molluscs, demographic stress can be assumed (Cohen 1977: 80).

In the Asturian case, there is no indication of a shift toward the exploitation of small game. Although insectivores, rodents, and lagomorphs occur in low frequencies in many Asturian sites, their remains may be accounted for by nonhuman predation, by occasional, opportunistic kills, and by natural deaths in cave entrances (many of these species either habitually or occasionally live in or near cave mouths). Birds and reptiles, while present, are extremely rare. Land snails (*Helix* spp.) occupy moist cave entrances as preferred habitats, so that their presence in Asturian middens probably has little to do with human predation.

7. When a group shifts from the consumption of organisms at high trophic levels to those at lower trophic levels (in particular, when it shifts from animal to plant foods), population pressure may be assumed (Cohen 1977: 80).

As noted in Chapter 5, except for a few grinding stone fragments, there is little evidence in Asturian lithic industries to suggest the processing of plant foods, and, while occasional hazelnut and acorn fragments have been recovered from Asturian concheros, they are not sufficiently numerous to indicate systematic exploitation. Although factors of differential preservation may be important, and while palynological studies may alter our conception of Asturian subsistence, there are no direct indications that the Asturians were heavily dependent on plant foods, although logic dictates that they would have utilized the edible seeds and nuts in their environment.

8. When a shift occurs from the utilization of foods requiring little or no preparation to foods requiring increased preparation (cooking, grinding, pounding, leaching), population pressure is again indicated (Cohen 1977: 80).

Cohen argues that an increased investment in food preparation, while it increases the range of edible substances, is achieved only at a higher cost in labor. As noted above, there are few artifacts in Asturian assemblages that can be convincingly linked to food processing. Consequently, it would be difficult to detect such a transition archaeologically, even if it had occurred.

9. When there is evidence of environmental degradation suggesting human efforts (use of fire in land clearance), it may be argued that larger human populations are increasing their interference with natural ecosystems to augment the productivity of preferred (plant) foods (Cohen 1977: 80, 81).

There are no indications in the few Asturian pollen spectra available to date to support this kind of systematic interference with the landscape. Environmental degradation, resulting in the establishment of subclimax vegetation, evidently began in Roman times and became much accelerated in Cantabria during the Middle Ages (Chapter 2). The present landscape is a largely artificial one, produced mainly to meet the requirements of a large dairy industry. Agriculture remains a secondary economic pursuit in Asturias and Santander even today.

10. When skeletal evidence of malnutrition increases through time, it may be argued that demographic stress is resulting in reduced quantity-quality in the diet available to each individual (Cohen 1977: 81).

The corpus of human skeletal material from Asturian sites is so small that no data relevant to the rate of nutritional pathologies are yet available. It is worth noting, however, that the burial from Colombres was that of an individual supposedly afflicted with rickets and caries.

11. When the size or quality of individuals exploited from a particular species shows a steady decline through time (when the size of molluscs decreases), it may be argued that human populations are consuming resources beyond their carrying capacity, resulting in the degradation of the exploited population (Cohen 1977: 81).

12. When an exploited species disappears from the archaeological record, it may be argued that the species was exploited beyond its carrying capacity (Cohen 1977: 81).

Limpets in general are significantly smaller in Asturian middens than in their Upper Paleolithic counterparts. At La Riera, this decline was first detected in the late Magdalenian (about 15,000 B.P.) and appeared to progress steadily until the end of the site sequence, which terminates with the formation of the Asturian conchero (8650 B.P.). Two factors influenced this decline: (1) the increasingly intensive exploitation of moderately wave-beaten coastal niches, where *P. vulgata* tend to be smaller than their estuarine counterparts, and (2) mixture with limpets of a different kind, *P. intermedia,* a species that is always smaller. There are a number of minor fluctuations in limpet size throughout the earlier part of the La Riera sequence that are probably due to overexploitation and subsequent recovery of local limpet populations.

With respect to possible extinctions, the near-total disappearance of the winkle (*L. littorea*) in middens of Asturian age is noteworthy, but is probably due more to paleoclimatic factors (specifically an increase in water temperature) than to human predation. It is significant that this species reappears in middens of post-Asturian date. In many previous publications, it had been supposed that the so-called "sautuola" limpet variant (*P. vulgata sautuola* = *P. vulgata mayor*) became extinct locally at about the end of the Pleistocene. It is now known, however, that this large and distinctive limpet still survives in small numbers in polluted estuarine waters where they are not subjected to human predation. Nevertheless, the disappearance of the "sautuola" variety from midden deposits at some time between 9000 and 10,000 B.P. is a striking fact, perhaps partly due to climatic change. Overexploitation by human groups in the area is also highly probable. It may be that increased human predation and paleoclimatic change coincident with the Pleistocene-Holocene boundary combined to cause the near-total disappearance of this subspecies.

In sum, the population pressure argument of Cohen, while designed primarily to account for the appearance of domestication economies, nevertheless helps to explain many of the features of Asturian archaeological assemblages in particular (and, I suspect, mesolithic adaptations in general). While none of the lines of evidence summarized are conclusive enough to demonstrate that population pressure was solely operative in causing the systemic changes noted in this essay, the co-occurrence of several of them is strongly suggestive that regional economies in Cantabrian Spain were coming under increasing stress during the Asturian period. When the particulars of the Asturian configuration are viewed in the long-term context of Upper Paleolithic developments in general, and especially when it is realized that simplistic paleoclimatic change arguments must be rejected as directly causing changes in Late and post-Pleistocene archaeological assemblages, population pressure emerges as the strongest single causal factor to explain the observed patterns.

Appendix A

POLLEN SAMPLES FROM LIENCRES

Geoffrey A. Clark and Josefa Menéndez-Amor

During the 1969 excavations, three pollen samples were taken from Levels 1 and 2 in Cuts 1 and 4. The samples were submitted, along with others from Asturian cave sites, to Dra. Josefa Menéndez-Amor, Laboratorio de Palinología, Museo Nacional de Ciencias Naturales, Madrid. Identifiable pollen grains were fairly abundant in the Level 1 samples; pollen was present in lower frequencies in the sample from Level 2 (Table A.1).

Sample 1 was taken from Cut 1, Level 2; it comes from the A horizon of the *terra fusca* soil described by Butzer and Bowman (1979). The sample was removed from a depth of 47 cm below ground surface, only a few centimeters above the limestone bedrock characteristic of the area. Only 50 grains were identified, and the low count makes detailed discussion of vegetation patterns dubious. Salient features include high relative frequencies of pine (*Pinus* spp., 28 percent), ericaceous shrubs (26 percent) like gorse (*Ulex* spp.) and heather (*Erica* spp.), and sedges (*Cyperus* spp., 18 percent). Except for low frequencies of hazel (*Corylus,* perhaps in shrub form) and alder (*Alnus*), no deciduous arboreal vegetation is represented.

The heather-gorse-sedge association corresponds well to the Spanish definition of lowland matorral, a climax vegetational association related to the excessively saline conditions prevalent along the Spanish coastal *rías* (Guinea Lopez 1953: 218–228; Clark 1971a: 43–47). Local soil type, parent material, exposure to sun and wind, and moisture regimen all play important roles in determining matorral composition. A heather-gorse matorral covers the dolina adjacent to the site and occurs on the hillslopes above it, suggesting that the shrubby aspect of the local vegetation has changed little since the end of the Pleistocene. Pockets of matorral are presently confined to the immediate coast; rolling pasture lands on terrain formerly forested are the dominant vegetational type in the area today.

The presence of pine in quantity is in keeping with a pre-Boreal (10,300-9500 B.P.) or Boreal (9500-8200 B.P.) phase date (Butzer 1971a: 531). Of interest is the pollen spectrum from the Azilian Level 1 at Cueva Morín (Leroi-Gourhan 1971). The Morín Azilian is thought to date to the Older Dryas-Allerod boundary (about 12,200 B.P.); it effectively marks the end of cultural deposition in

TABLE A.1
Pollen Samples from Levels 1 and 2 at Liencres

	Alnus (alder)	*Betula* (birch)	*Pinus* (pine)	*Salix* (willow)	*Quercus* (oak)	*Ulmus* (elm)	*Corylus* (hazel)	Ericaceae (gorse, heather)	Gramineae (grasses)	Cyperaceae (sedges)	Filicales (ferns)	Compositae Liguliflorae	Compositae Flos.	Various	Arboreal Pollen (%)	Nonarboreal Pollen (%)
LIENCRES CUT 1 LEVEL 1 136 GRAINS	8 0.058	1 0.007	6 0.044		1 0.007	1 0.007	7 0.051	52 0.380	6 0.044	24 0.176	6[a] 0.044	9 0.066	7 0.051	8 0.058	0.174	0.826
LIENCRES CUT 4 LEVEL 1 139 GRAINS	16 0.115	1 0.007	21 0.151	1 0.007	3 0.022		17 0.122	30 0.216	5 0.036		19[b] 0.137	6 0.043		20 0.144	0.424	0.576
LIENCRES CUT 1 LEVEL 2 50 GRAINS	2 0.040		14 0.280				2 0.040	13 0.260	1 0.020	9 0.180	3[c] 0.060	3 0.060		3 0.060	0.360	0.640

a. 5 grains (Filices in general); 1 grain (Polypodium); (0.037, 0.007).
b. 9 grains (Filices in general); 9 grains (Polypodium); 1 grain (Athyrium); (0.065, 0.065, 0.007).
c. 1 grain (Filices in general); 2 grains (Polypodium); (0.020, 0.040).

the sequence. At Morín, the arboreal pollen frequency is extremely low (on the order of 4 percent), and no pine is represented. Compositae and Cichoridae predominate; the fauna are cold-loving forms. A cold, treeless environment is well documented for the preceding Final Magdalenian levels in the area as well (El Otero, González Echegaray and others 1966: 83–85; El Pendo). A pre-Boreal or Boreal date is indicated for Level 2 at Liencres, given the evidence for post-Pleistocene pedogenesis described above (see also Butzer and Bowman 1979). There are no indications of the arctic environment characteristic of Younger Dryas times (11,400-10,300 B.P.). A pre-Boreal or Boreal phase date for Level 2 is also in accord with the Asturian industry found predominantly in Level 1. Radiocarbon determinations for the Asturian of the caves range between 8909 B.P. and 7004 B.P.

Sample 2 was taken from Cut 4, Level 1 (Square 09,19). It also pertains to the A horizon and was removed from a depth of 25 to 30 cm below ground surface. Salient features include statistically equivalent frequencies of alder (*Alnus* spp., 11.5 percent), pine (*Pinus* spp., 15 percent), and hazel (*Corylus* spp., 12 percent); ericaceous shrubby plants (21.6 percent) continue to be prevalent, and there is a notable increase in the Filicales (true ferns, 13.7 percent). The matorral configuration seems to be a stable element in the Liencres series. The incidence of deciduous vegetation and ferns stands in marked contrast with that of Level 2, and may indicate the replacement of a coniferous forest-matorral combination by a mixed deciduous coniferous forest-matorral configuration. A mixed forest on the coastal plain would be more compatible with the formation of microenvironmental niches suitable for fern development than would

the coniferous forest of Level 2 times. The incidence of pine pollen is noticeably diminished.

Sample 3 was taken from Cut 1, Level 1, at a depth of 8 to 20 cm. below the surface. Salient features of this sample include a radical decline in the arboreal fraction (to 17.4 percent), and a concomitant increase in the frequency of nonarboreal pollen. No arboreal species is present with a frequency greater than 6 percent; pine (*Pinus* spp.) declines from 15 percent to 4.4 percent, alder (*Alnus* spp.) from 11.5 percent to 5.8 percent, and hazel (*Corylus* spp.) from 12.2 percent to 5.1 percent. Ericaceous shrubs become dominant (38 percent), accompanied by increases in the frequency of grass and sedge pollen.

It is difficult to escape the impression that the Sample 3 spectrum describes essentially contemporaneous vegetation. The decline in the frequency of fern pollen would be congruent with the fact that ferns occur only in sheltered locales and moisture traps in the area today (for example, dolina walls, floors). Gorse, heather, and sedge are common in the immediate vicinity of the site. Stands of pine occur within 10 km of Liencres; isolated individuals and small clusters of trees are found within 2 or 3 km of the site. Stands of alder and hazel are commonly found throughout Cantabria wherever the original climax or paraclimax vegetation has been preserved intact (Guinea Lopez 1953: 49, 338). In sum, the Level 1 samples seem to indicate a vegetational configuration not unlike that of the Cantabrian coastal plain prior to the Middle Ages, when extensive deforestation began to alter the landscape, ultimately creating the artificial pasture lands that are the predominant form of cover today.

Appendix B

LIENCRES: THE 1972 SURFACE COLLECTION

In August, 1972, I visited Liencres again with several members of the Burgos archaeological survey group. More than three years had elapsed since the site was tested. The erosional processes that led to the initial discovery of the site had continued unabated; as a result, a considerable amount of artifact material was exposed on the surface. The test pit locations were easily discernible, and some of the original grid stakes were located. A second surface collection was undertaken. As in 1969, the horizontal location of each artifact was plotted; artifacts were classified according to the format developed for the initial project. Some 231 additional pieces were recovered, bringing the total artifact yield from Liencres to 1833. Retouched pieces collected from this single component site now total 162, or 8.8 percent of the artifact inventory. All material recovered from Liencres is stored in the Museo Provincial de Prehistoria y Arqueología, Juan de la Cosa, 1, Santander, Spain.

Table B.1 summarizes the lithic inventory from the 1972 surface collection. Categories correspond with those given in the main body of the text with one important exception: shatter flakes (Clark 1971a: 265). Shatter flakes are small, sharply angular blocky fragments of flint or quartzite produced by percussion flaking. Although they may not exhibit any of the commonly recognized characteristics of flakes (Bordes 1968: 26), it is clear that they are artificial and accidental byproducts of the manufacturing process. Shatter flakes generally do not preserve any cortical material on any surface. In Tables 4.1 and 4.5, they are included in the category "plain flakes." Figure B.1 indicates the lateral dispersion of common flint artifact types across the site surface; Figure B.2 shows the distribution of quartzite tools and debitage. Types occurring in extremely low frequencies are not represented, nor are the few artifacts that occurred on the slopes below the site proper. Figure B.3 illustrates some of the retouched pieces recovered in 1972.

Inspection of Figures B.1 and B.2 indicates a rather marked east-west trending linear scatter. The artifact alignment partially coincides with and partially parallels a narrow footpath that extends along the edge of the cliff above the inlet. The cluster sampled by Cut 4 was gratifyingly absent, although the densest part of the linear scatter is adjacent to and north-northwest of Cut 4. No lithic debris was observed weathering out of the floors of the old excavations, but the 1969 soundings were partly filled with fine sediments washed or blown in from the surrounding land surfaces. Probably the cultural deposits were effectively exhausted in the areas sampled by Cuts 2 and 4; in Cut 1 (where bedrock was reached), artifact material seldom occurred below a depth of 25 or 30 cm. Cut 6 samples the dolina fill and may still contain cultural deposits.

With respect to type distributions, few salient clusters are apparent. Exceptions include a dense concentration of decortication, plain, and trimming flakes along the south edge of Cut 4 (18/19,08), which may represent a primary knapping area. Flake clusters also occur at the base of Cut 2 (12,02), and due north of Cut 4 (21/22, 03/04). In all three cases, flint artifacts predominate. The quartzite fraction is low (13.8 percent), and is comparable to the 1969 surface collection (14.4 percent) and Level 1 (13.5 percent).

In terms of composition, the 1972 surface pickup differs little from that of 1969. The major constituent consists of various debitage categories, among which plain, secondary decortication, trimming, and shatter flakes are the most common elements. Flint bladelets are also prevalent. Retouched pieces numbered only 19; as before, nucleiform endscrapers, notches, backed bladelets, and continuously retouched flakes predominate, but type frequencies are so low that they preclude detailed comparison.

The 1972 surface collection provided few surprises, either with respect to composition or distribution. Type frequencies replicate reasonably well those obtained from the collections made in 1969. The corpus of artifactual data from the site was increased to over 1800 pieces, which constitute the best collection of material available to date from an Asturian or Asturian-like site.

TABLE B.1
Liencres: Surface Collection, 1972
Inventory of Lithic Material

Types	Material		
	Quartzite	Flint	% Total
Unworked cobbles	1		0.004
Unworked pebbles	4		0.017
Split cobble segments	3		0.013
Amorphous broken chunks	2	8	0.043
Nuclei (all types)	1	8	0.039
Flakes, plain	2	23	0.108
Flakes, primary decortication	2	5	0.030
Flakes, secondary decortication	6	39	0.195
Flakes, trimming	8	44	0.225
Flakes, shatter		36	0.156
Flakes, core renewal		2	0.009
Pebble hammerstones	1		0.004
Blades, bladelets		18	0.078
Denticulates	1		0.004
Chopper	1		0.004
Point, projectile		1	0.004
Knife, naturally backed		1	0.004
Notches		3	0.013
Becs, typical		1	0.004
Bladelets, backed		2	0.009
Endscraper, simple (atypical)		1	0.004
Endscraper, nucleiform		3	0.013
Pièce esquillée		1	0.004
Pieces with continuous retouch on one or more edges		2	0.009
Burin spalls		1	0.004
Total	32	199	0.997

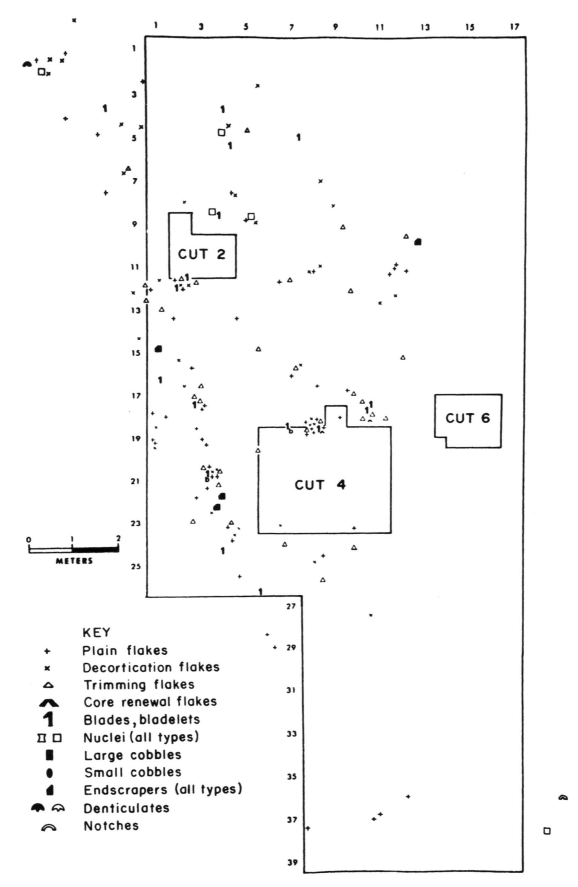

KEY

+ Plain flakes
× Decortication flakes
△ Trimming flakes
⌃ Core renewal flakes
1 Blades, bladelets
⊟ ▢ Nuclei (all types)
▮ Large cobbles
● Small cobbles
◢ Endscrapers (all types)
▲ ⌢ Denticulates
⌒ Notches

Figure B.1. Distribution of flint artifacts in the
1972 surface collection, Liencres.

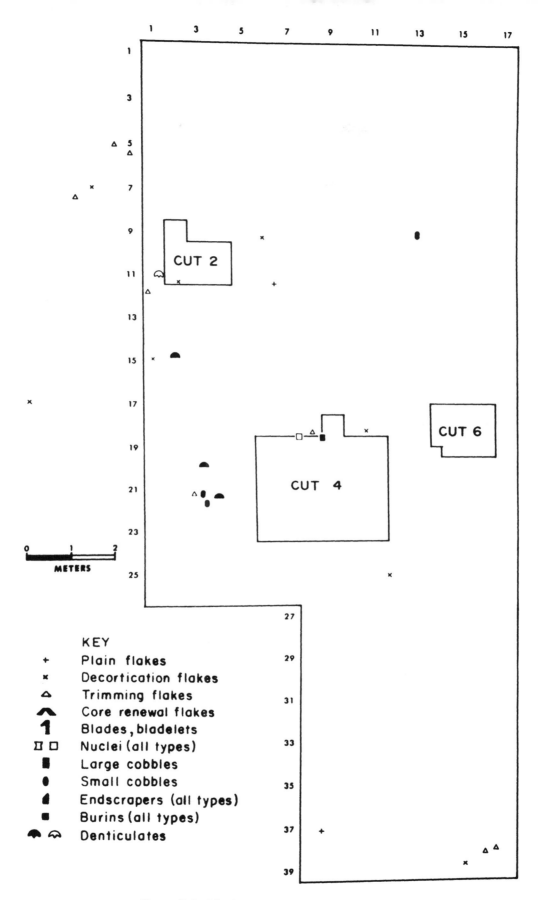

Figure B.2. Distribution of quartzite artifacts in the 1972 surface collection, Liencres.

[155]

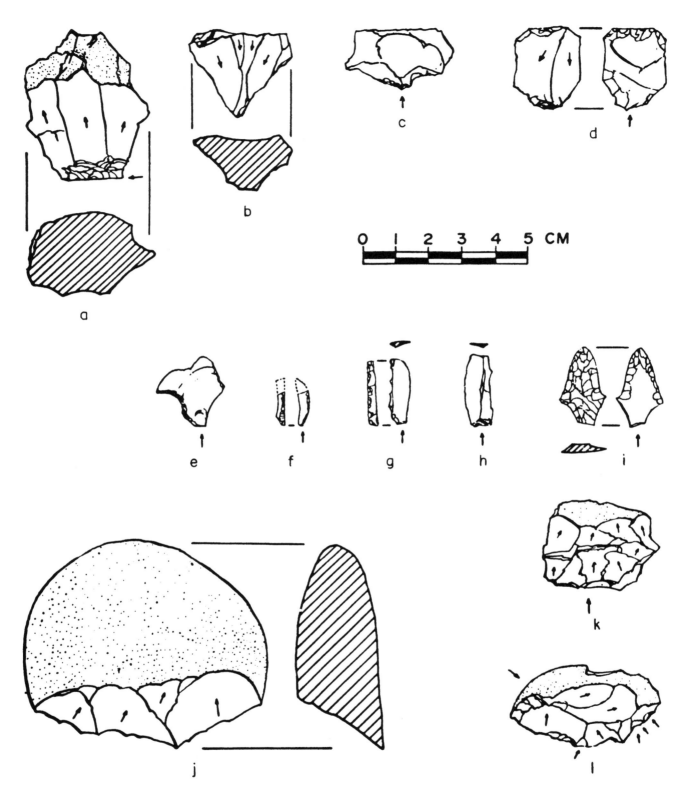

Figure B.3. Flint and quartzite artifacts in the 1972 surface collection, Liencres: *a*, nucleiform endscraper made on a blade-bladelet core (arrow on right indicates point of detachment of platform renewal flake); *b*, mixed flake-bladelet core; *c*, atypical perforator (bec); *d*, pièce esquillée (dorsal on left, ventral on right; *e*, flake notch (retouched semiabruptly on ventral surface);*f, g*, backed bladelets; *h*, bladelet; *i*, partially bifacial projectile point (possibly broken or unfinished); *j*, chopper; *k*, pick trimming flake (note evidence of prior retouch, piece was probably detached from the edge of an Asturian pick); *l*, flake denticulate. Material: *a–i*, flint; *j–l*, quartzite.

Appendix C

Site, Excavator, and Storage Location
of Illustrated Artifacts

Figure	Site	Excavator	Storage Location
5.1a	Arnero	Vega del Sella and Obermaier, 1919	Museo Arqueológico Provincial, Oviedo
b	Fonfría	Vega del Sella, 1915	Museo Arqueológico Nacional, Madrid
c	Colombres	Carballo, 1926	Museo Provincial de Prehistoria y Arqueología, Santander
d	Cueto de la Mina	Vega del Sella, 1914, 1915	Museo Arqueológico Provincial, Oviedo
e	La Loja	Vega del Sella, 1916–1920	Museo Arqueológico Provincial, Oviedo
f	Bricia	Jordá, 1953	Museo Arqueológico Provincial, Oviedo
g	Coberizas	Vega del Sella and Obermaier, 1919	Museo Arqueológico Nacional, Madrid
h	Balmori	Vega del Sella and Obermaier, 1914–1917	Museo Arqueológico Provincial, Oviedo
i	Penicial	Vega del Sella, 1914	Museo Arqueológico Provincial, Oviedo
j	Liencres	Clark, 1969	Museo Provincial de Prehistoria y Arqueología, Santander
k	Lledías	Jordá, 1953	Museo Arqueológico Provincial, Oviedo
l	La Riera	Clark, 1969	Museo Arqueológico Provincial, Oviedo
m	La Riera	Vega del Sella and Obermaier, 1917	Museo Arqueológico Provincial, Oviedo
n	Cuartamentero	Giles, 1967	Museo Arqueológico Nacional, Madrid
o	Tres Calabres	Vega del Sella, 1922	Museo Arqueológico Provincial, Oviedo
p	Infierno	Vega del Sella, 1916–1920	Museo Arqueológico Provincial, Oviedo
5.2a	Lledías	Jordá, 1953	Museo Arqueológico Provincial, Oviedo
b	La Riera	Vega del Sella and Obermaier, 1917	Museo Nacional de Ciencias Naturales, Madrid
c	La Riera	Clark, 1969	Museo Arqueológico Provincial, Oviedo
d	Fonfría	Vega del Sella, 1915	Museo Arqueológico Provincial, Oviedo
e	Arnero	Clark, 1969	Museo Arqueológico Provincial, Oviedo
f	Penicial	Vega del Sella, 1914	Museo Nacional de Ciencias Naturales, Madrid
g	Fonfría	Vega del Sella, 1915	Museo Arqueológico Provincial, Oviedo
h	La Franca	Vega del Sella, 1915	Museo Nacional de Ciencias Naturales, Madrid
i	Penicial	Vega del Sella, 1914	Museo Nacional de Ciencias Naturales, Madrid
j	Tres Calabres	Vega del Sella, 1922	Museo Arqueológico Provincial, Oviedo
k	Colombres	Carballo, 1926	Museo Provincial de Prehistoria y Arqueología, Santander
l	Cuartamentero	Giles, 1967	Museo Arqueológico Nacional, Madrid
m	Fonfría	Vega del Sella, 1915	Museo Nacional de Ciencias Naturales, Madrid

Appendix C

(continued)

Figure	Site	Excavator	Storage Location
n	La Riera	Vega del Sella and Obermaier, 1917	Museo Arqueológico Provincial, Oviedo
o	Fonfría	Vega del Sella, 1915	Museo Arqueológico Provincial, Oviedo
p	La Franca	Vega del Sella, 1915	Museo Provincial de Prehistoria y Arqueología, Santander
q	La Loja	Vega del Sella, 1916–1920	Museo Arqueológico Provincial, Oviedo
r	Cuartamentero	Giles, 1967	Museo Arqueológico Nacional, Madrid
s	La Franca	Vega del Sella, 1915	Museo Provincial de Prehistoria y Arqueología, Santander
t	Balmori	Clark, 1969	Museo Arqueológico Provincial, Oviedo
5.3*a*	Arnero	Vega del Sella and Obermaier, 1919	Museo Arqueológico Provincial, Oviedo
b–c	Balmori	Clark, 1969	Museo Arqueológico Provincial, Oviedo
d	Liencres	Clark, 1969	Museo Provincial de Prehistoria y Arqueología, Santander
e	La Riera	Clark, 1969	Museo Arqueológico Provincial, Oviedo
f	Liencres	Clark, 1969	Museo Provincial de Prehistoria y Arqueología, Santander
g–h	La Riera	Clark, 1969	Museo Arqueológico Provincial, Oviedo
i–n	Liencres	Clark, 1969	Museo Provincial de Prehistoria y Arqueología, Santander
o	La Riera	Clark, 1969	Museo Arqueológico Provincial, Oviedo
p	Fonfría	Vega del Sella, 1915	Museo Arqueológico Provincial, Oviedo
q	Liencres	Clark, 1969	Museo Provincial de Prehistoria y Arqueología, Santander
r	Balmori	Clark, 1969	Museo Arqueológico Provincial, Oviedo
s	La Riera	Clark, 1969	Museo Arqueológico Provincial, Oviedo
t–u	Liencres	Clark, 1969	Museo Provincial de Prehistoria y Arqueología, Santander
v	La Riera	Clark, 1969	Museo Arqueológico Provincial, Oviedo
w	Liencres	Clark, 1969	Museo Provincial de Prehistoria y Arqueología, Santander
x	La Riera	Clark, 1969	Museo Arqueológico Provincial, Oviedo
y–z	Liencres	Clark, 1969	Museo Provincial de Prehistoria y Arqueología, Santander
a'	Fonfría	Vega del Sella, 1915	Museo Arqueológico Provincial, Oviedo
b'	Balmori	Clark, 1969	Museo Arqueológico Provincial, Oviedo
c'–d'	Liencres	Clark, 1969	Museo Provincial de Prehistoria y Arqueología, Santander
e'	Balmori	Clark, 1969	Museo Arqueológico Provincial, Oviedo
f'	La Riera	Clark, 1969	Museo Arqueológico Provincial, Oviedo
g'	Penicial	Vega del Sella, 1914	Museo Arqueológico Provincial, Oviedo

Appendix C

(continued)

Figure	Site	Excavator	Storage Location
h'	Balmori	Clark, 1969	Museo Arqueológico Provincial, Oviedo
i'–j'	La Riera	Clark, 1969	Museo Arqueológico Provincial, Oviedo
k'–l'	Balmori	Clark, 1969	Museo Arqueológico Provincial, Oviedo
m'	La Riera	Clark, 1969	Museo Arqueológico Provincial, Oviedo
n'	Liencres	Clark, 1969	Museo Provincial de Prehistoria y Arqueología, Santander
o'	La Riera	Clark, 1969	Museo Arqueológico Provincial, Oviedo
p'–q'	Liencres	Clark, 1969	Museo Provincial de Prehistoria y Arqueología, Santander
r'	La Riera	Clark, 1969	Museo Arqueológico Provincial, Oviedo
s'	Tres Calabres	Vega del Sella, 1922	Museo Arqueológico Provincial, Oviedo
t'	La Riera	Clark, 1969	Museo Arqueológico Provincial, Oviedo
u'	La Loja	Vega del Sella, 1916–1920	Museo Arqueológico Provincial, Oviedo
5.4*a–g*	Liencres	Clark, 1969	Museo Provincial de Prehistoria y Arqueología, Santander
h	La Riera	Clark, 1969	Museo Arqueológico Provincial, Oviedo
i	Liencres	Clark, 1969	Museo Provincial de Prehistoria y Arqueología, Santander
j–l	La Riera	Clark, 1969	Museo Arqueológico Provincial, Oviedo
m	Liencres	Clark, 1969	Museo Provincial de Prehistoria y Arqueología, Santander
n–o	La Riera	Clark, 1969	Museo Arqueológico Provincial, Oviedo
p–r	Liencres	Clark, 1969	Museo Provincial de Prehistoria y Arqueología, Santander
s–u	La Riera	Clark, 1969	Museo Arqueológico Provincial, Oviedo
v	La Franca	Vega del Sella, 1915	Museo Arqueológico Provincial, Oviedo
w–x	La Riera	Clark, 1969	Museo Arqueológico Provincial, Oviedo
y–c'	Liencres	Clark, 1969	Museo Provincial de Prehistoria y Arqueología, Santander
d'–e'	La Riera	Clark, 1969	Museo Arqueológico Provincial, Oviedo
f'	Liencres	Clark, 1969	Museo Provincial de Prehistoria y Arqueología, Santander
g'–h'	La Riera	Clark, 1969	Museo Arqueológico Provincial, Oviedo
i'–m'	Liencres	Clark, 1969	Museo Provincial de Prehistoria y Arqueología, Santander
n'	La Riera	Clark, 1969	Museo Arqueológico Provincial, Oviedo
o'	Liencres	Clark, 1969	Museo Provincial de Prehistoria y Arqueología, Santander
p'	La Riera	Clark, 1969	Museo Arqueológico Provincial, Oviedo

REFERENCES

Aguirre, Emiliano de
1964 Las Gándaras de Budiño (Porriño, Pontevedra). *Excavaciones Arqueológicas en España* 31. Madrid.
Aguirre, Emiliano de, and Karl W. Butzer
1967 A problematical Pleistocene artifact assemblage from northwestern Spain. *Science* 157(3787): 430, 431.
Alcalde del Rio, Hermilio, Henri Breuil, and Paul Sierra
1911 *Les Cavernes de la Region Cantabrique*. Monaco: Imprimerie Albert Ièr.
Almagro-Basch, Martin
1960 *Manual de Historia Universal*. Vol. 1 (Prehistoria). Madrid: Espasa-Calpé.
1963 El Paleolítico Español. Chapter 3 in *Historia de España* (3rd edition), edited by Ramón Menéndez-Pidal. Madrid: Espasa-Calpé.
Altuna, Jesús
1972 Fauna de mamíferos de los yacimientos prehistoricos de Guipúzcoa, con catálogo de los mamíferos cuaternarios del Cantábrico y Pirineo Occidental. *Munibe* 24: 1–464.
1976 Los mamíferos del yacimiento prehistorico de Tito Bustillo. In *Excavaciones en la Cueva de Tito Bustillo (Asturias)*, edited by J. Moure and M. Cano, pp. 151–194. Oviedo: Instituto de Estudios Asturianos.
1980 Historia de la domesticación animal en el País Vasco desde sus origenes hasta la Romanización. *Munibe* 32: 1–163.
Altuna, Jesús, and Lawrence Straus
1976 The Solutrean of Altamira: the artifactual and faunal evidence. *Zephyrus* 26–27: 175–182.
Anderez, Valeriano
1953 La cueva prehistorica de "Meaza:" estado actual de su exploración. Sección "Investigaciones Prehistoricas" in *Miscelánea Comillas* 19. Palencia: Publicaciones de la Universidad Pontífica de Comillas.
Andrews, F. C.
1954 Asymptotic behavior in some rank tests of analysis of variance. *Annals of Mathematical Statistics* 25: 724–736.
Apellaniz, Juan
1974 El grupo de Los Husos durante la prehistoria con cerámica. *Estudios de Arqueología Alavesa* 7: 1–409.
1975 Neolítico y Bronce en la Cornisa Cantábrica. In *La Prehistoria de la Cornisa Cantábrica*, edited by M.-A. García Guinea, pp. 201–222. Santander: Institución Cultural de Cantabria.
Aranguren-Sabas, Félix
1966 *Mapa Geológico de la Península Ibérica, Baleares y Canarias*. 2nd edition. Madrid.
Arkin, Herbert, and Raymond Colton
1967 Tables for Statisticians. *Barnes and Noble College Outline Series* 75, 2nd edition. New York: Barnes and Noble.
Ashton, E. H., M. J. R. Healey, and S. Lipton
1957 The descriptive use of discriminant functions in physical anthropology. *Proceedings of the Royal Society* 146: 552–572, Series, B. London.

Bailey, Geoffrey N.
1973 Concheros del norte de España: una hipótesis préliminar. *Actas del 12º Congreso Nacional de Arqueología* (Jaén, 1971), pp. 73–84. Zaragoza.
1978 Shell middens as indicators of postglacial economies: a territorial perspective. In *The Early Postglacial Settlement of Northern Europe*, edited by P. Mellars, pp. 37–63. London: Duckworth.
1981a Concepts, time-scales and explanations in economic prehistory. In "Economic Archaeology: Towards an Integration of Ecological and Social Approaches," edited by A. Sheridan and G. Bailey, pp. 97–117. *British Archaeological Reports* S–96. Oxford.
1981b Concepts of resource exploitation: continuity and discontinuity in paleoeconomy. *World Archaeology* 13(1): 1–15.
Barras de Aragon, Felix
1898 Cráneos prehistóricos de Val-de-Dios (Oviedo). *Boletín de la Sociedad Española de Historia Natural* 31. Madrid.
Bartlett, M. S.
1965 Multivariate Statistics. In *Theoretical and Mathematical Biology*, edited by S. Waterman and D. Morowitz, pp. 201–223. New York: McGraw-Hill.
Biberson, Pierre, Georges Choubert, Maurice Faure-Mauret, and Georges Lecointre
1960 Contribution à l'Etude de la "Pebble Culture" du Maroc Atlantique. *Bulletin Arquéologique Marocaine* 3. Marseille.
Binford, Lewis R.
1968 Post-Pleistocene adaptations. In *New Perspectives in Archeology*, edited by Sally Binford and Lewis Binford, pp. 313–342. Chicago: Aldine.
1972 Contemporary model building: paradigms and the current state of Paleolithic research. In *Models in Archaeology*, edited by D. Clarke, pp. 109–166. London: Methuen.
1973 Interassemblage variability—the Mousterian and the 'functional' argument. In *The Explanation of Culture Change: Models in Prehistory*, edited by Colin Renfrew, pp. 227–254. Pittsburgh: University of Pittsburgh Press.
1976 Forty-seven trips—A case study in the character of some formation processes of the archaeological record. In "Contributions to Anthropology: The Interior Peoples of Northern Alaska," edited by E. Hall, pp. 299–351. *Archaeological Survey of Canada Paper* 49. Ottawa: National Museum of Canada.
1978a *Nunamiut Ethnoarchaeology*. New York: Academic Press.
1978b Dimensional analysis of behavior and site structure: learning from an Eskimo hunting stand. *American Antiquity* 43(3): 330–361.
1980 Willow smoke and dogs' tails: hunter-gatherer settlement systems and archaeological site formation. *American Antiquity* 45(1): 4–20.

Binford, Lewis, and Sally Binford
1966   A preliminary analysis of functional variability in the Mousterian of Levallois facies. *American Anthropologist* 68(2): 238–295.

Binford, Sally, and Lewis Binford
1969   Stone tools and human behavior. *Scientific American* 220(4): 70–84.

Blalock, Hubert
1972   *Social Statistics.* 2nd edition. New York: McGraw-Hill.

Blas Cortina, Miguel-Angel, Manual González, Maria del Carmen Marquez, and J. Rodriguez
1978   Picos Asturienses de yacimientos al aire libre en Asturias. *Boletin del Instituto de Estudios Asturianos* 93–94: 335–356.

Bordes, François
1961   Typologie du paléolithique ancien et moyen. *Publications de L'Institut de Préhistoire de l'Université de Bordeaux Memoire* 1. Bordeaux: Imprimeries Delmas.
1968   *The Old Stone Age.* New York: McGraw-Hill.

Bordes, François, and Denise de Sonneville-Bordes
1970   The significance of variability in Paleolithic assemblages. *World Archaeology* 2(1): 61–73.

Boserup, Ester
1965   *The Conditions of Agricultural Growth.* Chicago: Aldine.

Braidwood, Robert J.
1962   Southwestern Asia beyond the lands of Mediterranean littoral. In "Courses Toward Urban Life," edited by Robert Braidwood and Gordon Willey, pp. 132–146. *Viking Fund Publications in Anthropology* 32. Chicago: Aldine.

Braidwood, Robert, and Charles Reed
1957   The achievement and early consequences of food production. *Cold Spring Harbor Symposia on Quantitative Biology* 22: 19–31.

Breuil, Henri, and Georges Zybszewski
1942   Contribution à l'étude des industries Paléolithiques du Portugal et leurs rapports avec la géologie du Quaternaire. *Comunicacões dos Servicos Geológicos de Portugal* 23(1). Lisboa.
1945   Contribution à l'étude des industries Paléolithiques du Portugal et leurs rapports avec la géológie du Quaternaire. *Comunicacões dos Servicos Geológicos de Portugal* 26(2). Lisboa.

Brinch Petersen, Erik
1971   Ølby Lyng. En ostsjaellandsk kystboplads med Ertebøllekultur. *Aarbøger for Nordisk Oldkyndighed og Historie,* pp. 5–42. Oslo.
1973   A survey of the Late Paleolithic and the Mesolithic of Denmark. In *The Mesolithic in Europe,* edited by Stefan Kozłowski, pp. 77–128. Warsaw: Warsaw University Press.

Brothwell, Donald
1972   Paleodemography of earlier British populations. *World Archaeology* 4(1): 75–87.

Brown, J. A.
1893   On the continuity of the Palaeolithic and Neolithic periods. *Journal of the Royal Anthropological Institute* 22: 66–98.

Burkitt, Miles C.
1931   Notes on a journey through north-west Spain and Portugal. *Publications of the Prehistoric Society of East Anglia* 6. London.

Butzer, Karl W.
1964   *Environment and Archaeology: An Introduction to Pleistocene Geography.* Chicago: Aldine.
1967   Geomorphology and stratigraphy of the Paleolithic site of Budiño (Province of Pontevedra, Spain). *Eiszeitalter und Gegenwart* 18: 82–103.
1970   Preliminary observations on the geomorphologic setting and stratigraphy of Cueva Morín (province of Santander, Spain). Ms, University of Chicago, Chicago.
1971a   *Environment and Archaeology: An Ecological Approach to Prehistory.* 2nd edition, revised. Chicago and New York: Aldine-Atherton.
1971b   Comunicación préliminar sobre la geología de Cueva Morín (Santander). In "Cueva Morín: Excavaciones 1966–1968," edited by Joaquín González Echegaray and Leslie Freeman, pp. 345–358. *Publicaciones del Patronato de las Cuevas Prehistoricas de la Provincia de Santander Memoria* 6. Santander.

Butzer, Karl, and Daniel Bowman
1975   Algunos sedimentos de niveles arqueológicos asturienses de yacimientos de la España cantábrica. *Cuadernos de Arqueología* 3: 60–66.
1979   Some sediments from Asturian archaeological levels from sites in Cantabrian Spain. *Quaternaria* 21: 287–291.

Butzer, Karl, and Bruce Gladfelter
1968   Quartz grain micromorphology. In *Desert and River in Nubia,* by Karl Butzer and Carl Hansen, pp. 473–481. Madison: University of Wisconsin Press.

Butzer, Karl, and Carl Hansen
1968   *Desert and River in Nubia.* Madison: University of Wisconsin Press.

Carballo, Jesus
1924   *Prehistoria Universal y Especial de España.* Madrid.
1926   *El Esqueleto Humano Más Antiguo de España.* Published privately by the author, Santander.
1960   *Investigaciones Prehistoricas II.* Santander: Publicaciones del Museo Provincial de Prehistoria.

Chapa, Teresa
1975   Magdaleniense medio y superior de Cueto de la Mina. *Boletin del Instituto de Estudios Asturianos* 86: 755–780.

Childe, V. Gordon
1927   *The Dawn of European Civilisation.* London: Kegan Paul.
1931   The forest cultures of northern Europe: a study in evolution and diffusion. *Journal of the Royal Anthropological Institute* 61: 325–348.

Clark, Geoffrey A.
1971a   The Asturian of Cantabria: a re-evaluation. MS, doctoral dissertation, University of Chicago, Chicago.
1971b   The Asturian of Cantabria: subsistence base and the evidence for post-Pleistocene climatic shifts. *American Anthropologist* 73(5): 1244–1257.
1972   El Asturiense de Cantabria: bases sustentadores y evidencias de los cambios climáticos Post-Pleistocenos. *Trabajos de Prehistoria* 29: 17–30. Madrid: Consejo Superior de Investigaciones Científicas.
1974a   Excavations in the Late Pleistocene cave site of Balmori, Asturias (Spain). *Quaternaria* 18: 383–426.
1974b   La ocupación Asturiense de la cueva de La Riera (Asturias, España). *Trabajos de Prehistoria* 31: 9–38. Madrid: Consejo Superior de Investigaciones Científicas.
1975a   Liencres: una estación al aire libre de estilo Asturiense cerca de Santander. *Cuadernos de Arqueología* 3: 1–84. Bilbao: Seminario de Arqueología, Universidad de Deusto.
1975b   El hombre y su ambiente a comienzos del Holoceno en la Región Cantábrica. *Boletin del Instituto de Estudios Asturianos* 85: 363–387.
1976a   El Asturiense Cantábrico. *Bibliotheca Praehistorica Hispana* 13: 1–372. Madrid: Consejo Superior de Investigaciones Científicas.
1976b   L'Asturien des Cantabres: état de la recherche actuelle. *Actes du 20ᵉ Congrès Préhistorique de France,* edited by Max Escalon de Fonton, pp. 84–101. Paris: Centre National de la Recherche Scientifique.

162   *References*

Clark, Geoffrey A. *(continued)*
1976c More on contingency table analysis, decision making criteria and the use of log linear models. *American Antiquity* 41(3): 259–273.
1979a Spatial association at Liencres, an early Holocene open site on the Santander coast, north-central Spain. In "Computer Graphics in Archaeology," edited by S. Upham, pp. 121–144. *Arizona State University Anthropological Research Papers* 15. Tempe.
1979b Liencres, an open station of Asturian affinity near Santander, Spain. *Quaternaria* 21: 249–286, 292–304.
1979c Editor. The North Burgos Archaeological Survey: Bronze and Iron Age Archaeology on the Meseta del Norte (Province of Burgos, North-Central Spain). *Arizona State University Anthropological Research Papers* 19. Tempe.
1981 On preagricultural coastal adaptations. *Current Anthropology* 22(4): 444–446. Chicago.
1982 Boreal phase settlement-subsistence models for Cantabrian Spain. In *Hunter-Gatherer Economy in Prehistory*, edited by G. Bailey, pp. 96–110. Cambridge: Cambridge University Press.

Clark, Geoffrey A., and Thomas Cartledge
1973a Excavaciones en la cueva de Coberizas, Asturias (España). *Noticiario Arqueológico Hispanico, Serie Prehistorica* 2: 10–37. Madrid: Consejo Superior de Investigaciones Científicas.
1973b Recent excavations at the cave of Coberizas (Province of Asturias, Spain). *Quaternaria* 17: 387–411.

Clark, Geoffrey A., and Valerie J. Clark
1975 La cueva de Balmori (Asturias, España): nuevas aportaciones. *Trabajos de Prehistoria* 32: 35–77. Madrid: Consejo Superior de Investigaciones Científicas.

Clark, Geoffrey A., Richard Effland, and Joel Johnstone
1977 Quantitative spatial analysis: computer applications of Nearest Neighbor analysis to objects distributed across Two-dimensional space. In *Computer Applications in Archaeology*, edited by S. Laflin, pp. 27–44. Birmingham: University of Birmingham.

Clark, Geoffrey A., and Shereen Lerner
1980 Prehistoric resource utilization in early Holocene Cantabrian Spain. *Anthropology UCLA* 10(1–2): 53–96. Los Angeles.

Clark, Geoffrey A., and Josefa Menéndez-Amor
1975 Appendice II: Muestras de polen de Liencres, Niveles 1 y 2. *Cuadernos de Arqueología* 3: 67–71. Bilbao: Seminario de Arqueología, Universidad de Deusto.

Clark, Geoffrey A., and Linda Richards
1978 Late and post-Pleistocene industries and fauna from the cave site of La Riera (Province of Asturias, Spain). In *Views of the Past*, edited by Leslie Freeman, pp. 117–152. The Hague: Mouton.

Clark, Geoffrey A., and Lawrence G. Straus
1977a La Riera Paleoecological Project: preliminary report, 1976 excavations. *Current Anthropology* 18(2): 354, 355.
1977b Cueva de la Riera: objetivo del 'Proyecto Paleoecológico' e informe préliminar de la campaña de 1976. *Boletin del Instituto de Estudios Asturianos* 91: 489–505.
1977c Algunas observaciones sobre 'Revisión Estratigráfica de la Cueva de la Riera.' *Boletin del Instituto de Estudios Asturianos* 91: 507, 508.
1982 Late Pleistocene hunter-gatherer adaptations in Cantabrian Spain. In *Hunter-Gatherer Economy in Prehistory*, edited by G. Bailey, pp. 131–147. Cambridge: Cambridge University Press.

Clark, Geoffrey A., and Seonbok Yi
1982 Niche-width variation in Late Pleistocene–Early Holocene archaeofaunas from Cantabrian Spain. In *Animals and Archaeology: Hunters and Their Prey*, edited by Juliet Clutton-Brock and Caroline Grigson. Oxford: British Archaeological Reports.

Clark, J. Grahame D.
1932 *The Mesolithic Age in Britain*. Cambridge: Cambridge University Press.
1936 *The Mesolithic Settlement of Northern Europe*. Cambridge: Cambridge University Press.
1948 The development of fishing in prehistoric Europe. *Antiquaries Journal* 28: 44–85.
1953 The economic approach to prehistory. *Proceedings of the British Academy* 39: 215–238.
1972 *Star Carr: A Case Study in Bioarchaeology*. Anthropology Module 10. Reading, Massachusetts: Addison-Wesley Modular Publications.
1973 Seasonality and the interpretation of lithic assemblages. In *Estudios Dedicados al Profesor Luis Pericot*, edited by J. Maluquer, pp. 39–56. Barcelona.
1975 *The Earlier Stone Age Settlement of Scandinavia*. Cambridge: Cambridge University Press.
1978 Neothermal orientations. In *The Early Postglacial Settlement of Northern Europe*, edited by P. Mellars, pp. 1–10. London: Duckworth.
1980 *Mesolithic Prelude: The Palaeolithic-Neolithic Transition in Old World Prehistory*. Edinburgh: Edinburgh University Press.

Clark, J. Grahame D., S. Warren, H. Godwin, and W. Macfayden
1934 An early mesolithic site at Broxbourne sealed under Boreal peat. *Journal of the Royal Anthropological Institute* 64: 101–128.

Clark, J. Grahame D., D. Walker, H. Godwin, G. Fraser, and J. King
1954 *Excavations at Star Carr, An Early Mesolithic Site Near Seamer, Scarborough, Yorkshire*. Cambridge: Cambridge University Press.

Clark, Phillip J., and Francis Evans
1954 Distance to Nearest Neighbour as a measure of spatial relationships in Populations. *Ecology* 35(4): 445–453.

CLIMAP
1976 The surface of the Ice-Age earth. *Science* 191(4232): 1131–1137.

Cohen, Mark N.
1975 Archaeological evidence of population pressure in pre-agricultural societies. *American Antiquity* 40(4): 471–474.
1977 *The Food Crisis in Prehistory*. New Haven: Yale University Press.

Collins, Desmond
1969 Culture traditions and the environment of early man. *Current Anthropology* 10(2): 267–296.
1970 Stone artifact analysis and the recognition of culture traditions. *World Archaeology* 2(1): 17–27.

Corbet, G. B.
1966 *The Terrestrial Mammals of Western Europe*. London: G. T. Foulis.

Corchón, Maria S.
1971a *El Solutrense en Santander*. Santander: Institución Cultural de Cantabria.
1971b Notas en torno al arte mueble asturiano. *Publicaciones del Seminario de Prehistoria y Arqueología de la Universidad de Salamanca*. Salamanca.

Cornwall, Ian W.
1968 *Prehistoric Animals and Their Hunters*. London: Faber and Faber.

Crusafont Pairo, Manuel
1963 ¿Es la industria "Asturiense" una evolucionada "Pebble Culture"? *Speleón* 14(1–4): 77–88.

Dacey, Michael F.
1960 The Spacing of River Towns. *Annals of the Association of American Geographers* 50: 59–61.

Darling, F. Fraser
1963 *A Herd of Red Deer: A Study in Animal Behavior*. London: Oxford University Press.

Davidson, Iain
1981 Can we study prehistoric economy for fisher-gatherer-hunters? An historical approach to Cambridge 'paleoeconomy.' In "Economic Archaeology: Towards an Integration of Ecological and Social Approaches," edited by A. Sheridan and G. Bailey, pp. 17–33. *British Archaeological Reports* S–96. Oxford.

Dixon, W. J., editor
1975 *BMD (Biomedical Computer Programs)*. Berkeley: University of California Press.

Ellerman, J. R., and T. C. S. Morrison-Scott
1966 *Checklist of Palearctic and Indian Mammals: 1758–1946*. Second edition. London: Publications of the British Museum (Natural History).

Escalon de Fonton, Max
1966 Du Paléolithique supérieur au Mésolithique dans le Midi meditérranean. *Bulletin de la Société Préhistorique Française* 63(1): 66–180.

Escortell Ponsoda, Matilde
1973 Dos puñales de la Edad de Bronce en el Puerto de Gumial (Alto Aller). *Boletín del Instituto de Estudios Asturianos* 79: 411–420.

Everitt, B.
1974 *Cluster Analysis*. London: Heinemann Educational Books.

Eyre, S. R.
1963 *Vegetation and Soils: A World Picture*. Chicago: Aldine.

Ferembach, Denise
1974 *Le Gisement Mésolithique de Moita do Sebastião (Muge, Portugal): Anthropologie*. Lisboa: Publiçāoes do Direcçāo-Geral dos Assuntos Culturais.

Ferrier, Jaques
1949 Contribution à l'Étude de l'Asturien—I. *Bulletin de la Société Préhistorique Française* 46: 193–203.
1950 Contribution à l'Étude de l'Asturien—II. *Bulletin de la Société Préhistorique Française* 47: 74–89.

Fisher, Ronald A.
1938 The use of multiple measurements in taxonomic problems. *Annals of the Eugenics Society of London* 7: 179–188.

Flannery, Kent
1967 Culture history versus cultural process: a debate in American archaeology. *Scientific American* 217(2): 119–122.
1973 Archaeology with a capital S. In *Research and Theory in Current Archaeology*, edited by C. Redman, pp. 47–58. New York: Wiley Interscience.

Fleming, Andrew
1972 The genesis of pastoralism in European prehistory. *World Archaeology* 4(2): 179–191.

Fontela, Juan Dominguez
1925 La estación paleolítica de la Guardia. *Boletín de la Comisión Provincial de Monumentos Historicos y Artísticos de Orense* 7(160): 241–244.

Fraga-Torrejón, E. de
1958 Catálogo bibliográfico de la fauna cuaternaria asturiana. *Monográfias Geológicas* 8: 1–75. Oviedo: Instituto de Geología Aplicada.

Francis, Julie, and Geoffrey Clark
1979 Toward a model of subsistence and settlement: archaeological site catchment analysis of Bronze and Iron Age survey data from north Burgos Province, north-central Spain. *Arizona State University Anthropological Research Papers* 19: 210–246. Tempe.

Freeman, Leslie G.
1964 Mousterian developments in Cantabrian Spain. MS, doctoral dissertation, University of Chicago, Chicago.
1968 A theoretical framework for interpreting archaeological materials. In *Man the Hunter*, edited by R. Lee and I. deVore, pp. 262–267. Chicago: Aldine.
1973 The significance of mammalian faunas from Paleolithic occupations in Cantabrian Spain. *American Antiquity* 38(1): 3–44.

Fretter, Vera, and Alastair Graham
1962 *British Prosobranch Molluscs: Their Functional Anatomy and Ecology*. London: Ray Society.

Garcia Guinea, Miguel-Angel
1976 Primeros sondéos estratigráficos en la cueva de Tito Bustillo (Ribadesella, Asturias). *Publicaciones del Patronato de Cuevas Prehistoricas de Santander* 12. Santander.

Garner, B. J.
1967 Models of urban geography and settlement location. In *Economic Models in Geography*, edited by R. Chorley and P. Haggett, pp. 303–360. London: Methuen.

Garrod, Dorothy A. E., L. H. Buxton, G. E. Smith, and D. M. A. Bate
1928 Excavations at a Mousterian Rock Shelter at Devil's Tower, Gibraltar. *Journal of the Royal Anthropological Institute* 58: 33–114.

Gavelas, Antonio J.
1980 Sobre nuevos concheros asturienses en los concejos de Ribadesella y Llanes (Asturias). *Boletín del Instituto de Estudios Asturianos* 101: 675–718.

Gómez Tabanera, José M.
1976 Revisión estratigráfica de la cueva de La Riera. *Boletín del Instituto de Estudios Asturianos* 88–89: 855–910.

González, José Manuel
1965 Localización de un pico asturiense en Luarca (Asturias). *Valdedios*, pp. 35–39. Oviedo.
1976 *Antiguos Pobladores de Asturias: Protohistoria.* Gijón: Ediciones Ayalga.

González Echegaray, Joaquín
1966 Sobre la cronología de la glaciación Würmiense en la Costa Cantábrica. *Ampurias* 28: 1–12.
1971 Apreciaciones cuantitatívas sobre el Magdaleniense III de la Costa Cantábrica. *Munibe* 23: 323–327.
1972– Consideraciones climáticas y ecológicas sobre el Mag-
1973 daleniense III en el norte de España. *Zephyrus* 23–24: 167–187.
1975 Clima y ambiente durante el paleolítico. In *La Prehistoria de la Cornisa Cantábrica*, edited by M. A. Garcia Guinea and M. A. Puente, pp. 35–62. Santander: Institución Cultural de Cantabria.

González Echegaray, Joaquín, and Leslie G. Freeman
1971 Cueva Morín: Excavaciones 1966–1968. *Publicaciones del Patronato de las Cuevas Prehistóricas de la Provincia de Santander Memoria* 6. Santander: Diputación Provincial de Santander.
1973 Cueva Morín: Excavaciones 1969. *Publicaciones del Patronato de las Cuevas Prehistoricas de la Provincia de Santander Memoria* 10. Santander: Diputación Provincial de Santander.

González Echegaray, Joaquín, Miguel-Angel García Guinea, and A. Begínes Ramirez
1966 La Cueva de Otero. *Excavaciones Arqueológicas en España* 53. Madrid: Consejo Superior de Investigaciones Científicas.

González Morales, Manuel
1978 Excavaciones en el conchero Asturiense de la Cueva de Mazaculos II (La Franca, Ribadedeva, Asturias). *Boletín del Instituto de Estudios Asturianos* 93–94: 369–383.

González Morales, Manuel, and Maria del Carmen Marquez
1974 Nota sobre la cueva de "El Quintanal" (Balmori, Llanes) y sus grabados rupestres. *Boletín del Instituto de Estudios Asturianos* 81: 235–246.
1978 The Asturian shell midden of Cueva de Mazaculos II (La Franca, Asturias, Spain). *Current Anthropology* 19(3): 614–615.

Goodman, A., and J. S. Ratti
1971 *Finite Mathematics With Applications*. New York and London: Macmillan.

Gorchkov, G., and A. Yakouchova
1967 *Géologie Générale*. Moscou: Editions Mir.

Graham, John M.
1970   Discrimination of British Lower and Middle Paleolithic handaxe groups using canonical variates. *World Archaeology* 1(3): 321–342.

Guerra Delgado, Antonio, F. Guitián Ojea, G. Paneque Guerrero, A. García Rodríguez, J. A. Sánchez Fernández, F. Monturiol Rodríguez, and J. L. Mudarra Gómez
1968   *Mapa de Suelos de España: Península y Baleares: Descripciones de las Asociaciones y Tipos Principales de Suelos.* Madrid: Instituto Nacional de Edafología y Agrobiología.

Guinea Lopez, Ernesto
1953   *Geográfia Botánica de Santander.* Santander: Diputación Provincial de Santander.

Haggett, Peter
1965   *Locational Analysis in Human Geography.* London: Edward Arnold.

Hainard, R.
1948   *Les Mammifères Sauvages d'Europe I: Insectivores, Cheiroptères, Carnivores.* Neuchâtel: Delachaux et Niéstle.
1949   *Les Mammifères Sauvages d'Europe II: Pinnipèdes, Rongeurs, Ongulés, Cétacés.* Neuchâtel: Delachaux et Niéstle.

Hernández Pacheco, Francisco
1944   Físiografia, geología y glaciarismo cuaternario de las Montañas de Reinosa. *Memoria de la Real Academia de Ciencias* 10, *Série Ciencias Naturales.* Madrid.

Hernández Pacheco, Francisco, Noël Llopis-Lladó, Francisco Jordá-Cerdá, and J. A. Martinez
1957   Livret-guide à l'excursion N₂ — le quaternaire de la región Cantabrique. *INQUA: 5e Congrès International.* Oviedo: Diputación Provincial de Asturias.

Hidalgo, Joaquín González
1890   Obras malacológicas; estudios préliminares sobre los moluscos terrestres y marinos de España, Portugal y las Baleares: Part II (Part I: 1887). *Memorias de la Real Academia de Ciencias Exactas, Físicas y Naturales de Madrid* 25. Madrid: Imprenta Luis Aguado.

Hodder, Ian, and Clive Orton
1976   *Spatial Analysis in Archaeology.* London: Cambridge University Press.

Hodson, Roy
1970   Cluster analysis and archaeology: some new developments and applications. *World Archaeology* 1(3): 299–320.

Houston, J. M.
1967   *The Western Mediterranean World: An Introduction to Its Regional Landscapes.* New York: Frederick A. Praeger.

Hoyos-Sainz, Luis de
1963   Antropología Prehistórica Española. In *Historia de España,* third edition, edited by Ramón Menéndez-Pidal. Madrid: Espasa-Calpé.

Jacobi, Roger
1973   Aspects of the "Mesolithic Age" in Great Britain. In *The Mesolithic in Europe,* edited by Stefan Kozłowski, pp. 237–266. Warsaw: Warsaw University Press.

Janssens, Paul, Joaquín González Echegaray, and P. Azpeitia
1958   *Memoria de las Excavaciones de la Cueva del Juyo (1955–56).* Santander: Patronato de las Cuevas Prehistoricas de la Provincia de Santander.

Jalhay, Eugénio
1925   El Asturiense en Galicia. *Boletin de la Comisión Provincial de Monumentos Historicos y Artisticos de Orense* 8(165): 341–352.
1928   La estación Asturiense de la Guardia. *Boletin de la Comisión Provincial de Monumentos Historicos y Artisticos de Orense* 8(179): 169–186.
1933   ¿Serán pre-asturienses las estaciones prehistóricas del litoral galaico-portugûes próximo al Miño? *Boletin de la Comisión Provincial de Monumentos Historicos y Artisticos de Orense* 10(208).

Jalhay, Eugénio, and Afonso do Paço
1941   Páleo e Mesolítico Português. *Anais de la Academia Portuguesa da Historia* 4: 1–140. Lisboa: Publicações Commemorativas do Duplo Centenário da Fundação e Restauração de Portugal.

Jarman, Michael R.
1972   A territorial model for archaeology: a behavioral and geographical approach. In *Models in Archaeology,* edited by David Clarke, pp. 705–734. London: Methuen.

Jarman, Michael R., Claudio Vita-Finzi, and Eric Higgs
1972   Site catchment analysis in archaeology. In *Man, Settlement and Urbanism,* edited by P. Ucko, Ruth Tringham, and G. Dimbleby, pp. 61–66. London: Gerald Duckworth.

Jochim, Michael
1976   *Hunter-Gatherer Subsistence and Settlement: A Predictive Model.* New York: Academic Press.

Johnson, Gregory
1977   Aspects of regional analysis in archaeology. *Annual Review of Anthropology* 6: 479–508.

Johnstone, Joel, Richard Effland, and Geoffrey A. Clark
1977   The Arizona State University nearest neighbor program; documentation and discussion. In *Computer Applications in Archaeology,* edited by S. Laflin, pp. 45–54. Birmingham: University of Birmingham.

Jordá-Cerdá, Francisco
1953   La cueva de Tres Calabres y el Solutrense en Asturias. *Boletin del Instituto de Estudios Asturianos* 18: 46–58.
1954   La cueva de Bricia (Asturias). *Boletin del Instituto de Estudios Asturianos* 22: 169–195.
1955   *El Solutrense en España y sus Problemas.* Oviedo: Diputación Provincial de Asturias.
1957   *Prehistoria de la Región Cantábrica.* Oviedo: Diputación Provincial de Asturias.
1958   *Avance al Estudio de la Cueva de la Lloseta (Ardines, Ribadesella).* Oviedo: Publicaciones de la Diputación Provincial de Asturias.
1959   Revisión de la cronología del Asturiense. *5° Congreso Arqueológico Nacional,* pp. 63–66. Zaragoza: Universidad de Zaragoza.
1960   El complejo cultural Solutrense-Magdaleniense en la region cantábrica. *Primer Symposium de Prehistoria de la Península Ibérica.* Pamplona: Universidad de Pamplona.
1963   El Paleolítico Superior cantábrica y sus industrias. *Saitabi* 8: 3–22. Oviedo.
1967   La España de los tiempos paleolíticos. In *Las Raices de España,* edited by J. M. Gómez Tabanera, pp. 1–26. Oviedo: Instituto Español de Antropología Aplicada.
1975   El Paleolítico Hispano; notas sobre el Asturiense. *Las Ciencias* 40(2): 87–93.
1977   *Prehistoria de Asturias.* Gijón: Ediciones Ayalga.

King, L. J.
1961   A multivariate analysis of the spacing of urban settlements in the United States. *Annals of the Association of American Geographers* 51: 222–233.
1962   A quantitative expression of the pattern of urban settlements in selected areas of the United States. *Tijdschrift Voor Economische en Sociale Geografie* 53: 1–7. Amsterdam.

Kozłowski, Stefan K.
1973   Introduction to the History of Europe in the Early Holocene. In *The Mesolithic in Europe,* edited by Stefan Kozłowski, pp. 331–366. Warsaw: Warsaw University Press.

Kubiena, Walter L.
1953   *The Soils of Europe: Illustrated Diagnosis and Systematics.* Consejo Superior de Investigaciones Científicas de Madrid. London: Thomas Murby.

Kurt, Fred
1968   *Das Sozialverhalten des Rehes (Capreolus capreolus L.): Eine Feldstudie.* Berlin: Verlag Paul Parey.

Kurtén, Bjorn
1968   *Pleistocene Mammals of Europe*. Chicago: Aldine
Lautensach, H.
1932   *Portugal Auf Grund Eisgener Reisen und der Litteratur*.
        Vols. I, II. Gotha: Petermanns Mitt.
1940   Die Minhoterrassen und ihre Beziehungen zu den
        eiszeitlichen Problemem. *Congresso do Mundo Por-
        tugués* 1: 62–99. Lisboa.
Laville, Henri, and Jean-Phillipe Rigaud
1973   The Perigordian V industries in Perigord: typological
        variations, stratigraphy and relative chronology.
        World Archaeology 4(3): 330–338.
Leroi-Gourhan, Arlette
1971   Análisis Polínico de Cueva Morín. In "Cueva Morín:
        Excavaciones 1966–1968," edited by J. González
        Echegaray and Leslie Freeman, pp. 359–368. *Pub-
        licaciones del Patronato de las Cuevas Prehistoricas de
        la Provincia de Santander* 6. Santander.
Lewis, J. R.
1964   *The Ecology of Rocky Shores*. London: Hodder and
        Stoughton.
Llopis-Lladó, Noël
1953   Estudios Hidrogeológicos y Prehistóricos en Posada
        (Llanes). *Speleón* 4(3–4). Oviedo.
Llopis-Lladó, Noël, and Francisco Jordá-Cerdá
1957   Mapa del Cuaternario de Asturias. *INQUA, 5° Con-
        greso Internacional de Antropología, Pre-y Proto His-
        tórica*. Oviedo: Diputación Provincial de Asturias.
Lubbock, John
1865   *Prehistoric Times*. London: Williams and Norgate.
Lumley, Henry de
1966   Les Fouilles de Terra Amata à Nice: Premièrs Ré-
        sultats. *Bulletin du Musée d'Anthropologie Préhistor-
        ique de Monaco, Fasc* 13. Monaco: Imprimerie
        Nationale de Monaco.
Madariaga, Benito
1967   El género *Patella* en la bahia de Santander: carac-
        teristicas biológicas y bromatológicas. *Anales de la
        Facultad de Veterinaria de Leon*, pp. 355–422. Leon:
        Universidad de Leon.
1976   Consideraciones acerca de la utilización del 'pico
        marisquero' del Asturiense. In *40° Aniversario del
        Centro de Estudios Montañeses* 3: 437–451. San-
        tander: Institución Cultural de Cantabria.
Mapa de la Provincia de Oviedo
1968   Diputación Provincial de Asturias, Edición Especial,
        Escala 1:200,000. Oviedo: Talleres del Instituto Geo-
        gráfico y Catastral.
Mapa Forestal de España
1966   Ministerio de Agricultura: Dirección General de
        Montes, Caza y Pesca Fluvial; Escala 1:400,000.
        Madrid.
Mapa Geológico de España: Península Ibérica, Baleares y
Canarias.
1966   Instituto Geológico y Minero de España, 5ª Edición,
        Escala 1:1,000,000. Madrid.
Mapas de la Dirección General del Instituto Geográfico y
Catastral
1940/42   Primera Edición, Escala 1:50,000, Núms. 31, 32,
        34, 35. Madrid: Talleres del Instituto Geográfico y
        Catastral.
Marquez, Maria del Carmen
1974   Trabajos de campo realizados por el Conde de la Vega
        del Sella. *Boletin del Instituto de Estudios Asturianos*
        83: 811–836.
Martínez Alvarez, J. A.
1965   *Rasgos Geológicos de la Zona Oriental de Asturias*.
        Oviedo: Diputación Provincial de Asturias.
Maury, Jean
1968   Essai de classement des gâlets amenagés des plages
        portugaises entre Rio Lima et Rio Minho. *Travaux de
        l'Institute d'Art Préhistorique de l'Université de
        Toulouse* 10: 166–180.
1973   Le monoface pièce méconnue de l'Asturien du Portu-

gal. *Travaux de l'Institute d'Art Préhistorique de l'Uni-
        versité de Toulouse* 14: 257–269.
1974   La position stratigraphique de l'Asturien des plages
        portugaises entre Lima et Minho. *Travaux de l'In-
        stitute d'Art Préhistorique de l'Université de Toulouse*
        16: 217–238.
1976   Profil archéologique de l'Asturien de Portugal. *Trav-
        aux de l'Institute d'Art Préhistorique de l'Université de
        Toulouse* 18.
1977   The Asturian in Portugal. *British Archaeological Re-
        ports, Supplementary Series* 21. Oxford.
Mayor, Matías, and Tomas Diaz
1977   *La Flora Asturiana*. Gijón: Ediciones Ayalgas.
McCollough, Major Charles Ross
1971   Perigordian Facies in the Upper Paleolithic of Can-
        tabria. MS, doctoral dissertation, University of Penn-
        sylvania, Philadelphia.
Mellars, Paul
1973   The character of the middle-upper paleolithic transi-
        tion in the southwest of France. In *The Explanation of
        Culture Change*, edited by Colin Renfrew, pp. 255–
        276. Pittsburgh: University of Pittsburgh Press.
1978   Editor. *The Early Postglacial Settlement of Northern
        Europe*. London: Duckworth.
Menéndez-Pidal, Ramón, editor
1963   *História de España*. Madrid: Espasa-Calpé.
Morris, Desmond
1965   *The Mammals: A Guide to Living Species*. London:
        Hodder and Staughton.
de Mortillet, Gabriel
1883   *Le Préhistorique Antiquité de l'Homme*. Paris: Aca-
        demie des Sciences.
Morton, J. E.
1967   *Molluscs*. Fourth edition, revised. London:
        Hutchinson.
Newell, Raymond R.
1973   The Post-Glacial Adaptations of the Indigenous Popu-
        lation of the Northwest European Lowland Plain. In
        The Mesolithic in Europe, edited by Stefan Kozlowski,
        pp. 399–440. Warsaw: Warsaw University Press.
Newell, Raymond, V. Pye, and M. Ahsanullah
1971   The effect of thermal acclimation on the heat toler-
        ance of the intertidal prosobranches *Littorina littorea*
        (L.) and *Monodonta lineata* (da Costa). *Journal of Ex-
        perimental Biology* 54: 525–533.
Noval, Alfredo
1976   *La Fauna Salvaje Asturiana*. Gijón: Ediciones Ayalga.
Obermaier, Hugo
1914   Estudio de los glaciares de los Picos de Europa. *Traba-
        jos del Museo Nacional de Ciencias Naturales Memo-
        ria* 9 (Serie Geológico). Madrid.
1924   *Fossil Man in Spain*. New Haven: Yale University
        Press.
1925   El Hombre Fosil. *Comisión de Investigaciones Paleon-
        tológicas y Prehistóricas Memoria* 9. 2nd edition.
        Madrid: Museo Nacional de Ciencias Naturales.
Paço, Afonso do
1937   Paleo e mesolítico português: descobrimentos-bibli-
        ografia: I. *Revista de Guimarães*, Vols. 46–47.
        Guimarães.
1940a   Paleo e mesolítico português: descobrimentos-bibli-
        ografia: II. *Broteria* 31. Lisboa.
1940b   Revisão dos problemas do paleolítico, mesolítico e
        asturiense. *Publicações do Congreso do Mundo Por-
        tugués* 1: 129–158. Lisboa.
Parmalee, Paul, and Walter Klippel
1974   Freshwater mussels as a prehistoric food resource.
        American Antiquity 39(3): 421–434.
Passemard, Emile
1924   L'industrie des tourbes de Mouligna. *Bulletin de la
        Société Préhistorique Française* 17(11): 263–267.
Pérez, Manuel
1974   Tipología del pico asturiense. *Boletin del Instituto de
        Estudios Asturianos* 81: 217–233.

Pericot García, Luis
  1934   Epocas primitiva y romana. *Historia de España*, Vol. 1. Barcelona.
  1954   *El Paleolítico y Epipaleolítico en España*. 4° Congreso Internacional de Ciencias Prehistóricas y Protohistóricas. Madrid.
  1956   Sobre los Hallazgos del Montgrí. In *Homenaje al Conde de la Vega del Sella*. Oviedo: Diputación Provincial de Asturias.
  1964   *Medio Siglo de Prehistória Hispánica*. Discurso Inaugural del Año Academico 1964–1965. Barcelona: Universidad de Barcelona.

Piette, Edouard
  1889   L'époque de transition intermédiaire entre l'âge du renne et l'époque de la pierre polie. *Congrès International d'Anthropologie et d'Archéologie Préhistorique*, Comptes Rendus, 10th Session. Paris.

Piggott, Stuart
  1965   *Ancient Europe*. Edinburgh: Edinburgh University Press.

Plog, Frederick T.
  1968   Archaeological Surveys: A New Perspective. MS, master's thesis, Department of Anthropology, University of Chicago, Chicago.

Price, T. Douglas
  1973   A proposed model for procurement systems in the Mesolithic of northwestern Europe. In *The Mesolithic in Europe*, edited by Stefan Kozlowski, pp. 455–476. Warsaw: Warsaw University Press.

Prior, Richard
  1968   *The Roe Deer of Cranborne Chase: An Ecological Survey*. New York and Toronto: Oxford University Press.

Quirós Linares, Francisco, and Emilio Murcia Navarro
  1977   El marco geográfico Asturiano. In *Historia de Asturias: Prehistoria*, edited by F. Jordá, pp. vi–xxix. Gijón: Ediciones Ayalga.

Rao, C. R.
  1973   *Linear Statistical Inference and its Applications*. 2nd edition. New York: Wiley and Sons.

Rappaport, Roy
  1969   Some suggestions concerning concept and method in ecological anthropology. *National Museum of Canada Bulletin* 230. Ottawa.

Ricketts, E. F., and Jack Calvin
  1948   *Between Pacific Tides*. Revised edition. Palo Alto: Stanford University Press.

Roche, Jean
  1951   *L'Industrie Préhistorique du Cabeço d'Amoreira (Muge)*. Instituto para a Alta Cultura, Centro de Estudos de Etnología Peninsular. Pôrto: Imprensa Portuguesa.
  1952   Les fouilles des amas coquilliers de Muge (leur importance pour la chronologie du Mésolithique). *Boletin da Sociedade Geológica de Portugal* 10: 145–150.
  1954   Resultats des dernières campagnes de fouilles executés à Moita do Sebastião (Muge). *Revista da Faculdade de Ciencias de Lisboa* 4(1): 179–186.
  1956   Recentes Decouvertes au Gisement de Moita do Sebastião Muge, Portugal. *Cronica del 4° Congreso Internacional de Ciencias Prehistoricas y Protohistoricas* (Madrid: 1954), pp. 155–161. Zaragoza.
  1966   Balance de un siglo de excavaciones en los concheros mesoliticos de Muge. *Ampurias* 28: 13–48.

Rodríguez Asensio, J. Adolfo
  1978a Nota préliminar sobre las excavaciones en el yacimiento de Bañugues (Gozón-Asturias). *Boletín del Instituto de Estudios Asturianos* 93–94: 357–368.
  1978b The early paleolithic site of Bañugues (Gozón, Asturias, Spain). *Current Anthropology* 19(3): 615, 616.

Roe, Derek A.
  1968a A gazetteer of British Lower and Middle Palaeolithic sites. *Council for British Archaeology Research Report* 8.
  1968b British Lower and Middle Palaeolithic handaxe groups. *Proceedings of the Prehistoric Society* 34: 1–82.
  1970   Comments on the results obtained by J. M. Graham. *World Archaeology* 1(3): 338–342.

Rogers, J.
  1920   *The Shell Book*. New York: Doubleday, Page and Co.

Rozoy, J. G.
  1978   *Les Dernièrs Chasseurs*. Vols. 1, 2. Special number of the Bulletin de la Société Archéologique Champenoise (June). Reims.

Santa-Olalla, Julio Martinez
  1941   Sobre el Neolítico Antiguo en España. *Atlantis* 16 (1–2): 90–105.

Sautuola, Marcelino S., El Marqués de
  1880   Breves apuntes sobre algunos objetos prehistoricos de la Provincia de Santander. Published privately by the author. Santander.

Savory, Hubert N.
  1968   *Spain and Portugal: The Prehistory of the Iberian Peninsula*. New York: Praeger.

Scheitlin, Thomas, and Geoffrey Clark
  1978   Three-dimensional surface representations of lithic categories at Liencres. *Newsletter of Computer Archaeology* 13(3): 1–13.

Sehested, N. F. B.
  1884   *Archaeologiske Undersøgelser 1878–1881*. København.

Serpa-Pinto, Rui de
  1928   O Asturiense em Portugal. *Trabalhos da Sociedade Portuguesa de Antropología e Etnología* 4(1). Pôrto.
  1929   Notulas asturienses—I. *Trabalhos da Sociedade Portuguesa de Antropología e Etnología* 4(2). Pôrto.
  1930   Bibliográfia do Asturiense. *Portucale* 3(17). Pôrto.
  1931   Notulas asturienses—III. *Trabalhos da Sociedade Portuguesa de Antropología e Etnología* 5(2). Pôrto.

Service, Elman R.
  1962   *Primitive Social Organization: An Evolutionary Perspective*. New York: Random House.

Siegel, Sidney
  1956   *Nonparametric Statistics for the Behavioral Sciences*. New York: McGraw-Hill.

Simon, H. A.
  1945   *Administrative Behaviour: A Study of Decision-Making Processes in Administrative Organization*. Glencoe: Free Press.

Smith, Carol, editor
  1976a *Regional Analysis: Economic Systems*. New York: Academic Press.
  1976b *Regional Analysis: Social Systems*. New York: Academic Press.

Sokal, Robert R., and F. James Rohlf
  1969   *Biometry: The Principles and Practice of Statistics in Biological Research*. San Francisco: W. H. Freeman.

Sonneville-Bordes, Denise de
  1963   Upper Paleolithic Cultures in Western Europe. *Science* 142(3590): 347–355.

Sonneville-Bordes, Denise de, and Jean Perrot
  1953   Essai d'adaptation des méthodes statistiques et paléolithiques, I: Grattoirs, II: Outils Solutréens. *Bulletin de la Société Préhistorique Française* 50: 323–333.
  1954   Lexique Typologique du Paléolithique Superieur. *Bulletin de la Société Préhistorique Française* 51: 327–334.
  1955   Lexique Typologique du Paléolithique Superieur. *Bulletin de la Société Préhistorique Française* 52: 76–78.

1956 Lexique Typologique du Paléolithique Superieur. *Bulletin de la Société Préhistorique Française* 53: 547–579.
Spooner, Brian, editor
1972 *Population Growth: Anthropological Implications.* Cambridge: M.I.T. Press.
Stafford, Barbara
1977 Burin manufacture and utilization: an experimental study. *Journal of Field Archaeology* 4(2): 235–246.
1979 A Technofunctional Study of Lithics from Payson, Arizona. MS, doctoral dissertation, Department of Anthropology, Arizona State University, Tempe.
Straus, Lawrence, G.
1975a A Study of the Solutrean in Vasco-Cantabrian Spain. MS, doctoral dissertation, Department of Anthropology, University of Chicago, Chicago.
1975b ¿Solutrense o Magdaleniense Inferior cantábrico? Significado de las 'differencias.' *Boletin del Instituto de Estudios Asturianos* 86: 781–791.
1977 Of deerslayers and mountain men: paleolithic faunal exploitation in Cantabrian Spain. In *For Theory Building in Archaeology,* edited by L. Binford, pp. 41–76. New York: Academic Press.
1978a Observaciones préliminares sobre la variabilidad de las puntas Solutrenses. *Trabajos de Prehistoria* 35. Madrid: Consejo Superior de Investigaciones Cientí ficas.
1978b Of Neanderthal hillbillies, origin myths and stone tools: notes on Upper Paleolithic assemblage variability. *Lithic Technology* 7(2): 36–39.
1978c Thoughts on Solutrean concave base point distribution. *Lithic Technology* 6(3): 32–35.
1979a Variabilité dans les industries solutréenes de l'Espagne cantabrique. *Bulletin de la Société Préhistorique Française* 76: 276–280.
1979b Mesolithic adaptations along the northern coast of Spain. *Quaternaria* 21: 305–327.
Straus, Lawrence G., and Geoffrey A. Clark
1978a Prehistoric Investigations in Cantabrian Spain. *Journal of Field Archaeology* 5: 289–317.
1978b La Riera Paleoecological Project: preliminary report, 1977 excavations. *Current Anthropology* 19(2): 455–456.
1978c Four millennia: the Solutrean of Cantabrian Spain. *Antiquity* 152: 240, 241.
1979 La Riera Paleoecological Project, 1978 excavations. *Current Anthropology* 20(1): 235, 236.
Straus, Lawrence G., Geoffrey A. Clark, and Manuel González
1978 Cronología de las industrias del Würm Tardio y del Holoceno Temprano en Cantabria: contribuciones del Proyecto Paleoecológico de la Riera. In *C–14 y La Prehistoria de la Peninsula Iberica,* edited by M. Almagro-Gorbea and others, pp. 37–43. Madrid: Fundación Juan March.
Straus, Lawrence G., Federico Bernaldo, Victoria Cabrera, and Geoffrey A. Clark
1977 New radiocarbon dates for the Spanish Solutrean. *Antiquity* 51: 243.
Straus, Lawrence, Geoffrey A. Clark, Jesus Altuna, and Jesus Ortea
1980 Ice-age subsistence in northern Spain. *Scientific American* 242(6): 142–153.
Straus, Lawrence, Jesus Altuna, Geoffrey A. Clark, Manuel González, Henri Laville, Arlette Leroi-Gourhan, Miguel Menéndez, and Jesus Ortea
1981 Paleoecology at La Riera (Asturias, Spain). *Current Anthropology* 22(6): 655–682.
Sullivan Alan, and Michael Schiffer
1977 A critical examination of SARG. MS, on file with the Department of Anthropology, University of Arizona.

Tucson.
Thomas, R. A., D. Griffith, C. Wise, and R. Artusy, Jr.
1975 Environmental adaptation on Delaware's coastal plain. *Archaeology of Eastern North America* 3: 35–90.
Tresguerres, Juan
1976a Azilian burial from Los Azules, I, Asturias, Spain. *Current Anthropology* 17(4): 769, 770.
1976b Enterramiento Aziliense de la Cueva de Los Azules I (Cangas de Onis, Oviedo). *Boletin del Instituto de Estudios Asturianos* 87: 273–288.
Tringham, Ruth
1972 The Aims of Functional Analysis of Stone Tools. Paper presented at the 37th Annual Meeting of the Society for American Archaeology, Bal Harbour, Florida.
1973 The Mesolithic of Southeastern Europe. In *The Mesolithic in Europe,* edited by Stefan Kozlowski, pp. 551–572. Warsaw: Warsaw University Press.
Uría-Riú, Juan
1941 La caverna de Lledías (Llanes, Asturias). *Archivo Español de Arqueología, Memoria* 42. Madrid.
Utrilla, Pilar
1976a Las industrias del Magdaleniense Inferior y Medio de la Costa Cantábrica. *Publicaciones del Departamento de Historia Antigua.* Zaragoza: Universidad de Zaragoza.
1976b La region asturiana durante los inicios del Magdaleniense. *Boletin del Instituto de Estudios Asturianos* 88/89: 801–854.
Van den Brink, F. H.
1967 *A Field Guide to the Mammals of Britain and Europe.* London: William Collins and Sons.
Vaurie, Charles
1959 *The Birds of the Palearctic Fauna: A Systematic Reference (Order Passeriforms).* London: H. F. G. Witherby.
1965 *The Birds of the Palearctic Fauna: A Systematic Reference (Non-Passeriforms).* London: H. F. G. Witherby.
Vega del Sella, Ricardo Duque de Estrada y Martínez de Moratín, Conde de la
1914 La cueva del Penicial (Asturias). *Comisión de Investigaciones Paleontológicas y Prehistoricas, Memoria* 4. Madrid: Museo Nacional de Ciencias Naturales.
1915 Avance al estudio del Paleolítico Superior en la region Cantábrica. *Publicaciones del Congreso de Valladolid,* pp. 139–160. Madrid: Asociación Española para el Progreso de las Ciencias.
1916 El Paleolítico de Cueto de la Mina. *Comisión de Investigaciones Paleontológicas y Prehistoricas, Memoria* 13. Madrid: Museo Nacional de Ciencias Naturales.
1921 Notas para la climatología cuaternaria. *Comisión de Investigaciones Paleontológicas y Prehistoricas, Memoria* 29. Madrid: Junta para Ampliación de Estudios e Investigaciones Científicas.
1923 El Asturiense, nueva industria Pre-neolítica. *Comisión de Investigaciones Paleontológicas y Prehistoricas, Memoria* 32. Madrid: Museo Nacional de Ciencias Naturales.
1925 La transición al Neolítico en la costa Cantábrica. *Sociedad Española de Antropología, Etnografía y Prehistoria, Memoria* 40: 165–172. Madrid: Museo Antropológico Nacional.
1930 Las cuevas de La Riera y Balmori. *Comisión de Investigaciones Paleontológicas y Prehistoricas, Memoria* 38. Madrid: Museo Nacional de Ciencias Naturales.
1933 Asturienses, capsienses y vascos. In *Homenagem a Martins Sarmento,* pp. 405–410. Guimarães: Sociedade Martins Sarmento.
Viana, Abel
1940 Os Problemas do Asturiense Portugués. *Congreso do Mundo Portugués* 1: 167–194. Lisboa.

Viana, Abel *(continued)*
1956   Asturiense das Asturias e do Litoral Minhoto. In *Homenage al Conde de la Vega del Sella,* pp. 185–198. Oviedo: Diputación Provincial de Asturias.

Villar, Emilio H. del
1937   *Los Suelos de la Península Luso-Ibérica.* Madrid: Tipográfica Artística.

Vita-Finzi, Claudio, and Eric S. Higgs
1970   Prehistoric economy in the Mount Carmel area of Palestine: site catchment analysis. *Proceedings of the Prehistoric Society,* N.S. 36: 1–37. London.

Volman, Thomas
1978   Early archaeological evidence for shellfish collecting. *Science* 201: 911–913.

Voous, Karel H.
1960   *Atlas of European Birds.* London: Thomas Nelson and Sons.

Walker, Ernest P., F. Warnick, S. Hamlet, K. Lange, M. Davis, H. Vible, and P. Wright
1968   *Mammals of the World.* Vols. 1, 2. 2nd edition, edited by J. L. Paradiso. Baltimore: John Hopkins Press.

Wallis, W. Allen, and Harry V. Roberts
1967   *Statistics: A New Approach.* Glencoe: Free Press.

Waterbolk. H. Tjalling
1968   Food Production in Prehistoric Europe. *Science* 162: 1093–1102.

Willey, Gordon, and Jeremy Sabloff
1974   *A History of American Archaeology.* San Francisco: Freeman.

Wood, John J.
1974   A computer program for hierarchical cluster analysis. *Newsletter of Computer Archaeology* 9(4): 1–11.

Wymer, John, and Ronald Singer
1972   Archaeology of Klasies River Mouth, Cape Province, South Africa. In *Man, Settlement and Urbanism,* edited by P. Ucko, R. Tringham, and G. Dimbleby. London: Duckworth.

Zeuner, Frederick E.
1963   *A History of Domesticated Animals.* New York: Harper and Row.

Zipf, George
1949   *Human Behaviour and the Principle of Least Effort.* New York: Hafner Publishing.

INDEX

Acheulean, 26
Agrostis spp., 7, 111
Alcalde del Rio, H., 34
Alder. *See Alnus*
Alleröd period, 150
Almagro Basch, M., xi
Alnus glutinosa, 6, 111
Alnus sp. indet., 150, 151
Altamira, site of, 7, 20, 38, 40
Altuna, J., x, 110
Alvárez, A., 36, 37, 42
Ancora, site of, 48, 145
Animals. *See* Fauna
Antler tools. *See* Industry, bone and antler
Aramar, site of, 48, 49, 145
Arenaza, site of, 2
Arizona State University, xi
Arnero, site of, 17, 18, 108
   stratigraphy, 17, 18
      Aurignacian, 18
      Mousterian, 18
Arvicola amphibius, 14–16
Arvicola terrestris, 20
Ash. *See Fraxinus*
Astralium rugosus, 27
Asturian of Cantabria
   age of, 9, 10
   assemblage composition, 9
   base camps, 120
   catchment analysis, 120–139
   concheros, 9, 10
   contemporaneity with Azilian, 2, 145
   data sources, x
   fauna, 110–119
   geographical setting, 140, 141
   industry, 80–109
   literary usage, 1
   minor sites, 38, 39
   pollen, 150, 151
   radiocarbon dates, 118
   site inventory, 10–38
Atlantic period, 1, 44, 51, 84
Aurignacian, 9, 13, 14, 17, 18, 29, 39
Auroch. *See Bos primigenius*
Avifauna, 8, 26
Azilian, ix, 2, 3, 17, 20, 23, 27–29, 38, 40, 69, 70, 140–142, 150
   contemporaneity with Asturian, 2, 145

Badger. *See Meles meles*
Bailey, G., 145
Balmori, site of, x, 7, 20–25, 39, 56, 70, 85, 108, 109, 117–119
   Cut E sequence, 117–119
   sedimentology, 23, 25
   stratigraphy, 21–23
      Azilian, 23
      Magdalenian, 23
      Solutrean, 21
   Upper Paleolithic conchero, 40
Bañugues, site of, 48, 145
Barley, 2
Barnacles. *See Polliceps cornucopia*
Bear, brown. *See Ursus arctos*
Bear, cave. *See Ursus spelaeus*

Beech. *See Fagus silvatica*
Benfiça de Ribatejo, site of, 47
Bernaldo de Quirós, F., xi
Betula vulgaris, 6, 28, 111
Biarritz, 145
Birch. *See Betula vulgaris*
Birds. *See* Avifauna
Bison priscus, 14–16, 23, 26, 38
Boar. *See Sus scrofa*
Bone tools. *See* Industry, bone and antler
Boreal period, 1, 44, 51, 84, 150, 151
Bos-Bison indet., 12, 31, 34
Bos primigenius, 17, 18, 23, 27, 34
Bos taurus, 2
Braidwood, R., x, xi
Breuil, H., 34
Bricia, site of, 29–31
   geological sequence 30
      karstic rejuvenation 31
   stratigraphy, 30, 31
      Magdalenian 30
Bronze Age, 2, 142
Broom. *See Genista* spp.
Buccinum undatum, 16
Budiño, site of, 48, 49
Burial, at Colombres, 33. *See also* Skeletal remains
Butzer, K., x, 29, 36

Cabrera Valdes, V., xi
Calluna spp., 111
Cancer pagurus, 17, 27
Canis lupus, 16, 23, 25–27
Cantabria
   definition, 3
   faunas, 7, 8
      birds, 8
      mammals, 7, 128, 130
      molluscs, 7, 8, 131
   geomorphology, 4–7, 123
      climate 5, 6
      geological structure, 4, 123
      karst topography, 4, 5, 123
      soil types, 5
      vegetation, 6, 123
Capra ibex, 7, 12, 14–17, 20, 23, 25, 31, 33, 38, 110–113, 127
   density, 127
   diet, 111
   habitat, 111
   transhumance, 127
Capreolus capreolus, 7, 14, 16, 17, 20, 23, 26, 27, 34, 110–113, 126
   density, 126
   diet, 111
   habitat, 111
   transhumance, 127
Carballo, J., 9, 32, 33
Cardium edulis, 19, 27, 31, 43
Cardium mucronatum, 23
Cardium tuberculata, 16, 23
Carex spp., 111
Cariguela del Pinar, site of, 2
Carreço, site of, 48, 145
Castanea sativa, 6

Catchment analysis, 120–139, 144, 145
   assumptions, 120–123
   cluster analysis, 135, 136
   discriminant function analysis, 136–139
   homogeneity tests, 133, 134
   hypotheses, 133, 134
   methodology, 125, 126
   models, 132, 133
   site catchment, definition, 120
   site territory, definition, 121
   zone transformation algorithm, 124
Cattle. *See Bos taurus*
Cervus elaphus, 7, 14–17, 19, 20, 23, 25–27, 31, 33, 34, 38, 110–113, 126
   caloric yields, 127, 131
   density, 126
   diet, 111
   group composition, 111, 113
   habitat, 111
   transhumance, 126
Chamois. *See Rupicapra rupicapra*
Châteauneuf-lez-Martigues, site of, 142, 143
Chestnut. *See Castanea sativa*
Childe, V., ix
Choppers. *See* Industry, lithic
Chopping tools. *See* Industry, lithic
Ciriego, Playa de, 36
Clark, G., ii, x, 3, 13, 14, 27, 28, 36, 64, 85, 105, 109, 152
Clark, J. G. D., ix, 3, 140
Clark, V., xi
Coastal adaptations, 2
Coberizas, site of, x, 19, 20, 70, 85, 108, 109
   stratigraphy, 20
      Magdalenian, 20
      Solutrean, 20
Cocharrinho, site of, 47
Colombres, site of, 9, 32–34, 108
   burial at, 33
   stratigraphy, 33, 34
Concheiros, 48
Concheros, 9, 10, 17, 123, 124
   formation of, 17, 123, 124
   in Galicia, 48
   post-Asturian, 42–44
      La Lloseta, 38, 43, 44
      Les Pedroses, 42
      San Antonio, 42, 43
   Upper Paleolithic, 38–42
      Balmori, 40
      El Cierro, 39–40, 42
      La Lloseta, 41
Corylus avellana, 7, 28
Corylus sp. indet., 150, 151
Crabs. *See Cancer pagurus; Portunus puber*
Cuartamentero, site of, xi, 31, 32
   skeletal remains, 32
   stratigraphy, 32
Cuerquense, 34
Cueto de la Mina, site of, 12–17, 18, 25, 108
   historical importance, 15
   stratigraphy, 14–17
      Aurignacian-Perigordian, 14

[169]